Henry Hart Milman

Story of Latin Christianity Including that of the Popes to the

Pontificate of Nicolas 5.

Vol. 6

Henry Hart Milman

Story of Latin Christianity Including that of the Popes to the Pontificate of Nicolas 5.
Vol. 6

ISBN/EAN: 9783741162947

Manufactured in Europe, USA, Canada, Australia, Japa

Cover: Foto ©Thomas Meinert / pixelio.de

Manufactured and distributed by brebook publishing software
(www.brebook.com)

Henry Hart Milman

Story of Latin Christianity Including that of the Popes to the

Pontificate of Nicolas 5.

HISTORY

OF

LATIN CHRISTIANITY;

INCLUDING THAT OF

THE POPES TO THE PONTIFICATE OF NICOLAS V.

By HENRY HART MILMAN, D.D.,

DEAN OF ST. PAUL'S.

IN NINE VOLUMES.—VOL. VI.

THIRD EDITION.

LONDON:
JOHN MURRAY, ALBEMARLE STREET.
1864.

CONTENTS

OF

THE SIXTH VOLUME.

BOOK IX.—*continued.*

CHAPTER IX.

NEW ORDERS. — ST. DOMINIC.

CHAPTER X.

ST. FRANCIS.

BOOK X.

CHAPTER I.

Honorius III.— Frederick II.

CHAPTER II.

Honorius III. and England.

CHAPTER III

Frederick II. and Gregory IX.

CHAPTER IV.

Renewal of Hostilities between Gregory IX. and Frederick II.

CHAPTER V.

FREDERICK AND INNOCENT IV.

BOOK XI.

CHAPTER I.

ST. LOUIS.

CHAPTER II.

POPE ALEXANDER IV.

CHAPTER IV.

GREGORY X. AND HIS SUCCESSORS.

CHAPTER V.

SICILIAN VESPERS.

CHAPTER VI.

Coelestine V.

HISTORY

OF

LATIN CHRISTIANITY.

BOOK IX.—*continued.*

CHAPTER IX.

New Orders. St. Dominic.

THE progress of the new opinions in all quarters, their obstinate resistance in Languedoc, opinions, if not yet rooted out, lopped by the sword, and scared by the fire, had revealed the secret of the fatal weakness of Latin Christianity. Sacerdotal Christianity, by ascending a throne higher than all thrones of earthly sovereigns, by the power, the wealth, the magnificence of the higher ecclesiastics, had withdrawn the influence of the clergy from its natural and peculiar office. Even with the lower orders of the priesthood, that which in a certain degree separated them from the people, set them apart from the sympathies of the people. The Church might still seem to preach to all, but it preached in a tone of lofty condescension; it dictated rather than persuaded; but, in general, actual preaching had fallen into disuse; it was in theory the special privilege of the bishops, and the bishops were but few who had either the gift, the inclination, or the leisure from their secular, judicial, or warlike occupations to preach even in their cathedral cities; in the rest of their dioceses their presence was but occasional; a progress or visitation of pomp and form, rather than of popular instruction. The only general teaching of the people was the Ritual.

But the splendid Ritual, admirably as it was con-
The Ritual. stituted to impress by its words or symbolic forms the leading truths of Christianity upon the more intelligent, or in a vaguer way upon the more rude and uneducated, could be administered, and was administered, by a priesthood almost entirely ignorant, but which had just learned mechanically, not without decency, perhaps not without devotion, to go through the stated observances. Everywhere the bell summoned to the frequent service, the service was performed, and the obedient flock gathered to the chapel or the church, knelt, and either performed their orisons, or heard the customary chant and prayer. This, the only instruction which the mass of the priesthood could convey, might for a time be sufficient to maintain in the minds of the people a quiescent and submissive faith, nevertheless, in itself could not but awaken in some a desire of knowledge, which it could not satisfy. Auricular confession, now by Innocent III. raised to a necessary duty, and to be heard not only by the lofty bishop, but by the parochial priest, might have more effect in repressing the uneasy or daring doubts of those who begun to reason; doubts which would startle and alarm the uneducated priest, and which he would endeavour to silence at once by all the terrors of his authority. Though the lower priesthood were from the people, they were not of the people; nor did they fully interpenetrate the whole mass of the people. The parochial divisions, where they existed, were arbitrary, accidental, often not clearly defined; they followed in

general the bounds of royal or aristocratical domains. A church was founded by a pious king, noble, or knight, with a certain district around it ; but in few countries was there any approach to a systematic organisation of the clergy in relation to the spiritual wants and care of the whole Christian community.

The fatal question of the celibacy of the clergy worked in both ways to the prejudice of their autho-   *Celibacy of clergy.* rity. The married clergy, on the whole no doubt the more moral, were acting in violation of the rules of the Church, and were subject to the opprobrious accusation of living in concubinage. The validity of their ministrations was denied by the more austere ; the doctrines of men charged with such grievous error lost their proper weight. The unmarried obeyed the outward rule, but by every account, not the bitter satire of enemies alone but the reluctant and melancholy admission of the most gentle and devout, in general so flagrantly violated the severer principles of the Church, that their teaching, if they attempted actual teaching, must have fallen dead on the minds of the people.

The earlier monastic orders were still more deficient as instructors in Christianity. Their chief, if   *Monasticism.* not their sole exclusive and avowed object, was the salvation, or, at the highest, the religious perfection of themselves and of their own votaries. Solitude, seclusion, the lonely cell, their own unapproached, or hardly approached, chapel, was their sphere ; their communication with others was sternly cut off. The dominant, the absorbing thought of each hermit, of each coenobite, was his own isolation or that of his brethren from the dangerous world. But to teach the world they must enter the world. Their influence, therefore, beyond their convent walls was but subordinate and

accessory. The halo of their sanctity might awe, attract
others; the zeal of love might, as to their more immediate neighbours, struggle with the coercive and em-
prisoning discipline. But the admiration of their sanctity would act chiefly in alluring emulous votaries
within, rather than in extending faith and holiness
beyond their walls. Even their charities were to relieve
their own souls, to lay up for themselves treasures of
good works, rather than from any real sympathy for the
people. The loftier notion of combining their own
humiliation with the good of mankind first dawned upon
the founders of the Mendicant orders. In the older
monasteries beneficence was but a subsidiary and ancil-
lary virtue. The cultivation of the soil was not to
increase its fertility for the general advantage; it was
to employ their own dangerous energies, to subdue their
own bodies by the hard discipline of labour. At all
events, the limit of their influence was that of their
retainers, tenants, peasants, or serfs, bounded by their
own near neighbourhood. No sooner indeed had any
one of the older Orders, or any single monastery attained
to numbers, rank or influence, than it became more and
more estranged from the humbler classes; the vows of
poverty had been eluded, the severer rule gradually
relaxed; the individual might remain poor, but the
order or the convent became rich; narrow cells grew
into stately cloisters, deserts into parks, hermits into
princely abbots. It became a great religious aristocracy;
it became worldly, without impregnating the world with
its religious spirit; it was hardly less secluded from
popular intercourse than before; even where learning
was cultivated it was the high scholastic theology: theology which, in its pride, stood as much aloof from the
popular mind as the feudal bishop or the mitred abbot.

But just at this time that popular mind throughout
Christendom seemed to demand instruction. *Intellectual
movement.*
There was a wide and vague awakening and
yearning of the human intellect. It is impossible to
suppose that the lower orders were not to a certain
extent generally stirred by that movement which
thronged the streets of the universities of Paris, Auxerre,
Oxford, with countless hosts of indigent scholars, which
led thousands to the feet of Abelard, and had raised
logical disputations on the most barren metaphysical
subjects to an interest like that of a tournament. An
insatiate thirst of curiosity, of inquiry, at least for mental
spiritual excitement, seemed almost suddenly to have
pervaded society.

Here that which was heresy, or accounted to be
heresy, stepped in and seized upon the vacant
mind. Preaching in public and in private was *Heresy.*
the strength of all the heresiarchs, of all the sects.
Eloquence, popular eloquence became a new power
which the Church had comparatively neglected or disdained since the time of the Crusades; or had gone on
wasting upon that worn-out and now almost unstirring
topic. The Petrobussians, the Henricians, the followers
of Peter Waldo, and the wilder teachers at least tinged
with the old Manichean tenets of the East, met on this
common ground. They were poor and popular; they
felt with the people, whether the lower burghers of the
cities, the lower vassals, or even the peasants and serfs;
they spoke the language of the people, they were of
the people. If here and there one of the higher clergy,
a priest or a canon, adopted their opinions and mode of
teaching, he became an object of reverence and noto-
riety; and this profound religious influence so obtained
was a strong temptation to religious minds. But all

these sects were bound together by their common revolutionary aversion to the clergy, not only the wealthy, worldly, immoral, tyrannical, but the decent but inert priesthood, who left the uninstructed souls of men to perish. In their turn, they were viewed with the most jealous hatred by the clergy, not merely on account of their heterodox and daring tenets, but as usurping their office, which themselves had almost let fall from their hands. We have seen the extent to which they prevailed; nothing less might be apprehended (unless coerced by the obedient temporal power, and no other measure seemed likely to succeed) than a general revolt of the lower orders from the doctrines and rule of the hierarchy.

At this time, too, the rude dialects which had been slowly forming by the breaking up of the Roman Latin and its fusion with the Teutonic, were growing into regular and distinct languages. Latin, the language of the Church, became less and less the language of the people. In proportion as the Roman or foreign element predominated, the services of the Church, the speech in which all priests were supposed to be instructed, remained more or less clear and intelligible. It was more so where the Latin maintained its ascendancy; but in the Teutonic or Sclavonian regions, even the priesthood had learned Latin imperfectly, if at all; and Latin had ceased to be the means of ordinary communication; it was a strange, obsolete, if still venerable language. Even in Italy, in Northern and Southern France, in England where the Norman French kept down to a certain extent the old free Anglo-Saxon (we must wait more than a century for Wyclyffe and Chaucer), in Spain, Latin was a kindred, indistinctly significant tongue, but not that of common use, not that of the field, the street, the market, or the fair. But vernacular teaching was in all quarters coetaneous with the new opinions; versions of the sacred writings, or parts of the sacred writings, into the young languages were at once the sign of their birth, and the instrument of their propagation. These languages had begun to speak, at least in poetry, and not only to the knightly aristocracy. The first sounds of Italian poetry were already heard in the Sicilian court of the young Frederick II.; Dante was ere long to come. The Provençal had made the nearest approach perhaps to a regular language; and Provence, as has been seen, lent her Romaunt to the great anti-hierarchical movement. In France the Trouvères had in the last century begun their inexhaustible, immeasurable epopées; but these were as yet the luxuries of the court and the castle, heard no doubt by the people; but not what is fairly called popular poetry,[a] though here and there might even now be heard the tale or the fable. Germany, less poetical, was at once borrowing the knightly poems on Charlemagne, and King Arthur, and the Crusades; emulating France, reviving the old classical fables, among them the story of Alexander; while in Walter the Falconer[b] are heard tones more menacing, more ominous of religious revolution, more daringly expressive of Teutonic independence.

But this gradual encroachment of the vernacular

---

[a] See in the 22nd vol. of the Hist. Littéraire de la France the description and analysis of the innumerable Chansons de Geste, Poëmes d'Aventure. With all these were mingled up, both in Germany and France, an interminable hagiological romances, legends, and lives of saints, even the more modern Saints. See, e.g., the French poem on Thomas à Becket, edited in the Berlin Transactions by M. Bekker.

[b] Lachmann has edited the original Walter der Vogelweide with his usual industry; Simrock modernised him to the understanding of the less learned reader.

poetry on the Latin, the vain struggle of the Latin
to maintain its mastery, the growth and influence of
modern languages must be reserved for a later, more
full, and consecutive inquiry.

Just at this juncture arose almost simultaneously,
St. Dominic without concert, in different countries, two men
and St. Francis wonderfully adapted to arrest and avert the
danger which threatened the whole hierarchical system.
One seized and, if he did not wrest from the hands of
the enemy, turned against him with indefatigable force
his own fatal arms, St. Dominic, the founder of the Friar
Preachers. By him Christendom was at once over-
spread with a host of zealous, active, devoted men,
whose function was popular instruction. They were
gathered from every country, and spoke, therefore,
every language and dialect. In a few years, from the
sierras of Spain to the steppes of Russia; from the
Tiber to the Thames, the Trent, the Baltic Sea; the old
faith, in its fullest mediæval, imaginative, inflexible
rigour, was preached in almost every town and hamlet.
The Dominicans did not confine themselves to popular
teaching: the more dangerous, if as yet not absolutely
disloyal seats of the new learning, of inquiry, of intellectual movement, the universities, Bologna, Paris,
Oxford are invaded, and compelled to admit these stern
apostles of unswerving orthodoxy. Their zeal soon over-
leaped the pale of Christendom: they plunge fearlessly
into the remote darkness of heathen and Mohammedan
lands, from whence come back rumours, which are constantly stirring the minds of their votaries, of wonderful
conversions and not less wonderful martyrdoms.

The other, St. Francis of Assisi, was endowed with
that fervour of mystic devotion, which spread like an
epidemic with irresistible contagion among the lower

orders throughout Christendom. It was a superstition,
but a superstition which had such an earnestness, warmth,
tenderness, as to raise the religious feeling to an intense
but gentle passion; it supplied a never-failing counter
excitement to rebellious reasoning, which gladly fell
asleep again on its bosom. After the death of its author
and example, it raised a new object of adoration, more
near, more familiar, and second only, if second, to the
Redeemer himself. Jesus was supposed to have lived
again in St. Francis with at least as bright a halo of
miracle around him, in absolute, almost surpassing perfection.

In one important respect the founders of these new
orders fully agreed, in their entire identification with
the lowest of mankind. At first amicable, afterwards
emulous, eventually hostile, they, or rather their Orders,
rivalled each other in sinking below poverty into beg-
gary. They were to live upon alms; the coarsest
imaginable dress, the hardest fare, the narrowest cell,
were to keep them down to the level of the humblest.
Though Dominic himself was of high birth, and many
of his followers of noble blood, St. Francis of decent
even wealthy parentage, according to the irrepealable
constitution of both Orders they were still to be the
poorest of mankind, instructing or consorting in religious fellowship with the very meanest outcasts of
society. Both the new Orders differed in the same
manner, and greatly to the advantage of the hierarchical
faith, from the old monkish institutions. Their primary
object was not the salvation of the individual monk, but
the salvation of others through him. Though, therefore, their rules within their monasteries were strictly
and severely monastic, bound by the common vows of
chastity, poverty, and obedience, seclusion was no part

of their discipline. Their business was abroad rather
than at home; their dwelling was not like that of the
old Benedictines or others, in the uncultivated swamps
and forests of the North, on the dreary Apennino, or
the exhausted soil of Italy, in order to subdue their
bodies, and occupy their dangerously unoccupied time;
merely as a secondary consequence to compel the desert
into fertile land. Their work was among their fellow
men; in the village, in the town, in the city, in the
market, even in the camp. In every Dominican convent
the Superior had the power to dispense even with the
ordinary internal discipline, if he thought the brother
might be more usefully employed in his special avo-
cation of a Preacher. It might seem the ambition of
these men, instead of cooping up a chosen few in high-
walled and secure monasteries, to subdue the whole
world into one vast cloister; monastic Christianity would
no longer flee the world, it would subjugate it, or win it
by gentle violence.

In Dominic Spain began to exercise that remarkable
Dominic a
Spaniard. influence over Latin Christianity, to display
that peculiar character which culminated as
it were in Ignatius Loyola, in Philip II., and in Torque-
mada, of which the code of the Inquisition was the
statutory law; of which Calderon was the poet. The
life of every devout Spaniard was a perpetual crusade.
By temperament and by position he was in constant
adventurous warfare against the enemies of the Cross:
hatred of the Jew, of the Mohammedan, was the horror
under which he served; it was the oath of his chivalry:
that hatred, in all its intensity, was soon and easily
extended to the heretic. Hereafter it was to comprehend the heathen Mexican, the Peruvian. St. Dominic
was, as it were, a Cortez, bound by his sense of duty,

urged by an inward voice, to invade older Christendom.
And Dominic was a man of as profound sagacity as of
adventurous enthusiasm. He intuitively perceived, or
the circumstances of his early career forced upon him,
the necessities of the age, and showed him the arms in
which himself and his forces must be arrayed to achieve
their conquest.

St. Dominic was born in 1170, in the village of
Caluroga, between Aranda and Osma, in Old
Castile. His parents were of noble name, that
of Guzman, if not of noble race.* Prophecies (we must
not disdain legend, though manifest legend) proclaimed
his birth. It was a tenet of his disciples that he was
born without original sin, sanctified in his mother's
womb. His mother dreamed that she bore a dog with
a torch in his mouth, which set the world on fire. His
votaries borrowed too the old classical fable; the bees
settled on his lips, foreshowing his exquisite eloquence.
Even in his infancy, his severe nature, among other
wonders, began to betray itself. He crept from his soft
couch to lie on the hard cold ground. The first part of
his education Dominic received from his uncle, a
churchman at Gamiel d'Izan. At fifteen years old he
was sent to the university of Palencia; he studied,
chiefly theology, for ten years. He was laborious,
devout, abstemious. Two stories are recorded which
show the dawn of religious strength in his character.
During a famine, he sold his clothes to feed the poor:
he offered in compassion to a woman who deplored the
slavery of her brother to the Moors, to be sold for his
redemption. He had not what may be strictly called a

---

* This point is contested. The Father Brémond wrote to confute the
Bollandists, who had cast a profane doubt on the noble descent of Dominic.

monastic training.[4] The Bishop of Osma had changed
his chapter into regular canons, those who lived in common, and under a rule approaching to a monastic
institute. Dominic became a canon in this rigorous
house: there he soon excelled the others in austerity.
This was in his twenty-fifth year: he remained in Osma,
not much known, for nine years longer. Diego de
Azevedo had succeeded to the Bishopric of Osma. He
was a prelate of great ability, and of strong religious
enthusiasm. He was sent to Denmark to negotiate the
marriage of Alfonso VIII. of Castile with a
princess of that kingdom. He chose the congenial Dominic as his companion. No sooner had they
crossed the Pyrenees than they found themselves in the
midst of the Albigensian heresy; they could not close
their eyes on the contempt into which the
clergy had fallen, or on the prosperity of the
sectarians; their very host at Toulouse was an Albigensian; Dominic is said to have converted him before the
morning.

The mission of the Bishop in Denmark was frustrated
by the unexpected death of the Princess. Before he
returned to Spain, Azevedo, with his companion, resolved
upon a pilgrimage to Rome. The character of the
Bishop of Osma appears from his proposal to Pope
Innocent. He wished to abandon his tranquil bishopric,
and to devote himself to the perilous life of a missionary,
among the Cumans and fierce people which occupied
part of Hungary, or in some other infidel country. That

(margin) In Langue-
doc.

(margin) A.D. 1203.

---

[4] The Chapter of his order was
shocked by, and carefully erased from
the authorised Legend of the Saint,
a passage, "Ubi nonnihil acerrit
illost in integritate carnis divinâ gratiâ
conservatum, nondum illam imper-
fectionem reddere potuisse, quia magis
afficiebatur juvencularum colloquiis
quam affatibus r Mulierum."—Apud
Holland. c. 1.

Dominic would have been his companion in this adventurous spiritual enterprise none can doubt. Innocent
commanded the Bishop to return to his diocese. On
their way the Bishop and Dominic stopped at Montpel-
lier. There, as has been said, they encountered in all their pomp the three Legates of A.D. 1206.
the Pope, Abbot Arnold, the Brother Raoul, and Peter
of Castelnau. The Legates were returning discomfited,
and almost desperate, from their progress in Languedoc.
Then it was that Dominic uttered his bold and memorable rebuke: "It is not by the display of power and
pomp, cavalcades of retainers, and richly houseled pal-
froys, or by gorgeous apparel, that the heretics will
proselytes; it is by zealous preaching, by apostolic
humility, by austerity, by seeming, it is true, but yet
seeming holiness. Zeal must be met by zeal, humility
by humility, false sanctity by real sanctity; preaching
falsehood by preaching truth." From that day Dominic
devoted himself to preaching the religion which he
believed. Even the Legates were for a time put to
shame by his precept and example, dismissed their
splendid equipages, and set forth with bare feet; yet if
with some humility of dress and demeanour, with none
of language or of heart. As the preacher of orthodoxy,
Dominic is said in the pulpit, at the conference, to have
argued with irresistible force: but his mission at last
seems to have made no profound impression on the
obstinate unbelievers. Ere long the Bishop Azevedo
retired to Osma and died. Dominic remained alone.

But now the murder of Peter of Castelnau roused
other powers and other passions. That more irresistible preacher, the sword of the Crusader, was sent
forth: it becomes impossible to discriminate between
the successes of one and of the other. The voice of

the Apostle is drowned in the din of war; even the conduct of Dominic himself, the manner in which he bore himself amidst these unevangelic allies, is clouded with doubt and uncertainty. His career is darkened too by
Miracles. the splendour of miracle, with which it is invested. These miracles must not be passed by: they are largely borrowed from the life of the Saviour and those of the Saints; they sometimes sink into the ludicrous. A schedule, which he had written during one conference, of scriptural proofs, leaped out of the fire, while the discriminating flames consumed the writings of his adversaries. He exorcised the devil who possessed three noble matrons in the shape of a great black cat with large black eyes, who at last ran up the bell-rope and disappeared. A lady of extreme beauty wished to leave her monastery, and resisted all the preacher's arguments. She blew her nose, it remained in the handkerchief. Horror-stricken, she implored the prayers of Dominic: at his intercession the nose resumed its place; the lady remained in the convent. Dominic raised the dead, frequently fed his disciples in a manner even more wonderful than the Lord in the desert.[*] His miracles equal, if not transcend those in the Gospel. It must indeed have been a stubborn generation, to need besides these wonders the sword of Simon de Montfort.

Throughout the Crusade Dominic is lost to the sight:
Dominic in war. he is hardly, if at all, noticed by historian or poet. It is not till the century after his death that his sterner followers boast of his presence, if not of his activity, in exciting the savage soldiery in the day

---

[*] All these and much more may be found in the lives of St. Dominic, in the Bollandists and elsewhere.

of battle. He marches unarmed in the van of the army
with the cross in his hands, and escapes unhurt. The
cross was shown pierced everywhere with arrows or jave-
lins, only the form of the Saviour himself uninjured. In
modern times there comes another change over the history of St. Dominic; that, of which his contemporaries
were silent, which the next generation blazoned forth
as a boast, is now become a grave imputation. In later
writings, his more prudent admirers assert, that he never
appeared in the field of battle; he was but once with
the armies, during the great victory of Simon de Montfort, at Muret; and then he remained within the city in
fervent and uninterrupted prayer. All, perhaps, that is
certainly known is that he showed no disapprobation of
the character or of the deeds of Simon de Montfort.
He obeyed his call to bless the marriage of his son, and
the baptism of his daughter.

So, too, the presence of St. Dominic on the tribunals,
where the unhappy heretics were tried for their
lives, and the part which he took in delivering   In the
tribunals.
them over to the secular arm to be burned by hundreds,
is in the same manner, according to the date of the biographer, a cause of pride or shame, is boldly vaunted,
or tenderly disguised and gently doubted. The more
charitable silence at least of the earlier writers is sternly
repudiated by the Bollandists, who will not allow the
milder sense to be given to the title "Persecutor of
Heretics," assigned to him by the Inquisition of Toulouse. They quote St. Thomas of Aquino as an irrefragable authority on the duty of burning heretics.
They refute the more tolerant argument by a long line
of glorious bishops who have urged or assisted at holo-
causts of victims. "What glory, splendour, and dignity (bursts forth Malvenda) belong to the Order of

Preachers, words cannot express! for the Holy Inquisition
owes its origin to St. Dominic, and was propagated by
his faithful followers. By them heretics of all kinds,
the innovators and corrupters of sound doctrine, were
destroyed, unless they would recant, by fire and sword,
or at least awed, banished, put to the rout." The title
of Dominic, in its fiercer sense, even rests on Papal
authority, that of Sixtus V. in his bull for the canonisation of Peter Martyr.[f] That indeed which in modern
days is alleged in proof of his mercy, rather implies his
habitual attendance on such scenes without showing the
same mercy. Once he interfered to save a victim, in
whom he saw some hopes of reconciliation, from the
flames.[g] Calmer inquiry must rob him of, or release
him from, these questionable glories. His heroic acts,
as moving in the van of bloody battles; his title of
Founder of the Inquisition, belong to legend not to history. It is his Order which has thrown back its aggran-
dising splendour on St. Dominic. So far was the Church
from bowing down before the transcendant powers and
holiness of the future saints, or discerning with instanta-
neous sagacity the value of these new allies, both the
Father of the Friar Preachers and the Father of the
Minorites were at first received with cold suspicion or
neglect at Rome; the foundation of the two new Orders
was extorted from the reluctant Innocent. The Third
Lateran Council had prohibited the establishment of
new orders. Well-timed and irresistible visions (the
counsels of wiser and more far-sighted men) enlightened

f " Jam vero ne recrudescerent in
posteris malum, aut impia hæresis
repullularet ex cineribus suis saluber-
rimo consilio Romani Pontificis Sanctæ
Inquisitionis officium creari S. Domi-   nici instituerunt, ridemque B. viro et
Fratribus Prædicatoribus præcipue
detulerunt."—Relchinius (a Dominicus); Præf. in Monetam. p. xxi.
    g La Cordaire, S. Dominique.

the Pope, and gently impelled him to open his eyes, and to yield to the revocation of his unwise judgement. Dominic returned from Rome, before the battle of Muret, armed with the Papal permission to enrol the Order of Friar Preachers.

The earliest foundation of Dominic had been a convent of females. He had observed that the noble ladies of Languedoc listened, especially in early life, with too eager ears to the preachers of heretical doctrines. At Prouille, at the foot of the Pyrenees, between Fanjaux and Monreal, he opened this retreat, where their virgin minds might be safe from the dangerous contagion. The first monastery of the Order of Preachers was that of St. Ronain, near Toulouse. The brotherhood consisted but of sixteen, most of them natives of Languedoc, some Spaniards, one Englishman. It is remarkable, however, that the Order, founded for the suppression of heresy by preaching in Languedoc, was hardly organised before it left the chosen scene of its labours. Instead of fixing on Toulouse or any of the cities of Provence as the centre of his operations, Dominic was seized with the ambition of converting the world. Rome, Bologna, Paris, were to be the seats of his power. Exactly four years after the battle of Muret he abandoned Languedoc for ever. His sagacious mind might perhaps anticipate the unfavourable change, the fall if not the death of De Montfort, the return of Count Raymond as the deliverer to his patrimonial city. But even the stern Spanish mind might be revolted by the horrors of the Albigensian war; he may have been struck by the common grief for the fall of the noble Spanish King of Arragon. At all events, the preacher of the word in Languedoc could play but a secondary part to the preacher by the sword;

and now that the aim was manifestly not conversion,
but conquest, not the re-establishment of the Church,
but the destruction of the liberties of the land, not the
subjugation of the heretical Count of Toulouse, but the
expulsion from their ancestral throne of the old princely
house and the substitution of a foreign usurper, the
Castilian might feel shame and compunction, even the
Christian might be reluctant to connect the Catholic
faith which he would preach with all the deeds of a
savage soldiery. The parting address ascribed to St.

Sept. 13, 1217.

Dominic is not quite consistent with this more
generous and charitable view of his conduct.
It is a terrible menace rather than gentle regret or
mild reproof. At the convent of Prouille, after high
mass, he thus spake: "For many years I have spoken
to you with tenderness, with prayers, and tears; but
according to the proverb of my country, where the
benediction has no effect, the rod may have much.
Behold, now, we rouse up against you princes and prelates, nations and kingdoms! Many shall perish by the
sword. The land shall be ravaged, walls thrown down;
and you, alas! reduced to slavery. So shall the chastisement do that which the blessing and which mildness
could not do." [b]

Dominic himself took up his residence in Rome.[c] His
success as a preacher was unrivalled. His followers
began to spread rumours of the miracles which he
wrought. The Pope Honorius III. appointed him to
the high office, since perpetuated among his spiritual
descendants, Master of the Sacred Palace. He was
held in the highest honour by the aged Cardinal Ugo-

[b] MS. de Prouille, published by
Père Percin; quoted by La Cordaire,
Vie de S. Dominique, p. 404.

[c] He first established the monastery
of San Sisto on the Celian Hill, after-
ward that of Santa Sabina.

lino, the future Pope Gregory IX. For the propagation
of his Order this residence in Rome was a master-stroke
of policy. Of the devout pilgrims to Rome, men of all
countries in Christendom, the most devout were most
enraptured by the eloquence of Dominic. Few but
must feel that it was a preaching Order which was
wanted in every part of the Christian world. Dominic
was gifted with that rare power, even in those times, of
infusing a profound and enduring devotion to one object.
Once within the magic circle, the enthralled disciple
either lost all desire to leave it, or, if he struggled, Dominic seized him and dragged him back, now an unreluctant captive, by awe, by persuasion, by conviction,
by what was believed to be miracle which might be
holy art, or the bold and ready use of casual but natural
circumstances. "God has never," as he revealed in
secret (a secret not likely to be religiously kept) to the
Abbot of Casamore, "refused me anything that I have
prayed for." When he prayed for the conversion of
Conrad the Teutonic, was Conrad left ignorant that he
had to resist the prayers of one whom God had thus
endowed with irresistible efficacy of prayer?[a] Thus were
preachers rapidly enlisted and dispersed throughout the
world, speaking every language in Christendom. Two
Poles, Hyacinth and Ceslas, carried the rules of the
order to their own country. Dominican convents were
founded at Cracow, even as far as Kiow.

Dominic had judged wisely and not too daringly in
embracing the world as the scene of his labours. Rapid pro-
In the year 1220, seven years after he had left gress of the
Languedoc, he stood, as the Master-General of A.D. 1220.
his order, at the head of an assembly at Bologna. Italy,

---

[a] La Cordaire, p. 539.

Spain, Provence, France, Germany, Poland, had now their Dominican convents; the voices of Dominican preachers had penetrated into every land. But the great question of holding property or dependence on the casual support of mendicancy was still undecided. Dominic had accepted landed endowments: in Languedoc he held a grant of tithes from Fulk Bishop of Toulouse. But the Order of St. Francis, of which absolute poverty was the vital rule, was now rising with simultaneous rapidity. Though both the founders of the new Orders and the brethren of the Orders had professed and displayed the most perfect mutual respect, and even amity (twice, it was said, they had met, with great marks of reverence and esteem), yet both true policy and devout ambition might reveal to the prudent as well as ardent Dominic that the vow of absolute poverty would give the Franciscans an immeasurable superiority in popular estimation. His followers must not be trammelled with worldly wealth, or be outdone in any point of austerity by those of St. Francis. The universal suffrage was for the vow of poverty in the strongest sense, the renunciation of all property by the Order as well as by the individual Brother. How long, how steadfastly, that vow was kept by either Order will appear in the course of our history.

The second great assembly of the Order was held shortly before the death of Dominic. The Order was now distributed into eight provinces, Spain, the first in rank, Provence, France, Lombardy, Rome, Germany, Hungary, and England. In England the Prior Gilbert had landed with fourteen friars. Gilbert preached before the Archbishop of Canterbury. The Primate, Stephen Langton, was so edified by his eloquence, that he at once gave full licence to

A.D. 1221.

preach throughout the land. Monasteries rose at Canterbury, London, Oxford.

But tho great strength of these two new Orders was, besides the communities of friars and nuns (each associated with itself a kindred female Order), the establishment of a third, a wider and more *Tertiaries* secular community, who were bound to the two former by bonds of close association, by reverence and implicit obedience, and were thus always ready to maintain tho interests, to admire and to propagate the wonders, to subserve in every way the advancement of the higher disciples of St. Dominic or St. Francis. They were men or women, old or young, married or unmarried, bound by none of the monastic vows, but deeply imbued with the monastic, with the corporate spirit; taught to observe all holy days, fasts, vigils with the utmost rigour, inured to constant prayer and attendance on divine worship. They were organised, each under his own prior; they crowded as a duty, as a privilege, into the church wherever a Dominican ascended the pulpit, predisposed, almost compelled, if compulsion were necessary, to admire, to applaud at least by rapt attention. Thus the Order spread not merely by its own perpetual influence and unwearied activity; it had everywhere a vast host of votaries wedded to its interests, full to fanaticism of its corporate spirit, bound to receive hospitably or ostentatiously their wandering preachers, to announce, to trumpet abroad, to propagate the fame of their eloquence, to spread belief in their miracles, to lavish alms upon them, to fight in their cause. This lay coadjutory, these Tertiaries, as they were called, or among the Dominicans, the Soldiers of Jesus Christ as not altogether secluded from the world, acted more widely and more subtly upon the world. Their rules were not rigidly

laid down till by the seventh Master of the Order,
Munion de Zamora; it was then approved by Popes.[*]

Dominic died August 6th, 1221. He was taken ill
at Venice, removed with difficulty to Bologna,
where he expired with saintly resignation.

Death.

His canonisation followed rapidly on his death. Gregory IX., who in his internecine war with the
Emperor Frederick II. had found the advan-
tage of these faithful, restless, unscrupulous allies in the
realm, in the camp, almost in the palace of his adversary, was not the man to pause or to hesitate in his
grateful acknowledgements or prodigal reward. " I no
more doubt," said the Pope, " the sanctity of Dominic
than that of St. Peter or St. Paul." In the bull of
canonisation, Dominic is elaborately described as riding
in the four-horsed chariot of the Gospel, as it were
seated behind the four Evangelists (or rather in the
four chariots of Zechariah, long interpreted as signifying
the four Evangelists), holding in his hand the irresistible
bow of the Divine Word.

Canonisation.

The admiration of their founder, if it rose not with
the Dominicans so absolutely into divine adoration as
with the Franciscans, yet bordered close upon it. He,
too, was so closely approximated to the Saviour as to be
placed nearly on an equality. The Virgin Mother herself, the special protectress of the sons of Dominic,[*]

---

[*] Among the special privileges of
the Order (in the bull of Honorius)
was that in the time of interdict (so
common were interdicts now become)
the Order might still celebrate mass
with low voice, without bells. Conceive the influence thus obtained in a
religious land, everywhere else deprived of all its holy services.

[*] There is a strange story of the
especial protection extended over the
Order by the Virgin. It might seem
singularly ill-adapted for painting, but
painting has nevertheless ventured, at
least partially, to represent it. To
this the modesty of more modern
manners, perhaps not less real though
more scrupulous respect (respect which

might almost seem to sanction their bold raptures of
spiritual adulation, from which our most fervent piety
might shrink as wild profanation. Dominic was the
adopted Son of the Blessed Virgin.*

And this was part of the creed maintained by an
Order which under its fourth general, John of Wil-
deshausen (in Westphalia), in their Chapter-General at
Bordeaux, reckoned its monasteries at the number of
four hundred and seventy. In Spain thirty-five, in
France fifty-two, in Germany fifty-two, in Tuscany
thirty-two, in Lombardy forty-six, in Hungary thirty,
in Poland thirty-six, in Denmark twenty-eight, in England forty. They were spreading into Asia, into heathen
or Saracen lands, into Palestine, Greece, Crete, Abys-

---

falls far short of worship), proscribes
more than an allusion; The Virgin
is represented with the whole convent
host of Dominicans crowded under
her dress. In the vision of St. Bri-
gitta, the Virgin herself is made to
sanction this awful confusion. Though
in the vision there is an interpretation
which softens away that which is the
painting (which I have seen) becomes
actual fact.

* More than this, of the Father
himself, "Ego, dulcissima filia, istos
duos filios genui, unum naturaliter
generando, alium amabiliter et dulciter
adoptando, ... Sicut hic Filius a
me naturaliter et æternaliter genitus,
assumptâ naturâ humanâ, in omnibus
fuit perfectissime obediens mihi, usque
ad mortem, sic filius meus adoptivus
Dominicus. Omnis, quæ operatur est
ab infantiâ suâ usque ad terminum
vitæ suæ, fuerunt angulata secundum
obedientiam præceptorum mesorum,

nec unquam semel fuit transgressus
quodcunque præceptum meum, quia
virginitatem corporis et animi illibatam
servavit, et gratiam baptismi quæ
spiritualiter renatus est, semper con-
servavit." The parallel goes on between the apostles of the Lord and
the brethren of S. Dominic,—Apud
Bolland. xiv. p. 544. See also a passage about the Virgin in La Corbière,
p. 234. In another Vita S. Dominici,
apud Bolland. Aug. 4, is this :—
There was a prophetic picture at
Venice, in which appear St. Paul and
S. Dominic. Under the latter, "Fac-
Hur Iter per istum." The comment
of the biographer is : "Doctrina Pauli
sicut et cæterorum apostolorum erat
doctrina inducens ad fidem et observationem præceptorum, doctrina Dominici ad observationem consiliorum, et
idea facilius per ipsum Iter ad Chris-
tum."—n. vii.

sinia. Nor is it their number alone which grows with such wonderful fertility. They are not content with the popular mind. They invade the high places of human intellect: they are disputing the mastery in the Universities of Italy and Germany, in Cologne, Paris, and in Oxford. Before long they are to claim two of the greatest luminaries of the scholastic philosophy, Albert the Great and Thomas of Aquino.

CHAPTER X.

St. Francis.[a]

ST. FRANCIS was born in the romantic town of Assisi, of a family, the Bernardini, engaged in trade. His birth took place while his father was on a mercantile journey in France; on his return his new-born son was baptised by the name of Francis.[b] His mother, Picca, loved him with all a mother's tenderness for her first-born. He received the earliest rudiments of instruction from the clergy of the parish of St. George: he was soon taken to assist his father in his trade. The father, a hard, money-making man, was shocked at first by the vanity and prodigality of his son. The young Francis gave banquets to his juvenile friends, dressed splendidly, and the streets of Assisi rang with the songs and revels of the joyous crew; but even then his bounty

(margin note: Birth and youth. A.D. 1182.)

---

[a] The vast annals of the Franciscan Order, by Lucas Wadding, in seventeen folio volumes, are the great authority: for S. Francis himself the life by S. Bonaventura. I have much used the Chronique de l'Ordre du Père S. François, in quaint old French (the original is in Portuguese, by Marco di Lisbona), Paris, 1623. I have an epic poem, in twenty-five cantos, a kind of religious plagiary of Tasso, San Francesco, ó Gierusalemme Celeste Acquistata, by Agostino Gallucci (1617). The author makes S. Francis imbibe the Wickliffites. There is a modern life by M. Malan.

[b] When the disciples of S. Francis were fully possessed with the conformity of their founder with the Saviour, the legend grew up, assimilating his birth to that of the Lord. A prophetess foreshowed it; he was born by divine suggestion in a stable; angels rejoiced; even peace and good will were announced, though by a human voice. An angel, like old Simeon, bare him at the font. And all this is gravely related by a biographer of the 19th century, M. Malan.

to the poor formed a large part of his generous waste-
fulness. He was taken captive in one of the petty wars
which had broken out between Perugia and Assisi, and
remained a year in prison. He was then seized with a
violent illness: when he rose from his bed nature looked
cold and dreary; he began to feel disgust to the world.
The stirrings of some great but yet undefined purpose
were already awake within him. He began to see
visions, but as yet they were of war and glory: the
soldier was not dead in his heart. He determined to
follow the fortunes of a youthful poor knight who was
setting out to fight under the banner of the "Gentle
Count," Walter of Brienne, against the hated Germans.
At Spoleto he again fell ill; his feverish visions took
another turn. Francis now felt upon him that profound
religious thraldom which he was never to break, never
to desire to break. His whole soul became deliberately,
calmly, extatic faith. He began to talk mysteriously of
his future bride—that bride was Poverty. He resolved
never to refuse alms to a poor person. He found his
way to Rome, threw down all he possessed, no costly
offering, on the altar of St. Peter. On his return he
joined a troop of beggars, and exchanged his dress for
the rags of the filthiest among them. His mother heard
and beheld all his strange acts with a tender and prophetic admiration. To a steady trader like the father it
was folly if not madness. He was sent with a valuable
bale of goods to sell at Foligno. On his return he threw
all the money down at the feet of the priest of St.
Damian to rebuild his church, as well as the price of his
horse, which he likewise sold. The priest refused the
gift. In the eyes of the father this was dishonesty as
well as folly. Francis concealed himself in a cave, where
he lay hid for a month in solitary prayer. He returned

to Assisi, looking so wild and haggard that the rabble hooted him as he passed and pelted him with mire and stones. The gentle Francis appeared to rejoice in every persecution. The indignant father shut him up in a dark chamber, from which, after a time, he was released by the tender solicitude of his mother. Bernardini now despaired of his unprofitable and intractable son, whom he suspected of alienating other sums besides that which he had received for the cloth and the horse. He cited him before the magistrates to compel him to abandon all rights on his patrimony, which he was disposed to squander in this thriftless manner. Francis declared that he was a servant of God, and declined the jurisdiction of the civil magistrate. The cause came before the Bishop. The Bishop earnestly exhorted Francis to yield up to his father any money which he might possess, or to which he was entitled. "It might be ungodly gain, and so unfit to be applied to holy uses." "I will give up the very clothes I wear," replied the enthu- Gives up his inheritance. A.D. 1207. Ætat. 25. siast, encouraged by the gentle demeanour of the Bishop. He stripped himself entirely naked.* "Peter Bernardini was my father; I have now but one father, he that is in heaven." The audience burst into tears; the Bishop threw his mantle over him and ordered an old coarse dress of an artisan to be brought: he then received Francis into his service.

Francis was now wedded to Poverty; but poverty he would only love in its basest form—mendi- Embraces mendicancy. cancy. He wandered abroad, was ill used by robbers; on his escape he received from an old friend at Gubbio a hermit's attire, a short tunic, a leathern girdle, a staff and slippers. He begged at the gates of

---

* According to S. Bonaventura, he had haircloth under his dress.

monasteries; he discharged the most menial offices.
With even more profound devotion he dedicated himself
for some time in the hospital at Gubbio to that unhappy
race of beings whom even Christianity was constrained
to banish from the social pale—the lepers.[4] He tended
them with more than necessary affectionateness, washed
their feet, dressed their sores, and is said to have wrought
miraculous cures among them. The moral miracle of
his charity toward them is a more certain and more
affecting proof of his true Christianity of heart. It was
an especial charge to the brethren of St. Francis of Assisi
to choose these outcasts of humanity as the objects of
their peculiar care.[5]

On his return to Assisi he employed himself in the
restoration of the church of St. Damian. "Whoever
will give me one stone shall have one prayer; whoever
two, two; three, three." The people mocked, but
Francis went on carrying the stones in his own hands,
and the church began to rise. He refused all food
which he did not obtain by begging. His father
reproached him and uttered his malediction. He took
a beggar of the lowest class: "Do thou my father and
give me thy blessing." But so successful was he in
awakening the charity of the inhabitants of Assisi, that

---

4 There is something singularly
affecting in the service of the Church
for the seclusion of the lepers, whose
number is as sure a proof of the
wretchedness of those times, as the
care of them of the charity. The
stern duty of looking to the public
welfare is tempered with exquisite
compassion for the victims of this
loathsome disease. The service may
be found—it is worth seeking for—in
Marténe de Antiquis Ecclesiæ Ritibus.

It is quoted by M. Malan. Compare
on S. Francis and the Lepers, Mr.
Brewer's Preface to the Monumenta
Franciscana, p. xliii., et seqq.; and
Translation of the Testament of S.
Francis, p. 592.

5 S. Bonaventura says that he
healed one leper with a kiss; "Nescio
quidnam horum magis sit admirandum,
an humilitatis profunditas in osculo tam
benigno, an virtutis præclaritas in mira-
culo tam stupendo."—Vit. S. Francisci.

not only the church of St. Damian, but two others,
St. Peter and St. Maria dei Angeli (called the Portiuncula), through his means arose out of their ruins to
decency and even splendour. One day, in the church
of St. Maria dei Angeli, he heard the text, " Provide
neither gold, nor silver, nor brass in your purse.
Neither scrip for your journey, neither two coats, neither
shoes nor yet staves." He threw away his wallet, his
staff, and his shoes, put on the coarsest dark grey tunic,
bound himself with a cord, and set out through the city
calling all to repentance.

This strange but fervent piety of Francis could not
but, in that age, kindle the zeal of others. Wonder
grew into admiration, admiration into emulation, emulation into a blind following of his footsteps. Disciples,
one by one (the first are carefully recorded), began to
gather round him. He retired with them to a lonely
spot in the bend of the river, called Rivo Torto. A rule
was wanting for the young brotherhood. Thrice upon
the altar he opened the Gospels, which perhaps were
accustomed to be opened on these passages.[i] He read
three texts in reverence for the Holy Trinity. The
first was, " If thou wilt be perfect, sell all thou hast
and give to the poor ;"[g] the second, " Take nothing for
your journey ;"[h] the third, " If any one would come
after me, let him take up his cross and follow me."[i]
Francis made the sign of the cross and sent forth his
followers into the neighbouring cities, as if to divide the
world, to the east and west, the north and south. They
reassembled at Rivo Torto and determined to go to
Rome to obtain the authority of the Pope for the foundation of their order. On the way they met a knight

---

[i] The poet gives the date, St. Luke's day, Oct. 18, 1212.
[g] Matt. xix. 21.   [h] Mark vi. 8.   [i] Matt. xvi. 24.

in arms. "Angelo," said St. Francis, "instead of that
baldrick thou shalt gird thee with a cord; for thy sword
thou shalt take the cross of Christ; for the spurs, the
dirt and mire." Angelo made up the mystic number of
twelve, which the profound piety of his followers alleged
as a new similitude to the Lord.[b]

Innocent III. was walking on the terrace of the
Lateran when a mendicant of the meanest appearance
presented himself, proposing to convert the world by
poverty and humility. The haughty Pontiff dismissed
him with contempt. But a vision, says the legend,
doubtless more grave deliberation and inquiry, suggested
that such an Order might meet the heretics on their
own ground; the Poor Men of the Church might out-
labour and out-suffer the Poor Men of Lyons. He sent
for Francis, received him in the midst of the cardinals,
and listened to his proposal for his new Order. Some of
the cardinals objected the difficulty, the impossibility
of the vows. "To suppose that anything is difficult or
impossible with God," said the Cardinal Bishop of Sabina,
"is to blaspheme Christ and his Gospel."

The Order was now founded; the Benedictines of
Monte Subiaco gave them a church, called,
like that near Assisi, St. Maria dei Angeli, or
de la Portiuncula. In the difficulty, the seeming impossibility of the vows was their strength. The three vital
principles of the Order were chastity, poverty, obedience. For chastity, no one was to speak with a woman
alone, except the few who might safely do so (from age
or severity of character), and that was to urge penitence

---

[b] It was at this period that he was
said, or said himself that he was
transported to heaven, into the actual
presence of the Lord, who, according
to the poem, gave him a plenary indulgence for himself and his followers:—
"E plenaria indulgenza ogni dì dava."
c. vi. 41

or give spiritual counsel. Poverty was not only the
renunciation of all possessions, but of all property, even
in the clothes they wore, in the cord which girt them—
even in their breviaries.* Money was, as it were,
infected; they might on no account receive it in alms
except (the sole exception) to aid a sick brother; no
brother might ride if he had power to walk. They
were literally to fulfil the precept, if stricken on one
cheek, to offer the other; if spoiled of part of their
dress, to yield up the rest. Obedience was urged not
merely as obligatory and coercive : the deepest mutual
love was to be the bond of the brotherhood.

The passionate fervour of the preaching, the mystic
tenderness, the austere demeanour of Francis and his
disciples, could not but work rapidly and profoundly
among his female hearers. Clara, a noble virgin of
Assisi, under the direction of St. Francis, had in the
same manner to strive against the tender and affection-
ate worldliness, as she deemed it, of her family. But
she tore herself from their love as from a sin, entered
into a convent attached to the church of St. Damian,
and became the mother of the poor sisterhood of St.
Clare. Of Clara it is said that she never but once (and
that to receive the blessing of the Pope) so lifted her
eyelids that the colour of her eyes might be discerned.
Clara practised mortifications more severe than any of
her sex before. The life of the sisters was one long
dreary penance; even their services were all sadness.
The sisters who could read were to read the Hours, but
without chanting. Those who could not read were not
to learn to read. To the prayers of St. Clara it was

* At first, says S. Bonaventura, they had no books; their only book
was the cross.

attributed that, in later times, her own convent and the city of Assisi were preserved from the fierce Mohammedans which belonged to the army of Frederick II. The Order was confirmed by a bull of Innocent IV.

Francis, in the mean time, with his whole soul vowed to the service of God, set forth to subdue the world. He had hesitated between the contemplative and active life—prayer in the secluded monastery, or preaching the cross of Christ to mankind. The mission of love prevailed; his success and that of his ardent followers might seem to justify their resolution. They had divided the world, and some had already set forth into France and into Spain with the special design of converting the Miramamolin and his Mohammedan subjects. Everywhere they were heard with fanatic rapture. At their first Chapter, held in the church of the Portiuncula, only three years after the scene at Rivo Torto, it was necessary to ordain provincial masters in Spain, Provence, France and Germany: at a second Chapter of the Order in 1219 met five thousand brethren.

The holy ambition of St. Francis grew with his success. He determined to confront the great enemy of Christianity in his strength. He set off to preach to the Mohammedans of the East. The Christian army was encamped before Damietta. The sagacity of Francis anticipated from their discord, which he in vain endeavoured to reconcile, their defeat. His prophecy was too fully accomplished; but he determined not the less to proceed on his mission. On his way to the Saracen camp he met some sheep. It occurred to him, "I send you forth as sheep among the wolves." He was taken and carried before the Sultan. To the Sultan he boldly offered the way of salvation.

He preached (in what language we are not told) the
Holy Trinity and the Divine Saviour before these stern
Unitarians. The Mohammedans reverence what they
deem insanity as partaking of divine inspiration. The
Sultan is said to have listened with respect; his grave
face no doubt concealed his compassion. St. Francis
offered to enter a great fire with the priests of Islam,
and to set the truth of either faith on the issue. The
Sultan replied that his priests would not willingly submit to this perilous trial. "I will enter alone," said
Francis, "if, should I be burned, you will impute it to
my sins; should I come forth alive, you will embrace
the Gospel." The Sultan naturally declined these terms,
as not quite fair towards his creed. But he offered rich
presents to Francis (which the preacher of poverty rejected with utter disdain), and then sent him back in
honour to the camp at Damietta. Francis passed
through the Holy Land and the kingdom of Antioch,
preaching and winning disciples, and then returned to
Italy. His fame was now at its height, and wherever
he went his wondering disciples saw perpetual miracle.
In this respect the life of the Saviour is far surpassed
by that of St. Francis.

The Order soon had its martyrs. The Mohammedan
Moors of Africa were fiercer than those of
Egypt. Five monks, after preaching without   Martyrs.
success to the Saracens of Seville, crossed into Africa.
After many adventures (in one of which during an expedition against the Moorish tribes of the interior, Friar
Berard struck water from the desert rock, like Moses)
they were offered wealth, beautiful wives, and honours,
if they would embrace Mohammedanism. They spat on
the ground in contempt of the miscreant offer. The
King himself clove the head of one of them with a

sword; the rest were despatched in horrible torments.[*]
St. Francis received the sad intelligence with triumph,
and broke forth in gratulations to the convent of Alou-
quir, which had thus produced the first purple flowers of
martyrdom.

This was no hardness, or want of compassion, but
the counterworking of a stronger, more passionate emotion. Of all saints, St. Francis was
the most blameless and gentle. In Dominic and in his
disciples all was still rigorous, cold, argumentative;
something remained of the crusader's fierceness, the
Spaniard's haughty humility, the inquisitor's stern suppression of all gentler feelings, the polemic sternness.
Whether Francis would have burned heretics, happily
we know not, but he would willingly have been burned
for them: himself excessive in austerities, he would at
times mitigate the austerity of others. Francis was
emphatically the Saint of the people—of a poetic people
like the Italians. Those who were hereafter to chant
the Paradise of Dante, or the softer stanzas of Tasso,
might well be enamoured of the ruder devotional strains
in the poetry of the whole life of St. Francis. The
lowest of the low might find consolation, a kind of pride,
in the self-abasement of St. Francis even beneath the
meanest. The very name of his disciples, the Friar
Minors, implied their humility. In his own eyes (says
his most pious successor) he was but a sinner, while in
truth he was the mirror and splendour of holiness. It
was revealed, says the same Bonaventura, to a Brother,
that the throne of one of the angels, who fell from pride,

Character of St. Francis.

---

[*] See on these martyrs Southey's ballad :—
  "What news," / Queen Orraca,
    Of the martyrs five what news?
  Have the bloody Miramamolin
    Their burial yet refuse?"

was reserved for Francis, who was glorified by humility.
If the heart of the poorest was touched by the brotherhood in poverty and lowliness of such a saint, how was
his imagination kindled by his mystic strains? St.
Francis is among the oldest vernacular poets of Italy.°
His poetry, indeed, is but a long passionate ejaculation
of love to the Redeemer in rude metre; it has not even
the order and completeness of a hymn: it is a sort of
plaintive variation on one simple melody—an echo of
the same tender words, multiplied again and again, it
might be fancied, by the voices in the cloister walls.
But his ordinary speech is more poetical than his poetry.
In his peculiar language he addresses all animate, even
inanimate, creatures as his brothers; not merely the
birds and beasts; he had an especial fondness for lambs
and larks, as the images of the Lamb of God and of the
cherubim in heaven.ᵖ I know not if it be among the
Conformities, but the only malediction I find him to
have uttered was against a fierce swine which had killed
a young lamb. Of his intercourse with these mute
animals, we are told many pretty particularities, some
of them miraculous. But his poetic impersonation went
beyond this. When the surgeon was about to cauterise
him, he said, "Fire, my brother, be thou discreet and
gentle to me."ᵠ In one of his Italian hymns he speaks
of his brother the sun, his sister the moon, his brother
the wind, his sister the water.ʳ No wonder that in this
almost perpetual extatic state, unearthly music played

° M. de Montalembert is eloquent, as usual, on his poetry.—Preface to "La Vie d'Elizabeth d'Hongrie."

ᵖ Bonaventura, c. viii.

ᵠ The words were, "Fratel fuoco, da Dio creato più bello, più attivo, e più giovevole d'ogni altro elemento, sol tu mostra or nel cimento discret e mite."—Vita (Foligno), p. 15.

ʳ "Laudato sia el Dio, mio Signore con tute le Creature; specialmente Messer lo frate Sole. . . . Laudato sia il mio Signore per suor Luna, per frate vento, per suor acqua."

D 2

around him, unearthly light shone round his path. When
he died, he said, with exquisite simplicity, " Welcome,
sister Death." [a] St. Francis himself, no doubt, was but
unconsciously presumptuous, when he acted as under
divine inspiration, even when he laid the ground-work
for that assimilation of his own life to that of the Saviour,
which was wrought up by his disciples, as it were, into a
new Gospel, and superseded the old. His was the studious
imitation of humility, not the emulous approximation of
pride, even of pride disguised from himself; such pro-
faneness entered not into his thought. His life might
seem a religious trance. The mysticism so absolutely
absorbed him as to make him unconscious, as it were,
of the presence of his body. Incessantly active as was
his life, it was a kind of paroxysmal activity, constantly
collapsing into what might seem a kind of suspended
animation of the corporeal functions.[b] It was even said
that he underwent a kind of visible and glorious trans-
figuration.[c] But with what wonderful force must all
this have worked upon the world, the popular world
around him! About three years before his death, with
the permission of the Pope, he celebrated the Nativity
of the Lord in a new way. A manger was prepared,
the whole scene of the miraculous birth represented.
The mass was interpolated before the prayers. St.

---

[a] " Ben venga la sorella morte."

[b] " E tanto in lei (in Grea) sovrate
profondasi, tanto s' immerge, s' abissa,
e concentra, che assorto non vide, non
ascolta, non sente, e se opera carnal-
mente, sol conosca, non sel rammenta."
This state is thus illustrated : he was
riding on an ass ; he was almost torn
in pieces by devout men and women
shouting around him ; he was utterly
unconscious, like a dead man.—From

a modern Vita di S. Francesco, Foligno,
1824.

[c] " Ad conspectum sublimis Seraph
et humilis Crucifixi, fuit in vivæ
formæ effigiem, vi quâdam deiformi
et igneâ transformatus ; quemadmo-
dum testati sunt, tactis sacrosanctis
jurantes, qui palpaverunt, osculati
sunt, et viderunt."—S. Bonaventura,
in Vit. Minor. l.

Francis preached on the Nativity. The angelic choirs
were heard; a wondering disciple declared that he saw
a beautiful child reposing in the manger.

The order of St. Francis had, and of necessity, its
Tertiaries, like that of St. Dominic.[*] At his preaching,
and that of his disciples, such multitudes would have
crowded into the Order as to become dangerous and
unmanageable. The whole population of one town,
Canari in Umbria, offered themselves as disciples. The
Tertiaries were called the Brethren of Penitence; they
were to retain their social position in the world: but,
first enjoined to discharge all their debts, and to make
restitution of all unfair gains. They were then admitted
to make a vow to keep the commandments of God, and
to give satisfaction for any breach of which they might
have been guilty. They could not leave the order,
except to embrace a religious life. Women were not
admitted without the consent of their husbands. The
form and colour of their dress were prescribed, silk
rigidly prohibited. They were to keep aloof from all
public spectacles, dances, especially the theatre; to give
nothing to actors, jugglers, or such profane persons.
Their fasts were severe, but tempered with some lenity;
their attendance at church constant. They were not to
bear arms except in the cause of the Church of Rome,
the Christian faith, or their country, and that at the
licence of their ministers. On entering the Order, they
were immediately to make their wills to prevent future
litigation; they were to abstain from unnecessary oaths;
they were to submit to penance, when imposed by their
ministers.

But St. Francis had not yet attained his height even

* Chapter of Tertiaries, A.D. 1772; Chroniques, L. II. c. xxxii.

of worldly fame; he was yet to receive the last marks of
his similitude to the Redeemer, to bear on
his body actually and really the five wounds of
the Redeemer.

A.D. 1224.

That which was so gravely believed must be gravely
related. In the solitude of Monte Alverno (a
mountain which had been bestowed on the
Order by a rich and pious votary, and where a magnificent church afterwards arose) Francis had retired to
hold a solemn fast in honour of the Archangel Michael.
He had again consulted the holy oracle. Thrice the
Scriptures had been opened; thrice they opened on the
Passion of the Lord. This was interpreted, that even
in this life Francis was to be brought into some mysterious conformity with the death of the Saviour. One
morning, while he was praying in an access of the most
passionate devotion, he saw in a vision, or, as he supposed, in real being, a seraph with six wings. Amidst
these wings appeared the likeness of the Crucified.
Two wings arched over his head, two were stretched for
flight, two veiled the body. As the apparition disappeared, it left upon his mind an indescribable mixture
of delight and awe. On his body instantaneously appeared marks of the crucifixion, like those which he had
beheld. Two black excrescences, in the form of nails,
with the heads on one side, the points bent back on the
other, had grown out of his hands and feet. There was
a wound on his side, which frequently flowed with blood,
and stained his garment. Francis endeavoured, in his
extreme humility, notwithstanding the remonstrances of
his disciples, to conceal this wonderful sight; but the
wounds were seen, it is declared, at one time by fifty
brethren. Countless miracles were ascribed to their
power. The wound on his side Francis hid with peculiar

The Stig-
mata.

care. But it was seen during his life, as it is asserted;
the pious curiosity of his disciples pierced through every
concealment. Pope Alexander IV. publicly declared
that his own eyes had beheld the stigmata on the body
of St. Francis. Two years after St. Francis
died. He determined literally to realise the   Oct. 4, 1726.
words of the Scripture, to leave the world naked as he
entered it. His disciples might then, and did then, it
is said, actually satisfy themselves as to these signs: to
complete the parallel an incredulous Thomas was found
to investigate the fact with suspicious scrutiny. It became
an article of the Franciscan creed; though the now rival
Order, the Dominicans, hinted rationalistic doubts, they
were authoritatively rebuked. It became almost the
creed of Christendom.[7]

Up to a certain period this studious conformity of
the life of St. Francis with that of Christ,   Character
heightened, adorned, expanded, till it received   of Francis-
                                                      canism.
its perfect form in the work of Bartholomew of Pisa,
was promulgated by the emulous zeal of a host of disciples throughout the world. Those whose more reverential piety might take offence were few and silent; the
declaration of Pope Alexander, the ardent protector of
the Mendicant Friars, imposed it almost as an article of
the Belief. With the Franciscans, and all under the

[7] The Dominican Jacob de Voragine
assigns five causes for the stigmata;
they in fact resolve themselves into
the first, imagination. His illustra-
tions, however, are chiefly from preg-
ant women, whose children resemble
something which had violently impressed the mother's mind. He does
not deny the fact. "Summum ergo
Franciscum, in violone sibi facta imagina-
batur Seraphim Crucifixum, et tam

fortis imaginationis extitit, quod vulnera
passionis in carne sua impressit."—
Sermo iii. de S. Francisco. Compare
Gieseler, ii. 2, 349. Nicolas IV., too,
asserted the stigmata of St. Francis
(he was himself a Franciscan); he
silenced a Dominican, who dared to
assert that in Peter Martyr (Peter
was a Dominican) were signs Dei vivi,
in St. Francis only Dei mortui.—
Raynald, A.D. 1291.

dominion of the Franciscans, the lower orders throughout Christendom, there was thus almost a second Gospel, a second Redeemer, who could not but throw back the one Saviour into more awful obscurity. The worship of St. Francis in prayer, in picture, vied with that of Christ: if it led, perhaps, a few up to Christ, it kept the multitude fixed upon itself. But as soon as indignant religion dared lift up its protest (after several centuries!) it did so; and, as might be expected, revenged its long compulsory silence by the bitterest satire and the rudest burlesque.[a]

Franciscanism was the democracy of Christianity; but with St. Francis it was an humble, meek, quiescent democracy. In his own short fragmentary writings he ever enforces the most submissive obedience to the clergy;[b] those, at least, who lived according to the rule of the Roman Church. This rule would no doubt except the simoniac and the married clergy; but the whole character of his teaching was the farthest removed from that of a spiritual demagogue. His was a pacific passive mysticism, which consoled the poor for the inequalities of this life by the hopes of heaven. But ere long his more vehement disciple, Antony of Padua, sounded a dif-

---

[a] See the Alcoran des Cordeliers. Yet this book could hardly transcend the grave blasphemies of the Liber Conformitatum, e.g., Christ was transfigured once; S. Francis twenty times; Christ changed water into wine once, S. Francis three times; Christ endured his wounds a short time, S. Francis two years; and so with all the Gospel miracles.

[b] In his Testament he writes: "Postea dedit mihi Dominus, et dat tantam fidem in sacerdotibus, qui vivunt secundum Ordinem Sanctæ Romanæ ecclesiæ propter ordinem ipsorum, quod si facerent mihi persecutionem volo recurrere ad ipsos."— Op. S. Francisc. p. 20. "Il disoit que s'il rencontroit un Saint qui fust descendu du ciel en terre et un Prestre, qu'il baiseroit premièrement la main au Prestre, puis il feroit la reverence au Saint, recevant de celui-là le corps de nostre Seigneur Jesus Christ, pourquoi il méritoit plus d'honneur."— Chroniques, l. 4, lxxiv.

ferent note: he scrupled not to denounce the worldly
clergy. Antony of Padua was a Portuguese, born at
Lisbon. He showed early a strong religious temperament. The reliques of the five Franciscan martyrs,
sent over from Morocco, had kindled the most ardent
enthusiasm. The young Fernand (such was his bap-
tismal name) joined himself to some Franciscan friars,
utterly illiterate, but of burning zeal, and under their
guidance set forth deliberately to win the crown of martyrdom among the Moors. He was cast by a storm on
the coast of Sicily. He found his way to Romagna,
united himself to the Franciscans, retired into a hermitage, studied deeply, and at length was authorised by
the General of the Order to go forth and preach. For
many years his eloquence excited that rapture of faith
which during these times is almost periodically breaking
forth, especially in the north of Italy. Every class, both
sexes, all ages were equally entranced. Old enmities
were reconciled, old debts paid, forgotten wrong atoned
for; prostitutes forsook their sins, robbers forswore their
calling; such is said to have been the magic of his words
that infants ceased to cry. His voice was clear and
piercing like a trumpet; his Italian purer than that of
most natives. At Rimini, at Milan, in other cities, he
held disputations against the heretics, who yielded to
his irresistible arguments. But the triumph of his
courage and of his eloquence was his daring to stand
before Eccelin of Verona to rebuke him for his bloody
atrocities. Eccelin is said to have bowed in awe before
the intrepid preacher; he threw himself at the feet of
Antony, and promised to amend his life. The clergy
dared not but admire Antony of Padua, whom miracle
began to environ. But they saw not without terror that
the meek Franciscan might soon become a formidable

demagogue, formidable to themselves as to the enemies
of the faith,

But what is more extraordinary, already in the time of
St. Bonaventura the Franciscans had begun to be faithless to their hard bride, Poverty. Bonaventura himself
might have found it difficult to adduce authority for his
laborious learning in the rule of his Master. Franciscanism is in both respects more or less repudiating St.
Francis. The first General of the Order, Brother Elias
(General during the lifetime of the Saint), refused the
dignity, because his infirmities compelled him to violate
one of its rules, to ride on horseback. He was compelled
to assume the honour, degraded, resumed his office, was
again degraded; for Elias manifestly despised, and endeavoured to throw off, and not alone, the very vital
principle of the Order, mendicancy; he persecuted the
true disciples of St. Francis.[b] At length the successor
of St. Francis became a counsellor of Frederick II., the
mortal enemy of the Pope, especially of the Franciscan
Popes, above all of the first patron of Franciscanism,
Gregory IX.

The Rule had required the peremptory renunciation
of all worldly goods by every disciple of the
Order, and those who received the proselytes
were carefully to abstain from mingling in worldly
business. Not till he was absolutely destitute did the
disciple become a Franciscan. They might receive
food, clothes, or other necessaries, on no account money;
even if they found it they were to trample it under foot.
They might labour for their support, but were to be paid

The Rule.

---

b Compare Les Chroniques, part ii. c. v. p. 4. " Ainsi étoit cause de grand mal, le grand nombre des frères qui lui adheroient, lesquels comme les partisans le suivoient et l'imitoient, l'incitant à poursuivre les frères qui etoient zelés observateurs de la règle." —Rigal. cap. ii. p. 23.

in kind. They were to have two tunics, one with a hood, one without, a girdle and breeches. The fatal feud, the controversy on the interpretation of this stern rule of poverty, will find its place hereafter.

St. Francis rejected alike the pomp of ritual and the pride of learning. The Franciscan services were to be conducted with the utmost simplicity of devotion, with no wantonness of music. There was to be only one daily mass. It was not long before the magnificent church of Assisi began to rise; and the Franciscan services, if faithful to the form, began soon by their gorgeousness to mock the spirit of their master.

No Franciscan was to preach without permission of the Provincial of the Order, or if forbidden by the bishop of the diocese; their sermons were to be on the great religious and moral truths of the Gospel, and especially short. He despised and prohibited human learning, even human eloquence displayed for vanity and ostentation.[*] Bonaventura himself in his profoundest writings maintained the mystic fervour of his master; but everywhere the Franciscans are with the Dominicans vieing for the mastery in the universities of Christendom; Duns Scotus the most arid dialectician, and William of Ockham the demagogue of scholasticism, balance the fame of Albert the Great and Thomas of Aquino. A century has not passed before, besides the clergy, the older Orders are heaping invectives on the disciples of St. Francis, not only as disturbers of their religious

---

[*] " Je ne voudrais point de plus grands Docteurs de Théologie, que ceux qui enseignent leur prochain avec les œuvres, la douceur, la pauvreté, et l'humilité." He goes on to rebuke preachers who are filled with vain glory by the concourse of hearers, and the success of their preaching.—Chroniques, li. c. xiiv. I find the Saint goaded to one other malediction,—against a provincial, who encouraged profound study at the University of Bologna.—c. xviii. See above his contempt and aversion for books.

peace, as alienating the affections and reverence of their flocks or their retainers, but as their more successful rivals for the alms of dying penitents, as the more universal legatees of lands, treasures, houses, immunities.

The Benedictine of St. Alban's,[a] Matthew Paris, who at first wrote, or rather adopted language, highly commending the now-born zeal, and yet-admired holiness of the mendicants,[b] in all the bitter jealousy of a rival Order, writes thus:—"It is terrible, it is an awful presage, that in three hundred years, in four hundred years, even in more, the old monastic Orders have not so entirely degenerated as these Fraternities. The friars who have been founded hardly forty years have built, even in the present day in England, residences as lofty as the palaces of our kings. These are they, who enlarging day by day their sumptuous edifices, encircling them with lofty walls, lay up within them incalculable treasures, imprudently transgressing the bounds of poverty, and violating, according

Change in the Order.

---

[a] The first Franciscan foundation in England was at Abingdon.—Malan, p. 264. This statement in Paris is singularly illustrated by the documents in the Monumenta Franciscana. Mr. Brewer, in his remarkable Preface, enlarges on the self-devoting usage of the early Franciscans to fix their domicile in the mean, fœtid, unwholesome suburbs of the cities. This seems to have been peculiarly the case in England. In London their first residence is in "Stynkinge Lane," in the parish of St. Nicholas in Macelio. But ere long grant after grant is united of houses, lands, and messuages in the same quarter. Till in the reign of Edward I. rises their Church, 300 feet long, 85 wide, 64 high to the roof; the pillars all marble. To this the Queen contributes 200l. sterling. There is a long list of donors, who glazed their windows. At length rises their Library, which cost 556l. 18s. 8d. Richard Whyttyngton, Mayor, gave of this 400l. Multiply this sum by 15, in modern money it amounts to above 8000l. Mr. Brewer, in his fervent admiration of the saintly rise, closes his eyes on the rapid degeneracy of the Order, and their departure from their first principles.

[b] Wendover, ii. p. 210, sub ann. 1207.

to the prophecy of the German Hildegard, the very
fundamental rules of their profession.   These are they
who impelled by the love of gain, force themselves upon
the last hours of the Lords, and of the rich whom they
know to be overflowing with wealth ; and these, despising
all rights, supplanting the ordinary pastors, extort confessions and secret testaments, boasting of themselves
and of their Order, and asserting their vast superiority
over all others.   So that no one of the faithful now
believes that he can be saved, unless guided and directed
by the Preachers or Friar Minors.   Eager to obtain
privileges, they serve in the courts of kings and nobles,
as counsellors, chamberlains, treasurers, bridesmen, or
notaries of marriages ; they are the executioners of the
Papal extortions.   In their preaching they sometimes
take the tone of flattery, sometimes of biting censure :
they scruple not to reveal confessions, or to bring forward
the most rash accusations.   They despise the legitimate
Orders, those founded by holy fathers, by St. Benedict
or St. Augustine, with all their professors.   They place
their own Order high above all ; they look on the Cistercians as rude and simple, half laic or rather peasants ;
they treat the Black Monks as haughty Epicureans." [f]

Our history reverts to the close of Innocent III.'s
eventful pontificate.

In the full vigour of his manhood died Innocent III.
He, of all the Popes, had advanced the most   A.D. 1216.
exorbitant pretensions, and those pretensions Death of
                                               Pope Inno-
had been received by an age most disposed to   cent III.
accept them with humble deference.   The high and
blameless, in some respects wise and gentle character of
Innocent, might seem to approach more nearly than

---

[f] Paris reckons the forty years to his own time, sub ann. 1249.

any one of the whole succession of Roman bishops, to
the ideal height of a supreme Pontiff: in him, if ever,
might appear to be realised the churchman's highest
conception of the Vicar of Christ. Gregory VII. and
Boniface VIII., the first and the last of the aggressive
Popes, and the aged Gregory IX., had no doubt more
rugged warfare to encounter, fiercer and more unscrupulous enemies to subdue. But in all these there was
a personal sternness, a contemptuous haughtiness; theirs
was a worldly majesty. Hildebrand and Benedetto
Gaetani are men in whom secular policy obscures, and
throws back, as it were, the spiritual greatness; and
though the firmness with which they endure reverses
may be more lofty, yet there is a kind of desecration of
the unapproachable sanctity of their office in their personal calamities. The pride of Innocent was calmer,
more self-possessed; his dignity was less disturbed by
degrading collisions with rude adversaries; he died on
his unshaken throne, in the plenitude of his
seemingly unquestioned power. Yet if we
pause and contemplate, as we cannot but pause and
contemplate, the issue of this highest, in a certain sense
noblest and most religious contest for the Papal ascendancy over the world of man, there is an inevitable conviction of the unreality of that Papal power. With all
the grandeur of his views, with all the persevering
energy of his measures, throughout Innocent's reign,
everywhere we behold failure, everywhere immediate
discomfiture, or transitory success which paved the way
for future disaster. The higher the throne of the Pope
the more manifestly were its foundations undermined,
unsound, unenduring.

Even Rome does not always maintain her peaceful
subservience. Her obedience is interrupted, precarious;

Results of his Pontificate.

that of transient awe, not of deep attachment, or rooted reverence. In Italy, the tutelage of the young Frederick, suspicious, ungenerous, imperious, yet negligent, could not but plant deep in the heart of the young sovereign mistrust, want of veneration, still more of affection for his ecclesiastical guardian. What was there to attach Frederick to the Church? how much to estrange! As King of Sicily he was held under strict tributary control; his step-mother the Church watches every movement with jealous supervision; exacts the most rigid discharge of all the extorted signs of vassalage. It is not as heir of the Empire that he is reluctantly permitted or coldly encouraged to cross the Alps, and to win back, if he can, the crown of his ancestors, but as the enemy of the Pope's enemy. Otho had been so ungrateful, was so dangerous, that against him the Pope would support even a Hohenstaufen. The seeds of evil were sown in Frederick's mind, in Frederick's heart, to spring up with fearful fertility. In the Empire it is impossible not to burthen the memory of Innocent with the miseries of the long civil war. Otho without the aid of the Pope could not have maintained the contest for a year; with all the Pope's aid he had sunk into contempt, almost insignificance; he was about to be abandoned, if not actually abandoned, by the Pope himself. The casual blow of the assassin alone prevented the complete triumph of Philip, already he had extorted his absolution; Innocent was compelled to yield, and could not yield without loss of dignity.[*]   The

---

[*] Read the very curious Latin poem published by Leibnitz, R. Brunsw. S. II. p. 525, on the Disputatio between Roma and Pope Innocent on the destitution of Otho. Roma begins:—

"Tibi soli supplicat orbis, Et prece humanitas, to disputerole mortur."

Innocent, after some flattery of the greatness of Rome, urges:—

triumph of Otho leads to as fierce, and more perilous
resistance to the Papal power, than could have been
expected from the haughtiness of the Hohenstaufen.
The Pope has an irresistible enemy in Italy itself. Innocent is compelled to abandon the great object of the
Papal policy, the breaking the line of succession in the
house of Swabia, and to assist in the elevation of a
Swabian Emperor. He must yield to the union of the
crown of Sicily with that of Germany; and so bequeath
to his successors the obstinate and perilous strife with
Frederick II.

In France, Philip Augustus is forced to seem, yet
only seem, to submit; the miseries of his unhappy wife
are but aggravated by the Papal protection. The death
of Agnes of Meran, rather than Innocent's authority,
heals the strife. The sons of the proscribed concubine
succeed to the throne of France.

In England the Barons refuse to desert John when
under the interdict of the Pope; when the Pope becomes
the King's ally, resenting the cession of the realm, they
withdraw their allegiance. Even in Stephen Langton,
who owes his promotion to the Pope, the Englishman
prevails over the ecclesiastic; the Great Charter is
extorted from the King when under the express protection of the Holy See, and maintained resolutely against

---

"Quæ vos admiraveit Fryemis?
Ut sic manduwe relevare velitis Olympem,
Vultis ut Excisæ Romanæ præsto restrast,
Hæatis Catholicæ fidei, dominandi superius
Non solum factus, sed et ipse superbus."

Then follow several pages of dispute,
kindling into fierce altercation. The
Pope winds up:—

"Si te
Non movent super hæc assignate rationes
Per quas Othoni Fredericus substituatur.
Sic volo, sic fiat, sit pro ratione voluntas."

Rome bursts into invective:—

"Qualis
Servorum Christi Servus!
Non es apostolicus, sed apostaticus; atque
Pastor
Immo lupus, vocamus ipse grex."

Rome appeals to a General Council.
Rome, supposing the Council present,
addresses it. The Council replies:—
"Roma parens, non est nostrum deponere
Papam."

But the Council declares its right to
depose Frederick and to restore Otho.

the Papal sentence of abrogation; and in the Great Charter is laid the first stone of the religious as well as the civil liberties of the land.

Venice, in the Crusade, deludes, defies, baffles the Pope. The Crusaders become her army, besiege, fight, conquer for her interests. In vain the Pope protests, threatens, anathematises: Venice calmly proceeds in the subjugation of Zara. To the astonishment, the indignation of the Pope, the Crusaders' banners wave not over Jerusalem, but over Constantinople. But for her own wisdom, Venice might have given an Emperor to the capital of the East, she secures the patriarchate almost in defiance of the Pope; only when she has entirely gained her ends does she submit to the petty and unregarded vengeance of the Pope.

Even in the Albigensian war the success was indeed complete; heresy was crushed, but by means of which Innocent disapproved in his heart. He had let loose a terrible force, which he could neither arrest nor control. The Pope can do everything but show mercy or moderation. He could not shake off, the Papacy has never shaken off, the burthen of its complicity in the remorseless carnage perpetrated by the Crusaders in Languedoc, in the crimes and cruelties of Simon de Montfort. A dark and ineffaceable stain of fraud and dissimulation too has gathered around the fame of Innocent himself.[b] Heresy was quenched in blood; but the earth sooner or later gives out the terrible cry of blood for vengeance against murderers and oppressors.

---

[b] It is remarkable that Innocent III. was never canonised. There were popular rumours that the soul of Innocent, escaping from the fires of purgatory, appeared on earth, assorted by pursuing devils, taking refuge at the foot of the cross, and imploring the prayers of the faithful.—Chronic. Erfort. p. 243. Thom. Cantiprat, Vit. S. Luitgardæ, ap. Surium, Jan. 16.

The great religious event of this Pontificate, the foundation of the Mendicant Orders, that which perhaps perpetuated, or at least immeasurably strengthened, the Papal power for two centuries was extorted from the reluctant Pope. Both St. Dominic and St. Francis were coldly received, almost contemptuously repelled. It was not till either his own more mature deliberation, or wiser counsel which took the form of divine admonition, prevented this fatal error, and prophetically revealed the secret of their strength and of their irresistible influence throughout Christendom, that Innocent awoke to wisdom. He then bequeathed these two great standing armies to the Papacy; armies maintained without cost, sworn, more than sworn, bound by the unbroken chains of their own zeal and devotion to unquestioning, unhesitating service throughout Christendom, speaking all languages. They were colonies of religious militia, natives of every land, yet under foreign control and guidance. Their whole power, importance, perhaps possessions, rested on their fidelity to the See of Rome, that fidelity guaranteed by the charter of their existence. Well might they appear so great as they are seen by the eye of Dante, like the Cherubin and Seraphin in Paradise.[1]

---

[1] Paradiso, xi. 34, &c.

BOOK X.

E 2

CONTEMPORARY CHRONOLOGY.

POPES.	EMPERORS OF GERMANY.	KINGS OF FRANCE.	KING OF ENGLAND.
A.D. A.D.	1212 Frederic II. 1250	A.D. A.D.	A.D. A.D.
1216 Honorius III. 1227			1216 Henry III. 1272
		Philip Augustus	
		1223 Louis VIII. 1226	
1227 Gregory IX. 1241		1226 Louis IX. (Saint) 1270	ARCHBISHOPS OF CANTERBURY.
1241 Celestine IV. 1241			
1243 Innocent IV. 1254	1246 Henry Raspe (anti-emperor) 1247		Stephen Langton 1228
1254 Alexander IV. 1261	1247 William of Holland 1256		1229 Richard Weathershed 1234
			1234 Edmund Rich 1244
	1257 ??? Richard of Cornwall (?) Alfonso of Castile (?)		1244 Boniface of Savoy 1271
	ARCHBISHOPS OF MENTZ.		
	Conrad of Wittelsbach 1200		
	1200 Siegfried I. of Eppstein 1230		
	1230 Siegfried II. of Eppstein 1249		
	1249 Christian II. 1250		
	1250 Gerhard I.		

CONTEMPORARY CHRONOLOGY.

KINGS OF SCOTLAND.	KINGS OF SPAIN.	KINGS OF NAPLES.	EMPERORS OF THE EAST.
A.D. A.D.	A.D. A.D.	A.D. A.D.	A.D. A.D.
1214 Alexander II. 1249	*Castile.*		*Latin.*
	1217 Alfonso X. 1252		1217 Peter de Cour-
	1254 Ferdinand III. 1252		tenay 1220
	1252 Alfonso XI.,		1220 Robert 1228
	the Wise 1274		1228 Baldwin II. 1261
	Arragon.	Frederick II. 1250	*Greek.*
1249 Alexander III. 1286	1213 James I.		Theodore Las-
			caris 1222
	KINGS OF PORTUGAL.	1250 Conrad 1253	1222 John Ducas 1255
		1254 Manfred 1265	1255 Theodore 1259
	A.D. A.D.		1259 John IV.
	1212 Alfonso the		Bijo Michael Palæ-
	Fat, 1223	1265 Conrad II.—	logus
	1223 Sancho II. 1245	Charles of Anjou.	1282 Ammion.
	1245 Alfonso, III. 1279		

BOOK X.

CHAPTER I.

Honorius III.   Frederick II.

THE Pontificate of Honorius III. is a kind of oasis of
repose, between the more eventful rule of Innocent III. and that of Gregory IX. Honorius
was a Roman of the noble house of Savelli,
Cardinal of St. John and St. Paul. The Papacy having
attained its consummate height under Innocent III.,
might appear resting upon its arms, and gathering up
its might for its last internecine conflict, under Gregory
IX. and Innocent IV. with the most powerful, the ablest,
and when driven to desperation, most reckless antagonist, who had as yet come into collision with the
spiritual supremacy. During nearly eleven
years the combatants seem girding themselves
for the contest. At first mutual respect or common
interests maintain even more than the outward appearance of amity; then arise jealousy, estrangement,
doubtful peace, but not declared war. On one side
neither the power nor the ambition of the Emperor
Frederick II. are mature: his more modest views of
aggrandisement gradually expand; his own character
is developing itself into that of premature enlighten-
ment and lingering superstition; of chivalrous adventure and courtly elegance, of stern cruelty and generous

(margin notes) Honorius III. July 18, 1216. Consecrated July 24. — A.D. 1216 to 1227.

liberality, of restless and all-stirring, all-embracing
activity, which keeps Germany, Italy, even the East,
in one uninterrupted war with his implacable enemies
the Popes, and with the Lombard Republics, while he
is constantly betraying his natural disposition to bask
away an easy and luxurious life on the shores of his
beloved Sicily. All this is yet in its dawn, in its yet
unfulfilled promise, in its menace. Frederick has won
the Empire; he has united, though he had agreed to
make over Sicily to his son, the Imperial crown to
that of Sicily. Even if rumours are already abroad
of his dangerous freedom of opinion, this may pass for
youthful levity, he is still the spiritual subject of the
Pope.

Honorius III. stands between Innocent III. and Gregory IX., not as a Pontiff of superior wisdom and more
true Christian dignity, adopting a gentler and more
conciliating policy from the sense of its more perfect
compatibility with his office of Vicar of Christ, Mildness of Honorius
but rather from natural gentleness of character
bordering on timidity. He has neither energy of mind
to take the loftier line, nor to resist the high churchmen, who are urging him towards it; his was a tempor-
ising policy, which could only avert for a time the
inevitable conflict.

And yet a Pope who could assume as his maxim to
act with gentleness rather than by compulsion, by influence rather than anathema, nevertheless, to make no
surrender of the overweening pretensions of his function; must have had a mind of force and vigour of its
own, not unworthy of admiration: a moderate Pope is
so rare in these times, that he may demand some
homage for his moderation. His age and infirmities
may have tended to this less enterprising or turbulent

administration.[a] Honorius accepted the tradition of all
the rights and duties asserted by, and generally ascribed
to the successor of St. Peter, as part of his high office.
The Holy War was now become so established an article
in the Christian creed, that no Pope, however beyond
his age, could have ventured even to be remiss in urging
this solemn obligation on all true Christians. No cardinal not in heart a Crusader would have been raised to
the Papal See. The assurance of the final triumph of
the Christian arms became a point of honour, more than
that, an essential part of Christian piety; to deny it
was an impeachment on the valour of true Christians, a
want of sufficient reliance on God himself. Christ
could not, however he might try the patience of the
Christian, eventually abandon to the infidel his holy
sepulchre. All admonitions of disaster and defeat were
but the just chastisements of the sins of the crusaders;
the triumph, however postponed, was certain, as certain
as that Christ was the Son of God, Mohammed a false
prophet.

Honorius was as earnest, as zealous in the good cause,
as had been his more inflexible predecessor; this was

Honorius
urges the
Crusade.

the primary object of his ten years' Pontificate;
this, which however it had to encounter the
coldness, the torpor, the worn-out sympathies of Christendom, clashed with no jealous or hostile feeling. However severe the rebuke, it was rebuke of which Christendom acknowledged the justice; all men honoured the
Pope for his zeal in sounding the trumpet with the
fiercest energy, even though they did not answer to the
call. The more the enthusiasm of Christendom cooled

---

[a] "Cum esset corpore infirmus, et ultra modum debilis."—Raynald. sub
an.

down into indifference, the more ardent and pressing
the exhortation of the Popes. The first act of
Honorius was a circular address to Christen- <small>Dec. 4, 1216.</small>
dom, full of reproof, expostulation, entreaty to contri-
bute either in person or in money to the new campaign.
The only King who obeyed the summons was <small>Crusade of Andrew of Hungary.</small>
Andrew of Hungary. Some German princes
and prelates met the Hungarian at Spalatro, the Dukes
of Austria and Meran, the Archbishop of Saltzburg, the
Bishops of Bamberg, Zeitz, Munster, and Utrecht. But
notwithstanding the interdict of the Patriarch of Jerusalem, Andrew returned in the next year, though not
without some fame for valour and conduct, on the plea
of enfeebled health, and of important affairs of Hungary.[b] His trophies were reliques, the heads of St.
Stephen and St. Margaret, the hands of St. Bartholomew and St. Thomas, a slip of the rod of Aaron, one
of the water-pots of the Marriage of Cana. <small>A.D. 1218. Against Damietta.</small>
The expedition from the Holy Land against
Damietta, the flight of Sultan Kameel from that city,
its occupation by the Christians, raised the most exult-
ing hopes. The proposal of the Sultan to yield up
Jerusalem was rejected with scorn. But the fatal
reverses, which showed the danger of accepting a
Legate (the Cardinal Pelagius) as a general, too soon
threw men's minds back into their former prostration.
But even before this discomfiture, King Frederick II.
had centred on himself the thoughts and hopes of all
who were still Crusaders in their hearts, as the one
monarch in Christendom who could restore the <small>Frederick II.</small>
fallen fortunes of the Cross in the East. In
his first access of youthful pride, as having at eighteen

---

[b] This was the Crusade joined by S. Francis.—See Ch. X.

years of age won, by his own gallant daring, the Trans-
alpine throne of his ancestors; and in his grateful
devotion to the Pope, who, in hatred to Otho, had maintained his cause, Frederick II. had taken the Cross.
Nor for some years does there appear any reason to
mistrust, if not his religious, at least his adventurous
and ambitious ardour. But till the death of his rival
Otho, he could command no powerful force which would
follow him to the Holy Land, nor could he leave his
yet unsettled realm. The princes and churchmen, his
partisans, were to be rewarded and so confirmed in their
loyalty; the doubtful and wavering to be won; the refractory or resistant to be reduced to allegiance.

The death of Otho, in the castle of Wurtzburg, near
Goslar, had been a signal example of the power of religious awe. The battle of Bouvines and the desertion
of his friends had broken his proud spirit; his health
failed, violent remedies brought him to the brink of the
grave. Hell yawned before the outcast from the Church;
nothing less than a public expiation of his sins could
soothe his shuddering conscience. No bishop would
approach the excommunicated, the fallen Sovereign;
the Prior of Halberstadt, on his solemn oath upon the
reliques of St. Simon and St. Jude brought for that
purpose from Brunswick, that if he lived he would give
full satisfaction to the Church, obtained him absolution
and the Last Sacrament. The next day, the last of his
life, in the presence of the Empress and his family, the
nobles, and the Abbot of Hildesheim, he knelt almost
naked on a carpet, made the fullest confession of his
sins; he showed a cross, which he had received at
Rome, as a pledge that he would embark on a Crusade:
"the devil had still thwarted his holy vow." The cross
was restored to him. He then crouched down, exposed

his naked shoulders, and entreated all present to inflict the merited chastisement All hands were armed with rods; the very scullions assisted in the pious work of flagellation, or at least of humiliation. In the pauses of the Miserere the Emperor's voice was heard: "Strike harder, spare not the hardened sinner." So died the rival of Philip of Swabia, the foe of Innocent III., in the forty-third year of his age.[*]

With the death of Otho rose new schemes of aggrandisement before the eyes of Frederick II.; he must secure the Imperial crown for himself; for his son Henry the succession to the German kingdom. The Imperial crown must be obtained from the hands of the Pope; the election of his son at least be ratified by that power. A friendly correspondence began with Honorius III. The price set on the coronation of Frederick as Emperor was his undertaking a Crusade to the Holy Land. At the High Diet at Fulda, Frederick himself (so he writes to the Pope) had already summoned the princes of Germany to his great design: at the Diet proclaimed to be held at Magdeburg, he urged the Pope to excommunicate all who should not appear in arms on the next St. John's day. His chief counsellor seemed to be Herman of Salza, the Master of the Teutonic Order, as deeply devoted to the service of the Holy Land, as the Templars and Knights of St. John. On that Order he heaped privileges and possessions. But already in Rome, no doubt among the old austere anti-German party, were dark suspicions, solemn admonitions, secret warnings to the mild Pope, that no son of the house of Swabia could be

Promises to lead the Crusade.

Jan. 12, 1219.

---

* Otho died 19th May, 1218.—See lii. p. 1373. " Praecepit coquinariis Narratio de Morte Ottonis IV. apud ut in collum suum conculcarent."— Martene et Durand Thes. His. Anecdot. Albert. Stadens. Chron. p. 204.

otherwise than an enemy to the Church: the Imperial crown and the kingdom of Naples could not be in the possession of one Sovereign without endangering the independence of the Papacy. Frederick repelled these accusations of hostility to the Church with passionate vehemence. "I well know that those who dare to rise up against the Church of Rome have drunk of the cup of Babylon; and hope that during my whole life I shall never be justly charged with ingratitude to my Holy Mother. I design not, against my own declaration, to obtain the election of my son Henry to the throne of Germany in order to unite the two kingdoms of Germany and Sicily; but that in my absence (no doubt he implies in the Holy Land), the two realms may be more firmly governed; and that in case of my death, my son may be more certain of inheriting the throne of his fathers. That son remains under subjection to the Roman See, which, having protected me, so ought to protect him in his undoubted rights." [4] He then condescends to exculpate himself from all the special charges brought against him by Rome.

The correspondence continued on both sides in terms of amicable courtesy. Each had his object, of which he never lost sight. The Pope would even hazard the aggrandisement of the house of Swabia if he could send forth an overpowering armament to the East. Frederick, secure of the aggrandisement of his house, was fully prepared to head the Crusade. Honorius consented that, in case of the death of Henry the son of Frederick without heir or brother, Frederick should hold both the Empire and the king-

Sept. 6, 1212.
Correspondence with the Pope.
May 18, 1212.

---

[4] Regest. Hon., quoted from the Vatican archives by Von Raumer, iii. p. 324.

dom of Naples during his lifetime. Frederick desired
to retain unconditionally the investiture of both kingdoms; but on this point the Pope showed so much
reluctance that Frederick broke off the treaty by letter,
reserving it for a personal interview with the Pope.
"For who could be more obedient to the Church than
he who was nursed at her breast and had rested in her
lap? Who more loyal? Who would be so mindful of
benefits already received, or so prepared to acknowledge
his obligations according to the will and pleasure of his
benefactors?" Such were the smooth nor yet deceptive
words of Frederick.[*] Frederick had already consented,
even proposed, that the Pope should place all the German Princes who refused to take up the Cross under the
interdict of the Church, and thus, as the Pope reminds
him, had still more inextricably bound himself, who had
already vowed to take up that Cross. Frederick urged
Honorius to write individually to all the princes among
whom there was no ardour for the Crusade, to threaten
them with the ban if at least they did not maintain the
truce of God; he promised, protesting that he acted
without deceit or subtlety; to send forward his forces,
and follow himself as speedily as he might. The Pope
expressed his profound satisfaction at finding his beloved
son so devoted to God and to the Church. He urged
him to delay no longer the holy design: "Youth,
power, fame, your vow, the example of your ancestors,
summon you to fulfil your glorious enterprise. That
which your illustrious grandfather Frederick I. _March, 1226._
undertook with all his puissance, it is your
mission to bring to a glorious end. Three times have I

---

[*] All this I am not surprised to find by such writers as Höfler represented
as the most deliberate hypocrisy. I am sorry to see the same partial view in
Boehmer's Regesta.

consented to delay; I will even prolong the term to
the 1st of May. Whose offer is this?—Not mine; but
that of Christ! Whose advantage?—That of all his
disciples! Whose honour?—That of all Christians!
Are you not invited by unspeakable rewards? summoned
by miracles? admonished by examples?"

But, in the mean time, Frederick, without waiting the
assent of the Pope, had carried his great design, the
election of his son Henry to the crown of Germany.
His unbounded popularity, his power now that his rival
Otho was dead, the fortunate falling in of some great
fiefs (especially the vast possessions of Berthold of Zahringen, which enabled him to reward some, to win
others of the nobler houses), his affability, his
liberality, his justice, gave him command over
the suffrages of the temporal princes. By a
great measure of wisdom and justice, the
charter of the liberties of the German Church, on which
some looked with jealousy as investing him with dangerous power, he gained the support of the high ecclesiastica.[1] The King surrendered the unkingly right or usage
of seizing to his own use the personalities of bishops on
their decease. These effects, if not bequeathed by will,
went to the bishop's successor. The King consented to
renounce the right of coining money and levying tolls
within the territory of the bishops without their consent;
and to punish all forgeries of their coin. The vassals
and serfs of the prelates were to be received in no imperial city or fief of the Empire to their damage. The
advocates, under pretence of protection, were not to
injure the estates of the Church: no one was to occupy
by force an ecclesiastical fief. He who did not submit

Diet of Frankfort. April, 1220. Election of Henry as his successor. Apr. 26, 1220.

---

[1] Monument. Germ. iv. 235.

within six weeks to the authority of the Church fell
under the ban of the Empire, and could neither act as
judge, plaintiff, nor witness in any court. The Bishops,
on their side, promised to prosecute and to punish all who
opposed the will of the King. The King further stipulated that no one might erect castles or fortresses in the
lands of a spiritual prince. No officer of the King had
jurisdiction, could coin money, or levy tolls in the episcopal cities, except eight days before and eight days after
a diet to be held in such city. Only when the King was
actually within the city was the jurisdiction of the prince
suspended, and only so long as he should remain.

The election of Henry to the throne of Germany
without the consent of the Pope struck Rome with
dismay. Frederick made haste to allay, if possible, the
jealous apprehension. He declared that it was the spontaneous act of the Princes of the Empire during his
absence, without his instigation. They had seen, from
a quarrel which had broken out between the Archbishop
of Mentz and the Landgrave of Thuringia, the absolute
necessity of a King to maintain in Frederick's absence
the peace of the Empire. He had even delayed his own
consent. The act of election would be laid
before the Pope with the seals of all who had
been concerned in the affair.[a] He declared that this
election was by no means designed to perpetuate the
union of the kingdom of Naples with the Empire. "Even
if the Church had no right over the kingdom of Apulia
and Sicily, I would freely grant that kingdom to the
Pope rather than attach it to the Empire, should I die
without lawful heirs."[b] He significantly adds, that it

Nuremberg
July 12.

---

[a] Regest., quoted by Von Raumer, p. 335. Pertz, Monumenta.

[b] "Prius ipso regno Romanam Ecclesiam quam Imperium daturum us."—Ibid.

is constantly suggested to him that the love professed to
him by the Church is not sincere and will not be lasting,
but he had constantly refused to entertain such un-
grounded and dishonourable suspicions.

The Abbot of Fulda had, in the mean time, been
despatched to Rome to demand the coronation of Frederick as Emperor. This embassage had been usually the
office of one of the great prelates of Germany, but the
mild Honorius took no offence, or disguised it. At
the end of August Frederick descended the Alps into
the plain of Lombardy. Eight years before, a boy of
eighteen, he had crossed those Alps, almost alone, on
his desperate adventure of wresting the crown of his
fathers from the brow of Otho. He came back, in the
prime of life, one of the mightiest kings who had ever
occupied that throne; stronger in the attachment of all
orders, perhaps, than any former Swabian king; having
secured, it might seem, in his house, at least the Empire,
if not the Empire with all its rights in Italy; and with
the kingdom of Sicily, instead of a hostile power at the
command of the Popes, his own, if not in possession, in
attachment. During these eight years Italy had been
one great feud of city with city, of the cities within
themselves. Milan, released from fears of the Emperor,
had now begun a quarrel with the Church. The Podestà
expelled the Archbishop. Parma and many other cities
had followed this example; the bishops were driven out,
their palaces destroyed, their property plundered: the
great ability of the Cardinal Ugolino, afterwards Gregory IX., had restored something like order, but the fire
was still smouldering in its ashes.

Frederick passed on without involving himself in these
implacable quarrels: it was time to assert the Imperial
rights when invested in the Imperial crown. He had

crossed the Brenner, and moving by Verona and Mantua, so avoided Milan. The absence of the Archbishop from Milan was a full excuse for his postponing his coronation with the iron crown of Lombardy. He granted rights and privileges to Venice, Genoa, Pisa; overawed or conciliated some cities. On the thirtieth of September he was in Verona, on the fourth of October in Bologna. His Chancellor, Conrad of Metz, had arranged the terms on which he was to receive the Imperial crown. Frederick advanced with a great array of churchmen in his retinue—the Archbishops of Mentz, of Ravenna, the Patriarch of Aquileia, the Bishops of Metz, Passau, Trent, Brixen, Augsburg, Duke Louis of Bavaria, and Henry Count Palatine. Ambassadors appeared from almost all the cities of Italy: from Apulia, from the Counts of Celano, St. Severino, and Aquila; deputies from the city of Naples. The people of Rome were quiet and well pleased. The only untoward incident which disturbed the peace was a quarrel about a dog between the Ambassadors of Florence and Pisa, which led to a bloody war. On the twenty-second of November Frederick and his Queen were crowned in St. Peter's amid universal acclamations. Frederick disputed not the covenanted price to be paid for the Imperial crown. He received the Cross once more from the hand of Cardinal Ugolino. He swore that part of his forces should set forth for the Holy Land in the March of the following year, himself in August. He released his vassals from their fealty in all the territories of the Countess Matilda, and made over the appointment of all the podestàs to the Pope; some who refused to submit were placed by the Chancellor Conrad under the ban of the Empire. He put the Pope in possession of the whole region from Radicofani to

Ceperano, with the March of Ancona and the Duchy of
Spoleto.

His liberality was not limited to these grants. Two
laws concerning the immunities of ecclesiastics and
Laws in favour of ecclesiastics. the suppression of heretics might satisfy the
severest churchman. The first absolutely an-
nulled all laws or usages of cities, communities, or
ruling powers which might be or were employed against
the liberties of the churches or of spiritual persons, or
against the laws of the Church and of the Empire.
Outlawry and heavy fines were enacted not only against
those who enforced, but who counselled or aided in the
enforcement of such usages: the offenders forfeited, if
contumacious for a whole year, all their goods.[1] No
tax or burthen could be set upon ecclesiastics, churches,
or spiritual foundations. Whoever arraigned a spiritual
person before a civil tribunal forfeited his right to im-
plead; the tribunal which admitted such arraignment
lost its jurisdiction; the judge who refused justice three
times to a spiritual person in any matter forfeited his
judicial authority.

The law against heretics vied in sternness with that
Laws against heretics. of Innocent III., confirmed by Otho IV.[2] All
Cathari, Paterines, Leonists, Speronists, Ar-
noldists, and dissidents of all other descriptions, were
incapable of holding places of honour, and under ban.
Their goods were confiscated, and not restored to their
children; "for outrages against the Lord of Heaven
were more heinous than against a temporal lord."
Whoever, suspected of heresy, did not clear himself
after a year's trial was to be treated as a heretic. Every

[1] Constit. Frederici II. in Corp. Jur. tit. i. Bullar. Roman. i. 83.
[2] This law was renewed and made more severe, 1224. Raynald. sub ann. 1231.

magistrate on entering upon office must himself take
an oath of orthodoxy, and swear to punish all whom
the Church might denounce as heretics. If any temporal lord did not rid his lands of heretics, the true
believers might take the business into their own hands,
and seize the goods of the delinquent, provided that
the rights of an innocent lord were not thereby im-
peached. All who concealed, aided, protected heretics
were under ban and interdict; if they did not make
satisfaction within two years, under outlawry; they could
hold no office, nor inherit, nor enter any plea, nor bear
testimony.

Three other laws, based on the eternal principles of
morality, accompanied these acts of ecclesiastical legislation, or of temporal legislation in the spirit of the
Church. One prohibited the plundering of wrecks,
excepting the ships of pirates and infidels. **Other laws.**
Another protected pilgrims; they were to be
received with kindness; if they died, their property was
to be restored to their rightful heirs. The third protected the persons and labours of the cultivators of
the soil.

The Pope and the Emperor, notwithstanding some
trifling differences, parted in perfect amity. "Never,"
writes Honorius, "did Pope love Emperor as he loved
his son Frederick." Each had obtained some great
objects; the Pope the peaceable surrender of the Ma-
thildine territories, and the solemn oath that Frederick
would speedily set forth on the Crusade. The Emperor
retired in peace and joy to the beloved land of his
youth. The perilous question of his right to the kingdom of Sicily had been intentionally or happily
avoided; he had been recognised by the Pope as **Sept. 8.**
Emperor and King of Sicily. There were still brooding

causes of mutual suspicion and dissatisfaction. Frederick pursued with vigour his determination of repressing the turbulent nobles of Apulia; the castles of the partisans of Otho were seized; they fled, and, he bitterly complained, were received with more than hospitality in the Papal dominions. He spared not the inimical bishops; they were driven from their sees; some imprisoned. The Pope loudly protested against this audacious violation of the immunities of Churchmen. Frederick refused them entrance into the kingdom; he had rather forfeit his crown than the inalienable right of the sovereign, of which he had been defrauded by Innocent III., of visiting treason on all his subjects.[a]

Then in the next year came the fatal news from the East—the capture, the disasters which followed the capture of Damietta. The Pope and the Emperor expressed their common grief; the Pope was bowed with dismay and sorrow;[a] the tidings pierced as a sword to the heart of Frederick.[b] Frederick had sent forty triremes, under the Bishop of Catania and the Count of Malta; they had arrived too late. But this dire reverse showed that nothing less than an overwhelming force could restore the Christian cause in the East; and in those days of colder religious zeal, even the Emperor and King of Sicily could not at once summon such overwhelming force. Frederick was fully occupied in the Sicilian dominions. During his minority, and during his absence, the powerful Germans, Normans, Italians, even Churchmen, had

A.D. 1221. Loss of Damietta.

---

[a] "Chè prima si lascierebbe torre la corona, chè derogar in un punto da questi suoi diritti."—Giannone, l. xvi. c. 1.

[a] Letter of Pope Honorius, Nov. 1221.

[b] Epist. Honor. apud Raynald. Aug. 10, 1221.

usurped fiefs, castles, cities:[p] he had to resume by force
rights unlawfully obtained, to dispossess men whose only
title had been open or secret leanings to the Emperor
Otho; to punish arbitrary oppression of the people; to
destroy strong castles built without licence; to settle
ancient feuds and suppress private wars: it needed all
his power, his popularity, his firmness, to avert insurrection during these vigorous but necessary measures.
Two great assizes held at Capua and Messina [Dec. 1120 to
showed the confusion in the affairs of both May. 1121.
kingdoms. But from such nobles he could expect no
ready obedience to assemble around his banner for an
expedition to the Holy Land. Instead of a great fleet,
suddenly raised, as by the wand of an enchanter (this
the Pope seemed to expect), and a powerful army, in
April in the year 1222 the Pope and the [Meeting
Emperor met at Veroli to deliberate on the at Veroli.
Crusade. They agreed to proclaim a great assembly at
Verona in the November of that year, at which the
Pope and the Emperor were to be present. All princes,
prelates, knights, and vassals were to be summoned to
unite in one irresistible effort for the relief of the East.
The assembly at Verona did not take place; the illness
of the Pope, the occupations of the Emperor, were
alleged as excuses for the further delay. A second
time the Pope and the Emperor met at Feren- [At Ferentino,
tino; with them King John of Jerusalem, the March, 1222.
Patriarch, the Grand Master of the Knights Templars.
Frederick explained the difficulties which had impeded
his movements, first in Germany, now in Sicily. To
the opposition of his turbulent barons was now added
the danger of an insurrection of the Saracens in Sicily.

---

[p] Letter of Frederick to the Pope from Traoi, March 3, 1221.

Frederick himself was engaged in a short but obstinate
war.[a] Even the King of Jerusalem deprecated the
despatch of an insufficient force. Two full years were
to be employed, by deliberate agreement, in awakening
the dormant zeal of Christendom; but Frederick, now
a widower, bound himself, it might seem, in the inex-
tricable fetters of his own personal interest and ambition,
by engaging to marry Iolante, the beautiful daughter
of King John.

Two years passed away; King John of Jerusalem
travelled over Western Christendom, to England, France,
Germany, to represent in all lands the state of extreme
peril and distress to which his kingdom was reduced.
Everywhere he met with the most courteous and royal
reception; but the days of Peter the Hermit and St.
Bernard were gone by. France, England, Germany,
Spain, were involved in their own affairs; a few took
the Cross, and offered sums of money to no great
amount; and this was all which was done by the royal
preacher of the Crusade. Tuscany and Lombardy were
almost as indifferent to the expostulations of Cardinal
Ugolino, who had for some years received full power
from the Emperor to awaken, if possible, the sluggish
ardour of those provinces. King John and the Patriarch, after visiting Apulia, reported to the Pope the

---

[a] The two following passages show
that this was no feigned excuse:—
" Imperator in Sicilia de Mirabello
triumphavit, et de lymo et suis facit
quod eorum meruerat exigentia com-
missorum." — Richd. San. Germ.
" Dominus Fredericus erat cum magno
exercitu super Saracenos Jacæ, et cepit
Benavith cum filiis suis, et suspendit
apud Panormum."—Anon. Sic. He

afterwards transplanted many of them
to Lucera. So far was Frederick as
yet from any suspicious dealings with
the Saracens. The Parliament at
Messina had passed persecuting laws
against the Jews. A law of the same
year protected the churches and the
clergy from the burthens laid upon
them by the nobles.

absolute impossibility of raising any powerful armament by the time appointed in the treaty of Ferentino.

Honorius was compelled to submit; at San Germano was framed a new agreement, by two Cardinals commissioned by the Pope, which deferred for two years longer (till August, 1227) the final departure of the Crusade.[r] Frederick permitted himself to be bound by stringent articles. In that month of that year he would proceed on the Crusade, and maintain one thousand knights at his own cost for two years: for each knight who was deficient he was to pay the penalty of fifty marks, to be at the disposal of the King, the Patriarch, and the Master of the Knights Templars, for the benefit of the Holy Land. He was to have a fleet of 150 ships to transport 2000 knights, without cost, to Palestine. If so many knights were not ready to embark, the money saved was to be devoted to those pious interests. He was to place in the hands of the same persons 100,000 ounces of gold, at four several periods, to be forfeited for the same uses, if in two years he did not embark on the Crusade. His successors were bound to fulfil these covenants in case of his death. If he failed to perform any one of these covenants; if at the appointed time he did not embark for the Holy Land; if he did not maintain the stipulated number of knights; if he did not pay the stipulated sums of money; he fell at once under the interdict of the Church: if he left unfulfilled any other point, the Church, by his own free admission, had the power to pronounce the interdict.

Personal ambition, as well as religious zeal, or the policy of keeping on good terms with the spiritual power, might seem to mingle with the aspirations of the

At San Germano, July, 1225.

---

[r] Ric. San. Germ., sub ann.

Emperor Frederick for the Holy Land; to his great
Empire he would add the dominions of the East. In
the November of the same year, after the
signature of the treaty in San Germano, he
celebrated his marriage with Iolante, daughter
of the King of Jerusalem. No sooner had he done
this, than he assumed to himself the title of King of
Jerusalem: he caused a new great seal to be made, in
which he styled himself Emperor, King of Jerusalem
and Sicily. John of Jerusalem was King, he asserted,
only by right of his wife; on her death, the crown descended to her daughter; as the husband of Iolante
he was the lawful sovereign.* King John, by temperament a wrathful man, burst into a paroxysm of fury;
high words ensued; he called the Emperor the son of a
butcher; he accused him of neglecting his daughter, of
diverting those embraces due to his bride to one of her
attendants. He retired in anger to Bologna. Frederick
had other causes for suspecting the enmity of his father-
in-law. He was the brother of Walter of Brienne; and
rumours had prevailed that he intended to claim the
inheritance of his brother's wife, the daughter of the
Norman Tancred. But John filled Italy with dark
stories of the dissoluteness of the gallant Frederick:
that he abstained altogether from the bed of Iolante is
refuted by the fact that two years after she bore him a
son, which Frederick acknowledged as his own. They
appeared even during that year, at least with all outward
signs of perfect harmony.

---

* "Desponsata puellâ Imperator just at that time threw Iolante into
patrem requisivit; ut regna et regalia prison, and ravished her cousin, the
jura resignet—stupefactus ille obedit." daughter of Walter of Brienne. Was
—Jord. apud Raynald. Yet if we are this one of the tales told by the King
to believe the Chronicle of Tours, he of Jerusalem?

Nor was this the only event which crossed the designs
of Frederick, if he ever seriously determined to fulfil
his vow (where is the evidence, but that of his bitter
enemies, that he had not so determined?). Throughout
all his dominions, instead of that profound peace and
established order which might enable him, at the head
of the united knighthood of the Empire and of Italy, to
break with irresistible forces upon the East; in Germany the assassination of the wise and good Engelbert,
Archbishop of Cologne,[1] to whom Frederick had entrusted the tutelage of his son Henry, and the administration of the Empire, threatened the peace of the
realm. In Lombardy, Guelf and Ghibelline warred,
intrigued; princes against princes, Bonifazio of Montferrat and the house of Este against the Salinguerra,
and that cruel race of which Eccelin di Romano was
the head, Venice and Genoa, Genoa and Pisa,   State of
Genoa and Milan, Asti and Alexandria, Ra-   Italy.
venna and Ferrara, Mantua and Cremona, even Rome
and Viterbo, were now involved in fierce hostility, or
pausing to take advantage each of the other; and each
city had usually a friendly faction within the walls of
its rival. Frederick, who held the lofty Swabian notion
as to the prerogative of the Emperor, had determined
with a high hand to assert the Imperial rights. He
hoped, with his Ghibelline allies, to become again the
Sovereign of the north of Italy. He was prepared to
march at the head of his Southern forces; a Diet had
been summoned at Verona. Milan again set herself at
the head of a new Lombard League. In Milan the
internal strife between the nobles and the people, between the Archbishop and the Podestà, had been allayed

---

[1] Godfrei. Monarb. apud Boehmer Fontes, Nov. 7, 1225.

by the prudent intervention of the Pope, to whom the peace of Milan was of infinite importance, that the republic might put forth her whole strength as head of the Lombard League." Milan was joined by Bologna, Piacenza, Verona, Brescia, Faenza, Mantua, Vercelli, Lodi, Bergamo, Turin, Alessandria, Vicenza, Padua, Treviso." The mediation of Honorius averted the threatening hostilities. Yet the Imperialists accuse Honorius as the secret favourer of the League.'

With Honorius himself a rupture seemed to be imminent. The Emperor, even before the treaty of San Germano, had done the Pope the service of maintaining him against his hostile subjects, compelling the Capitanata and the Maremma to return to their allegiance, coercing the populace of Rome, who in one of their usual outbursts, had driven the Pontiff from the city. The deep murmurs of a coming storm might be heard by the sagacious ear. Frederick, in his determination to reduce his Apulian kingdom to subjection, had still treated the ecclesiastical fiefs as he did the civil; he retained the temporalities in his possession during vacancies, so that five of the largest bishoprics, Capua, Aversa, Brundusium, Salerno, and Cosenza, were without bishops. Honorius, soon after the treaty of San Germano, wrote to inform the Emperor that for the good of his soul and the souls of his subjects, he had

---

" The annual income of the Archbishop of Milan, according to Giulini, was 80,000 golden florins (Giulini, Memorie, I. xlviii.). This Giulini estimates at, in the 13th century, nearly 10 millions of lire Milanese. Cherrier reckons this sum at more than 7½ millions of francs.—Cherrier, II. p. 299.

" Compare the Chronicon Placentinum, particularly the strange poem, p. 69.

' "Cujus suggestione multæ civitates contra imperatorem conjuraverunt facientes collegium."—Gol. Muench. p. 395. Compare Chronicon Placentinum, p. 75.

appointed five learned and worthy Prelates to these
sees, natives of the kingdom of Naples, and who could
not, therefore, but be acceptable to the King. Frederick,
indignant at this compulsory nomination, without, as
was usual, even courteous consultation of the Sovereign,
refused to receive the Bishops, and even repelled the
Legates of the Pope from his court. He summoned, it
might seem in reprisal, the inhabitants of Spoleto to his
banner, to accompany him in his expedition to Lombardy. The Spoletines averred that, by the late treaty,
which the Emperor was thus wantonly violating, they
owed allegiance only to the Pope.

The correspondence betrayed the bitterness and rising wrath on both sides. Even Honorius Letter of
seemed about to resume the haughty tone of Honorius.
his predecessors. "If our writing hath filled you with
astonishment, how much more were we amazed by
yours! You boast that you have been more obedient
to us than any of the Kings of your race. Indeed, no
great boast! But if you will compare yourself with
those godly and generous Sovereigns, who have in word
and deed protected the Church, you will not claim superiority; you will strive to approach more nearly to
those great examples. You charge the Church with
treachery, that while she pretended to be your guardian,
she let loose your enemies on Apulia, and raised Otho
to the throne of your fathers: you venture on these
accusations, who have so repeatedly declared that to
the Church you owe your preservation, your life. Pro-
vidence must have urged you to these rash charges that
the care and prudence of the Church may be more
manifest to all men." To the Church, he insinuates, Frederick mainly owes the crown of June 5, 1226
Germany, which he has no right to call hereditary

in his family. "In all our negotiations with you we
have respected your dignity more than our own."
" Whatever irregularity there might be in the appointment of the bishops, it was not for the King's arbitrary
will to decide; and Frederick had been guilty of far
more flagrant encroachments on the rights of bishops
and of the lower clergy." Honorius exculpates himself
from having received the rebellious subjects of the King
in the territories of the See. " You accuse us of laying
heavy burdens on you, which we touch not ourselves
with the tip of our finger. You forget your voluntary
taking up the Cross, our prolongation of the period,
our free gifts of the tithes of all ecclesiastical property; our own contributions in money, the activity of
our brethren in preaching the Holy Vow. In fine, the
band of the Lord is not weakened in its power to
humble the haughty: be not dazzled by your prosperity, so as to throw off the lowliness which you professed
in times of trouble. It is the law of true nobility not
to be elated by success, as not to be cast down by adversity."

Honorius no doubt felt his strength; the Pope at the
head of the Guelfic interest in Lombardy had been
formidable to the designs of Frederick. The
Emperor, indeed, had assumed a tone of command, which the forces which he could array would
hardly maintain. At Borgo St. Domnino he had placed
all the contumacious cities under the ban of the Empire; the Papal Legate, the Bishop of Hildesheim, had
pronounced the interdict of the Church, as though their
turbulent proceedings impeded the Crusade. Both
parties submitted to the mediation of Honorius; Frederick condescended to receive the intrusive bishops whom
he had repelled: he declared himself ready to accept

July 11, 1226.

the terms most consistent with the honour of God, of the Church, of the Empire, and of the Holy Land. The Pope, whose whole soul was absorbed in the promotion of his one object, the Crusade, pronounced his award, in which he treated the Emperor and his rebellious subjects as hostile powers con- *Arbitration of Honorius. Nov. 17, 1226.* tending on equal terms. Each party was to suspend hostilities, to restore the prisoners taken, to forswear their animosities. The King annulled the act of the Imperial ban, and all penalties incurred under it; the Lombards stipulated to maintain at their own cost four hundred knights for the service of the Holy Land during two years, and rigidly to enforce all *Jan. 1227.* laws against heretics. This haughty arbitration, almost acknowledging the absolute independence of the Republics, was the last act of Honorius III.; he *Death of Honorius.* died in the month of March, a few months before the term agreed on in the treaty of San Germano was to expire, and the Emperor, under pain of excommunication, to embark for the Holy Land. The Apostolic tiara devolved on the Cardinal Ugolino, of the noble house of Conti, which had given to the Holy See Innocent III. The more lofty churchmen felt some disappointment that the Papacy was declined by Cardinal Conrad, the Count of Urach, the declared enemy of Frederick. They mistrusted only the feebleness of age in the Cardinal Ugolino. A Pope eighty years old, might seem no fitting antagonist for a Prince like Frederick, as yet hardly in the full maturity of his years. In all other respects the Cardinal Ugolino, in learning, in ability, in activity, in the assertion of the loftiest hierarchical principles, stood high above the whole conclave. Frederick himself, on a former occasion, had borne testimony to the distinguished character

of the Cardinal Ugolino. "He is a man of spotless
reputation, of blameless morals, renowned for piety,
erudition, and eloquence. He shines among the rest
like a brilliant star." The emperor's political astrology had not calculated the baleful influence of that
disastrous planet on his fortunes, his fame, and his
peace.

CHAPTER II.

Honorius III. and England.

THE relations of Honorius III. to the Empire and the
Emperor Frederick II. were no doubt of the most profound importance to Christendom; yet those to England
must find their place in an English history.* We revert
to the commencement of his Papacy. The first care,
indeed, of Pope Honorius was for the vassal kingdom of
England. The death of King John, three months after
that of Innocent III., totally changed the position of the
Pontiff. On his accession Honorius had embraced with
the utmost ardour the policy of Innocent. King John,
the vassal of the Papacy, must be supported against his
rebellious barons, and against the invasion of Louis of
France, by all the terrors of the Papal power. Louis
and all his army, the Barons and all their partisans,
were under the most rigorous form of excommunication.
But on John's death, the Pope is no longer the haughty
and unscrupulous ally and protector of an odious, feeble,
and irreligious tyrant; of one whose lusts had wounded

* Mr. Wm. Hamilton, when ambassador at Naples, rendered to the
country the valuable service of obtaining transcripts of the documents in
the Papal archives relating to Great
Britain and the See of Rome. These
documents, through the active zeal of
M. Panizzi, are now deposited in the
British Museum. They commence,
after one or two unimportant papers,
with the first year of Honorius. They
are not very accurately copied; many
are repetitions; whether they are full
and complete no one can know. Many
have been already printed in Rymer,
in Raynaldus, and elsewhere. Prynne
had seen some of the originals, some
which do not appear, in the Tower.
I cite these documents as MS. B. M.

the high chivalrous honour of many of the noblest
families; whose perfidy, backed by the absolving power
of the Pope, had broken the most solemn engagements,
and revoked the great Charter to which he had submitted at Runnymede; who was ravaging the whole
realm with wild foreign hordes, Brabanters, Poitevins,
freebooters of all countries, and had driven the nobles of
England into an unnatural alliance with Louis of France,
and a transference of the throne to a foreign conqueror.
The Pope was no longer the steadfast enemy of the
liberties of the realm. He assumed the lofty ground of
guardian, as liege lord, of the young heir to the throne
(Henry III. was but nine years old), the protector of a
blameless orphan whom a rebellious baronage and an
alien usurper were endeavouring to despoil of his ancestral crown. Honorius throughout speaks of the young
Henry as the vassal of the Church of Rome; of himself
as the suzerain of England.[b]   English loyalty and English independence hardly needed the Papal fulminations
to induce them to abandon the cause into which they
had plunged in their despair,[c] the cause of a foreign
prince, whose accession to the throne of England would
have reduced the realm to a province of France. Already
their fidelity to Louis had been shaken by rumours, or

---

[b] John he describes as "carissimum
in Christo filium nostrum J., Angliæ
regem illustrem crucesignatum et
vasallum nostrum."—p. 15. The
kingdom of England "specialis juris
apost. sedis existit,"—p. 27. The
Bulls of Honorius have been printed
in an appendix to the Royal Letters
of the time of Henry III., by Mr.
Shirley. Rolls Publications, 1862.

[c] Honorius admits that the Barons
might have had some cause for their

wickedness (malitia) in resisting under
John what they called the intolerable
yoke of servitude. Now that John is
dead, they have no excuse if they do
not return to their allegiance. He
gives power to the Legates, to the
Bishops of Winchester, Worcester,
Exeter, the Archbishops of Dublin and
Bordeaux (the Primate was still in
Rome), to absolve the Barons from
their oaths to Prince Louis.

more than rumours, that the ambitious and unscrupulous
Louis intended, so soon as he had obtained the crown,
to rid himself by banishment and by disinheritance of
his dangerous partisans; to expel the barons from the
realm.[d] The desertion of the nobles, the decisive battle
of Lincoln, seated Henry III. on the throne of the
Plantagenets. The Pope had only to reward with his
praises, immunities, grants, and privileges the few
nobles and prelates faithful to the cause of John and of
his son, W. Marcschal Earl of Pembroke, the Earl of
Arundel, Savary de Mauleon, Hubert de Burgh the
Justiciary, the Chancellor R. de Marisco, who became
Bishop of Durham.[e] He had tardily, sometimes ungra-
ciously, to relieve from the terrible penalties of excommunication the partisans of Louis;[f] to persuade or to
force the King of France to withdraw all support from
the cause of his son, who still continued either in open
hostility or in secret aggression on the continental dominions of Henry III.; and to maintain his lofty position
as Liege Lord and Protector of the King and of the
realm of England.

The Legate Gualo, the Cardinal of St. Marcellus, had
conducted this signal revolution with consummate address

---

[d] Shakspeare has given this plot, with its groundwork in the confession of the Count of Melun.—King John, Act v. Sc. 4.

[e] There are several letters (MS. B.M.) to these English nobles; one to Robert de Marisco empowered him to hold the chancellorship with the bishopric of Durham, and excused him from the fulfilment of his vow to take the cross in the Holy Land, his services being wanted in England. On R. de Marisco compare Collier, I.

p. 430.

[f] There are some curious instances (MS. B. M.) of the terror of the ex-communications. One of the subjects of France, in fear of his life from a fall from his horse, implores absolution for having followed his sovereign's son to the English war; the Pope would hardly excuse him from a journey to Rome. The Chancellor of the King of Scotland is excommunicate for obeying his King. So too the Archbishop of Glasgow,

and moderation.[a] From the coronation of Henry III. at
Gloucester by his hands, the Cardinal took the lead in
all public affairs: he was virtual if not acknowledged
Protector of the infant King. Before the battle of
Lincoln the Legate harangued the royal army, lavished
his absolutions, his promises of eternal reward; under
the blessing of God, bestowed by him, the army advanced to victory.[b] In the settlement of the kingdom,
in the reconciliation of the nobles, he was mild if lofty,
judicious if dictatorial. England might have owed a
deep debt of gratitude to the Pope and to the Legate, if
Gualo's fame had not been tarnished by his inordinate
rapacity.[i] To the nobles he was liberal of his free
absolution; the clergy must pay the penalty of their
rebellion, and pay that penalty in forfeiture, or the
redemption of forfeiture by enormous fines to the Pope
and to his Legate. Inquisitors were sent through the
whole realm to investigate the conduct of the clergy.[k]
The lower ecclesiastics, even canons, under the slightest
suspicion of the rebellion, were dispossessed of their
benefices to make room for foreign priests; the only
way to elude degradation was by purchasing the favour
of the Legate at a vast price. The Bishop of Lincoln

---

[a] Letter to the Abbots of Citeaux
and Clairvaux (MS. B. M. i. p. 43).
They are to use all mild means of persuasion, to threaten stronger measures.

[b] Wendover, p. 19.

[i] Compare the verse of Giles de
Corbeil, p. 69, on the avarice of Gualo
in France.

[k] Wendover, p. 33. The inquisitors
sent some "aecampanies ad legatum et
ab omni beneficio spoliatos, qui illorum
beneficia suis clericis abondanter dis-
tribuit atque de damnis aliorum suos

omnes divites fecit." Wendover gives
the case of the Bishop of Lincoln,
whose example was followed by others,
who "sumptibus nimis damnosis
gratiam sibi reconciliabant legati.
Clericorum vero et canonicorum secu-
larium ablque haustu tam immoderato
loculos evacuavit." &c. See also Math.
Westm. ann. 1218, who describes
Gualo returning to Rome, "clitellis
auro et argento refertis," having disposed ad libitum of the revenues
(redditus) of England.

for his restoration to his see paid 1000 marks to the
Pope, 100 to the Legate.[m]

Throughout the long reign of Henry III. England
was held by successive Popes as a province of the Papal
territory.   The Legate, like a prætor or proconsul of
old, held or affected to hold an undefined supremacy:
during the Barons' wars the Pope with a kind of feudal
as well as ecclesiastical authority condemned the rebels,
not only against their Lord, but against the vassal of
the Holy See.   England was the great tributary province, in which Papal avarice levied the most enormous
sums, and drained the wealth of the country by direct
or indirect taxation.   There were four distinct sources
of Papal revenue from the realm of England.

I. The ancient payment of Peter's Pence;[n] this

---

[m] Pope Honorius was not well
informed on the affairs of England.
When Henry was counselled to take
up arms to reduce the castles held by
the ruffian Fulk de Breauté in defiance
of the King and the peace of the realm,
the Primate had supported the King
and the nobles in this act of necessary
justice and order by ecclesiastical censures.   The Pope wrote a furious
letter of rebuke to Langton (MS.
B. M. ix. Aug. 1224), espousing the
cause of Fulk, who had through his
wealth influence at Rome.   Still later

Gregory IX. reproves and revokes
certain royal grants to Bishops and
Barons, as "in grave præjudicium
ecclesiæ Romanæ ad quam Regnum
Angliæ pertinere dinoscitur, et enor-
mem læsionem ejusdem regni,"—
MS. B. M. ad regem, vol. xiv. p.
77.

[n] The account of Cencius, the Pope's
chamberlain, of the assessment of
Peter's pence in the dioceses of Eng-
land, has been published before by Dr.
Lingard, but may be here inserted from
MS. B. M.:—

De Cantuariensi Ecclesia	xli. libræ	et xviii. solidos		
De Roffensi	v.	xii.	
De Londoniensi	xvi.	x.	
De Norwicensi	xxi.	x.	
De Eliensi	v.		
De Lincolniensi	xlii.		
De Cicestrensi	viii.		
De Wintoniensi	xvii.	vi.	et viii. denarios.
De Exoniensi	ix.	v.	
De Wigorniensi	v.	v.	
De Herefordensi	vi.		
De Bathoniensi	vi.	v.	
De Saresberiensi	xviii.		
De Coventriensi	x.	v.	
De Eboracensi	xi.	x.	

p. lil.

G 2

subsidy to the Pope, as the ecclesiastical sovereign, acknowledged in Saxon times, and admitted by the Conqueror, was regularly assessed in the different dioceses, and transmitted to Rome. Dignitaries of the Church were usually the treasurers who paid it over to Italian bankers in London, the intermediate agents with Rome.

II. The 1000 marks—700 for England, 300 for Ireland—the sign and acknowledgment of feudal vassalage, stipulated by King John, when he took the oath of submission, and made over the kingdom as a fief. Powerful Popes are constantly heard imperiously, necessitous Popes more humbly, almost with supplication, demanding the payment of this tribute and its arrears (for it seems to have been irregularly levied);[*] but during the whole reign of Henry III. and later, no question seems to have been raised of the Pope's right.

III. The benefices held by foreigners, chiefly Italians, and payments to foreign churches out of the property of the English church;[?] the invasion of the English sees by foreign prelates, with its inevitable consequences (or rather antecedents, for John began the practice of purchasing the support of Rome by enriching her Italian clergy), in crowding the English benefices with strangers, and burdening them with persons who never came near them. These abuses as yet only raised deep and suppressed murmurs, ere long to break out into fierce and obstinate resistance. Pandulph, the Papal Legate, be-

[*] Urban IV., MS. B. M. a. p. 29, Dec. 1261. Clement IV., ibid. 12, June 8, 1266.

[?] The convent of Viterbo has a grant of 30 marks from a moiety of the living of Holkham in Norfolk, i. 278; 50 marks from church of Wing-ham to convent of M. Aureo in Anagni, iii. 110. Claims of another convent in Anagni on a benefice in diocese of Winchester, vol. iv. 50. See the grants to John Peter Leone, and others, in Prynne, p. 83. MS. B. M.

came Bishop of Norwich. Pope Honorius writes to
Pandulph not merely authorising but urging him to
provide a benefice or benefices in his diocese of Norwich
for his own (the Bishop's) brother, that brother (a
curious plurality) being Archdeacon of Thessalonica.[*]
These foreigners were of course more and more odious
to the whole realm : to the laity as draining away their
wealth without discharging any duties ; still more to
the clergy as usurping their benefices ; though ignorant
of the language, affecting superiority in attainments ;
as well as from their uncongenial manners, and, if they
are not belied, unchecked vices. They were blood-
suckers, drawing out the life, or drones fattening on the
spoil of the land. All existing documents show that the
jealousy and animosity of the English did not exag-
gerate the evil.[′] At length, just at the close of his
Pontificate, even Pope Honorius, by his Legate Otho,
made the bold and open demand that two prebends in
every cathedral and conventual church (one from the
portion of the Bishop or Abbot, one from that of the
Chapter), or the sustentation of one monk, should be
assigned in perpetuity to the Church of Rome. On
this the nobles interfered in the King's name, inhibiting
such alienation. When the subject was brought before
a synod at Westminster by the Archbishop, the pro-

* Pandulph is by mistake made
cardinal ; he was sub-deacon of the
Roman Church. He is called in the
documents Master Pandulph. Many
letters to and from Pandulph, showing
his great power and influence, may be
read in the Royal Letters among the
Rolls Publications.

′ MS. B. M. E. g., grant of a church
to a consanguineus of the Pope, one
Gervaise, excommunicated for favour-
ing the Barons, having been ejected
from it, i. p. 333. Transfer from one
Italian to another, 235. Grant from
Bishop of Durham to Peter Saracen
(Civis Romanus) of 40 marks, charged
on the See for services done, ii. 158.
Requiring a canonry o' Lincoln for
Thebaldus, scriptor noster, 189.
Canonry of Chichester for a son of
a Roman citizen.

posal was received with derisive laughter at the avarice of the see of Rome. Even the King was prompted to this prudent resolution: " When the rest of Christendom shall have consented to this measure, we will consult with our prelates whether it be right to follow their example." The Council of Bourges, where the Legate Otho urged the same general demand, had eluded it with the same contemptuous disregard. It was even more menacingly suggested that such general oppression from Rome might lead to a general withdrawal of allegiance from Rome.[*]

A.D. 1226.

Five years after, the people of England seemed determined to take the affair into their own hands. Terrible letters were distributed by unseen means, and by unknown persons, addressed to the bishops and chapters, to the abbots and friars, denouncing the insolence and avarice of these Romans; positively inhibiting any payments to them from the revenues of their churches; threatening those who paid to burn their palaces and barns over their heads, and to wreak the same vengeance on them which would inevitably fall on the Italians.[†] Cencius, the Pope's collector of Peter's Pence, a Canon of St. Paul's, was suddenly carried off by armed men, with their faces hid under vizors: he returned with his bags well rifled, after five weeks' imprisonment. John of Florence, Archdeacon of Norwich, escaped the same fate, and concealed himself in London. Other aggressive measures followed. The barns of the Italian clergy were attacked; the corn sold or distributed to the poor.

* Wendover, p. 114, 121, 124. " Quis si omnibus emet universalis oppressio, posset timeri ne insolentia et generalis diaresis, quod Deus avertat."

† Gregory writes to the Archbishop of Canterbury (1234) that the English " ægre non ferunt si inter ipsos mercatores extranei, honores ibidem et beneficia consequantur, cum apud Deum non sit acceptio personarum."—MS. B. M.

It might seem almost a simultaneous rising: though the active assailants were few, the feelings of the whole people were with them." At one place (Wingham) the sheriff was obliged, as it appeared, to raise an armed force to keep the peace; the officers were shown letters-patent (forged as was said) in the King's name, autho-rising the acts of the spoiler: they looked on, not caring to examine the letters too closely, in quiet un-concern at the spoliation. The Pope (Gre-gory IX.) issued an angry Bull,[x] which not A.D. 1232. only accused the Bishops of conniving at these enor-mities, and of making this ungrateful return for the good offices which he had shown to the King; he bitterly complained of the ill usage of his Nuncios and officers. One had been cut to pieces, another left half dead; the Pope's Bulls had been trampled under foot. The Pope demanded instant, ample, merciless punish-ment of the malefactors, restoration of the damaged property. Robert Twenge, a bold Yorkshire knight, who under a feigned name had been the ringleader, appeared before the King, owned himself to have been the William Wither who had headed the insurgents: he had done all this in righteous vengeance against the Romans, who by a sentence of the Pope, fraudulently obtained, had deprived him of the right of patronage to a benefice. He had rather be unjustly excommunicated than despoiled of his right. He was recommended to go to Rome with testimonials from the King for absolu-tion, and this was all.[y] The abuse, however, will appear

" The Pope so far admitted the justice of these complaints as to issue a bull allowing the patrons to present after the death of the Italian incum-bents.—MS. B. M. iil. 138. Gregory IX. said that he had less frequently used this power of granting benefices in England.—Wilkin's Concilia, i. 269.
x Apud Rymer, dated Spoleto.
y Wendover, 292.

yet rampant, when we return to the history of the English Church.

IV. The taxation of the clergy (a twentieth, fifteenth, or tenth) as a subsidy for the Holy Land ; but a subsidy grudgingly paid, and not devoted with too rigid exclusiveness to its holy purpose. Some portion of this was at times thrown, as it were, as a boon to the King (in general under a vow to undertake a Crusade), but applied by him without rebuke or remonstrance to other purposes. This tax was on the whole property of the Church, of the secular clergy and of the monasteries. Favour was sometimes (not always) shown to the Cistercians, the Præmonstratensians, the Monks of Sempringham—almost always to the Templars and Knights of St. John. Other emoluments arose out of the Crusades ; compositions for vows not fulfilled ; besides what arose out of bequests, the property of intestate clergy, and other sources. The Popes seem to have had boundless notions of the wealth and weakness of England. England paid, murmured, but laid up deep stores of alienation and aversion from the Roman See.[a]

---

[a] Clement IV. (Viterbo, May 21, 1266) orders his collector to get in all arrears "de crucibus, denariis Sancti Petri, et debitis quibuscunque." Of these debts there is a long list. "Aut ea voto seu promisso, decimâ vel vicesimâ, seu redemptionibus votorum tam crucesignatorum quam aliorum, vel depositis vel testamentorum (sic) aut bonis clericorum decedentium ab intestato seu aliâ quâcunque ratione modo vel causâ eisdem vel Apostolicæ et terræ sanctæ vel aliter earum a quibuscunque pecunia debeatur." The collectors had power to excommunicate for non-payment. MS. B. M. sii.

CHAPTER III.

Frederick II. and Gregory IX.

THE Empire and the Papacy were now to meet in their last mortal and implacable strife; the two first acts of this tremendous drama, separated *Last strife of Papacy and Empire.* by an interval of many years, were to be developed during the Pontificate of a prelate who ascended the throne of St. Peter at the age of eighty. Nor was this strife for any specific point in dispute like the right of investiture, but avowedly for supremacy on one side, which hardly deigned to call itself independence; for independence, on the other, which remotely at least aspired after supremacy. Cæsar would bear no superior, the successor of St. Peter no equal. The contest could not have begun under men more strongly contrasted, or more determinedly oppugnant in character than Gregory IX. and Frederick II. Gregory *Gregory IX.* retained the ambition, the vigour, almost the activity of youth, with the stubborn obstinacy, and something of the irritable petulance of old age. He was still master of all his powerful faculties; his knowledge of affairs, of mankind, of the peculiar interests of almost all the nations in Christendom, acquired by long employment in the most important negotiations both by Innocent III. and by Honorius III.; eloquence which his own age compared to that of Tully; profound erudition in that learning which, in the mediæval churchman, commanded the highest admiration. No one was

his superior in the science of the canon law; the
Decretals to which he afterwards gave a more full and
authoritative form, were at his command, and they were
to him as much the law of God as the Gospels themselves or the primary principles of morality.   The
jealous reverence and attachment of a great lawyer to
his science strengthened the lofty pretensions of the
churchman.[a]

Frederick II. with many of the noblest qualities which
could captivate the admiration of his own age,
in some respects might appear misplaced, and
by many centuries prematurely born.   Frederick having
crowded into his youth adventures, perils, successes,
almost unparalleled in history, was now only expanding
into the prime of manhood.   A parentless orphan he
had struggled upward into the actual reigning monarch
of his hereditary Sicily; he was even then rising above
the yoke of the turbulent magnates of his realm, and
the depressing tutelage of the Papal See.   He had
crossed the Alps a boyish adventurer, and won, so much
through his own valour and daring that he might well
ascribe to himself his conquest, the kingdom of Germany, the imperial crown; he was in undisputed possession of the Empire, with all its rights in Northern Italy;
King of Apulia, Sicily, and Jerusalem.   He was beginning
to be at once the Magnificent Sovereign, the knight, the
poet, the lawgiver, the patron of arts, letters, and
science; the Magnificent Sovereign now holding his
court in one of the old barbaric and feudal cities of

Frederick II.

---

* Epist. Honor., 14th March, 1221.
He is described as " Forma decorus et
venustas aspectu, perspicacis ingenii
et fidelis memoriæ prærogativâ donatus,
liberalium artium et utriusque juris
peritiâ eminenter instructus, fluvius
eloquentiæ Tullianæ, sacræ paginæ diligens observator et doctor, zelator
fidei."—Cardin. Arragon, Vit. Greg.
IX.

Germany among the proud and turbulent princes of the
Empire, more often on the sunny shores of Naples or
Palermo, in southern and almost Oriental luxury; the
gallant Knight and troubadour Poet not forbidding himself those amorous indulgences which were the reward
of chivalrous valour, and of the "gay science;" the
Lawgiver, whose far-seeing wisdom seemed to anticipate
some of those views of equal justice, of the advantages of
commerce, of the cultivation of the arts of peace, beyond
all the toleration of adverse religions, which even in a
more dutiful son of the Church would doubtless have
seemed godless indifference.   Frederick **must appear**
before us in the course of our history in **the full de-**
velopment of all these shades of character; **but, besides**
all this, Frederick's views of the temporal sovereignty
were **as** imperious and autocratic as those of the
haughtiest churchman of the spiritual supremacy. The
ban of the Empire ought to be at least equally awful
with that of the Church; disloyalty to the Emperor was
as heinous a sin as infidelity to the head of Christendom;
the independence of the Lombard republics was as a great
and punishable political heresy. Even in Rome itself, as
head of the Roman Empire, Frederick aspired to **a**
supremacy which was not less unlimited because vague
and undefined, and irreconcileable with that of the
Supreme Pontiff. If ever Emperor might be tempted
by the vision of a vast hereditary monarchy to be perpetuated in his house, the princely house of Hohenstaufen, it was Frederick. He had heirs of his greatness; his eldest son was King of the Romans; from his
loins might yet spring an inexhaustible race of princes:
the failure of his imperial line was his last fear. The
character of the man seemed formed to achieve and
to maintain this vast design; he was at once terrible

and popular, courteous, generous, placable to his foes;
yet there was a depth of cruelty in the heart of Frederick
towards revolted subjects, which made him look on the
atrocities of his allies, Eccelin da Romano, and the
Salinguerras, but as legitimate means to quell insolent
and stubborn rebellion.

The loftier churchmen, if for a moment they had mis-
givings on account of his age, hailed the election of Cardinal Ugolino with the utmost satisfaction. The surpassing magnificence of his coronation
attested the unanimous applause of the clergy, and even
of the people of Rome.[b] Gregory had in secret murmured against the gentler and more yielding policy of
Honorius III. Of such weakness he could not accuse
himself. The old man at once threw down the
gauntlet; on the day of his accession[c] he
issued an energetic proclamation to all the sovereigns of
Christendom announcing his election to the pontificate,
and summoning them to enter on a new Crusade. That
addressed to Frederick was more direct, vehement, and
imperative, and closed not without some significant
hints that he would not long brook the delay with
which the Emperor had beguiled his predecessor.[d] The
King's disobedience might involve him in difficulties
from which the Pope himself, even if he should so will,
could hardly extricate him.[e]

Frederick, in the height of their subsequent contest,

Gregory IX.

Gregory's first act.

[b] "Tunc lugubres vestes mutavit Ecclesia, et urbis serenitate mœsta pristinum recepere fulgorem."—Cardin. Arragon. in Vit. See description of the inauguration.
[c] 1227, March 18. Raynaldi Annal.
[d] "Alloquia quantumcunque te sincerâ diligamus in Domino charitate, et tibi quantum in Domino possimus deferre velimus, id dissimulare nullâ poterimus ratione."—Epistol. ad Frederic. apud Raynaldi, March 27.
[e] "Nequaquam nos et tejum in illam novitatem inducam, de quâ forsan te de facili non poterimus, etiamsi voluerimus, expedire."—Ibid.

reproached the Pope as having been, while in the lower
orders of the Church, his familiar friend, but that no
sooner had he reached the summit of his ambition than
he threw off all gratitude, and became his determined
enemy.' Yet his congratulations on the accession of
Gregory were expressed in the most courtly tone. The
Bishop of Reggio, and Herman of Salza, the Grand
Master of the Teutonic order, were his ambassadors to
Rome. Gregory, on his side, with impartial severity,
compelled the Lombards to fulfil and ratify the treaty
which had been agreed to through the mediation of
Honorius. Frederick had already transmitted to Rome
the documents which were requisite for the full execution of the stipulations on his part, the general amnesty,
the revocation of the Imperial ban, the release of the
prisoners, the assent of King Henry. The Lombards
were not so ready or so open in their proceedings.
Gregory was constrained to send a strong
summons to the Lombards declaring that he   March 24.
would no longer be tampered with by their idle and
frivolous excuses : " If in this important affair ye despise,
mock, or elude our commands and those of God, nothing
remains for us but to invoke heaven and earth against
your insolence." [g]   The treaty arrived in Rome the day
after this summons had been despatched, wanting the
seal of the Marquis of Montferrat, and of many of the
cities; but Gregory would not be baffled; the Archbishop of Milan received orders to menace the cities

[f] " Iste novus athleta, elatis in Ecclesiam oblitus, statim post assump-
supplciis factus Pontifex Generalis, tam suam fidem cum tempore variam
amictus mater praecipuus dum in et novus cum dignitate commutans."—
minoribus ordinibus constitutus, bene- Petr. de Vineis, Epistol. L. xvi.
ficiorum omnium quibus Imperium   [g] Regest. Gregor., quoted by Von
Christianum sacrosanctam ditavit Raumer, p. 416.

with ecclesiastical censures, and the treaty came back with all the necessary ratifications. In this Gregory pursued the politic as well as the just course. The Emperor must not have this plausible excuse to elude his embarkation on the Crusade at the appointed day in August. The Lombards themselves were imperatively urged to furnish their proper contingent for the Holy War. Gregory IX. knew Lombardy well, it had been the scene of his own preaching of the Cross; and tho sagacious fears of the Church (the stipulations in the treaty of Honorius betrayed this sagacity and these fears) could not but discern that however these proud republics might be heartily Guelfic, cordially on the side of the Church, they were only so from their common jealousy of the Empire. But there was that tacit understanding, or at least unacknowledged sympathy, between civil and religious liberty, which must be watched with vigilant mistrust. It was manifest that the respect for their bishops in all those republics depended entirely on the political conduct of the prelates, not on the sanctity of their office. There was a remissness or reluctance in the suppression of heresy, and in the punishment of heretics, which required constant urgency and rebuke on the part of the Pope: "Ye make a great noise," writes Gregory, "about fines imposed, and sentences of exile against heretics; but ye quietly give them back their fines, and admit them again into your cities. In the mean time ye regard not the immunities of the clergy, neither their exemption from taxation nor their personal freedom; ye even permit enactments injurious to their defence of their liberties, enactments foolish and culpable, even to their banishment by the laity. Take heed, lest a more fearful interdict than that with which you have been punished (the ban of the Empire) fall upon you, the interdict of the Church."[b]

But the Pope was not content with general exhortations to the Emperor to embark on the Crusade: he assumed the privilege of his holy office and of his venerable age to admonish the young and brilliant Frederick on his life, and on the duties of his imperial dignity. The address was sent from Anagni, to which the Pope had retired from the heats of Rome, by the famous Gualo, one of the austere Order of Friar Preachers instituted by St. Dominic.[l] The letter dwelt in the highest terms on the wonderful mental endowments of Frederick, his reason quickened with the liveliest intelligence, and winged by the brightest imagination. The Pope entreats him not to degrade the qualities which he possesses in common with the angels, nor to sacrifice them to the lower appetites, which he has in common with the beasts and the plants of the earth. The love of sensual things debases the intellect, the pampering of the delicate body corrupts the affections. If knowledge and love, those twin lights, are extinguished; if those eagles which should soar in triumph stoop and entangle themselves with earthly pleasures, how canst thou show to thy followers the way of salvation? " Far be it from thee to hold up this fatal example of thraldom to the sensual life. Your justice should be the pillar of fire, your mercy the cooling cloud to lead God's chosen people into the land of promise." He proceeds to a strange mystic interpretation of the five great ensigns of the imperial power; the

---

[b] Regesta, ibid. p. 417.

[l] The Cardinal Ugolino had been the first to foresee the tremendous power of the new Orders. He had been their firm protector: they were bound to him, especially the Franciscans, not only by professed reverence, but by passionate personal attachment.

inward meaning of all these mysterious symbols, the
cross, the lance, the triple crown, the sceptre, and the
golden apple: this he would engrave indelibly with an
iron pen on the adamantine tablets of the king's heart.[a]

It were great injustice to the character of Gregory to
attribute this high-toned, however extravagantly mystic,
remonstrance to the unworthy motives of ambition or
animosity. The severe old man might, not
without grounds, take offence at the luxury,
the splendour, the sensuality of Frederick's Sicilian
court, the freedom at least, if not licence, of Frederick's
life. It was the zeal, perhaps of a monk, but yet the
honest and religious zeal. Frederick's predilection for
his native kingdom, for the bright cities reflected in the
blue Mediterranean, over the dark barbaric towns of
Germany, of itself characterises the man. The summer
skies, the more polished manners, the more elegant
luxuries, the knowledge, the arts, the poetry, the gaiety,
the beauty, the romance of the South, were throughout
his life more congenial to his mind than the heavier
and more chilly climate, the feudal barbarism, the ruder
pomp, the coarser habits of his German liegemen.
Among the profane sayings attributed to Frederick
(who was neither guarded nor discreet in his more
mirthful conversation, and as his strife with the Church
grew fiercer would not become more reverential), sayings caught up, and no doubt sharpened by his enemies,
was that memorable one—that God would never have
chosen the barren land of Judæa for his own people if
he had seen his beautiful and fertile Sicily. And no
doubt that delicious climate and lovely land, so highly
appreciated by the gay sovereign, was not without influ-

Court of Frederick.

---

[a] Epistola Gregor. apud Raynald., Annal., June 8.

ence on the state, and even the manners of his court, to
which other circumstances contributed to give a peculiar
and romantic character. It resembled probably (though
its full splendour was of a later period) Granada in its
glory, more than any other in Europe, though more
rich and picturesque from the variety of races, of manners, usages, even dresses, which prevailed within it.
Here it was that Southern and Oriental luxury began
to impart its mysteries to Christian Europe. The court
was open to the mingled population which at that time
filled the cities of Southern Italy. If anything of Gre-
cian elegance, art, or luxury survived in the West, it
was in the towns of Naples and Sicily. There the
Norman chivalry, without having lost their bold and
enterprising bearing, had yielded in some degree to the
melting influence of the land, had acquired Southern
passions, Southern habits. The ruder and more ferocious
German soldiery, as many as were spared by the climate,
gradually softened, at least in their outward demeanour.
The Jews were numerous, enlightened, wealthy. The
Mohammedan inhabitants of Sicily were neither the
least polished, nor the least welcome at the court of
Frederick: they were subsiding into loyal subjects of the
liberal Christian King; and Frederick was accused by
his enemies, and even then believed by the Asiatic
and Egyptian Mussulmen, to have approximated more
closely to their manners, even to their creed, than became a Christian Emperor. He spoke their tongue,
admired and cultivated their science, caused their philosophy to be translated into the Latin language. In
his court their Oriental manners yielded to the less
secluded habits of the West. It was one of the grave
charges, at a later period, that Saracen women were
seen at the court of Palermo, who by their licentious-

ness corrupted the morals of his Christian subjects.
Frederick admitted the truth of the charge, but asserted
the pure demeanour and chastity of these Mohammedan
ladies: nevertheless, to avoid all future scandal, he consented to dismiss them. This at a time when abhorrence of the Mohammedan was among the first articles
of a Christian's creed; when it would have been impious
to suppose a Mohammedan man capable of any virtue
except of valour, a Mohammedan female of any virtue
at all! The impression made by this inclination for the
society of miscreant ladies, its inseparable connexion
with Mohammedan habits, transpires in the Guelfic character of Frederick by Villani. The Florentine does
ample justice to his noble and kingly qualities, to the
universality of his genius and knowledge, "but he was
dissolute and abandoned to every kind of luxury. After
the manner of the Saracens he had many concubines,
and was attended by Mamelukes; he gave himself up
to sensual enjoyments, and led an epicurean life, taking
no thought of the world to come, and this was the
principal reason of his enmity to Holy Church and to
the hierarchy, as well as his avarice in usurping the
possessions and infringing on the jurisdiction of the
clergy."

It was in this Southern kingdom that the first rude
notes of Italian poetry were heard in the soft Sicilian
dialect. Frederick himself, and his Chancellor Peter
de Vineâ, were promising pupils in the gay science.
Among the treasures of the earliest Italian song are
several compositions of the monarch and of his poetic
rival. One sonnet indeed of Peter de Vineâ is perhaps
equal to anything of the kind before the time when

* Istorie Fiorentin. vi. c. 1.

Petrarch set the common thoughts of all these amorous
Platonists in the perfect crystals of his inimitable language. Of these lays most which survive are amatory,
but it is not unlikely that as the kindred troubadours of
Provence, the poets did not abstain from satiric touches
on the clergy. How far Frederick himself indulged in
more than poetic licence, the invectives of his enemies
cannot be accepted as authority. It was during his
first widowhood that he indulged the height of his passion for the beautiful Bianca Lancia; this mistress bore
him two sons, his best beloved Enzio, during so many
years of his more splendid career the pride, the delight
of his heart, unrivalled for his beauty, the valiant warrior, the consummate general, the cause, by his imprisonment, of the bitterest grief, which in the father's
decline bowed down his broken spirit. Enzio was born
at the close of the year in which Frederick wedded
Iolante of Jerusalem. The fact that Iolante died in
childbed giving birth to his son Conrad, is at least evidence that he had not altogether estranged her from
his affections. In public she had all the state and
splendour of his queen; nor is it known that during her
lifetime her peace was embittered by any more cherished
rivals.

Still if this brilliant and poetic state of society (even
if at this time it was only expanding to its fulness of
luxury and splendour) must appear dubious at least to
the less severe Christian moralist, how must it have
appeared to those who had learned their notions of
morals from the rule of St. Benedict rather than the
Gospel; the admirers of Francis and of Dominic; **men
in** whom human affections were alike proscribed **with**
sensual enjoyments, and in whose religious language, to
themselves at least, pleasure bore the same meaning as

sin; men, who had prayed, and fasted, and scourged
out of themselves every lingering sympathy of our
common nature? How, above all, to one in whom, as
in Gregory IX., age had utterly frozen up a heart,
already hardened by the austerest discipline of monk-
hood? It is impossible to conceive a contrast more
strong or more irreconcileable than the octogenarian
Gregory, in his cloister palace, in his conclave of stern
ascetics, with all but severe imprisonment within conventual walls, completely monastic in manners, habits,
views, in corporate spirit, in celibacy, in rigid seclusion
from the rest of mankind, in the conscientious determination to enslave, if possible, all Christendom to its
inviolable unity of faith, and to the least possible lati-
tude of discipline; and the gay, and yet youthful
Frederick, with his mingled assemblage of knights and
ladies, of Christians, Jews and Mohammedans, of poets
and men of science, met, as it were, to enjoy and minister
to enjoyment; to cultivate the pure intellect: where,
if not the restraints of religion, at least the awful authority of churchmen, was examined with freedom, sometimes ridiculed with sportive wit.

A few months were to put to the test the obedience
of Frederick to the See of Rome, perhaps his Christian
fidelity. By the treaty of San Germano, the August of
the present year had been fixed for his embarkation for the Holy Land. Gregory, it is
clear, mistrusted his sincerity; with what justice it is
hard to decide. However Frederick might be wanting
in fervent religious zeal, he was not in the chivalrous
love of enterprise; however he might not abhor the
Mohammedans with the true Christian cordiality of his
day, he would not decline to meet them in arms as
brave and generous foes; however the recovery of the

Saviour's tomb might not influence him with the fierce
enthusiasm which had kindled the hearers of Peter the
Hermit or St. Bernard, or perhaps that which sent forth
his grandsire Barbarossa: yet an Oriental kingdom,
which he claimed in the right of his wife, a conquest
which would have commanded the grateful admiration
of Christendom, was a prize which his ambition would
hardly disdain, or rather at which it would grasp with
bold eagerness. Frederick was personally brave; but
neither was his finer, though active and close-knit frame,
suited to hew his way through hosts of unbelievers; he
aspired not, and could not hope, to rival the ferocious
personal prowess of our Richard Cœur de Lion, or to
leave his name as the terror of Arabian mothers. Nor
would his faith behold Paradise as the assured close of
a battle-field with the Infidels, the remission of sins as
the sure reward of a massacre of the believers in Islam.
Frederick was not averse to obtain by negotiation (and
surely, with the warnings of all former Crusades, especially that of his grandsire Barbarossa, not unwisely),
and by taking advantage of the feuds between the
Saracen princes, those conquests which some would
deem it impious to strive after but by open war.
Frederick had already received an embassy from Sultan
Malek-al-Kameel of Egypt (of this the Pope could
hardly be ignorant). Between the Egyptian and Damascene descendants of the great Saladin there was implacable hostility. Kameel had now recovered Damietta;[*] he had made a treaty with the discomfited

---

* In the fierce invectives of their
later controversy, the Papal party
attributed to the tardiness, even to the
treachery of Frederick, the disastrous
loss of Damietta. If he had accomplished the first German division of
the German Crusaders, the Christians
would not have been without a leader;
and with his fame and power he might,
by the conquest of Egypt, have re-

Crusaders. He hated his rival of Damascus even more bitterly than he did the Christians. His offers to Frederick were the surrender of the kingdom of Jerusalem, on condition of close alliance against the Sultan of Damascus. Frederick had despatched to the East an ambassador of no less rank than the Archbishop of Palermo. The Prelate bore magnificent and acceptable presents, horses, arms, it was said the Emperor's own palfrey.[c] In the January of the following year the Archbishop had returned to Palermo, with presents, according to the Eastern authority, of twice the value of his own; many rare treasures from India, Arabia, Syria, and Irak. Among these, to the admiration of the Occidentals, was a large elephant.[f] To the Pope, the negotiations themselves were unanswerable signs of Frederick's favour to the Infidels, and his perfidy to the cause of the Christians.[?]

Negotiations with Sultan Kameel.

Yet Frederick seemed earnestly determined to fulfil his vow. Though the treaty with the Lombard cities was hardly concluded, he had made vast preparations. He had levied a large tax from the whole kingdom of Sicily for the maintenance of his forces;[r] a noble fleet

---

established, and for ever, the Christian dominion in the East. But Frederick certainly could not have gone at that time with a force equal to this great enterprise.

[c] Ebn Ferah, quoted in Michaud's Bibliographie des Croisades, p. 727.

[f] Michd. de S. German. p. 1004. Makrizi apud Reinaud. Hugo Plagon.

[?] The letter of Gregory IX. in Matth. Paris. "Quod detestabilis est, cum Soldano et aliis Saracenis nefandis (Fredericus) contrahens partimes, illis favorem, Christianis odium

exhibuit manifeste." — Sub ann. 1228, p. 348. On these rumours of the understanding between the Emperor and Sultan Kameel no doubt Gregory founded his darker charge of Frederick's having compelled the surrender of Damietta, not only by withholding all relief from the Christians when masters of it, but by direct and treacherous intercourse with the Soldan.

[r] Richard de S. German. p. 1103. Alberic. ad ann. 1227. The monastery of San Germano was assessed at 450 ounces.

rode in the harbour of Brundusium : Frederick himself, with his Empress Iolante, passed over from Sicily and took up his abode in Otranto.

Pilgrims in the mean time had been assembling from various quarters. In Germany, at a great Diet at Aix-la-Chapelle, in the presence of King Henry, many of the Princes and Prelates had taken the Cross. Some of these, especially the Duke of Austria, alleged excuses from their vow. But the Landgrave of Thuringia, the husband of Elizabeth of Hungary, afterwards sainted for her virtues, tore himself from his beloved wife in the devotion to what both esteemed the higher duty.[*] The Bishops of Augsburg, Bamberg, and Ratisbon accompanied the Landgrave to Italy. France seemed for once to be cold in the Holy cause (Louis IX. was in his infancy), but in England there had been a wide-spread popular movement. On the vigil of John the Baptist's day it was rumoured abroad, that the Saviour himself had appeared in the heavens, bleeding, pierced with the nails and lance, on a cross which shone like fire.[*] It was to encourage forty thousand pilgrims, who were said already to have taken the Cross. This was seen more than once in different places, in order to confute the incredulous gainsayers. But of those forty thousand who were enrolled, probably no large proportion reached Southern Italy.

The Emperor, hardly released from the affairs of Northern Italy, was expected to have provisions and ships ready for the transport of all this vast undisciplined rout, of which no one could calculate the numbers.

---

[*] Montalembert, Vie de St. Elizabeth de Hoogrie.
[*] Wendover, p. 144. The reading in Paris for quadraginta is seraginta. Ed. Coxe, p. 144.

Delays took place, which the impatient Pope, ignorant
no doubt of the difficulties of maintaining and embarking
a great armament, ascribed at once to the remissness or
the perfidy of Frederick. The heats came on with more
than usual violence, they were such, it is said, as might
have melted solid metal.[*] A fever broke out fatal, as
ever, to the Germans.[a] The Landgrave of Thuringia,
the Bishops of Augsburg and of Angers were among its
victims; the pilgrims perished by thousands. The death
of the Landgrave was attributed not only to the wanton
delay, but even to poison administered by the orders of
Frederick, who, in his insatiate rapacity, coveted the
large possessions of the Prince. About the appointed
day Frederick himself embarked; the fleet set sail; it
lost sight of the shore;—but three days after the Imperial ship was seen returning hastily to the haven of
Otranto; Frederick, alleging severe illness, returned
to the baths of Pozzuoli, to restore his strength. The
greater part of the fleet either dispersed or, following
the Emperor's example, returned to land.

Gregory heard at Anagni (the year of Gregory's
accession had not yet expired) the return of Frederick,
the dissolution of the armament. On St.
Michael's Day, surrounded by his Cardinals
and Prelates, he delivered a lofty discourse,
on the text, "It must needs be that offences come, but
woe unto him through whom they come." He pronounced the excommunication, which Frederick had
incurred by his breach of the agreement at San Ger-

Excommun-
ication of
Frederick.
Sept. 29.

---

[*] "Cujus ardoribus ipsa fere solida
metalla liquescunt."—Card. Arragon.
in Vit. Greg. IX.

[a] An impostor placed himself on
the steps of St. Peter's, in the attire
and character of the Pope, and publicly
sold indulgences, releasing the pilgrims
from their vows. After carrying on
this strange bold fraud for some days,
he was apprehended, and paid the
penalty of his imposture.—Raynald.
sub ann.

mano. Nothing was wanting to the terror. All the
bells joined their most dissonant peals; the clergy,
each with his torch, stood around the altar. Gregory
implored the eternal malediction of God against the
Emperor. The clergy dashed down their torches: there
was utter darkness. The churchmen saw in this sentence the beginning of the holy strife, of the triumph
of St. Michael over the subtle and scaly dragon. The
sentence was followed by an address to the Apulian
bishops, the subjects of Frederick. "The little bark
of St. Peter, launched on the boundless ocean, though
tossed by the billows, is submerged but never lost, for
the Lord is reposing within her: he is awakened at
length by the cries of his disciples; he commands the
sea and the winds, and there is a great calm. From
four quarters the tempests are now assailing our bark;
the armies of the Infidels are striving with all their
might that the land, hallowed by the blood of Christ,
may become the prey of their impiety; the rage of
tyrants, asserting their temporal claims, proscribes
justice and tramples under foot the liberties of the
Church: the folly of heretics seeks to rend the seam-
less garment of Christ, and to destroy the Sacraments
of the faith; false brethren and wicked sons, by their
treacherous perversity, disturb the bowels and tear open
the sides of their mother." "The Church of Christ,
afflicted by so many troubles, while she thinks that she
is nursing up her children, is fostering in her bosom fire
and serpents and basilisks,[r] which would destroy everything by their breath, their bite, and their burning.
To combat these monsters, to triumph over hostile
armies, to appease these restless tempests, the Holy

---

[r] Regulae.

Apostolic See reckoned in these latter times on a nursling whom she had brought up with the tenderest care. The Church had taken up the Emperor Frederick, as it were, from his mother's womb, fed him at her breasts, borne him on her shoulders; she had often rescued him from those who sought his life; instructed him, educated him with care and pain to manhood; invested him with the royal dignity; and to crown all these blessings, bestowed on him the title of Emperor, hoping to find in him a protecting support, a staff for her old age. No sooner was he King in Germany than, of his own accord, unexhorted, unknown to the Apostolic See, he took the Cross and made a vow to depart for the Holy Land; he even demanded that himself and all other Crusaders should be excommunicated if they did not set forth at the appointed time. At his coronation as Emperor we ourselves, then holding an inferior office under the most Holy Honorius, gave him the Cross, and received the renewal of his vows. Three times at Veroli, at Ferentino, at San Germano, he alleged delays; the Church in her indulgence accepted his excuses. At San Germano he made a covenant, which he swore by his soul to accomplish; if not, he incurred by his own consent the most awful excommunication. How has he fulfilled that covenant? When many thousands of pilgrims, depending on his solemn promises, were assembled in the port of Brundusium, he detained the armament so long, under the burning summer heats, in that region of death, in that pestilent atmosphere, that a great part of the pilgrims perished, the noble Landgrave of Thuringia, the Bishops of Augsburg and Angers. At length, when the ships began to return from the Holy Land, the pilgrims embarked on board of them, on the Nativity of the Blessed

Virgin, expecting the Emperor to join their fleet. But
he, breaking all his promises, bursting every bond,
trampling under foot the fear of God, despising all
reverence for Christ Jesus, scorning the censures of the
Church, deserting the Christian army, abandoning
the Holy Land to the Unbelievers, to his own disgrace
and that of all Christendom, withdrew to the luxuries
and wonted delights of his kingdom, seeking to palliate
his offence by frivolous excuses of simulated sickness.[*]

"Behold, and see if ever sorrow was like unto the
sorrow" of the Apostolic Pontiff. The Pope describes
in pathetic terms the state of the Holy Land; attri-
butes to the base intrigues of Frederick with the Unbelievers, the fatal issue of the treaty of Damietta;
"but for him, Jerusalem might have been recovered in
exchange for that city. That we may not be esteemed
as dumb dogs, who dare not bark, or fear to take vengeance on him, the Emperor Frederick, who has
caused such ruin to the people of God, we proclaim the
said Emperor excommunicate; we command you to
publish this our excommunication throughout the
realm; and to declare, that in case of his contumacy,
we shall proceed to still more awful censures. We
trust, however, that he will see his own shame; and
return to the mercy of his mother the Church, having
given ample satisfaction for all his guilt."

---

[*] Compare with this statement, Frederick's own account, published to the world three months after. Both he and the Landgrave had been ill; both had a relapse; both returned to Otranto, where the Landgrave died. "Præterea nondum resumptâ convalescentiâ, galeas ingressi sumus, nos et dilectus consanguineus noster Lant- gravius, vestigia præcedentium secuti. Ubi tanta subito invasit utrumque turbatio, quod et nos in graviorem decidimus recidivam, et idem Lantgravius post accessum nostrum apud Idruntium de medio, proh dolor! est ereptus."— Epist. Frederic. If this was untrue, it was a most audacious and easily confuted untruth.

Gregory IX. had been on the throne of St. Peter not eight months before he uttered the fulminating decree; in which some truth is so confounded and kneaded up with falsehood and exaggeration; and there is so much of reckless wrath, such want of calm, statesman-like dignity, such deliberate, almost artful determination to make the worst of everything. The passionate old man might seem desperately to abandon all hopes of future success in the Holy Land; and to take vindictive comfort in heaping all the blame on Frederick.[a]

Gregory returned to Rome; Frederick had already sent ambassadors solemnly to assert that his illness was real and unfeigned, the Bishops of Bari and Reggio, and Reginald of Spoleto. By one account, the Pope refused to admit them to his presence: at all events he repelled them with the utmost scorn, and so persisted in branding the Emperor in the face of Christendom as a hypocrite and a liar.[b]

Twice again, on St. Martin's Day and on Christmas Day, the Pope, amid all the assembled hierarchy, renewed and confirmed the excommunication. Frederick treated the excommunication itself with utter contempt; either through love or fear the clergy of the kingdom of Naples performed as usual all the sacred offices. At Capua he held a Diet of all the Barons of Apulia; he assessed a tax on both the kingdoms for an expedition to the Holy Land, appointed for the ensuing May. He

---

[a] "Hic (Gregorius IX.) tanquam superbus primo anno pontificatus sui coepit excommunicare Fredericum Imperatorem pro causis frivolis et falsis."
—Abb. Urspergens. p. 247.

[b] There is a letter to Frederick, quoted in Raynaldus, in the milder tone, declaring that the Pope had been blamed for the magnitude of his proceedings; because he had not also censured him for many acts of tyranny and invasion on the rights of the Church in Naples and Sicily.

summoned an assemblage of all his Italian subjects to
meet at Ravenna, to take counsel for this common Crusade. From Capua came forth his defiant appeal to
Christendom.[c] In this appeal Frederick replied to the
unmeasured language of the Pope in language not less
unmeasured. He addressed all the Sovereigns of Christendom; he urged them to a league of all temporal
Kings to oppose this oppressive league of the Pope and
the Hierarchy. He declared that he had been prevented from accomplishing his vow, not, as the Pope
falsely averred, by frivolous excuses, but by serious illness; he appealed to the faithful witness in Heaven for
his veracity; he declared his fixed determination, immediately that God should restore him to health, to
proceed on that holy expedition. "The end of all is at
hand; the Christian charity which should rule and
maintain all things is dried up in its fountain not in its
streams, not in its branches, but in its stem. Has not
the unjust interdict of the Pope reduced the Count of
Toulouse and many other princes to servitude? Did
not Innocent III. (this he especially addressed to King
Henry of England) urge the noble Barons of England
to insurrection against John, as the enemy of the
Church? But no sooner had the humiliated King
subjected his realm, like a dastard, to the See of Rome,
than, having sucked the fat of the land, he abandoned
those Barons to shame, ruin, and death. Such is the
way of Rome, under words as smooth as oil and honey
lies hid the rapacious blood-sucker: the Church of
Rome, as though she were the true Church, calls herself
my mother and my nurse, while all her acts have been
those of a stepmother. The whole world pays tribute

[c] Rich. de San Germ.

to the avarice of the Romans. Her Legates travel
about through all lands, with full powers of ban and
interdict and excommunication, not to sow the seed of
the word of God, but to extort money, to reap what
they have not sown. They spare not the holy churches,
nor the sanctuary of the poor, nor the rights of the
prelates. The primitive Church, founded on poverty
and simplicity, brought forth numberless Saints: she
rested on no foundation, but that which had been laid
by our Lord Jesus Christ. The Romans are now rolling
in wealth; what wonder that the walls of the Church
are undermined to the base, and threaten utter ruin ?" [a]
The Emperor concluded with the solemn admonition to
all temporal Sovereigns to make common cause against
the common adversary : " Your house is in danger when
that of your neighbour is on fire." But in all this strife
of counter proclamations, the advantage was with the
Pope. Almost every pulpit in Christendom might propagate to the end of the earth the Papal fulminations:
every wandering friar might repeat them in the ears of
men. The Emperor's vindication, the Imperial ban
against the Pope, might be transmitted to Imperial
officers, to municipal magistrates, even to friendly prelates or monks: they might be read in diets or burgher
meetings, be affixed on town-halls or market places, but
among a people who could not read ; who would tremble
to hear them.[b]

[a] Matth. Paris, sub ann. 1228.
Written no doubt at the end of
1227, Dec. 6 ; received in England in
1228.

[b] " D'ailleurs les moyens de pub-
licité faciles et puissans dans les mains
du Pape, étaient presque nuls dans
celles des princes séculiers, qui avant

l'imprimerie ne pouvaient que diffi-
cilement se faire entendre des masses
populaires. Dans cette lutte de paroles
l'avantage devoit rester au Saint Siège,
puisque la chaire dont il disposoit
était la seule tribune de ce temps."—
Cherrier, Lutte des Papes et des Em-
pereurs, ii. p. 739.

Yet the Emperor had allies, more dangerous to the
Pope than the remote Sovereigns of Christendom.
Gregory, on his return from Anagni, had been received
in Rome with the acclamations of the clergy, and part
at least of the people. But in Rome there had always
been a strong Imperialist party, a party hostile to the
ruling Pontiff. Gregory had already demolished the
palaces and castle towers of some of the Roman nobles,
which obstructed his view, and no doubt threatened his
security in the Lateran :[f] he had met with no open resistance, but such things were not done in Rome without
more dangerous secret murmurs. Frederick, by timely
succours during a famine in the last winter, had won the
hearts of many of the populace. He had made himself
friends, especially among the powerful Frangipani, by
acts of prodigal generosity. He had purchased the
lands of the heads of that family, and granted them
back without fine as Imperial fiefs. The Frangipanis
became the sworn liegemen of the Emperor's family.
Roffrid of Benevento, a famous professor of Jurisprudence in Bologna, appeared in Rome and read in public,
with the consent of the Senate and people of Rome, the
vindication of the Emperor.

On Thursday in the Holy Week the Pope proceeded
to his more tremendous censures on the im-   March 22.
penitent Frederick. "His crimes had now   Second excommunication.
accumulated in fearful measure. To the triple   A.D. 1239.
offence, which he had committed in the breach of the
treaty of San Germano—that he had neither passed
the sea to the Holy Land, nor armed and despatched
the stipulated number of knights at his own cost, nor
furnished the sums of money according to his obligation

---

[f] Card. Arragon. in Vita.

—were added other offences. He had prevented the
Archbishop of Tarento from entering his See; he had
seized all the estates held by the Knights Templars and
Knights of St. John within his realm; he had broken
the treaty entered into and guaranteed by the See of
Rome with the Count of Celano and Reginald of Acerra;
he had deprived the Count Roger, though he had taken
the Cross, of his followers and of his lands, and thrown
his son into prison, and had refused to release him at
the representation of the Holy See." All these were,
in Frederick's estimation, his rebellious subjects, visited
with just and lawful penalties. These aggravated crimes
—for crimes they were assumed to be on the irrefragable grounds of Papal accusation—called for aggravated
censures. The Pope declared every place in which
Frederick might be, under interdict; all divine offices
were at once to cease; all who dared to celebrate such
offices were deprived of their functions and of their
benefices. If he himself should dare to force his way
into the ceremonies of the Church he was threatened
with something worse. If he did not desist from the
oppression of the churches and of ecclesiastical persons,
if he did not cease from trampling under foot the ecclesiastical liberties, and from treating the excommunication with contempt, all his subjects were at once
absolved from their allegiance. He was menaced with
the loss of his fief, the kingdom of Naples, which he
held from, and for which he had done homage to, the
See of Rome. The holy ceremonies passed away undisturbed; but on the Wednesday in Easter week, while
the Pope was celebrating the mass, there was suddenly
heard a fierce cry, a howl as Gregory describes
it; and the whole populace rose in insurrection. The storm was for a time allayed; but after

Gregory
driven from
Rome.

some weeks Gregory found it necessary to leave Rome.
He retired first to Rieti, afterwards to Perugia.[a]

Frederick, in the mean time, although under excommunication, celebrated his Easter with great
pomp and rejoicing at Baroli. Tidings had   March 20.
arrived of high importance from the Holy Land.
Gregory had received, and had promulgated throughout
Christendom, the most doleful accounts of the state of
the Christians in Palestine. A letter addressed to the
Pope by Gerold the Patriarch, Peter Archbishop of
Cæsarea (the Pope's Legate), the Archbishop of Narbonne, the Bishops of Winchester and Exeter, the Grand
Masters of the Templars and of St. John, announced,
that no sooner had the news of the Emperor's abandonment of the Crusade arrived in Syria, than the pilgrims,
to the number of forty thousand, re-embarked for the
West. Only eight hundred remained, who were retained with difficulty, and were only kept up to the
high pitch of enthusiasm by the promise of the Duke of
Limbourg, then at the head of the army, to break the
existing treaties, and march at once upon Jerusalem.
On the other hand, a letter from Thomas Count of
Acerra, the Lieutenant of Frederick in the Holy Land,
who now held the city of Ptolemais, announced the
death of the Sultan Moadhin of Damascus.[b] Moadhin
was the most formidable enemy of the Christians; he
had been at the head of a powerful army; his implacable
hatred of the Christians had brought all the more warlike
Saracens under his banner: he had destroyed many of
the strongholds, which, if in the power of the Crusaders,

a Rich. San Germ. "Quociens
Idem (the Frangipani) reversi cum
Papa rursus excommunicari et imper-
torum, servunt ut a populo pelleretur   turpiter extra civitatem."—Conrad.
Ureperg. Compare Vit. Greg. IX.
b The Christians called him Cen-
radin.—Rich. San Germ.

might be of military importance: he had subjected
Jerusalem itself to further ravage.

All the acts of Frederick now showed his determination to embark before the spring was passed
for the Holy Land. He would convince the
world, the Pope himself, of his sincerity. Already had
he despatched considerable reinforcements to the Count
of Acerra; the taxes for the armament were levied with
rigour; the army which was to accompany him was
drawn together from all quarters. The death of the
Empress Iolante in childbirth did not delay
these warlike proceedings. To Baroli he summoned all the magnates of the kingdom, to hear his
final instructions, to witness his last will and testament,
in case he should not return alive from his expedition.
No building could contain the vast assemblage: a tribune was raised in the open air, from which the Imperial mandates were read aloud. He exhorted all the
barons and prelates with their liegemen to live at peace
among themselves, as in the happy days of William II.
Reginald Duke of Spoleto was appointed Bailiff of the
realm; his elder son Henry was declared heir both of
the Empire and of the kingdom of Sicily;[1] if he died
without heirs, then Conrad; afterwards any surviving
son of Frederick by a lawful wife. This, his last will,
could only be annulled by a later authentic testament.
The Duke of Spoleto, the Grand Justiciary Henry de
Morro, and others of the nobles, swore to the execution
of this solemn act.

The more determined Frederick appeared to fulfil his
vow, the more resolute became the Pope in his hostility.
He had interdicted the payment of all taxes to the ex-

_____

[1] Ric. de San Germ. p. 1003.

communicated sovereign by all the prelates, monasteries, and ecclesiastics of his realm.[b] Pilgrims who passed the Alps to join the army were plundered by the Lombards; at the instigation (so, no doubt, it was falsely rumoured, but the falsehood is significant) of the Pope himself.[c] The border of the Neapolitan kingdom was violated by the Pope's subjects of Rieti; the powerful Lords of Polito in the Capitanata renounced their allegiance to the King. Frederick went down to Brundusium; his fleet, only of twenty galleys, rode off the island of St. Andrew.[a] Messengers from the Pope arrived peremptorily inhibiting his embarkation on the Crusade till he should have given satisfaction to the Church, and been released from her ban. Frederick paid no attention to the mandate; he sailed to Otranto; as he left that harbour, he sent the Archbishop of Bari and Count Henry of Malta to the Pope, to demand the abrogation of the interdict: they were rejected with scorn by Gregory.[c]

Frederick set sail with his small armament of twenty galleys, which contained at most six hundred knights, more, the Pope tauntingly declared, *Frederick sets sail.* like a pirate than a great sovereign. He could not await, perhaps he had no inclination to place himself at the head of a great Crusade, assembled from all quarters of the world, and so involve himself in a long war which he could not abandon without disgrace. He could not safely withdraw the main part of his forces, and expose his kingdom of Naples to the undisguised hostility of the Pope, with malcontents of all classes,

[b] Ric. de San Germ.   [c] Urspergen, sub ann. 1228.
[a] Jordanus, in Raynaldi, sub ann, Andreas Dandolo, apud Muratori, xii. 344, June or July.
[c] Reg. Gregor., quoted by Von Raumer, p. 443.

I 2

especially the clergy, whom he had been forced to keep
down with a strong hand. He was still in secret intelligence with the Sultan of Egypt, still hoped to acquire
by peaceful negotiations what his predecessors had not
been able to secure by war.[p] Frederick, after a prospe-

In Cyprus.
rous voyage, landed at Cyprus: there, by acts
of violence and treachery (the only account of
these transactions is from hostile writers) he wrested the
tutelage of the young King from John of Ibelin, whom
he invited to a banquet, treated with honour as his own
near kinsman, and then compelled to submit to his
terms. But as the young King was cousin to his Empress Iolante, his interference, which was solicited by
some of the leading men in the island, may have rested
on some asserted right as nearest of kin.[q] From Cyprus
he sailed to Ptolemais (Acre): he was received with the

At Ptole-
mais.
Sept. 7.
utmost demonstrations of joy. The remnant
of the pilgrims who had not returned to Europe
welcomed their tardy deliverer as about to lead them to
conquest; the clergy and the people came forth in
long processions; the Knights of the Temple and St.
John knelt before the Emperor and kissed his knee;
but (inauspicious omen!) the clergy refused the kiss of
peace, and declined all intercourse with one under the
ban of the Church.[r] At the head of a great force
Frederick might have found it difficult to awe into concord the conflicting factions which divided the Christians
in the Holy Land: they seemed to suspend their

Frederick
landed
Sept. 7.
mutual animosities in their common jealousy
of Frederick. The old estrangement of the
clergy quickened rapidly into open hostility. The

[p] See above, p. 100.

[q] The mother of Henry of Cyprus
was half-sister to Maria Iolante, the

mother of the Empress.

[r] Matth. Paris. Urspergens. sub
ann.

active hatred of the Pope had instantly pursued the
Emperor, even faster than his own fleet, to the Holy
Land. Two Franciscan friars had been despatched in a
fast sailing bark, to proclaim to the Eastern Christians
that he was still under excommunication; that all were
to avoid him as a profane person. The Patriarch, the
two Grand Masters of the Orders, were to take measures
that the Crusade was not desecrated by being under the
banner of an excommunicated man, lest the affairs of
the Christians should be imperilled. The Master of
the Teutonic Order was to take the command of the
German and Lombard pilgrims; Richard the Marshal
and Otho Peliard of the troops of the kingdoms of
Jerusalem and Cyprus; in his own camp the Emperor
was to be without power, nothing was to be done in his
name.[a]

The Knights Templars and Knights of the Hospital
hardly required to be stimulated by the Papal
censures to the hatred of Frederick. These
associations, from bands of gallant knights
vowed to protect the pilgrims to the Holy Sepulchre,
and to perform other Christian services, had rapidly
grown into powerful Orders, with vast possessions in
every Christian kingdom; and, themselves not strong
enough to maintain the kingdom of Jerusalem, were
jealous of all others. As yet they were stern bigots,
and had not incurred those suspicions which darkened
around them at a later period in their history. Frederick had placed them under severe control, with all
the other too zealous partisans of the Church, in his
realm of Naples and Sicily. This was one of the acts
which appears throughout among the charges of tyran-

Opposition of the clergy. The Templars and Hospitallers.

---

[a] Richard de San Germano, p. 1003.

nical maladministration in the Apulian kingdom. These
religious Orders claimed the same exemptions, the same
immunities, with other ecclesiastics: the mere fact that
they were submitted to the severe and impartial taxation of Frederick would to them be an intolerable
grievance. Their unruly murmurs, if not resistance,
would no doubt provoke the haughty sovereign; his
haughtiness would rouse theirs to still more inflexible
opposition. Perhaps Frederick's favour to the Teutonic
Order might further exasperate their jealousy. They
had already filled the ears of the Pope with their
clamours against Thomas of Acerra, the Lieutenant of
Frederick. Gregory had proclaimed to Christendom,
to France where the Templars were in great power,
that "the worthy vicegerent of Frederick, that minister
of Mahomet who scrupled not to employ his impious
Saracens of Nocera against Christians and Churchmen
in his Apulian kingdom, had openly taken part with the
unbelievers against these true soldiers of the Cross."
The Saracens, when the suspension of arms was at an
end, had attacked a post of the Knights Templars, and
had carried off a rich booty. The Templars had pursued the marauders, and rescued part of the spoil ; when
Thomas of Acerra appeared at the head of his troops,
and, instead of siding with the Christians, had compelled
them to restore the booty to the Infidels. Such was
their version of this affair,[a] eagerly accredited by the
Pope. It is more probable that the Lieutenant of the
Emperor acted as General of the Christian forces; and
that this whole proceeding was in violation of his orders,

[a] Letter of Gregory to the Legate in France, in Matth. Paris. Compare
Hugo Plagon. where the Marshal Richard is represented as in command of
the pilgrims.

as it clearly was on both sides, of the existing treaty.
The Knights Templars and Hospitallers held themselves
as entirely independent powers; fought or refused to
fight according to their own will and judgement; formed
no part of one great Christian army: were amenable, in
their own estimation, to no superior military rule. If
they had refused obedience to the Lieutenant of the
Emperor or the King of Jerusalem, they were not likely
to receive commands from one under excommunication.
Frederick himself soon experienced their utter contumacy. He commanded them to evacuate a castle
called the Castle of the Pilgrims, which he wished to
garrison with his own troops. The Templars closed the
gates in his face, and insultingly told him to go his way,
or he might find himself in a place from whence he
would not be able to make his way.[a]

Frederick, however, with the main army of the pilgrims
was in high popularity; they refused not to march under
his standard; he appeared to approve of their determination to break off the treaty, and to advance at once
upon Jerusalem. Frederick, to avoid this perpetual collision with his enemies, pitched his camp at Recordana,
some distance without the gates of Ptolemais. He then
determined to take possession of Joppa (Jaffa), and to
build a strong fortress in that city. He summoned all
the Christian forces to join him in this expedition. The
Templars peremptorily refused, if the war was to be
carried on, and the orders issued to the camp, in the
name of the excommunicated Emperor. Frederick commenced his march without them; but mistrusting the
small number of his forces, was obliged to submit that
all orders should be issued in the name of God and of

---

[a] Hugo Plagon.

120   LATIN CHRISTIANITY.   Book X.

Christianity. Frederick's occupation of Joppa, the port
nearest to Jerusalem, was not only to obtain possession
of a city in which he should be more completely master
than in Ptolemais, and to strengthen the Christian
cause by the erection of a strong citadel; but as the
jealous vigilance of his enemies discerned, to bring
himself into closer neighbourhood with the Sultan of
Egypt. Kameel, the Babylonian Sultan, as he was
called from the Egyptian Babylon (Cairo), was encamped in great force near Gaza. The old amity, and
more than the amity, something like a close league
between the Sultan of Egypt and the Emperor Frederick, now appeared almost in its full maturity.
Already, soon after the loss of Damietta and its recovery from the discomfited Christians, Sultan Kameel
had sent his embassy to Frederick, avowedly because
he was acknowledged to be the greatest of the Christian
powers, and in Sicily ruled over Mohammedan subjects
with mildness, if not with favour. The interchange of
presents had been such as became two such splendid
sovereigns.* The secret of their negotiations, carried
on by the mission of the Archbishop of Palermo to
Cairo, of Fakreddin the favourite of Sultan Kameel to
Sicily, could be no secret to the watchful emissaries of
the Pope.

There had been mortal feud between Malek Kameel
of Egypt and Malek Moadhin of Damascus. Malek
Moadhin had called in the formidable aid of Gelal-eddin,
the Sultan of Kharismia, who had made great conquests
in Georgia, the Greater Armenia, and Northern Syria.
Sultan Kameel had not scrupled to seek the aid of the
Christian against Moadhin; no doubt to Frederick the

---

* See the Arabian history of the Patriarchs of Alexandria.

lure was the peaceful establishment of the kingdom of
Jerusalem, in close alliance with the Egyptian Sultan.[f]
On the death of Moadhin the Damascene, Sultan
Kameel had marched at once into Syria, occupied Jerusalem, and the whole southern district: he threatened
to seize the whole dominions of Moadhin. But a third
brother, Malek Ashraf, Prince of Khelath, Edessa, and
Haran on the Euphrates, took up the cause of David,
the young son of Moadhin. The Christians, reinforced
by Frederick's first armament under Thomas of Acerra,
upon this had taken a more threatening attitude; had
begun to rebuild Sidon, to man other fortresses, and to
make hostile incursions. Sultan Kameel affected great
dread of their power: he addressed a letter to his
brother Ashraf, expressing his fears lest, to the disgrace
of the Mohammedan name, the Christians should wrest
Jerusalem, the great conquest of Saladin, from the
hands of the true believers. Ashraf was deceived, or
chose to be deceived; he abandoned the cause of the
young Sultan of Damascus; he agreed to share in his
spoils; Sultan Kameel was to remain in Palestine master
of Jerusalem, to oppose the Christians; while Ashraf
undertook the siege of Damascus. Such was the state
of affairs when Frederick suddenly landed at Ptolemais.
Sultan Kameel repented that he had invited him; he
had sought an ally, he feared a master. The name of
the Great Christian Emperor spread terror among the
whole Mohammedan population.[s] Had Frederick, even
though he had brought so inconsiderable a force, at
once been recognised as the head of the Crusade; had
he been joined cordially by the Knights of the Temple
and of the Hospital, his name had still been imposing,

[f] Abulfeda.   [s] Ibid.

he might have dictated his own terms. The dissensions of the Christians were fatal—dissensions which could not be disguised from the sagacious Mohammedans.

Almost the first act of King Frederick on his arrival in Palestine was an embassy, of Balian Prince of Tyre and Thomas of Acerra his Lieutenant, to the camp of his old ally Sultan Kameel; they were received with great pomp; the army drawn up in array. The embassy returned to Ptolemaïs with a huge elephant and other costly presents. The negotiations began at the camp of Recordana; they were continued at Joppa. The demands of Frederick were no less than the absolute surrender of Jerusalem and all the adjacent districts; the restoration of his kingdom to its full extent. The Sultan, as much in awe of the zealots of Mohammedanism as Frederick of the zealots of Christianity, alleged almost insuperable difficulties. The Emir Fakreddin, the old friend of Frederick, and another named Shems Eddin, were constantly in the Christian camp. They not merely treated with the accomplished Emperor, who spoke Arabic fluently, on the subjects of their mission, but discussed all the most profound questions of science and philosophy. Sultan Kameel affected the character of a patron of learning; Frederick addressed to him a number of those philosophic enigmas which exercise and delight the ingenious Oriental mind. Their intercourse was compared to that of the Queen of Sheba and Solomon. There were other Eastern amusements not so becoming the Christian Emperor. Christian ladies met the Mohammedan delegates at feasts, it was said with no advantage to their virtue. Among the Sultan's presents was a bevy of dancing girls, whose graceful feats the Emperor beheld with too great interest, and was not, it was said, insensible to their beauty.

The Emperor wore the Saracen dress; he became, in the estimation of the stern Churchmon, a Saracen.[a]

The treaty dragged slowly on. Sultan Kameel could not be ignorant of the hostility against Frederick in the Christian camp: if he had been ignorant, the knowledge would have been forced upon him. The Emperor, by no means superior even to the superstition of the land, had determined to undertake a pilgrimage almost alone, and in a woollen robe, to bathe in the Jordan. The Templars wrote a letter to betray his design to the Sultan, that he might avail himself of this opportunity of seizing and making Frederick prisoner, or even of putting him to death. The Sultan sent the letter to the Emperor.[b] From all these causes, the tone of the Sultan naturally rose, that of Frederick was lowered, by the treason of which he was obliged to dissemble his knowledge, as he could not revenge it. Eastern interpreters are wont to translate all demands made of their sovereigns into humble petitions. The Arabian historian has thus, perhaps, selecting a few sentences out of a long address, toned down the words of Frederick to Sultan Kameel to abject supplication. "I am thy friend. Thou art not ignorant that I am the greatest of the Kings of the West. It is thou that hast invited me to this land; the Kings and the Pope are well informed of my journey. If I return having obtained nothing, I shall forfeit all consideration with

Negotiations with Sultan Kameel

[a] "Quod cum maxima verecundia referimus et rubore, Imperatori Soldanus audirem quod secundum morem Saracenicum se haberet, misit cantatrices quae et saltatrices dicuntur, et joculatores, personas quidem non solum infames verum etiam de quibus inter Christianos haberi mentio non debet. Cum quibus idem princeps hujus mundi vigiliis, potationibus, et inde-mentis, et omni modo Saracenis se gerebat."—Epist. Gerold. apud Raynald. 1220, v.

[b] Matthew Paris, and the Arabian historians in Reinaud, p. 429. Addi tion to Michaud.

them. And after all, Jerusalem, is it not the birthplace
of the Christian religion? and have you not destroyed
it? It is in the lowest state of ruin; out of your good-
ness surrender it to me as it is, that I may be able to
lift up my head among the kings of Christendom. I renounce at once all advantages which I may obtain from
it." To Fakreddin, in more intimate converse, he
acknowledged, according to another Eastern account,
" My object in coming hither was not to deliver the
Holy City, but to maintain my estimation among the
Franks." He had before made large demands of commercial privileges, the exemption of tribute for his
merchants in the ports of Alexandria and Rosetta. The
terms actually obtained, at their lowest amount, belie
this humiliating petition. The whole negotiation was a
profound secret to all but Frederick and the immediate
adherents to whom he condescended to communicate it.

At length Frederick summoned four Syrian Barons;
he explained to them that the state of his
affairs, the utter exhaustion of his finances,
made it impossible for him to remain in the Holy Land.
There were still stronger secret reasons for hastening
the conclusion of the treaty. A fast-sailing vessel had
been despatched to Joppa, which announced that the
Papal army had broken into Apulia, and were laying
waste the whole land, and threatened to wrest from
Frederick his beloved kingdom of Sicily. The Sultan
of Babylon, he told the Barons, had offered to surrender
Jerusalem, and other advantageous conditions. He
demanded their advice. The Barons replied that under
such circumstances it might be well to accept
the terms; but they insisted on the right of
fortifying the walls of Jerusalem. The Emperor then

summoned the Grand Masters of the Temple and the
Hospital and the English Bishops of Winchester and
Exeter; he made the same statement to them. They
answered that no such treaty could be made without
the assent of the Patriarch of Jerusalem, in his double
capacity as head of the Syrian Church and Legate of
the Pope.   Frederick superciliously replied that he
could dispense with the assent of the Patriarch. Gerold,
before his adversary, became his most implacable foe.

One week after the first interview the treaty was
signed: there is much discrepancy in the articles between the Mohammedan and Christian   Feb. 18.
accounts; the Mohammedans restrict, the Christians
enlarge the concessions. The terms transmitted by the
Patriarch to the Pope, translated from the Arabic into
the French, were these:—I. The entire surrender of
Jerusalem to the Emperor and his Prefects. II. Except
the site of the Temple, occupied by the Mosque of Omar,
which remained absolutely in the power of the Saracens:
they held the keys of the gates. III. The Saracens were
to have free access as pilgrims to perform their devotions at Bethlehem. IV. Devout Christians were only
permitted to enter and pray within the precincts of the
Temple on certain conditions. V. All wrong committed
by one Saracen upon another in Jerusalem was to be
judged before a Mussulman tribunal. VI. The Emperor was to give no succour to any Frank or Saracen,
who should be engaged in war against the Saracens, or
suffer any violation of the truce.   VII. The Emperor
was to recall all who were engaged in any invasion of
the territory of the Sultan of Egypt, and prohibit to the
utmost of his power every violation of such territory.
VIII. In case of such violation of the treaty, the Emperor was to espouse and defend the cause of the Sultan

of Egypt.   IX. Tripoli, Antioch, Karak, and their
dependencies were not included in this treaty.[*]

The German pilgrims rejoiced without disguise at this
easy accomplishment of their vows; they were eager to
set out to offer their devotions in the Holy Sepulchre.
Frederick himself determined to accomplish his own

Frederick in Jerusalem. March 11. pilgrimage, and to assume in his capital the
crown of the kingdom of Jerusalem. Attended
by the faithful Master of the Teutonic Knights, Herman
of Salza, and accompanied by Shems Eddin, the Saracen
Kadi of Naplous, he arrived on the eve of Sunday, the
19th of March, in Jerusalem: he took up his lodging in
the neighbourhood of the Temple, now a Mohammedan
mosque, under the guardianship of the Kadi; there were
fears lest he should be attacked by some Mohammedan
fanatic. But the Emperor had not arrived in Jerusalem
before the Archbishop of Cæsarea appeared with instructions from the Patriarch of Jerusalem to declare him
under excommunication, and to place the city of Jerusalem under the ban. Even the Sepulchre of the Lord
was under interdict; the prayers of the pilgrims even in
that holiest place were forbidden, or declared unholy.
No Christian rite could be celebrated before the Christian Emperor, and that disgrace was inflicted in the
face of all the Mohammedans!

Immediately on his arrival the Emperor visited the
Church of the Holy Sepulchre. The church was silent:

---

[*] These articles are obviously incom-
plete; they do not describe the extent
of the concessions, which, according
to other statements, included, with
Jerusalem, Bethlehem, Nazareth, and
the whole district between Joppa and
Jerusalem. There is nothing said, if
anything was definitively agreed, as to
the right of the Emperor to rebuild
the walls of Jerusalem; nor of the
condition that the Saracens were only
to enter Jerusalem unarmed, and not to
pass the night within the walls. The
important stipulation of the surrender
of all Christian prisoners without
ransom is altogether omitted.

not a priest appeared: during his stay no mass was
celebrated within the city or in the suburbs.   An
English Dominican, named Walter, performed one solitary service on the morning of the Sunday.   Frederick
proceeded again in great pomp and in all his imperial
apparel to the Church of the Sepulchre.   No prelate,
no priest of the Church of Jerusalem was there who
ventured to utter a blessing.   The Archbishops of
Palermo and of Capua were present, but seem *Coronation of Frederick.*
to have taken no part in the ceremony.   The
imperial crown was placed on the high altar; Frederick
took it up and with his own hands placed it on his
head.   The Master of the Teutonic Order delivered an
address in the name of the Emperor, which was read in
German, in French, in Latin, and in Italian.   It ran in
this strain: "It is well known that at Aix-la-Chapelle
I took the Cross of my own free will.   Hitherto insuperable difficulties have impeded the fulfilment of my
vow.   I acquit the Pope for his hard judgement of me
and for my excommunication: in no other way could he
escape the blasphemy and evil report of men.   I exculpate him further for his writing against me to Palestine
in so hostile a spirit, for men had rumoured that I had
levied my army not against the Holy Land, but to
invade the Papal States.   Had the Pope known my real
design, he would have written not against me, but in my
favour: did he know how many are acting here to the
prejudice of Christianity, he would not pay so much
respect to their complaints and representations . . . . .
I would willingly do all which shall expose those real
enemies and false friends of Christ who delight in discord, and so put them to shame by the restoration
of peace and unity.   I will not now think of the high
estate which is my lot on earth, but humble myself

before God to whom I owe my elevation, and before
him who is his Vicar upon earth."[4] The Emperor
returned through the streets wearing the crown of
Jerusalem. The same day he visited the site of the
Temple, whereon stood the Mosque of Omar.

The zealous Mohammedans were in bitter displeasure
with Frederick, as having obtained from their easy
Sultan the possession of the Holy City; yet their religious pride watched all his actions, and construed every
word and act into a contempt of the Christian faith, and
his respect, if not more than respect, for Islam. The
Emir Shems Eddin, so writes the Arabic historian, had
issued rigid orders that nothing should be done which
could offend the Emperor. The house where the
Emperor slept was just below the minaret from which
the Muezzin was wont to proclaim the hour of prayer.
But in Jerusalem the Muezzin did more. He read
certain verses of the Korán; on that night the text,
" How is it possible that God had for his son Jesus the
son of Mary?" The Kadi took alarm; he silenced
altogether the officious Muezzin. The Emperor listened
in vain for that sound which in the silent night is so
solemn and impressive. He inquired the reason of this
silence, which had continued for two days. The Kadi
gave the real cause, the fear of offending the Christian
Emperor. " You are wrong," said Frederick, " to
neglect on my account your duty, your law, and your
religion. By God, if you should visit me in my realm,

[4] If this is the genuine speech, quoted by Von Raumer from the un-published Regesta in the Papal archives, it may show the malice of the Patriarch Gerold, who thus describes it :—" Ita coronatus reddit in cathedrâ Patriar-chatus excusando militiam suam et accusando ecclesiam Romanam, im-potens et quod iojustè processerat contra eum ; et notabilem eam secreta invectivâ et reprehensivâ de immutabili et simoniali avaritiâ."

you will find no such respectful deference." The Emperor had declared that one of the chief objects of his visit to the Holy Land was to behold the Mohammedans at prayer. He stood in wondering admiration before the Mosque of Omar; he surveyed the pulpit from which the Imaun delivered his sermons. A Christian priest had found his way into the precincts with the book of the Gospels in his hand; the Emperor resented this as an insult to the religious worship of the Mohammedans, and threatened to punish it as a signal breach of the treaty. The Arabic historian puts into his mouth these words: " Here we are all the servants of the Sultan; it is he that has restored to us our Churches." So writes the graver historian.[e] There is a description of Frederick's demeanour in the Temple by an eye-witness, one of the ministering attendants, in which the same ill-suppressed aversion to the uncircumcised is mingled with the desire to claim an imperial proselyte. " The Emperor was red-haired and bald, with weak sight; as a slave he would not have sold for more than 200 drachms."

Frederick's language showed (so averred some Mohammedans) that he did not believe the Christian religion; he did not scruple to jest upon it. He read without anger, and demanded the explanation of the inscription in letters of gold, " Saladin, in a certain year, purified the Holy City from the presence of those who worship many Gods."[f] The windows of the Holy Chapel were closely barred to keep out the defilements of the birds. " You may shut out the birds," said Frederick, " how will ye keep out the swine?" At noon, at the hour of prayer, when all the faithful fall on

---

[e] Makrizi, in Reinaud.
[f] The Mohammedans a define the worshippers of the Trinity.

their knees in adoration, the Mohammedans in attendance on Frederick did the same; among the rest the aged preceptor of Frederick, a Sicilian Mussulman who had instructed him in dialectics. Frederick, in this at least not going beyond the bounds of wise tolerance, betrayed neither surprise nor dissatisfaction.

After but two days the Emperor retired from the interdicted city; if he took no steps to restore the walls, some part of the blame must attach to his religious foes, who pursued him even into the Holy City with such inexorable hostility.

Both the Emperor and the Sultan had wounded the Unpopularity of the treaty. pride and offended the religious prejudices of the more zealous among their people. To some the peaceful settlement of the war between Christian and Mussulman was of itself an abomination, a degenerate infringement of the good old usage, which arrayed them against each other as irreclaimable enemies: the valiant Christians were deprived of the privilege of obtaining remission of their sins by the pillage and massacre of the Islamites: the Islamites of winning Paradise by the slaughter of Christians. The Sultan of Egypt, so rude was the shock throughout the world of Islam, was obliged to send ambassadors to the Caliph of Bagdad and to the Princes on the Euphrates to explain his conduct. The surrender of Jerusalem was the great cause of affliction and shame. The Sultan in vain alleged that it was but the unwalled and defenceless city that he yielded up; there were bitter lamentations among all the Moslems, who were forced to depart from their homes; sad verses were written and sung in the streets. The Imauns of the Mosque of Omar went in melancholy procession to the Sultan to remonstrate. They attempted to overawe him by proclaiming **an** unusual hour of prayer. Kameel treated them with great indignity, and sent them back stripped of their silver lamps and other ornaments of the Mosque. In Damascus was the most loud and bitter lamentation. The Sultan of Damascus was besieged in his capital by Malek el Ashraf. The territory, now basely yielded to the Christians, was part of his kingdom; he was the rightful Lord of Jerusalem. There an Imaun of great sanctity, the historian Ibn Dschusi himself, was summoned to preach to the people on this dire calamity. The honour of Islam was concerned; he mounted the pulpit: "So then the way to the Holy City is about to be closed to faithful pilgrims: you who love communion with God in that hallowed place can no longer prostrate yourself, or water the ground with your tears. Great God! if our eyes were fountains, could we shed tears enough? If our hearts were cloven, could we be afflicted enough?" The whole assembly burst into a wild wail of sorrow and indignation.*

Frederick announced this treaty in Western Christendom in the most magnificent terms. His letter to the King of England bears date on the day of his entrance into Jerusalem. He ascribes his triumph to a miracle wrought by the Lord of Hosts, who seemed no longer to delight in the multitude of armed men. In the face of two great armies, that of the Sultan of Egypt and of Sultan Ashraf encamped near Gaza, and that of the Sultan (David) of Damascus at Naplous, Jerusalem, Bethlehem, Nazareth, the district of Sharon, and Sidon, had been freely ceded to him: the Mohammedans were only by sufferance to enter the Holy City. The Sultan had bound himself to surrender all prisoners, whom he

---

* Reinaud. Extrait des Auteurs Arabes.—Wilken, vi. p. 493.

onght to have released by the treaty of Damietta, and
all who had been taken since.[b] The seal of this letter
bore a likeness of the Emperor, with a scroll: over his
head " the Emperor of the Romans," on the right
shoulder "the King of Jerusalem," on the left " the
King of Sicily."

Far different was the reception of the treaty by the
Pope, and by all who sided with, or might be expected
to side with, the Pope. It was but a new manifestation
of the perfidy, the contumacy, the ingratitude to the
Church, the indifference of the Emperor to religion, if
not of his apostasy. A letter arrived, and was actively
promulgated through Western Christendom, from
Gerold, Patriarch of Jerusalem, describing in the
blackest colours every act of the Emperor. In the
treaty the dignity, the interests of religion and of the
Church, the dignity and interests of the Patriarch, had
been, it might seem studiously neglected; even in the
territory conceded by the Sultan some of the lands
belonging to the Knights Templars were comprehended,
none of those claimed by the Patriarch. Gerold overlooked his own obstinate hostility to Frederick, while he
dwelt so bitterly on that of Frederick to himself. The
letter began with Frederick's occupation of
Joppa; his avowed partiality to the interests
of the Mohammedans, his neglect, or worse, of the
Christians. At least five hundred Christians had fallen
since his arrival, not ten Saracens. All excesses, all
breaches of the truce were visited severely on the
Christians, connived at or disregarded in the Mohammedans. A Saracen who had been plundered was sent
back in splendid apparel to the Sultan. All the

[b] The letter in Matthew Paris.

Emperor's suspicious intercourse with the Saracens, his Mohammedan luxuries, his presents of splendid arms to be used by Infidels against true Believers, were recounted; the secresy of the treaty and its acceptance, with the signature of the Sultan as its sole guarantee. The Master of the Teutonic Order had insidiously invited him (the Patriarch) to accompany the Emperor to Jerusalem. He had demanded first to see the treaty. There he found that the Sultan of Damascus, the true Lord of Jerusalem, was no party to the covenant; "there were no provisions in favour of himself or of the Church; how could he venture his holy person within the power of the treacherous Sultan and his unbelieving host?" The letter closed with a strong complaint that the Emperor had left the city without rebuilding the walls. But the Patriarch admitted that Frederick had consulted the Bishops of Winchester and Exeter, the Master of the Hospitallers, the Præceptor of the Temple, to advise and aid him in this work: their reply had been cold and dilatory; and Frederick departed from the city.[1]

Even before the arrival of Gerald's letters, the Pope, in a letter to the Archbishop of Milan and his suffragans, all liegemen of the Emperor, had denounced the treaty as a monstrous reconciliation of Christ and Belial; as the establishment of the worship of Mohammed in the Temple of God; and thus "the antagonist of the Cross, the enemy of the faith, the foe of all chastity, the condemned to hell, is lifted up for adoration, by a perverse judgement, to the intolerable contumely of the Saviour, the inexpiable disgrace of the Christian name, the contempt of all

Letter of Gregory to Archbishop of Milan.

---

[1] Epist. Gerold. Patriarchæ, apud Matth. Paris.

the martyrs who have laid down their lives to purify
the Holy Land from the worldly pollutions of the
Saracens."[k]

Albert of Austria was the most powerful enemy who
might be tempted to revolt against Frederick in his
German dominions, the greatest and most dangerous
vassal of the Empire. Him the Pope addressed at
greater length, and with a more distinct enu-

June 16. meration of four flagitious enormities with
which he especially charged the Emperor. First, he
had shamelessly presented the sword and other arms
which he had received from the altar of St. Peter,
blessed by the Pope himself, for the defence of the

Letter to Albert of Austria. faith, and the chastisement of the wicked, to
the Sultan of Babylon, the enemy of the faith,
the adversary of Christ Jesus, the worshipper of Mohammed the son of Perdition; he had promised not to
bear arms against the Sultan, against whom as Emperor
he was bound to wage implacable war. The second was
a more execrable and more stupendous offence. In the
Temple of God, where Christ made his offering, where
he had sat on his cathedral throne in the midst of the
doctors, the Emperor had cast Christ forth, and placed
Mohammed, that son of Perdition; he had commanded
the law of God to keep silence, and permitted the free
preaching of the Koran: to the Infidels he had left the
keys of the Sanctuary, so that no Christian might enter
without their sufferance. Thirdly, he had excluded the
Eastern Christians of Antioch, Tripoli, and other strong
places, from the benefit of the treaty, and so betrayed
the Christian cause in the East to the enemy. Lastly,
he had so bound himself by this wicked league, that if

---

[k] Ad Epist. Mediol. June 13, 1229.

the Christian army should attempt to revenge the
insult done to the Redeemer, to cleanse the Temple
and the City of God from the defilements of the Pagans,
the Emperor had pledged himself to take part with the
foe. Albert of Austria was exhorted to disclaim all
allegiance to one guilty of such capital treason against
the majesty of God, to hold himself ready at the
summons of the Church to take up arms against the
Emperor.

The last acts of Frederick in Palestine are dwelt
upon both by the Patriarch and the Pope; they are
known almost entirely by these unfriendly representations. Frederick returned from Joppa to Ptolemais in
no placable mood with his implacable enemies leagued
against him in civil war.* The Patriarch had attempted
to raise an independent force at his own command: if
the pilgrims should retire from the Holy Land he would
need a body-guard for his holy person. He proposed,
out of some large sums of money left for the benefit of
the sacred cause by Philip-Augustus of France, to enrol
a band of knights, a new Order, for this end. Frederick
declared that no one should levy or command soldiers
within his realm without his will and consent. With
the inhabitants of Ptolemais Frederick had obtained,
either by his affable demeanour or by his treaty, great
popularity. He summoned a full assembly of all
Christian people on the broad sands without the city.
There he arose and arraigned the Patriarch and the

---

* "Præterea qualiter contra ipsum
Imperatorem, apud Acon, postmodum
redeuntem, prædicti Patriarchæ, Magi-
tri domuum hospitalis et templi se
gesserint, utpote qui contra ipsum,
intentius bella moverint in civitate
prædicta, his qui interfuerunt hæc
chrius extitit manifestum." —Rich.
San Germ. It is remarkable how many
privileges and grants be made to the
Teutonic Order: it is manifest that his
object was to raise up a loyal counter-
poise to the Templars and Hospitallers.
—Bœhmer, Regesta, sub ann.

Master of the Templars as having obstinately thwarted all his designs for the advancement of the Christian Cause, and having pursued him with their blind and obstinate hostility. He summoned all the pilgrims, having now fulfilled their vows, to depart from the Holy Land, and commanded his Lieutenant, Thomas de Acerra, to compel obedience to these orders. He was deaf to all remonstrance; on his return to the city he seized all the gates, manned them with his crossbowmen, and while he permitted all the Knights Templars to leave the city, he would admit none. He took possession of the churches, and occupied them with his archers. The Patriarch assembled all his adherents and all the Templars still within the city, and again thundered out his excommunication. Frederick kept him almost as a prisoner in his palace; his partisans were exposed to every insult and attack, even those who were carrying provisions to the palace. Two bold Franciscans, who on Palm Sunday denounced Frederick in the Church, were dragged from the pulpit, and scourged through the streets. But these violences availed not against the obstinate endurance of the Churchmen. After some vain attempts at reconciliation, the Patriarch placed the city of Ptolemais under interdict. These are not all the charges against Frederick; it was made a crime that he destroyed some of his ships, probably unserviceable: his arms and engines of war he is said to have sent to the Sultan of Egypt.

On the day of St. Peter and St. Paul the Emperor set sail for Europe; his presence was imperiously required. In every part of his dominions the Pope, with the ambitious activity of a temporal sovereign, and with all the tremendous arms wielded by

the spiritual power, was waging a war either in open
day, or in secret intrigues with his unruly and disaffected
vassals. The ostensible cause of the war was the aggression of Frederick's vicegerent in Apulia,   War in
Reginald Duke of Spoleto. Frederick had   Apulia.
left Reginald to subdue the revolt of the powerful family
of Polito. These rebels had taken refuge in the Papal
territory : they were pursued by Reginald. But once
beyond the Papal frontier the Duke of Spoleto extended
his ravages, it might seem reviving certain claims of his
own on the Dukedom of Spoleto. Frederick afterwards
disclaimed these acts of his lieutenant, and declared that
he had punished him for the infringement of his orders.[a]
But the occasion was too welcome not to be seized by
the Pope. He levied at once large forces, placed them
under the command of Frederick's most deadly enemies,
his father-in-law, John de Brienne, the ejected King of
Jerusalem, and the Cardinal John Colonna, with the
King's revolted subjects, the Counts of Celano and of
Aquila; the martial Legate Pelagius, who had commanded the army of Damietta, directed the whole force.
A report of Frederick's death in Palestine (a fraud of
which he complains with the bitterest indignation) was
industriously disseminated. John de Brienne even ventured to assert that there was no Emperor but himself.
The Papal armies at first met with great success; many
cities from fear, from disaffection to Frederick, from
despair of relief, opened their gates. The soldiers of
the Church committed devastations almost unprecedented even in these rude wars. But Gregory was not
content with this limited war; he strove to arm all

---

[a] The most particular account of these wars is in Rich. de San Germano,
apud Muratori, t. vii.

Christendom against the contumacious Emperor who defied the Church. From the remotest parts, from Wales, Ireland, England, large contributions were demanded, and in many cases extorted, for this holy war. Just at this juncture England contributed in a peculiar manner, even beyond her customary tribute, to the Papal treasury : the whole of such revenue was devoted to this end.

A dispute was pending in the Court of Rome concerning the See of Canterbury. On the death of Archbishop Stephen, the monks of Canterbury elected Walter of Hevesham to the primacy. The King refused his assent, and the objections urged were sufficiently strange, whether well-founded or but fictitious, against a man chosen as the successor of Becket. The father of Walter, it was said, had been hanged for robbery, and Walter himself, during the interdict, had embraced the party opposed to King John. The suffragan bishops (they always resented their exclusion from the election) accused Walter of having debauched a nun, by whom he had several children. Appeal was made to Rome ; the Pope delayed his sentence for further inquiry. The ambassadors of the King, the Bishops of Chester and Rochester, and John of Newton in vain laboured to obtain the Papal decision. One only argument would weigh with the Pope and the Cardinals. At length they engaged to pay for this tardy justice the tenth of all moveable property in the realm of England and Ireland in order to aid the Pope in his war against the Emperor. Even then the alleged immoralities were put out of sight ; the elected Primate of England was examined by three Cardinals on certain minute points of theology, and condemned as unworthy of so august a see, " which

Election to
Arch-
bishopric of
Canterbury.
July 1228.

ought to be filled by a man noble, wise, and modest."[a]
Richard, Bishop of Lincoln, was proposed in the name
of the King and the suffragan bishops, and received his
appointment by a Papal Bull. In France, besides the
exertions of the Legate, the Archbishops of Sens and of
Lyons were commanded by the Pope himself to publish
the grave offences of Frederick against the Holy See,
and to preach the Crusade against him. In Germany,
Albert of Austria had been urged to revolt; in the
North and in Denmark the Legate, the Cardinal Otho,
preached and promulgated the same Crusade.[b] He laid
Liège under an interdict, and King Henry raised an
army to besiege the Cardinal in Strasburg. The Pope
praised, as inspired by the Holy Ghost, the chivalrous
determination of the Prince of Portugal, to take up arms
in defence of the Church of Christ. The Lombards, on
the other hand, were sternly rebuked for their tardiness
in sending aid against the common enemy, the Pope
gave them a significant hint that the deserters of the
cause of the Church might be deserted in their turn in
their hour of need.

The rapid return of the Emperor disconcerted all
these hostile measures. With two well-armed barks he
landed at Astore, near Brundusium; many of the brave
German pilgrims followed after and rapidly May 10 and
July 13, 1220.
Return of .
Frederick.
grew to a formidable force. His first act was
to send ambassadors to the Pope, the Archbishop of Bari, the Bishop of Reggio and Herman de

---

[a] He was asked whether our Lord
descended into hell, in the flesh or not
in the flesh; on the presence of Christ
in the sacrament; how Rachel, being
already dead, could weep for her
children; on the power of an excommunication, unrightly pronounced; on
a case of marriage, where one of the
parties had died in infidelity. To
all these questions his answers were
wrong.

[b] Raynald. in notâ.

Salza, the master of the Teutonic order. The overtures were rejected with scorn. An excommunication even more strong and offensive had been issued by the Pope at Perugia.[t] The first clause denounced all the heretics with names odious to all zealous believers. After the Cathari, the Publicans, the Poor Men of Lyons, the Arnoldists, and under the same terrific anathema as no less an enemy of the Church, followed the Emperor Frederick; his contumacious disregard of the excommunication pronounced by the Cardinal of Albano was thus placed on the same footing with the wildest opinions and those most hostile to the Church. After the recital of his offences, the release of all his subjects from their allegiance, came the condemnation of his adherents, Reginald of Spoleto and his brother Bertoldo. With the other enemies of the Church were mingled up the Count de Foix, and the Viscount of Beziers; the only important names which now represented the odious heresy of Southern France. Some lesser offenders were included under the comprehensive ban. These were all, if not leagued together under the same proscription, alike denounced as enemies of God and of the Church. The conquering army of the Pope was on all sides arrested, repelled, defeated; the rebellious barons and cities returned to their allegiance; Frederick marched to the relief of Capua; the strength of the Papal force broke up in confusion. Frederick moved to Naples where he was received in triumph. In Capua he had organised the Saracens whom he had removed from Sicily, where they had been a wild mountain people, untameably and utterly lawless, to Nocera: there he

---

[t] This bull must have been issued in June, not in August. See Barthour, p. 335. Raynaldus, sub ann.

had settled them, foreseeing probably their future use
as inhabitants of walled cities and cultivators of the
soil. This was a force terrible to the rebellious churchmen who had espoused the Papal cause. From San
Germano Frederick sent forth his counter appeal to the
Sovereigns of Europe, representing the violence, the
injustice, the implacable resentment of the Pope. The
appeal could not but have some effect.

Christendom, even among the most devout adherents
of the Papal supremacy, refused to lend itself Christendom
to the fiery passions of the aged Pontiff. The Pope.
Pope was yet too awful to be openly condemned, but
the general reluctance to embrace his cause was the
strongest condemnation. Men throughout the Christian
world could not but doubt by which party the real
interests of the Eastern Christians had been most betrayed and injured. The fierce enthusiasm which would
not receive advantages unless won from the unbeliever
at the point of the sword had died away: men looked
to the effect of the treaty, they compared it with the
results of all the Crusades since that of Godfrey of
Bouillon. Jerusalem, the Holy Sepulchre, were in
the power of the Christians: devout pilgrims might
perform unmolested their pious vows; multitudes
of Christians had taken up their abode in seeming
security in the city of Sion. But if, thus trammelled,
opposed, pursued by the remorseless excommunication
into the Holy Sepulchre itself, Frederick by the awe
of his imperial name, by his personal greatness, had
obtained such a treaty; what terms might he not have
dictated, if supported by the Pope, the Patriarch, and
Knights Templars.* Treaties with the Mohammedan

* It has been observed that the three | Paris, the Abbot Ursperensis, and
contemporary historians, Matthew | Richard of San Germano, are all

powers were nothing new; they had been lately made
by Philip Augustus, and by the fierce Richard Cœur de
Lion.   The Christians had never disdained the policy of
taking advantage of the feuds among the Mohammedan
sovereigns and allying themselves with the Sultan of
Egypt or the Sultan of Damascus.   Even the Pope
himself had not disdained all peaceful intercourse with
the Unbelievers.   Frederick positively asserted that he
had surprised and had in his possession letters addressed
by the Pope to Sultan Kameel, urging him to break off
his negotiations with the Emperor.   Gregory afterwards
denied the truth of this charge; but it was publicly
averred, and proof offered, in the face of Christendom.[a]
Frederick had appealed to witnesses of all his acts, and
they, at all events the English Bishops of Winchester
and Exeter, the Master of the Hospitallers, the Master
of the Teutonic Order, had given no countenance to the
envious and rancorous charges of the Patriarch.

There was a deeper cause of dissatisfaction throughout that Hierarchy, to which the Pope had always
looked for the most zealous and self-sacrificing aid.
The clergy felt the strongest repugnance to the levy of
a tenth demanded by the Pope throughout Christendom,
to maintain wars, if not unjust, unnecessary, against the
Emperor.   No doubt the lavish and partial favour with

against the Pope.   "Verisimile enim
videtur, quod si tunc Imperator ejus
gratiâ se pace Romanæ Ecclesiæ tran-
misisset, longa multûm et affluentia pros-
peralium fuisset negotiûm Terræ
Sanctæ,"—Richard de San Germano
adds, that if the Sultan had not known
that Frederick was excommunicated by
the Pope, and hated by the Patriarch,
he would have granted much better
terms.   Compare Muratori, Annal.

d'Italia, sub ann.; and in Wilken the
extract from Themsehunk [a]—

[a] Waren dein Kaiser die gesandten,
Die sind die Ehre wanken (?) (?)
Das Grab und die Heer Land;
Die stunden gar in seiner Hand;
Nazareth und Bethlem,
Die Jordan und Jerusalem,
Dazu manig heilig Star,
Da Gott weit seinem Namen trat,
Syria und Juda," &c.
—Wilken, vi. p. 509.
[b] Epist. Petr. de Vineâ.

which he treated the Preaching and Begging Friars had
already awakened jealousy. Gregory had sagaciously
discerned the strength which their influence in the
lowest depths of society would gain for the Papal cause.
He had solemnly canonised Francis of Assisi   Oct. 4, 1722.
—one of his most confidential counsellors was
the Dominican Gualo.[1]   So active had the Friars been
in stirring up revolt in the kingdom of Naples, that the
first act of Reginald of Spoleto had been their expulsion
from the realm.

Christendom had eagerly rushed into a Crusade
against the unbelievers; it had not ventured to disap-
prove a Crusade against the heretics of Languedoc; but
a Crusade (for under that name Gregory IX. levied this
war) against the Emperor, and that Emperor the re-
storer of the Kingdom of Jerusalem, was encountered
with sullen repugnance or frank opposition. It was
observed as a strange sight that when Frederick's troops
advanced against those of the Pope, they still wore the
red crosses which they had worn in Palestine. The
banner of the Cross, under which Mohammedans fought
for Frederick, met the banner with the keys of St.
Peter.[2]

The disapprobation of silent disobedience, at best of
sluggish and tardy sympathy if not of rude disavowal
and condemnation, could not escape the all-watchful
ear of Rome. Gregory had no resource but in his own
dauntless and unbroken mind, and in the conviction of
his power. The German Princes had refused to dethrone King Henry: some of the greatest influence,

---

[1] Gualo was his emissary, if not his
Legate, in Lombardy. He was active
in framing the peace of San Germano.
—Epist. Gregor., Oct. 9, 1226.

[2] " Imperator cum crucesignatis
contra clarigeros hostes properat."—
Rich. de San Germano, p. 1013.

Leopold Duke of Austria, the Duke of Moravia, the
Archbishops of Saltzburg and of Aquileia, the Bishop of
Ratisbon, were in Italy endeavouring to mediate a
peace. The Lombards did not move; even if the
Guelfs had been so disposed, they were everywhere controlled by a Ghibelline opposition. One incident alone
was of a more encouraging character. Gregory was
still at Perugia an exile from rebellious Rome. But a
terrific flood had desolated the city. The religious
fears of the populace beheld the avenging hand of God
for their disobedience to their spiritual father; the
Pope returned to Rome in triumph.[1]

Peace was necessary to both parties, negotiations
Nov. 1228. were speedily begun. The Pope was suddenly
May. 1229. seized with a sacred horror of the shedding
human blood. A treaty was framed at San Germano
which maintained unabased the majesty of the Pope.[2]
In truth, by the absolution of the Emperor with but a
general declaration of submission to the Church, without satisfaction for the special crime for which he had
undergone excommunication, the Pope, virtually at
least, recognised the injustice of his own censures. Of
Treaty of San the affairs of the Holy Land, of the conduct
Germano.
June 14, 1229. of the Emperor, of the treaty with the Sultan,
denounced as impious, there was a profound and cautious silence. In other respects the terms might seem
humiliating to the Emperor; he granted a complete
amnesty to all his rebellious subjects, the Archbishop of
Tarentum and all the bishops and churchmen who had

---

[1] Not only was there a great destruction of property, of corn, wine,
cattle, and of human life, but a great
quantity of enormous serpents were cast
on shore, which rotted and bred a pesti-
lency. This is a story more than once
repeated in the later annals of Rome
—on what founded?—Gregor. VII.

[2] Albumari Episcopo, apud Raynald,
1229.

fled the realm; even the reinstatement of the insurgent
Counts of Celano and Aversa in their lands and domains in Germany, in Italy, in Sicily; he consented to
restore all the places he occupied in the Papal dominions, and all the estates which he had seized belonging
to churches, monasteries, the Templars, the Knights of
the Hospital, and generally of all who had adhered to
the Church. He renounced the right of judging the
ecclesiastics of his realm by the civil tribunals, excepting
in matters concerning royal fiefs; he gave up the right
of levying taxes on ecclesiastical property, as well that
of the clergy as of monasteries. It is said, but it appears
not in the treaty, that he promised to defray the enormous charges of the war, variously stated at 120,000
crowns and 120,000 ounces of gold; but in those times
promises to pay such debts by no means ensured their
payment. Frederick never fulfilled this covenant. If
to obtain absolution from the Papal censures Frederick
willingly yielded to these terms, it shows either that his
firm mind was not proof against the awe of the spiritual
power which enthralled the rest of Europe, or that he
had the wisdom to see that the time was not come to
struggle with success against such tyranny. He might
indeed hope that, ere long, to the stern old man who
now wielded the keys of St. Peter with the vigour of
Hildebrand or Innocent III., might succeed some feebler
or milder Pontiff. Already was Gregory approaching
to or more than ninety years old.[1] He was himself in
the strength and prime of manhood, nor could he expect
that this same aged Pontiff would rally again for a
contest, more long, more obstinate, and though not

[1] I confess that this extreme old age of Gregory IX. does not seem to me quite clearly made out. At all events, after every deduction, he was of an extraordinary age to display such activity and firmness.

terminated in his lifetime, more fatal to the Emperor
and to the House of Hohenstaufen. Frederick had been
released from the ban of excommunication at Ceperano

Aug. 28.
Sept. 1, 1230. by the Cardinal John of St. Sabina; he visited
the Pope at Anagni. They met, Frederick
with dignified submission, the Pope with the calm majesty of age and position, held a conference of many
hours, appeared together at a splendid banquet, and
interchanged the kiss of peace; the antagonists whose
mortal quarrel threatened a long convulsion throughout Christendom proclaimed to the world their mutual
amity.[a]

Nearly nine years elapsed before those two anta-

Sept. 1, 1239.
to 1239. Palm
Sunday. gonists, the Pope Gregory IX. and the Emperor Frederick II. resumed their immitigable
warfare,—years of but dubious peace, of open amity yet
secret mistrust, in which each called upon the other for
aid against his enemies; the Pope on Frederick against
the unruly Romans, Frederick on the Pope against
the rebellious Lombards and his rebellious son; but

[a] Frederick describes the interview —
"I cinde ut post absolutionem ex præ-
sentia corporum mediante serenitas
sequeretur, primo Septembris apostolicam sedem adivimus, et sanctissimum
patrem dominum Gregorium, Dei
gratiâ summum Pontificem, vidimus
reverenter. Qui affectione paternâ nos
recipiens, et pace cordium mente occulta
federatâ, tam benevola, tam benigne
propositum nobis suæ intentionis aperuit
ib ipsis quæ procurerant nil omittens,
et singula prosequens evidentis judicio
rationis, quod etsi nos procelens causm
commoverit, vel maturem potuerit
aliquem attulisse, sic benevolentis,
quam promovimus in eodem, contram
motum lenivit animi, et nostram asseilo
rancore serenavit adeo voluntatem, ut
non relictum ulterius præterita com-
morari quæ severitas intulit, ut virtus
es benmedtate prudens operaretur gratiam ampliorem."—Monument. Germ.
iv. 275. There is something very
striking in this. The generous awe
and reverence of Frederick for the holy
old man, considering his deep injuries
(I envy not those who can see nothing
but specious hypocrisy in Frederick),
and the Christian amenity of the Pope,
considering that Frederick, a short
time before, had been called a godless
heretic, almost a Mohammedan. Their
mutual amity is lost in mutual respect.

where each suspected a secret understanding with those
enemies. It is remarkable that both Frederick
and the Pope betook themselves in this interval of suspended war to legislation. Frederick to
the promulgation of a new jurisprudence for his kingdom
of Naples and Sicily; Gregory of a complete and authoritative code of the Decretals which formed the statute
law by which the Papacy and the sacerdotal order ruled
the world, and administered the internal government
of the Church. During the commencement of this
period Frederick left the administration of affairs in
Germany, though he still exercised an imperial control,
to his son Henry. The rebellion of Henry alone seemed
to compel him to cross the Alps and resume the
sway. His legislation aspired to regulate the
Empire; but in Germany from the limits imposed on
his power, it was not a complete and perfect code, it
was a succession of remedial laws. His earliest and
most characteristic work of legislation was content to
advance the peace, prosperity, and happiness of his own
Southern realm.

The constitution of his beloved kingdom was thus the
first care of Frederick. As a legislator he commands
almost unmingled admiration; and the aim and temper
of his legislation whether emanating from himself, or
adopted from the counsel of others, may justly influence
the general estimate of a character so variously represented by the passions of his own age, passions which
have continued to inflame, and even yet have not died
away from the heart of man.[b] The object of Frederick's

---

[b] Even in our own day M. Höfler, for instance, seems to revive all the rancour of the days of Innocent IV. Even Boehmer is not above this fatal influence. This part of my work was finished before the publication of the "Regesta Imperii," to which, nevertheless, I am bound to acknowledge much obligation.

jurisprudence was the mitigation, as far as possible the suppression, of feudal violence and oppression; the assertion of equal rights, equal justice, equal burthens; the toleration of different religions; the promotion of commerce by wise, almost premature regulations; the advancement of intellectual culture among his subjects by the establishment of universities liberally endowed, and by the encouragement of all the useful and refined arts. It is difficult to suppose a wise, equitable and humane legislator, a blind, a ruthless tyrant; or to reconcile the careful and sagacious provision for the rights and well-being of all ranks of his subjects with the reckless violation of those rights, and with heavy and systematic oppression; more especially if that jurisprudence is original and beyond his age. The legislator may himself be in some respects below the lofty aim of his laws; Frederick may have been driven to harsh measures to bring into order the rebellious magnates of the realm, whom his absence in Asia, the invasion and the intrigues of the Papal party, cast loose from their allegiance; the abrogation of their tyrannical privileges may have left a deep and brooding discontent, ready to break out into revolt and constantly enforcing still more rigorous enactments. The severe guardian of the morals of his subjects may have claimed to himself in some respects a royal, an Asiatic indulgence; he may have been compelled by inevitable wars to lay onerous burthens on the people, he may have been compelled to restrict or suspend the rights of particular subjects, or classes of subjects, by such determined hostility as that of the clergy to himself and to all his house; but on the whole the laws and institutions of the kingdom of Naples are an unexceptionable and imperishable testimony at least to his lofty designs for the good of man-

kind; which history cannot decline, or rather receives
with greater respect and trust than can be claimed by
any contemporary view of the acts or of the character
of Frederick II.   It is in this light only as illustrating the
life of the great antagonist of the Church that they belong
to Christian history, beyond their special bearing on religious questions, and the rights and condition of the clergy.[c]

The groundwork of Frederick's legislation was the
stern supremacy of the law; the submission of all, even
the nobles, who exercised the feudal privilege of separate jurisdictions, to a certain extent of the clergy, to
the king's sole and exclusive justice.   This was the great
revolution through which every feudal kingdom must
inevitably pass sooner or later.[d]   The crown must become the supreme fountain of justice and law.   The
first, and most difficult, but necessary step was the uni-
formity of that law.   There was the most extraordinary
variety of laws and usages throughout the realm, Roman,
Greek, Gothic, Lombard, Norman, Imperial-German
institutes; old municipal and recent seignorial rights.[e]
The Jews had their special privileges, the Saracens their
own customs and forms of procedure.   The majestic
law had to overawe to one system of obedience, with
due maintenance of their proper rights, the nobles, the
clergy, the burghers, and the peasants, even the Jews

---

[c] The constitutions of the Emperor
Frederick may be read in Cianciani,
vol. i. sub fine.   I am much indebted
for a brief, it appears to me very
sensible and accurate comment in the
Considerazioni sopra la Storia di Sicilia,
by the Canonico Gregorio (Palermo,
1805), and to my friend M. von Raul-
mer's earliest and best work, Geschichte
der Hohenstaufen.

[d] King Roger (see the Canonico Gregorio, t. iii.) had already vindicated a
certain supremacy for the King's Judi-
ciary.   King Roger's legislation is
strikingly analogous to, Gregorio thinks
borrowed from, that of his remote kinsman William, our Norman Conqueror.
In France this was among the great
steps first decisively taken by St. Louis.
[e] Cianciani, Preface.

and the Mohammedans. Frederick wisely determined
not to aspire so much to be the founder of an absolutely
new jurisprudence, as to select, confirm, and harmonise
the old institutions.[f]

The religious ordinances of the Sicilian constitution
demand our first examination. Frederick maintained the immunities of the worshippers of
other religions, of the Jews and the Arabians, with such
impartial equity, as to incur for this and other causes
the name of Jew and Saracen. But the most faithful
son of the Church could not condemn the heretic with
more authoritative severity, or visit his offence with
more remorseless punishment.[g] Heresy was described
as a crime against the offender himself, against his
neighbour, and against God, a more heinous crime even
than high treason. The obstinate heretic was condemned
to be burned, his whole property confiscated, his children
were incapable of holding office or of bearing testimony.
If such child should merit mercy by the denunciation
of another heretic, or of a concealer of heretics, the
Emperor might restore him to his rank. Schismatics
were declared outlaws, incapable of inheriting, liable to
forfeiture of their goods. No one might petition in
favour of a heretic: yet the repentant heretic might
receive pardon; his punishment, after due investigation
of the case by the ecclesiastical power, was to be adjudged by the secular authority. But these laws were

Laws relating to religion.

[f] The code was published at Amalfi, Sept. 1231: Rich. San Germ. sub ann. 1231; in Sicily by Richard de Monte-negro, High Justiciary, during the same year. Append. ad Malter. p. 231. Gregorio, iii. 14.

[g] Compare the edicts issued at Ravenna, Feb. 22, 1232, and March, against the Lombard heretics. They might have satisfied S. Dominic or Simon de Montfort. Re-enacted at Cremona, 1238; at Padua, 1239.—Monument. Germ. iv. 287, 288. Also letter of June 15, ex Regest. Greg. IX. in Höfler, p. 344.

directed against a particular class of men, dangerous it
was thought no less to the civil than to the religious
power; actual rebels against the Church, rebels likewise
against the Emperor, who was still the conservator of
pure orthodoxy, and betraying at least rebellious inclinations, if not designs hostile towards all power. They
were neither enacted nor put in force against the Greek
Christians who were still in considerable numbers in the
kingdom of Sicily, had their own priests, and celebrated
undisturbed their own rites. They were those heretics
which swarmed under various denominations, Cathari
or Paterins, from rebellious and republican Lombardy,
the hated and suspected source of all these opinions.
In all the states of the Pope, in Rome itself, not merely
were there hidden descendants of the Arnoldists, but
all the wild sects which defied the most cruel persecutions in the North of Italy, spread their doctrines even
within the shadow of the towers of St. Peter. Naples
and Averm were full of them,[b] and derived them from
rebellious Lombardy; and Frederick, whose notions of
the imperial power were as absolute as Gregory's of the
Papal, not only would not incur by their protection such
suspicions, as would have inevitably risen, of harbouring
or favouring heretics, he scrupled not to assist in the
extermination of these insolent insurrectionists against
lawful authority.[l]

---

[b] "Adeo quod ab Italiæ finibus,
præsertim a partibus Longobardiæ in
quibus pro certo præpradiemus ipsorum
nequitiam amplius abundare, jam usque
ad regnum nostrum suæ perfidiæ
rivulos derivarunt." — I. i. tit. i.
"Quod dolentes referimus, in regno
nostro Siciliæ Neapolis, et Avernam,
parteque vicinas dicitur infectam." —

Frederic. Epist. apud Epist. Gregor. iv.
131.

[l] Gregor. Vit. Richard de San Germ.
See also the Edict of the Senator and
people of Rome. —Apud Raynald. 1231.
Compare (afterwards) Frederick's letter
commanding the heretics throughout
Lombardy to be committed to the
flames.

The Constitution of Frederick endeavoured to reduce
the clergy into obedient and loyal subjects at once by
the vigorous assertion of the supreme and impartial law,
and by securing and extending their acknowledged immunities. The clergy were amenable to the general
law of the realm as concerned fiefs, could be impleaded
in the ordinary courts concerning occupancy of land,
inheritances, and debts: they had jurisdiction over their
own body, with the right of inflicting canonical punish-
ments: but besides this they were amenable to the
secular laws, especially for treason, or all crimes relating
to the person of the King.[a] They were not exempt
from general taxation; they were bound to discharge
all feudal obligations for their fiefs. On the other
hand, the crown abandoned its claim to the revenues
of vacant bishoprics and benefices:[a] three unexceptionable persons belonging to the Church were appointed
receivers on behalf of the successor. On the election
of bishops the law of Innocent III. was recognised; the
chapter communicated the vacancy to the Crown, and
proceeded to elect a fit successor; that successor could
not be inaugurated without the consent of the King, nor
consecrated without that of the Pope. Tithes were
secured to the Church from all lands, even from the
royal domains:[a] the Crown only enforced the expenditure of the appointed third on the sacred edifices, the
churches and chapels. All special courts of the higher
ecclesiastics as of the barons were abrogated; the crown
would be the sole fountain of justice: but the holders
of the great spiritual fiefs sat with the great Barons
under the presidency of the high Chancellor. Except-

* i. 42. A law of King William.
* iii. 28. Serfs and villains were not to be ordained, iii. 1, 8.   * i. 7.

ing in cases of marriage, no separate jurisdiction of the
clergy was recognised over the laity.[a] Appeals to Rome
were allowed, but only on matters purely ecclesiastical;
and these during wars with the Pope were absolutely
forbidden. The great magnates of the realm received
likewise substantial benefits in lieu of the privileges
wrested from them, which were perilous to the public
peace.[b] All their separate jurisdictions of noble or
prelate were abolished; the King's justiciary was alone
and supreme. But their fiefs were made hereditary,
and in the female line and to collaterals in the third
degree.[c]

The cities were emancipated from all the jurisdictions
of nobles or of ecclesiastics; but the municipal authorities were not absolutely left to   Cities.
their free election. The Sicilian King dreaded the fatal
example of the Lombard Republics: all the superior
governors were nominated by the Crown; the cities
only retained in their own hands the inferior appointments, for the regulation of their markets and havens.[f]
The law overlooked not the interest of the free peasants,
who constituted the chief cultivators of the
soil; or that of the serfs attached to the soil.   Peasants.
Absolute slavery was by no means common in Sicily;
the serfs could acquire and hold property. The free
peasants were numerous; the measures of Frederick
tended to raise the serfs to the same condition. He absolutely emancipated all those on the royal domain.

---

* Frederick asserted and exercised
the right of declaring the children of
the clergy, who by the canon law were
spurious, legitimate, with full title to
a share in all the inheritances of all the
goods of their parents, unless they were
fiefs; and capability of attaining to all

civil offices and honours. For this
privilege they paid an annual tax of
five per cent. to the royal exchequer.
This implied the marriage of the clergy
to a great extent.—Pet. de Vin. vi. 18.
Constitut. iii. 25.

[b] i. 46.   [c] iii. 23, 24.   [f] i. 47.

The establishment of his courts enabled all classes to
obtain justice at an easy and cheap rate against their
lords; the extraordinary aids to be demanded by the
lord were limited by law, that of the lay feudal superior,
to aids on the marriage of a daughter or sister, the arm-
ing the son when summoned to the service of the King,
and his ransom in captivity; that of the higher ecclesiastics and monasteries, to the summons to the King's
service, and receiving the King at free quarters;
journeys to Church Councils summoned by the Pope,
and Consecrations. Frederick was so desirous to promote the cultivation of the soil, that he exempted new
settlers in Sicily from taxes for ten years; only the
Jews, who took refuge from Africa, were obliged to pay
such taxes, and compelled to become cultivators of the
land.

But of all institutions, the most advanced was the
system of representative government, for the
first time regularly framed by the laws of
the realm. Besides the ancient Parliaments, at which
the magnates of the realm, the great ecclesiastical and
secular vassals of the Crown assembled when summoned
by the King's writ, two annual sessions took place, on
the 1st of March and the 1st of August, of a Parliament
constituted from the different orders of the realm.* All
the Barons and Prelates appeared in person; each of
the larger cities sent four representatives, each smaller
city two, each town or other place one; to these were
joined all the great and lesser Bailiffs of the Crown.
The summons to the Barons and Prelates was directly
from the King, that of the cities and towns from the

marginal note: Parliaments

---

* One of the cities appointed for the meeting of Parliament in Apulia was
Lentini; in Sicily, Piazza. Compare Gregorio, iii. p. 82.

judge of the province. They were to choose men of
probity, good repute, and impartiality. A Commissioner
from the Crown opened the Parliament, and conducted
its proceedings, which lasted from eight to ten days.
Every clerk or layman might arraign the conduct of
any public officer, or offer his advice for the good of his
town or district. The determinations which the royal
Commissioner, with the advice of the most distinguished
spiritual and temporal persons, approved, were delivered
signed and sealed by him directly to the King, excepting in unimportant matters, which might be regulated
by an order from the Justiciary of the Province.

The criminal law of Frederick's constitution was,
with some remarkable exceptions, mild beyond pre-
cedent; and also administered with a solemnity, impartiality, and regularity, elsewhere unknown. The Chief
Justiciary of the realm, with four other judges, formed
the great Court of Criminal Law; and the Crown
asserted itself to be the exclusive administrator of criminal justice.[1] Besides its implacable abhorrence of
heresy, it was severe and inexorable against all disturbers of the peace of the realm, and those who endangered the public security. Private war,[2] and the execution of the law by private hands, was rigidly forbidden. Justice must be sought only in the King's
courts. The punishment for every infringement of this
statute was decapitation and forfeiture of goods. Arms
were not to be borne except by the King's officers,
employed in the court or on the royal affairs,[3] or by
knights, knights' sons, and burghers, riding abroad from

[1] Gregorio, l. iii. c. iv. "Nobis
aliquando, quibus solum ordinationem
justitiariorum, ubicunque fuerimus, re-
servamus."—l. i. t. 95. This was part
of the "merum imperium" of the
sovereign.—i. t. 49.
[2] i. 8.   [3] l. 9.

their own homes. Whoever drew his sword on another
paid double the fine imposed for bearing it; whoever
wounded another lost his hand; whoever killed a man,
if a knight, was beheaded, if of lower rank, hanged. If
the homicide could not be found, the district paid a
heavy fine, yet in proportion to the wehrgeld of the
slain man; but Christians paid twice as much as Jews
or Saracens, as, no doubt, bound more especially to
know and maintain the law. The laws for the preservation of female chastity were singular and severe.
Even rape upon a common prostitute was punished by
beheading, if the charge was brought within a certain
time:[?] whoever did not aid a woman suffering violence
was heavily fined. But in these cases a false accusation
was visited with the same punishment. Mothers who
betrayed their daughters to whoredom had their noses
cut off;[a] men who connived at the adultery of their
wives were scourged. A man caught in adultery might
be slain by the husband; if not instantly slain, he paid
a heavy fine. The trials by battle and ordeal were
abolished as vain and superstitious: the former allowed
only in cases of murder, poisoning, or high treason,
where there was strong suspicion but not full proof. It
was designed to work on the terror of the criminal; but
if the accuser was worsted, he was condemned in case of
high treason to the utmost penalty; in other cases to
proportionate punishment. Torture was only used in
cases of heavy suspicion against persons of notoriously
evil repute.[a]

[?] i. 20.   [a] iii. 48, 50.

[a] Frederick's legislation was not content with abolishing these barbarous forms of testimony, almost the only available testimony in rude unlettered times. He laid down rules on written evidence; documents must be on parchment, not on perishable paper; he prohibited a certain kind of obscure and intricate writing, in use at Naples, Amalfi, and Sorrento; and ordered the notaries to write all deeds legibly and

These are but instances of the spirit in which Frederick framed his legislation, which aimed rather to advance, enrich, enlighten his subjects than to repress their free development by busy and perpetual interference. His regulations concerning commerce were almost prophetically wise: he laid down the great maxim that commercial exchange benefited both parties; he permitted the export of corn as the best means of fostering its cultivation. He entered into liberal treaties with Venice, with Asia, Genoa, and the Greek Empire, and even with some of the Saracen powers in Africa. By common consent, both parties condemned the plundering of wrecks, and pledged themselves to mutual aid and friendly reception into their harbours. The King himself was a great merchant; the royal vessels traded to Syria, Egypt, and other parts of the East. He had even factors who traded to India.[b] He encouraged internal commerce by the establishment of great fairs and markets;[c] manufactures of various kinds began to prosper.

But that which—if the constitution of Frederick had continued to flourish, if the institutions had worked out in peace their natural consequences—if the house of Hohenstaufen had maintained their power, splendour and tendencies to social and intellectual advancement—if they had not been dispossessed by the dynasty of Charles of Anjou, and the whole land thrown back by many centuries—might have enabled the Southern kingdom

---

clearly. The Emperor himself laid down regulations to test the authenticity of a certain document.—Gregorio, ill. p. 61.

[b] "Fredericus II. erat omnibus Soldanis Orientis partceps in mercimoniis, et amicissimus, ita ut usque ad Indos

mercibus ad commodum suum, tam per mare, quam per terram, institores."—Matth. Par. 544.

[c] See edict for annual fairs at Salmona, Capua, Lucera, Bari, Tarentum, Cosenza, Reggio, Jan. 1234.—Rich. San Germ.

to take the lead, and anticipate the splendid period of
Italian learning, philosophy, and art, was the Universities; the establishments for education; the encourage-
ments for all learned and refined studies, imagined by
this accomplished King. Even the revival of Greek
letters might not have awaited the conquest of Constantinople by the Turks four centuries later. Greek was
the spoken language of the people in many parts of the
kingdom; the laws of Frederick were translated into
Greek for popular use; the epitaph of the Archbishop
of Messina in the year 1175 was Greek.[4] There were
Greek priests and Greek congregations in many parts
of Apulia and Sicily; the privileges conferred by the
Emperor Henry VI. on Messina had enacted that one of
the three magistrates should be a Greek. Hebrew, and
still more Arabic, were well known, not merely by Jews
and Arabians but by learned scholars. Frederick himself spoke German, Italian, Latin, Greek, Arabic, and
Hebrew. He declared his own passionate love for
learned and philosophical studies. Nothing after the
knowledge of affairs, of laws and of arms, became a monarch so well; to this he devoted all his leisure hours,
these were the liberal pursuits which adorned and dignified human life.[e] In Syria, and in his intercourse
with the Eastern monarchs, he had obtained great col-
lections of books; he caused translations to be made
from the Arabic, and out of Greek into Latin, of some
of the philosophic works of Aristotle and the Almagest
of Ptolemy.[f] The University of Naples was his great

---

[4] Von Raumer, p. 356.
[e] Peter de Vinca, iii. 67.
[f] He employed the celebrated Michael
Scott (the fabled magician) in the
translation of Aristotle. Among the

Papal documents relating to England
in the British Museum are several
letters concerning this remarkable man,
patronised alike by Frederick and by
the Pope. Honorius III. writes

foundation; Salerno remained the famous school of
medicine; but the University in the capital was encouraged by liberal endowments, and by regulations with
regard to the relations of the scholars and the citizens;
the price of lodgings was fixed by royal order; sums of
money were to be advanced to youths at low interest,
and could not be exacted during the years of study.
The King held out to the more promising students
honourable employments in his service. Philosophical
studies appeared most suited to the genius of Frederick;
natural history and the useful sciences he cultivated
with success; but he had likewise great taste for the
fine arts, especially for architecture, both ornamental
and military. He restored the walls of many of the
greatest cities; built bridges and other useful works.
He had large menageries, supplied from the East and
from Africa. He sometimes vouchsafed to send some of
the more curious animals about for the instruction and
amusement of his subjects. The Ravennese were delighted with the appearance of some royal animals. He
was passionately fond of field sports, of the chase with
the hound and the hawk; his own book on falconry is
not merely instructive on that sport, but is a scientific
treatise on the nature and habits of those birds, and of
many other animals. The first efforts of Italian sculp-
ture and painting rose under his auspices; the beautiful
Italian language began to form itself in his court: it
has been said above that the earliest strains of Italian

(Jan. 16, 1225, p. 214) to the Archbishop of Canterbury to bestow preferment on Michael Scott "Quod
inter literatos dono vigeat scientiæ
singulari." M. Scott (p. 229) has
a licence to hold pluralities. (P. 246,
he is named by the Pope Archbishop of

Cashel, and to hold his other benefices.
(P. 253) he refuses the Archbishopric:
"Dum linguam terræ filius se ignorare
dicerel." He is described as not only
a great Latin scholar, but as familiar
with Hebrew and Arabic.

poetry were heard there: Peter de Vineâ, the Chancellor of Frederick, the compiler of his laws, was also the writer of the earliest Italian sonnet. Nor was Peter de Vineâ the only courtier who emulated the King in poetry: his beloved son Enzio, many of his courtiers, vied with their King and his ministers in the cultivation of the Italian language; and its first fruits the rich harmonious Italian poetry.[a]

His own age beheld with admiring amazement the magnificence of Frederick's court, the unexampled progress in wealth, luxury, and knowledge. The realm was at peace, notwithstanding some disturbance by those proud barons, whose interest it was to maintain the old feudal and seignorial rights; the reluctance of the clergy to recede from the complete dominion over the popular mind; and the taxation, which weighed, especially as Frederick became more involved in the Lombard war, on all classes. The world had seen no court so splendid, no system of laws so majestically equitable; a new order of things appeared to be arising; an epoch to be commencing in human civilisation. But this admiration was not universal: there was a deep and silent jealousy, an intuitive dread in the Church,[b] and in all

[a] Some of these poems I have read in a collection of the Poeti del Primo Secolo, Firenze, 1814. A small volume has been published by the Literary Union of Stuttgard (1843), Italienische Lieder des Hohenstaufischen Hofes in Sicilien. It contains lays by thirteen royal and noble authors. Dante, in his book De Vulgari Eloquentia, traces to the court of Frederick the origin of the true and universal Italian language. We return to this subject.

[b] The Pope seemed to consider that Frederick's new constitutions must be inimical to the Church. "Intelleximus siquidem quod vel proprio motu, vel seductus inconsultis consiliis perversorum, novas edere constitutiones intendis ex quibus necessario sequitur ut dicaris Ecclesiæ persecutor et obrutor publicæ libertatis."—Lib. v. Epist. 91, apud Raynald. 1231. He reproaches the Archbishop of Capua as "Frederico constitutiones destructivas salutis et institutivas enormium scandalorum edenti voluntarius obsequens."—Apud Hofler ii. p. 333.

the faithful partisans of the Church of remote, if not
immediate danger; of a latent design, at least a latent
tendency in the temporal kingdom to set itself apart,
and to sever itself from the one great religious Empire,
which had now been building itself up for centuries.
There was, if not an avowed independence, a threatening disposition to independence. The legislation, if it
did not directly clash, yet seemed to clash, with the
higher law of the Church; if it did not make the clergy
wholly subordinate, it degraded them in some respect to
the rank of subjects; if it did not abrogate, it limited
what were called the rights and privileges, but which
were in fact the separate rule and dominion of the
clergy; at all events, it assumed a supremacy, set itself
above, admitted only what it chose of the great Canon
Law of the Church; it was self-originating, self-asserting,
it had not condescended to consult those in whom for
centuries all political as well as spiritual wisdom had
been concentered: it was a legislation neither emanating
from, nor consented to by, the Church. If every nation
were thus to frame its own constitution, without regard
to the great unity maintained by the Church, the vast
Christian confederacy would break up, Kings might
assume the power of forbidding the recurrence to Rome
as the religious capital of the world; independent kingdoms might aspire to found independent churches. This
new knowledge too was not less dangerous because its
ultimate danger was not clearly seen; at all events, it
was not knowledge introduced, sanctioned, taught by
the sole great instructress, the Church. Theology, the
one Science, was threatened by a rival, and whence did
that rival profess to draw her wisdom? from the Heathen,
the Jew, the Unbeliever; from the Pagan Greek, the
Hebrew, the Arabic. That which might be in itself

harmless, edifying, improving, when taught by the
Church, would but inflame the rebellious pride of the
human intellect. What meant this ostentatious toleration of other religions, if not total indifference to Christ
and God; if not a secret inclination to apostasy? What
was all this splendour, but Epicurean or Eastern luxury?
What this poetry, but effeminate amatory songs? Was
this the life of a Christian King, of a Christian nobility,
of a Christian people? It was an absolute renunciation
of the severe discipline of the Church, of that austere
asceticism, which however the clergy and religious men
alone could practise its angelic, its divine perfection,
was the remote virtue after which all, even Kings (so
many of whom had exchanged their worldly robes for
the cowl and for sackcloth) ought to aspire, as to the
ultimate culminating height of true Christianity. It
was Mohammedan not merely in its secret indulgences,
its many concubines, in which the Emperor was still
said to allow himself Mohammedan licence; some of
his chosen companions, his trusted counsellors, at least
his instructors in science and philosophy were Mohammedans; ladies of that race and religion appeared, as
has been said, at his court (in them virtue was a thing
incredible to a sound churchman). The Saracens whom
he had transplanted to Nocera were among his most
faithful troops, followed him in his campaigns; it was
even reported, that after his marriage with Isabella of
England, he dismissed her English ladies, and made her
over to the care of Moorish eunuchs.

Such to the world was the fame, such to the Church
the evil fame of Frederick's Sicilian court; exaggerated
no doubt as to its splendour, luxury, licence, and learning, as well by the wonder of the world, as by the abhorrence of the Church. Yet, after all, out of his long life

(long if considered not by years but by events, by the
civil acts, the wars, the negotiations, the journeyings,
the vicissitudes, crowded into it by Frederick's own
busy and active ambition and by the whirling current of
affairs) the time during which he sunned himself in this
gorgeous voluptuousness must have been comparatively
short, intermittent, broken. At eighteen years of age
Frederick left Sicily to win the Imperial crown; he had
then eight years of the cold German climate and the
rude German manners during the establishment of his
Sovereignty over the haughty German Princes and
Prelates. Then eight years in the South, but A.D. 1220 to
during the first four the rebellious Apulian and 1228.
Sicilian nobles were to be brought under control, the
Saracens to be reduced to obedience, and trans- A.D. 1228 to
ported to Apulia: throughout the later four, 1228.
was strife with the Lombard cities, strife about the
Crusade, and preparation for the voyage. Then came
his Eastern campaign, his reconciliation with the Church.
Four years followed of legislation; and perhaps the
nearest approach to indolent and luxurious A.D. 1220 to
peace. Then succeeded the revolt of his son. 1234.
Four years more to coerce rebellious Germany, to attempt in vain to coerce rebellious Lombardy: A.D. 1234 to
all this was to close, with his life, in the unin- 1238.
terrupted immitigable feud with Gregory IX. and
Innocent IV.

The Pope Gregory IX. (it is impossible to decide
how far influenced by the desire of overawing The Decre-
this tendency of temporal legislation to assert tals.
its own independence) determined to array the higher
and eternal law of the Church in a more august and
authoritative form. The great code of the Papal
Decretals constituted this law; it had now long recog-

M 2

nised and admitted to the honours of equal authority
the bold inventions of the book called by the name of
Isidore; but during the Pontificate of Innocent III.
there had been five distinct compilations, conflicting in
some points, and giving rise to intricate and insoluble
questions.[1] Gregory in his old age aspired to be the
Justinian of the Church. He entrusted the compilation
of a complete and regular code to Raimond da Pennaforte, a noble Spaniard, related to the royal house of
Arragon, of the Dominican Order, and now the most
distinguished jurist in the University of Bologna.
Raimond da Pennaforte was to be to the Canon what
Imerius of Bologna had been to the revived Roman
Law. It is somewhat singular that Raimond had been
the most famous antagonist of the Arabian school of
learning, the most admired champion of Christianity, in
his native Spain.

The first part of these Decretals comprehended the
whole, in a form somewhat abbreviated; abbreviations
which, as some complained, endangered the rights of the
Church on important points; but were defended by the
admirers of Raimond of Pennaforte, who declared that
he could not err, for an angel from Heaven had constantly watched over his holy work.[k] The second contained the Decretals of Gregory IX. himself. The
whole was promulgated as the great statute law of
Christendom, superior in its authority to all secular
laws as the interests of the soul were to those of the

---

[1] " Sane diversæ constitutiones, et
decretales epistolæ, prædecessorum
nostrorum in diversa sparsæ volumina,
quarum aliquæ propter nimiam simili-
tudinem, et quædam propter contrarie-
tatem, nonnullæ etiam propter suam
prolixitatem, confusionem indocere

ridebantur; aliquæ vero ingrabantur
extra volumina supradicta, quæ tanquam incertæ frequenter in judiciis
vacillabant."—In Præfat.

[k] Chiflet, quoted by Schmeck, xxvii.
64. Raimond da Pennaforte was
canonized by Clement VIII., in 1601.

body, as the Church was of greater dignity than the
State ; as the Pope higher than any one temporal sovereign, or all the sovereigns of the world. Though especially the law of the clergy, it was the law binding likewise on the laity as Christians, as religious men, both
as demanding their rigid observance of all the rights,
immunities, independent jurisdictions of the clergy, and
concerning their own conduct as spiritual subjects of the
Church. All temporal jurisprudence was bound to
frame its decrees with due deference to the superior
ecclesiastical jurisprudence ; to respect the borders of
that inviolable domain ; not only not to interfere with
those matters over which the Church claimed exclusive
cognisance, but to be prepared to enforce by temporal
means those decrees which the Church, in her tenderness for human life, in her clemency, or in her want of
power, was unwilling or unable herself to carry into
execution. Beyond that sacred circle temporal legislation might claim the full allegiance of its temporal
subjects ; but the Church alone could touch the holy
person, punish the delinquencies, control the demeanour
of the sacerdotal order ; could regulate the power of the
superior over the inferior clergy, and choose those who
were to be enrolled in the order. The Church alone
could administer the property of the Church ; that property it was altogether beyond the province of the civil
power to tax ; even as to feudal obligations, the Church
would hardly consent to allow any decisions but her
own : though compelled to submit to the assent of the
crown in elections to benefices which were temporal
fiefs, yet that assent was, on the other hand, counter-
balanced by her undoubted power to consecrate or to
refuse consecration. The Book of Gregory's Decretals
was ordered to be the authorised text in all courts and

in all schools of law; it was to be, as it were, more and more deeply impressed into the minds of men. Even in its form it closely resembled the Roman law yet un-abrogated in many parts of Europe; but of course it comprehended alike those who lived under the different national laws, which had adopted more or less of the old Latin jurisprudence; it was the more universal statute-book of the more wide-ruling, all-embracing Rome.

CHAPTER IV.

Renewal of hostilities between Gregory IX. and Frederick II.

DURING the nine years of peace between the Empire and the Papacy, Pope Gregory IX. at times poured forth his flowery eloquence in the praise, almost the adulation, of the Emperor; the Emperor proclaimed himself the most loyal subject of the Church. The two potentates concurred only with hearty zeal in the persecution of those rebels against the civil and ecclesiastical power, the heretics.*

Peace of nine years. Aug. 1230 to 1239, Palm Sunday.

---

* During this period of peace an obscure heresy, that of the Stedinger, appeared or grew to its height in the duchy of Oldenburg; the Pope and the Emperor would concur in inflicting customary punishment on these rebels. Hartwig, the Archbishop of Bremen, had long appealed to Rome. On one occasion he returned with full power to subdue his refractory spiritual subjects, bearing, as he boasted, a singular and significant relique,—the sword with which Peter had struck off the ear of Malchus. More than thirty years after, Archbishop Gerhard, Count de la Lippe, a martial prelate, turned not his spiritual but his secular arms against them. Among their deadly feuds was the refusal to pay tithes. The Pope recites the charges against them, furnished of course by their mortal enemies. They wor-

shipped the Evil One now as a toad, which they kissed behind and on the mouth, and licked up its foul venom; now as a man, with a face wonderfully pale, haggard, with coal-black eyes. They kissed him; his kiss was cold as ice, and with his kiss oozed away all their Catholic faith. The Pope would urge the Emperor to take part in the war against these wretches. Conrad of Marburg, the hateful persecutor of the saintly Elizabeth of Hungary, now the Holy Inquisitor, was earnest and active in the cause. The Stedinger withstood a crusading army of 40,000 men; were defeated with the loss of 6000. Many fled to other lands; the rest submitted to the Archbishop. The Pope released them from the excommunication: but it is curious to observe, he only conceives their disobedience and insurrection;

At Rome multitudes of meaner religious criminals were
burned; many priests and of the lower orders of clergy
degraded and sent to Monte Casino and other rigid
monasteries as prisoners for life.[b] The Pope issued an
act of excommunication rising in wrath and terror above
former acts. Persons suspected of heresy were under
excommunication; if within a year they did not prove
themselves guiltless, they were to be treated as heretics.
Heretics were at once infamous; if judges, their acts
were at once null; if advocates, they could not plead;
if notaries, the instruments which they had drawn were
invalid. All priests were to be publicly stripped of
their holy dress and degraded. No gifts or oblations
were to be received from them; the clerk who bestowed
Christian burial on a heretic was to disentomb him with
his own hands, and cast him forth from the cemetery,
which became an accursed place unfit for burial. No
lay person was to dispute in public or in private concerning the Catholic faith: no descendant of a heretic
to the second generation could be admitted to holy
orders. Annibaldi, the senator of Rome and the Roman people, passed a decree enacting condign punishment on all heretics. The Emperor, not content with
suppressing these insurgents in his hereditary dominions, had given orders that throughout Lombardy,
their chief seat, they should be sought out, delivered to
the Inquisitors,[c] and there punished by the secular arm.[d]
One of his own most useful allies, Eccelin da Romano,

---

he is silent of their heresy.—Raynaldus, sub ann. 1233; Schroeck, xxii,
641, &c. The original authorities
are Albert. Stad. Ger. Monach. apud
Kochmer—above all the Papal letters.

[b] Vit. Gregor. IX. Rich. San
Germ. Raynald. sub ann. 1231.

[c] Gregory in one letter insinuates
that Frederick had burned some good
Catholics, his enemies, as pretending
that they were or had been heretics.—
Epist. 244. Raynald. p. 85.

[d] See ante, note, p. 151.

was in danger. Eccelin's two sons, Eccelin and Alberic, offered to denounce their father to the Inquisition. There was, what it is difficult to describe but as profound hypocrisy, or worse, on the part of the Pope: he declared his unwillingness to proceed to just vengeance against the father of such pious sons, who by his guilt would forfeit, as in a case of capital treason, all their inheritance; the sons were to persuade Eccelin to abandon all connexion with heresy or with heretics: if he refused, they were to regard their own salvation, and to denounce their father before the Papal tribunal.[*] It is strange enough that the suspected heretic, suspected perhaps not unjustly, took the vows, and died in the garb of a monk; the pious son became that Eccelin da Romano whose cruelty seems to have defied the exaggeration of party hatred.

But in all other respects the Pope and the Emperor were equally mistrustful of each other; peace was disguised war. Each had an ally in the midst of the other's territory whom he could not avow, yet would not abandon. Even in these perverse times the conduct of the Romans to the Pope is almost inexplicable. No sooner had the Pope, either harassed or threatened by their unruly proceedings, withdrawn in wrath, or under the pretext of enjoying the purer and cooler air, to Rieti, Anagni, or some other neighbouring city, than Rome began to regret his absence, to make overtures of submission; and still received him back with more rapturous demonstrations of joy.[f] In a few months they began to be

---

[*] The age may be pleased in favour of Gregory IX. What is to be said of the comment of the Papal annalist, Raynaldus?—"Nec mirum cuiquam videri potest datum hoc filiis adversus parentem consilium, cum nominis, a quo descendit omnis paternitas, sacra humanis affectibus debet anteferri."—p. 41. Raynald. 1231.

[f] Rich. de S. Germ., sub ann. 1231.

weary of their quiet: his splendid buildings for the defence and ornament of the city lost their imposing power, or became threatening to their liberties; he was either compelled or thought it prudent to retire. Viterbo had become to the Romans what Tusculum had been in a former century; the Romans loved their own liberty, but their hate of Viterbo was stronger than their love; the fear that the Pope might take part with Viterbo brought them to his feet; that he did not aid them in the subjugation of Viterbo rekindled their hostility to him. More than once the Pope called on the Emperor to assist him to put down his insurgent subjects: Frederick promised, eluded his promise;[a] his troops were wanted to suppress rebellions not feigned, but rather of some danger, at Messina and Syracuse. He had secret partisans everywhere: when Rome was papal, Viterbo was Imperialist; when Viterbo was for the Pope, Rome was for the Emperor. If Frederick was insincere in his maintenance of the Pope against his domestic enemies, Gregory was no less insincere in pretending to renounce all alliance, all sympathy with the Lombards.[b] But this connexion of the Pope with the Lombard League required infinite management and

1233. He returned to Rome, March, 1233. He was again in Anagni in August !

[a] Rebellion, reconciliation, 1233. New rebellion, beginning of 1234. "Quæ Fredericus imperator apud sanctam Germanam orta relatione comparta, qui fidelis defensionis presidiotis ecclesiæ Romanæ promiserat, et fidei et majestatis obliatus, Messanam properans, nullo prærequisite decessit, hostibus tanti favoris auxilium et consiliano daturus."—Vit. Gregor. Compare Pope's letter (Feb. 3, from Anagni, and Feb. 10). But in fact there was a dangerous insurrection in Messina; the King's Justiciary had been obliged to fly. Frederick had to put down movements also at Syracuse and Nicenia.—Ann. Sicul. Rich. San Germano.

[b] The Chronicon Placentinum has revealed a renewal of the Lombard League at Bologna, Oct. 26, 1231, and a secret mission to the Pope. p. 60.

dexterity: the Lombard cities swarmed with heretics, and so far were not the most becoming allies of the Pope.' Yet this alliance might seem an affair, not of policy only, but of safety. Gregory could not disguise to himself that so popular, so powerful a sovereign had never environed the Papal territories on every side. If Frederick (and Frederick's character might seem daring enough for so impious an act) should despise the sacred awe which guarded the person of the Pope, and scorn his excommunications, he was in an instant at the gates of Rome, of fickle and treacherous Rome. He had planted his two colonies of Saracens near the Apulian frontier; they at least would have no scruple in executing his most irreverent orders. The Pope was at his mercy, and friendless, as far as any strong or immediate check on the ambition or revenge of the Emperor. The Pope in supporting the Lombard republics, assumed the lofty position of the sacred defender of liberty, the asserter of Italian independence, when Italy seemed in danger of lying prostrate under one stern and despotic monarchy, which would extend from the German Ocean to the further shore of Sicily. At first his endeavours were wisely and becomingly devoted to the maintenance of peace—a peace which, so long as the Emperor refrained from asserting his full imperial rights, so long as the Guelfs ruled undisturbed in those cities in which their interests predominated, the republics were content to

' A modern writer, rather Papal, thus describes the state of Italy at that time: "Alle Kreise und Stände derjenigen Theils der Nation, den man als den eigentlichen Träger der Intelligenz in Italien betrachten müsste, waren geistig frei und mächtig genug, wo ihre Interessen denen der Kirche entgegen waren, die letzteren mit Füssen zu treten, nicht bloss einzelne Potentaten, oder das Geld-interesse des gemeinen Volkes, sondern oft alle gebildeten Städtebewohner wagten es, hock den Demokrahlen des Papstes hohn zu sprechen."—Leo, Geschichte der Italien, ii. 234.

observe; the lofty station of the mediator of such peace
became his sacred function, and gave him great weight
with both parties. But nearly at the same time an insurrection of the Pope's Roman subjects, more
daring and aggressive than usual, compelled
him to seek the succour of Frederick, and Frederick
was threatened with a rebellion which the high-minded
and religious Pope could not but condemn, though
against his fearful adversary.

For the third or fourth time the Pope had been compelled to retire to Rieti. Under the senatorship of Luca di Sabelli the senate and people
of Rome had advanced new pretensions, which tended
to revolutionise the whole Papal dominions. They had
demolished part of the Lateran palace, razed some of
the palaces of the cardinals, proclaimed their open
defiance of the Pope's governor, the Cardinal Rainier.
They had sent justiciaries into Tuscany and the Sabine
country to receive oaths of allegiance to themselves, and
to exact tribute. The Pope wrote pressing letters
addressed to all the princes and bishops of Christendom,
imploring succour in men and money; there was but
one near enough at hand to aid, had all been willing.
The Pope could not but call on him whose title as
Emperor was protector of the Church, who as King
of Naples was first vassal of the papal see.
Frederick did not disobey the summons: with
his young son Conrad he visited the Pope at Rieti.
The Cardinal Rainier had thrown himself with the
Pope's forces into Viterbo; the army of Frederick sat
down before Respampano, a strong castle which the

Affairs of Rome.

May, 1234.

May 20, 1234.

[footnote] See the letter to Frederick, in which he assumes the full power of
arbitration between the Emperor and the League.—Monument. Germ. iv.
299, dated June 5, 1243.

Romans occupied in the neighbourhood as an annoyance, and as a means, it might be, of surprising and taking Viterbo. But Respampano made resistance; Frederick himself retired, alleging *Sept. 1231.* important affairs, to his own dominions. The Papalists burst into a cry of reproach at his treacherous abandonment of the Pope. Yet it was entirely by the aid of some of his German troops that the Papal army inflicted a humiliating defeat on the Romans, who were compelled to submit to the terms of peace dictated by *April 14,* the Pope,[*] and enforced by the Emperor, who *1233.* was again with the Pope at Rieti. Angelo Malebranca; "by the grace of God the illustrious senator of the gentle city" (such were the high-sounding phrases), by the decree and authority of the sacred senate, by the command and instant acclamation of the famous people, assembled in the Capitol at the sound of the bell and of the trumpet, swore to the peace proposed by the three cardinals, between the Holy Roman Church, their Father the Supreme Pontiff, and the Senate and people of Rome. He swore to give satisfaction for the demolition of the Lateran palace and those of the cardinals, the invasion of the Papal territories, the exaction of oaths, the occupation of the domains of the Church. He swore that no clerks or ecclesiastical persons belonging to the families of the Pope or cardinals should be summoned before the civil tribunals (thus even in Rome there was a strong opposition to those immunities of the clergy from temporal jurisdiction for temporal offences).

---

* "Milites in civitate Viterbio collocaris, quorum quotidianis insultibus et depredationibus Romani adeo sunt vexati, ut non nolle pact cum Papâ pacem subirent."—Cod. Colm. The author of the life of Gregory says that the Emperor, instead of aiding the Pope, idled his time away in hunting; "Majestatis titulum in officium venatoris commutans . . . . in captarum avium sollicitabat aquilas triumphalem."

This did not apply to laics who belonged to such house-
holds. He swore to protect all pilgrims, laymen as well
as ecclesiastics, who visited the shrines of the Apostles.[*]
The peace was re-established likewise with the Emperor
and his vassals—with Anagni, Segni, Velletri, Viterbo,
and other cities of the Papal territories. But even during
this compulsory approximation to the Emperor, the
Pope, to remove all suspicion that he might be won to
desert their cause, wrote to the Lombards to reassure
them. However, he might call upon them not to
impede the descent of the Imperial troops from the Alps,
those troops were not directed against their liberties,
but came to maintain the liberties of the Church.

But if the rebels against the Pope were thus his
immediate subjects the Romans, the rebel against
Frederick was his own son. Henry had been left to
rule Germany as king of the Romans; the causes and
indeed the objects of his rebellion are obscure.[*] Henry
appears to have been a man of feeble character; so long as he was governed by wise
counsellors, filling his high office without blame; released from their control, the slave of his own loose
passions, and the passive instrument of low and design-
ing men. The only impulse to which the rebel son
could appeal was the pride of Germany, which would
no longer condescend to be governed from Italy, and to

Rebellion of King Henry.

* Apud Raynald. ann. 1235.
* In the year 1232 Frederick begun
to entertain suspicions of his son, and
to be discontented with his conduct,
Henry (but 20 years old) met his
father at Aquileia, promised amend-
ment, and to discard his evil counsellors.—Huba. Collect. Monument. i.
222. Frederick might remember the
fatal example of the Franconian house;

the conduct of Henry V. to Henry IV.
The chief burthen of Henry's vindication, addressed, Sept. 1236, to Bishop
Conrad of Hildesheim, is that the
Emperor had annulled some of his
grants, interfered in behalf of the
house of Bavaria (Louis of Bavaria
had been guardian of the realm during
his minority).

be a province of the kingdom of Apulia. Unlike some
of his predecessors, Pope Gregory took at once the high
Christian tone: he would seek no advantage from the
unnatural insurrection of a son against his father. All
the malicious insinuations against Gregory are put to
silence by the fact that, during their fiercest war of
accusation and recrimination, Frederick never charged
the Pope with the odious crime of encouraging his son's
disobedience. Frederick passed the Alps with
letters from the Pope, calling on all the   May, 1234.
Christian prelates of Germany to assert the authority
of the King and of the parent. Henry had held a
council of princes[p] at Boppart to raise the standard of
revolt, and had entered into treasonable league with
Milan and the Lombard cities. The rebellion was as
weak as wanton and guilty; Frederick entered
Germany with the scantiest attendance; the   July, 1234.
affrighted son, abandoned by all his partisans, met him
at Worms, and made the humblest submission.[q] Frederick renewed his pardon; but probably some new
detected intrigues, or the refusal to surrender his
castles, or meditated flight,[r] induced the Emperor to
send his son as a prisoner to the kingdom of Naples.
There he remained in such obscurity that his death
might have been unnoticed but for a passionate lamentation which Frederick himself sent forth, in which he
adopted the language of King David on the loss of his
ungrateful but beloved Absalom.[s]

[p] God. Colen. Chron. Erphurd. apud Bochmer Fontes R. G.

[q] " Ipso mense, nullo obstante, Ale-mannism intuens, Henricum regem filium suum ad mandatum suum recepit, quem duci Bavariæ custodiro-dum commisit."—Rich. San Germ.

[r] God. Col. Annal. Erphurd. Quotation from Ann. Argentin. in Bochmer's Regesta, p. 254.

[s] Besides this pathetic letter in Peter de Vineä, iv. 1, see the more extraordinary one, quoted by Höfler, addressed to the people of Messina.

Worms had beheld the sad scene of the ignominious arrest and imprisonment of the King of the Germans: that event was followed by the splendid nuptials of the Emperor with Isabella of England.

But though the Pope was guiltless, we believe he was guiltless, the Lombards were deep in this conspiracy against the power and the peace of Frederick. They, if they had not from the first instigated, had inflamed the ambition of Henry:[1] they had offered, if he would cross the Alps, to invest him at Monza with the iron crown of Italy." Frederick's long-suppressed impatience of Lombard freedom had now a justifiable cause for vengeance. The Ghibelline cities—Cremona, Parma, Pisa, and others; the Ghibelline Princes Eccelin and Alberic, the two sons of the suspected heretic Eccelin II. (who had now descended from his throne, and taken the habit of a monk, though it was rumoured that his devotion was that of an austere Paterin rather than that of an orthodox recluse) summoned the Emperor to relieve them from the oppressions of the Guelfic league, and to wreak his just revenge on those aggressive rebels. Frederick's declaration of war was drawn with singular subtlety. His chief object, he declared, was the suppression of heresy. The wide prevalence of heresy the Pope could not deny; to espouse the Lombard cause was to espouse that at least of imputed heresy; it was

(margin notes: Lombards concerned in King Henry's rebellion; May 1, 1236; Aug. 1236)

[1] Galvaneo Fiamma has these words: "Henricus composuit cum Mediolanensibus ad petitionem Domini Papæ."—c. 264. "Et tunc facta est liga fortis inter Henricum et Mediolanenses ad petitionem Papæ contra Imperatorem patrem suum."—Annal. Mediolan., Muratori, xvi. 624. These are Milanese, certainly not Ghibelline writers!

[2] During this year (1235) Frederick assisted with seemingly deep devotion at the translation to Marborg of the remains of St. Elizabeth of Hungary. 1,200,000 persons are said to have been present.—Montalembert, Vie de St. Elisabeth d'Hongrie.

to oppose the Emperor in the exercise of his highest
imperial function, the promotion of the unity of the
Church. The Emperor could not leave his own dominions in this state of spiritual and civil revolt to wage
war in foreign lands: so soon as he had subdued the
heretic he was prepared to arm against the Infidel.
Lombardy reduced to obedience, there would be no
obstacle to the reconquest of the Holy Land. Yet
though thus embarrassed, the Pope, in his own defence,
could not but interpose his mediation; he commanded
both parties to submit to his supreme arbitration.
Frederick yielded, but resolutely limited the time; if
the arbitration was not made before Christmas, he was
prepared for war. To the most urgent remonstrances
for longer time he turned a deaf and contemptuous ear:
he peremptorily challenged the Legate whom the Pope
had appointed, the Cardinal Bishop of Præneste, and
refused to accept as arbiter his declared enemy.[1] Frederick had already begun the campaign: Verona had
opened her gates; he had stormed Vicenza,
and laid half the city in ashes. He was re-   Nov. 1, 1236.
called beyond the Alps by the sudden insurrection of
the Duke of Austria. Gregory so far yielded, that in
place of the obnoxious Cardinal of Præneste, he named
as his Legates the Cardinals of Ostia and of
San Sabina. He commended them with high   March, 1237.
praise to the Patriarchs of Aquileia and of Grado, to
the Archbishops of Genoa and Ravenna, whom, with the
suffragans and all the people of Northern Italy, he exhorted to join in obtaining the blessings of peace. But
already he began to murmur his complaints of those

---

[1] Compare the letter, apud Raynald. sub ann. 1236 ; more complete in
Höfler, p. 357, and 360.

grievances which afterwards darkened to such impious crimes. The Frangipanis were again breaking out into turbulence in Rome:[7] it was suspected and urged that they were in the pay of Frederick. Taxes had been levied on the clergy in the kingdom of Naples; they had been summoned before civil tribunals; the old materials of certain churches had been profanely converted by the Saracens of Nocera to the repair of their mosques. The answer of Frederick was lofty and galling. He denied the truth of the Pope's charges; he appealed to the conscience of the Pope. Gregory demanded by what right he presumed to intrude into that awful sanctuary.[8] "Kings and princes were humbly to repose themselves on the lap of priests; Christian Emperors were bound to submit themselves not only to the supreme Pontiff, but even to other bishops. The Apostolic See was the judge of the whole world; God had reserved to himself the sole judgement of the manifest and hidden acts of the Pope. Let the Emperor dread the fate of Uzzah, who laid his profane hands on the ark of God." He urged Frederick to follow the example of the great Constantine, who thought it absolutely wicked that, where the Head of the Christian religion had been determined by the King of Heaven, an earthly Emperor should have the smallest power, and had therefore surrendered Italy to

[7] "Hoc anno Petrus Fratgipane, 1236, in urbe Româ pro parte Imperatoris guerram movit contra Papam et Senatorem."—Rich. San Germ.

[8] "Quod nequaquam inirate ad judicanda novtria conscientia nostrae ... avolaamo; cum regum colis et principum vicina gentibus sacerdotum, et Christiani Imperatores subdire ... delicnel executiones suas non solum Romano Pontifici, quin etiam aliis prasulibus non profetre, hec nos Dominus sedem apostolicam, cujus judicio orbem terrarum subjicit, in occultis et manifestis a nemine judicandam, soli suo judicio reservavit."—Greg. Epist. 10, 252, Oct. 23, 1236, apud Raynald.

the Apostolic government, and chosen for himself a new residence in Greece.[*]

Frederick returned from Germany victorious over the rebellious Duke of Austria; his son Conrad had been chosen King of the Romans. He crossed the Alps with three thousand German men-at-arms, besides the forces of the Ghibelline cities: he was joined by ten thousand Saracens from the South. His own ambassadors, Henry the Master of the Teutonic Order and his Chancellor Peter de Vineâ, by whom he had summoned the Pope to his aid against the enraged Lombards, had returned from Rome without accomplishing their mission. At the head of his army he would not grant audience to the Roman legates, the Cardinal Bishop of Ostia and the Cardinal of St. Sabina, who peremptorily enjoined him to submit to the arbitration of the Pope. The great battle of Corte Nuova might seem to avenge the defeat of his ancestor Frederick Barbarossa at Legnano. The Lombard army was discomfited with enormous loss; the Carroccio of Milan, defended till nightfall, was stripped of its banners, and abandoned to the conqueror. Frederick entered Cremona, the palaces of which city would hardly contain the captives, in a splendid ovation. The Podestà of Milan, Tiepolo, son of the Doge of Venice, was bound on the captive Carroccio; which was borne, as in the pomp of an Eastern potentate, on an elephant, followed by a wooden tower, with trumpeters and the Imperial standard. The pride of Frederick at this victory was at its height; he supposed that it would prostrate at once the madness of the rebels; he called upon the world to rejoice at the resto-

Second descent into Italy.

Aug. 1237.

Nov. 21, 1237.

---

[*] Ibid.

M 2

ration of the Roman Empire to all its rights.[b] The Carroccio was sent to Rome as a gift to the people of the
gentle city: it was deposited in the Capitol, a significant menace to the Pope.[c] But where every city was
a fortress, inexpugnable by the arts of war then known,
a battle in the open field did not decide the fate of a
league which included so many of the noblest cities of
Italy. Frederick had passed the winter at Cremona;
the terror of his arms had enforced at least outward submission from many of the leaguers. Almost all Piedmont, Alexandria, Turin, Susa, and the other cities
raised the Ghibelline banner. Milan, Brescia, Piacenza,
Bologna, remained alone in arms; even they made overtures for submission. Their offers were in some respects
sufficiently humiliating; to acknowledge themselves
rebels, to surrender all their gold and silver, to place
their banners at the feet of the Emperor, to furnish one
thousand men for the Crusades; but they demanded in
return a general amnesty and admission to the favour
of the Emperor, the maintenance of the liberties of the
citizens and of the cities. Frederick haughtily de-

---

[b] See the letter in Peter de Vineâ.
" Exultet jam Romani Imperii cultura
. . . mundus gaudeat universus . . .
confundatur rebellio hominis."—Frederick disguised not, he boasted of the
aid of his Saracens. He describes the
Germans reddening their swords with
blood, Pavia and Cremona wreaking
vengeance on the tyrannous Milanese,
" et suas evacuaverunt pharetras
Saraceni."

[c] " Quando illam ad almæ urbis
populum destinavit." A marble monument of this victory was shown in
1727.—Muratori, Dissert. xxvl. t. ii.
p. 491. The inscription was:—

" Ergo triumphorum urbis summæ cató
　　primorum,
Quem tibi militibant reges qui bella gere-
　　bant."

—Francisc. Pipin. apud Muratori,—
Compare the (Ghibelline) Chronicon
de Rebus in Italiâ gestis, discovered
by M. Pauizzi in the British Museum,
and printed with the Chronicon Placentinum at Paris, 1856. " Quod
carocrium cum apud Romam dimi-
sent, dominus papa usque ad mortem
doluit." The Pope would have prevented its admission into the city, but
was overawed by the Imperialist party.
—p. 172.

manded absolute and unconditional surrender.   They feared, they might well fear, Frederick's severity against rebels. With mistimed and impolitic rigour he had treated the captive Podestà of Milan as a rebel; Tiepolo was sent to Naples, and there publicly executed. The Republics declared that it was better to die by the sword than by the halter, by famine, or by fire.[a] Frederick, in the summer of the next year, under- ^{Aug. 8 to Oct.} took the siege of Brescia; at the end of two ^{1238.} months, foiled by the valour of the citizens and the skill of their chief engineer, a Spaniard, Kalamandrino, he was obliged to burn his besieging machines, and retire humiliated to Padua.[b] But without aid the Lombard liberties must fall: the Emperor was master of Italy from the Alps to the straits of Messina; the knell of Italian independence was rung; the Pope a vassal at the mercy of Frederick.

The dauntless old man rose in courage with the danger. Temporal allies were not absolutely wanting. Venice, dreading her own safety, and enraged at the execution of her noble son, Tiepolo, sent proposals for alliance to the Pope. The treaty was framed; Venice agreed to furnish 25 galleys, 300 knights, 2000 foot-soldiers, 500 archers; she was to obtain, as the price of this aid, Dari and Salpi in Apulia, and all that she could conquer in Sicily.[c]

The Pope wrote to the confederate cities of Lombardy and Romagna, taking them formally under the protection of the Holy See.[d] Genoa, under the same fears as Venice, and jealous of Imperialist Pisa, was prepared with her fleets to join the cause. During these nine

---

[a] Rich. de San Germ.
[c] Dandolo, 356. Marin. iv. 223.

[b] See B. Museum Chronicon, p. 177.
[d] Greg. Epist. apud Hahn. xviii.

years of peace, even if the former transgressions of
Frederick were absolutely annulled by the treaty and
absolution of San Germano, collisions between two
parties both grasping and aggressive, and with rights
the boundaries of which could not be precisely defined,
had been inevitable: pretexts could be found, made, or
exaggerated into crimes against the spiritual power,
which would give some justification to that power to
put forth, at such a crisis, its own peculiar weapons; and
to recur to its only arms, the excommunication, the
interdict, the absolution of subjects from their allegiance. Over this power Gregory had full command, in
its employment no scruple.

On Palm Sunday, and on Thursday in Holy week,
with all the civil and ecclesiastical state which
he could assemble around him, Gregory pronounced excommunication against the Emperor; he gave over his body to Satan for the good of
his soul, absolved all his subjects from their allegiance,
laid under interdict every place in which he might be,
degraded all ecclesiastics who should perform the services of the Church before him, or maintain any intercourse with him; and commanded the promulgation of
this sentence with the utmost solemnity and
publicity throughout Christendom. These were
the main articles of the impeachment published
some months before:—I. That in violation of his oath,
he had stirred up insurrection in Rome against the
Pope and the Cardinals. II. That he had arrested the
Cardinal of Prenesto while on the business of the
Church among the Albigenses. III. That in the kingdom of Sicily he had kept benefices vacant to the ruin
of men's souls; unjustly seized the goods of churches
and monasteries, levied taxes on the clergy, imprisoned,

banished, and even punished them with death. IV. That he had not restored their lands or goods to the Templars and Knights of St. John. V. That he had ill-treated, plundered, and expelled from his realm all the partisans of the Church. VI. That he had hindered the rebuilding of the church of Sora, favoured the Saracens, and settled them among Christians. VII. That he had seized and prevented the nephew of the King of Tunis from proceeding to Rome for baptism, and imprisoned Peter, Ambassador of the King of England. VIII. That he had taken possession of Massa, Ferrara, and especially Sardinia, being part of the patrimony of St. Peter. IX. That he had thrown obstacles in the way of the recovery of the Holy Land and the restoration of the Latin Empire in Constantinople, and in the affairs of the Lombards rejected the interposition of the Pope.

Frederick was at Padua, of which his most useful ally, Eccelin da Romano, had become Lord by all his characteristic treachery and barbarity. There were great rejoicings and festivities on that Palm Sunday; races and tournaments in honour of the Emperor. But some few Guelfs were heard to murmur bitterly among themselves, " This will be a day of woe to Frederick; this day the Holy Father is uttering his ban against him, and delivering him over to the devil!" On the arrival of the intelligence from Rome, Frederick for a time restrained his wrath. Peter de Vincá, the great Justiciary of the realm of Naples, pronounced in the presence of Frederick, who wore his crown, a long exculpatory sermon to the vast assembly, on a text out of Ovid—" Punishment when merited is to be borne with patience, but when it is undeserved, with sorrow." [b]

<hr>

[b] " Leniter ex merito quicquid patiare ferendo est
Quæ venit indignæ pœna dolenda venit."

He declared, " that since the days of Charlemagne, no

Frederick's
confutation of
the charges.

Emperor had been more just, gentle, and magnanimous, or had given so little cause for the
hostility of the Church." The Emperor himself rose
and averred, that if the excommunication had been
spoken on just grounds, and in a lawful manner, he
would have given instant satisfaction. He could only
lament that the Pope had inflicted so severe a censure,
without grounds and with such precipitate haste; even
before the excommunication he had refuted with the
same quiet arguments all these accusations. His first

Nov. 13,38.

reply had been in the same calm and dignified
tone.[1] The Pope had commissioned the Bishops
of Wurtzburg, Worms, Vercelli, and Parma to admonish
the Emperor previous to the excommunication. In
their presence, and in that of the Archbishops of Palermo and Messina, the Bishops of Cremona, Lodi,
Novara, and Mantua, many abbots, and some Dominican and Franciscan friars, he had made to all their
charges a full and satisfactory answer, and delivered his
justification to the Bishops:—I. He had encouraged no
insurrection in Rome; he had assisted the Pope with
men and money; he had no concern in the new feuds.
II. He had never even dreamed of arresting the Cardinal of Praeneste, though he might have found just
cause, since the Cardinal, acting for the Pope, had
inflamed the Lombards to disobedience and rebellion.
III. He could give no answer to the vague and unspe-
cified charges as to the oppression of the clergy in the
realm of Naples; and as to particular churches he
entered into long and elaborate explanations.[b] IV. He

---

[1] Peter de Vineis, l. 21, p. 156.
The refutation of the charges, according to Matthew Paris (sub ann. 1239),

was anterior to the excommunication.

[b] See especially, in a letter in

had restored all the lands to which the Templars and
Knights of St. John had just claim; all but those which
they had unlawfully received from his enemies during
his minority; they had been guilty of aiding his
enemies during the invasion of the kingdom, and some
had incurred forfeiture: their lands, in certain cases,
were assessable; were this not so, they would soon
acquire the whole realm, and that exempt from all
taxation. V. No one was condemned as a partisan of
the Pope; some had abandoned their estates from fear
of being prosecuted for their crimes. VI. No church
had been desecrated or destroyed in Lucera; that
of Sora was an accident, arising out of the disobedience
of the city; he would rebuild that, and all which had
fallen from age.   The Saracens, who lived scattered
over the whole realm, he had settled in one place, for
the security of the Christians, and to protect rather than
endanger the faith. VII. Abdelasis had fled from the
court of the King of Tunis; he was not a prisoner, but
living a free and pleasant life, furnished with horses,
clothes, and money by the Emperor. He had never
(he appealed to the Archbishops of Palermo and Messina) expressed any desire for baptism. Had he done
so, no one would have rejoiced more than the Emperor.
Peter was no Ambassador of the King of England.
VIII. The pretensions of the Pope to Massa and Ferrara
were groundless, still more to Sardinia, his son Enzio
had married Adelasia, the heiress of that island; he was
the rightful King. IX. The King prevents no one
from preaching the Crusade; he only interferes with

Höfler, his justification for the refusal
to rebuild the church at Sora. The
city had rebelled, had been razed,
church and all, and sown with salt.

Frederick had sworn that the city
should never be again inhabited: why
build a church for an uninhabited
wilderness?

those who, under pretence of preaching a Crusade, preach rebellion against the Sovereign, or, like John of Vicenza, usurp civil power. As to the affairs of Lombardy, the Pope had but interposed delays, to the frustration of his military plans. He would willingly submit to just terms; but after the unmeasured demands of the Lombards, and such manifest hostility on the part of the Pope, it would be dangerous and degrading to submit to the unconditional arbitration of the Pope.

The indignation of Frederick might seem to burst out with greater fury from this short, stern suppression. He determined boldly, resolutely, to measure his strength, the strength of the Emperor, the King of Sicily, so far the conqueror (notwithstanding the failure before Brescia) of the Lombard republics, against the strength of the Popedom. The Pope had declared war on causes vague, false or insignificant; the true cause of the war, Frederick's growing power and his successes in Lombardy, the Pope could not avow; Frederick would appeal to Christendom, to the world, on the justice of his cause and the unwarranted enmity of the Pope. He addressed strong and bitter remonstrances to the Cardinals, to the Roman people, to all the Sovereigns of Christendom. To the Cardinals he had already written, though his letter had not reached Rome before the promulgation of the excommunication, admonishing them to moderate the hasty resentment of the Pope. He endeavoured to separate the cause of the Pope from that of the Church; but vengeance against Gregory and the family of Gregory could not satisfy the insulted dignity of the Empire; if the authority of the Holy See, and the weight of their venerable college, thus burst all restraint, he must use all measures of

March 19.

defence; injury must be repelled with injury.[a] Some
of the Cardinals had endeavoured to arrest the precipitate wrath of Gregory: he treated their timid prudence with scorn. To the Romans the Emperor expressed his indignant wonder that Rome being the head
of the Empire, the people, without reverence for his
majesty, ungrateful for all his munificence, had heard
tamely the blasphemies of the Roman Pontiff against
the Sovereign of Rome; that of the whole tribe of
Romulus there was not one bold patrician, of so many
thousand Roman citizens not one, who uttered a word of
remonstrance, a word of sympathy with their insulted
Lord. He called on them to rise and to revenge the
blasphemy upon the blasphemer, and not to allow him to
glory in his presumption, as if they consented to his audacity.[b] As he was bound to assert the honour of Rome,
so were they to defend the dignity of the Roman Emperor.

Before all the temporal Sovereigns of the world, the
Emperor entered into a long vindication of all
his acts towards the Church and the Pope;
he appealed to their justice against the unjust
and tyrannous hierarchy. "Cast your eyes around!
lift up your ears, O sons of men, that ye may hear!
behold the universal scandal of the world, the dissensions of nations, lament the utter extinction of justice!
Wickedness has gone out from the Elders of Babylon,
who hitherto appeared to rule the people, whilst judgement is turned into bitterness, the fruits of justice into
wormwood. Sit in judgement, ye Princes, ye People

Appeal to the Princes of Christendom, April III.

---

[a] Apud Petrum de Vineâ, L. vi.

[b] "Quia cum idem blasphemator noster ausus non fuisset in nostri nominis blasphemiam prorumpere, de tantâ praesumptione gloriari non possit,

quod valentibus et videntibus Romanis, contra nos talia perpetrasset," &c.— Apud Petr. de Vin. L. vii. Math. Par. 332.

take cognisance of our cause; let judgement go forth
from the face of the Lord and your eyes behold equity."
The Papal excommunication had dwelt entirely on
occurrences subsequent to the peace of San Germano.
The Emperor went back to the commencement of the
Pope's hostility: he dwelt on his ingratitude, his cause-
less enmity. "He, who we hoped thought only of
things above, contemplated only heavenly things, dwelt
only in heaven, was suddenly found to be but a man;
even worse, by his acts of inhumanity is not only a
stranger to truth, but without one feeling of humanity."
He charged the Pope with the basest duplicity;[a] he
had professed the firmest friendship for the Emperor,
while by his letters and his Legates he was acting the
most hostile part.[b] This charge rested on his own letters, and the testimony of his factious accomplices.
The Pope had called on the Emperor to defy, and wage
war against, the Romans on his behalf, and at the same
time sent secret letters to Rome that this war was
waged without his knowledge or command, in order to
excite the hatred of the Romans against the Emperor.
Rome, chiefly by his power, had been restored to the
obedience of the Pope; what return had the Pope
made? — befriending the Lombard rebels in every
manner against their rightful Lord![c] No sooner had

---

[a] "Asserens quod nobis omnia
placabimus faciebat, cujus contrarium
per conscium et literas manifeste pro-
curaret; prout constat testimonio
plurium nostrorum fidelium qui tunc
temporis erant omnium consilii velut
ex eis quidam participes, et alii principes factiosis."

[b] He brought the charge against
the Pope of writing letters to the
Sultan, dissuading him from making

peace, letters which he declared had
fallen into his hands.

[c] "Audite mirabilem circumven-
tionis modum ad depressionem nostræ
justitiæ excogitatum. Dum pacem
cum nobis habere velle se simularet
ut Lombardos ad tempos, per treugar-
rum suffragia, respirantes, contra nos
fortius postmodum in rebelliones con-
firmet."—Epist. ad H. R. Angliæ.
Rymer, sub ann. 1238.

he raised a powerful army of Germans to subdue these
rebels, than the Pope inhibited their march, alleging
the general truce proclaimed for the Crusade.   The
Legate, the Cardinal of Præneste, whose holy life the
Pope so commended, had encouraged the revolt of Piacenza.   Because he could find no just cause for his
excommunication, the Pope had secretly sent letters
and Legates through the Empire, through the world,
to seduce his subjects from their allegiance.   He had
promised the ambassadors of Frederick, the Archbishop
of Palermo, the Bishops of Florence and Reggio, the
Justiciary Thaddeus of Suessa, and the Archbishop of
Messina, that he would send a Legate to the Emperor
to urge the Lombards to obedience; but in the mean
time he sent a Legate to Lombardy to encourage and
inflame their resistance.   Notwithstanding his answer
to all the charges against him, which had made the
Bishops of the Papal party blush by their completeness;[f] notwithstanding this unanswerable refutation,
the Pope had proceeded on Palm Sunday, and on
Thursday in the Holy Week, to excommunicate him
on these charges; this at the instigation of a few Lombard Cardinals, most of the better Cardinals, if report
speaks true, remonstrating against the act.   "Be it
that we had offended the Pope by some public and
singular insult, how violent and inordinate these proceedings, as though, if he had not vomited forth the
wrath that boiled within him, he must have burst!   We
grieve from our reverence for our Mother the Church!
Could we accept the Pope, thus our avowed enemy, no
equitable judge, to arbitrate in our dispute with Milan;

---

[f] " Quamquam de patris instabilitate confusos et filii reputasset, ao vere-
cundiâ capitis rubor ora perfunderet."—p. 156.

Milan, favoured by the Pope, though by the testimony
of all religious men, swarming with heretics?"[*]   "We
hold Pope Gregory to be an unworthy Vicar of Christ,
an unworthy successor of St. Peter; not in disrespect
to his office, but of his person, who sits in his court like
a merchant weighing out dispensations for gold, himself
signing, writing the bulls, perhaps counting the money.
He has but one real cause of enmity against me, that I
refused to marry to his niece my natural son Enzio,
now King of Sardinia.   But ye, O Kings and Princes
of the earth, lament not only for us, but for the whole
Church; for her head is sick; her prince is like a
roaring lion; in the midst of her sits a frantic prophet,
a man of falsehood, a polluted priest!"   He concludes
by calling all the princes of the world to his aid; not
that his own forces are insufficient to repel such injuries,
but that the world may know that when one temporal
prince is thus attacked the honour of all is concerned.

Another Imperial address seems designed for a lower
class, that class whose depths were stirred to
hatred of the Emperor by the Preachers and
the Franciscans.   Its strong figurative language, its
scriptural allusions, its invective against that rapacity
of the Roman See which was working up a sullen discontent even among the clergy, is addressed to all
Christendom.   Some passages must illustrate this strange
controversy.   "The Chief Priests and the Pharisees
have met in Council against their Lord, against the
Roman Emperor.   'What shall we do,' say they, 'for
this man is triumphing over all his enemies?   If we
let him alone, he will subdue the glory of the Lom-

Appeal to the commonalty.

---

[*] This very year Frederick renewed his remorseless edicts against the Lombard heretics.—Feb. 22.   Monument. Germ. i. 326, 7, 8.

lords; and, like another Cæsar, he will not delay to take away our place and destroy our nation. He will hire out the vineyard of the Lord to other labourers, and condemn us without trial, and bring us to ruin.' . . . 'Let us not await the fulfilment of these words of our Lord, but strike him quickly,' say they, 'with our tongues; let our arrows be no more concealed, but go forth; so go forth as to strike, so strike as to wound; so be he wounded as to fall before us, so fall as never to rise again; and then will he see what profit he has in his dreams.'" Thus speak the Pharisees who sit in the seat of Moses. . . . "This father of fathers, who is called the servant of servants, shutting out all justice, is become a deaf adder; refuses to hear the vindication of the King of the Romans; hurls malediction into the world as a stone is hurled from a sling; and sternly, and heedless of all consequences, exclaims, 'What I have written, I have written.'"

In better keeping Frederick alludes to the words of our Lord to his disciples after his resurrection, "That Master of Masters said not, 'Take arms and shield, the arrow, and the sword;' but, 'Peace be with you.'" On the avarice of the Pope he is inexhaustible. "But thou having nothing, but possessing all things, art ever seeking what thou mayest devour and swallow up; the whole world cannot glut the rapacity of thy maw, for the whole world sufficeth thee not. The Apostle Peter, by the Beautiful Gate, said to the lame man, 'I have neither silver nor gold;' but thou, if thy heap of money, which thou adorest, begins to dwindle, immediately beginnest to limp with the lame man, seeking anxiously what is of this world.' . . . Let our Mother

---

¹ In one place he calls him "Gregorius gregis disgregator pessimus."

Church then bewail that the shepherd of the flock is become a ravening wolf, eating the fatlings of the flock; neither binding up the broken, nor bringing the wanderer home to the fold; but a lover of schism, the head and author of offence, the father of deceit; against the rights and honour of the Roman King he protects heretics, the enemies of God and of all the faithful in Christ; having cast aside all fear of God, all respect of man. But that he may better conceal the malice of his heart, he cherishes and protects these enemies of the Cross and of the faith, under a certain semblance of piety, saying that he only aids the Lombards lest the Emperor should slay them, and should judge more rigorously than his justice requires. But this fox-like craft will not deceive the skilful hunter. . . . O grief! rarely dost thou expend the vast treasures of the Church on the poor! But, as Anagni bears witness, thou hast commanded a wonderful mansion, as it were the Palace of the Sun, to be built, forgetful of Peter, who long had nothing but his net; and of Jerusalem, which lies the servant of dogs, tributary to the Saracens; 'All power is from God,' writes the Apostle; 'whoso resists the power resists the authority of God.' Either receive, then, into the bosom of the Church her elder son,[*] who without guile incessantly demands pardon; otherwise, the strong lion, who feigns sleep, with his terrible roar will draw all the fat bulls from the ends of the earth, will plant justice, take the rule over the Church, plucking up and destroying the horns of the proud."[a]

The Pope, in his long and elaborate reply, exceeded even the violence of this fierce Philippic. It is thus

---

"Filium singularem."   [a] Peter de Vineâ, l. 1.

that the Father of the Faithful commences his manifesto against the Emperor in the words of the
Apocalypse: "Out of the sea is a beast arisen, Pope's reply.
whose name is all over written 'Blasphemy;' he has
the feet of a bear, the jaws of a ravening lion, the
mottled limbs of the panther. He opens his mouth to
blaspheme the name of God; and shoots his poisoned
arrows against the tabernacle of the Lord, and the
saints that dwell therein. . . . Already has he laid
his secret ambush against the Church; he openly sets
up the battering engines of the Ishmaelites; builds
schools for the perdition of souls;' lifts himself up
against Christ the Redeemer of man, endeavouring to
efface the tablets of his testament with the pen of
heretical wickedness. Cease to wonder that he has
drawn against us the dagger of calumny, for he has
risen up to extirpate from the earth the name of the
Lord. Rather, to repel his lies by the simple truth, to
refute his sophisms by the arguments of holiness, we
exorcise the head, the body, the extremities of this
beast, who is no other than the Emperor Frederick."

Then follows a full account of the whole of Frederick's former contest with Gregory, in which the Emperor is treated throughout as an unmeasured liar.
"This shameless artisan of falsehood lies when he says
that I was of old his friend." The history of the preparation for the Crusade, and the Crusade is related with
the blackest calumny. To Frederick is attributed the
death of the Crusaders at Brundusium, and the poisoning of the Landgrave of Thuringia insinuated as the
general belief. The suppression of heresy in Lombardy
could not be entrusted to one himself tainted by heresy.

---

^f Gregory no doubt alludes to the universities founded by Frederick.

The insurrections in Lombardy are attributed to the
Emperor's want of clemency; the oppressions of the
Church are become the most wanton and barbarous
cruelties; "the dwellings of Christians are pulled down
to build the walls of Babylon; churches are destroyed
that edifices may be built where divine honours are
offered to Mohammed." The kingdom of Sicily, so
declares the Pope, is reduced to the utmost distress.[1]
By his unexampled cruelties, barons, knights, and others
have been degraded to the state and condition of slaves;
already the greater part of the inhabitants have nothing to
lie upon but hard straw, nothing to cover their nakedness but the coarsest clothes; nothing to appease their
hunger but a little millet bread. The charge of dilapi-
dation of the Papal revenues, of venal avarice, the Pope
repels with indignation: "I, who by God's grace have
greatly increased the patrimony of the Church. He
falsely asserts that I was enraged at his refusing his
consent to the marriage of my niece with his natural
son." He lies more impudently when he says that I

---

[1] Read the Cardinal Gregorio's
sensible account of the taxation of
Sicily by Frederick II. "Occupato
di continuo nelle guerre Italiane, in-
tento a reprimere nei suoi stati i
movimenti dei fazioni, e dalla impla-
cabile ira dei suoi nemici oppresso e
dai Romani Pontefici sempre conter-
nato, ebbe cosi varia e travagliata for-
tuna, e fu in tali angustie di continuo
ridotto, ed ai suoi molti e presenti e
sempre nuovi bisogni più non trovò
gli ordinari proventi della corona, e le
antiche rendite del regno sufficienti,
indi avvenne, che da quel tempo in
poi fu costretto ad ordinare i più
sottili modi, perchè accrescere le
pubbliche entrate, e nuove contri-
buzioni, conservebbè fosse, si procacciasse;
anzi le cose in processo di tempo sopra-
mente e per molta irritazion di animo
si esacerbarono."—t. iii. p. 110. No
doubt, as his finances became more
and more exhausted by war, the burthens must have been heavier. But
the flourishing state of Sicilian commerce and agriculture during the
peaceful period but now elapsed, con-
futes the virulent accusation of the
Pope.

[2] This is not strictly a denial of the
fact of such proposals, or at least of
advances by the Pope. This charge
of early nepotism is curious.

have in return pledged my faith to the Lombards against
the Empire." Throughout the whole document there is
so much of the wild exaggeration of passion, and at the
same time so much art in the dressing out of facts; such
an absence of the grave majesty of religion and the
calm simplicity of truth, as to be surprising even when
the provocations of Frederick's addresses are taken into
consideration. But the heaviest charge was reserved
for the close. " In truth this pestilent King maintains
to use his own words, that the world has been deceived
by three impostors;[b] Jesus Christ, Moses, and Mahomet: the two of these died in honour, the Charge about
the three im-
postors.
third was hanged on a tree. Even more, he
has asserted distinctly and loudly that those are fools
who aver that God, the Omnipotent Creator of the
world, was born of a Virgin."

Such was the blasphemy of which the Pope arraigned
the Emperor before Christendom. Popular rumour had
scattered abroad through the jealousy of the active
priesthood, and still more through the wandering Friars,
many other sayings of Frederick equally revolting to
the feelings of the age; not merely that which contrasted the fertility of his beloved Sicily with the Holy
Land, but sayings which were especially scornful as to
the presence of Christ in the sacrament. When he
saw the host carried to a sick person, he is accused of
saying, "How long will this mummery last?"[c] When a
Saracen prince was present at the mass, he asked what
was in the monstrance: "The people fable that it is
our God." Passing once through a corn-field, he said,

---

[b] A book was said to have existed
at this time, with this title; it has
never been discovered. I have seen

a vulgar production with the title, of
modern manufacture.

[c] " Quam diu durabit Truffa ista?"

"How many Gods might be made out of this corn?"
"If the princes of the world would stand by him he
would easily make for all mankind a better faith and
better rule of life."[4]

Frederick was not unconscious of the perilous work-
ings of these direct and indirect accusations upon the
popular mind. He hastened to repel them; and to
turn the language of the Apocalypse against his accuser.
He thus addressed the bishops of Christendom.
After declaring that God had created two great
lights for the guidance of mankind, the Priesthood and
the Empire:—"He, in name only Pope, has called us
the beast that arose out of the sea, whose name was
Blasphemy, spotted as the panther. We again aver that
he is the beast of whom it is written, 'And there went
out another horse that was red, and power was given to
him that sat thereon to take away peace from the earth,
that the living should slay each other.' For from the
time of his accession this Father, not of mercies but of
discord, not of consolation but of desolation, has plunged
the whole world in bitterness. If we rightly interpret
the words, he is the great anti-Christ, who has deceived
the whole world, the anti-Christ of whom he declares
us the forerunner. He is a second Balaam hired by
money to curse us; the prince of the princes of darkness who have abused the prophecies. He is the angel
who issued from the abyss having the vials full of wormwood to waste earth and heaven." The Emperor dis-
claims in the most emphatic terms the speech about the
three impostors; rehearses his creed, especially concern-

(marginal note) Frederick's rejoinder.

---

4 Peter de Vineâ, i. 31. He was said also to have laid down the maxim,
"Homo nihil aliud debet credere, nisi quod potest vi et ratione naturæ pro-
bare."—Apud Raynald.

ing the Incarnation, in the orthodox words; expresses
the most reverential respect for Moses: "As to Mahomet, we have always maintained that his body is
suspended in the air, possessed by devils, his soul tor-
mented in hell, because his works were works of darkness and contrary to the laws of the Most High." The
address closed with an appeal to the sounder wisdom of
the Prelates, and significant threats of the terrors of his
vengeance.

The effect of **this war of** proclamations, **addressed,**
only with a separate superscription, to every
King in Christendom, circulated in every   July 1.
kingdom, **was** to fill the hearts of the faithful **with**
terror, amazement, and perplexity. Those who **had**
espoused neither the party of the Emperor nor of **the**
Pope fluctuated in painful doubt. The avarice of **the**
Roman See had alienated to a great extent the devotion
of mankind, otherwise the letter of the Pope would
have exasperated the world to madness; they would
have risen in one wide insurrection against the   Public
declared adversary of the Church, as the   opinion in
                                             Christendom.
enemy of Christ. "But alas!" so writes a contemporary
historian, "many sons of the Church separated themselves from their father the Pope, and joined the Emperor, well knowing the inexorable hatred between the
Pope and the Emperor, and that from that hatred sprung
these fierce, indecent and untrustworthy invectives.
The Pope, some said, pretends that from his love to
Frederick he had contributed to elevate him to the
Empire, and reproaches him with ingratitude. But it is
notorious that this was entirely out of hatred to Otho,
whom the Pope persecuted to death for asserting the
interests of the Empire, as Frederick now asserts them.
Frederick fought the battle of the Church in Palestine,

which is under greater obligation to him than he to the
Church. The whole Western Church, especially the
monasteries, are every day ground by the extortions of
the Romans; they have never suffered any injustice
from the Emperor. The people subjoined, 'What means
this? A short time ago the Pope accused the Emperor
of being more attached to Mohammedanism than to
Christianity, now he is accused of calling Mohammed
an impostor. He speaks in his letters in the most
Catholic terms. He attacks the person of the Pope,
not the Papal authority. We do not believe that he
has ever avowed heretical or profane opinions; at all
events he has never let loose upon us usurers and plun-
derers of our revenues.'"*

This was written in an English monastery. In England as most heavily oppressed, there was the strongest
discontent. The feeble Henry III., though brother-in-
law of the Emperor, trembled before the faintest whisper
of Papal authority. But the nobles, even the Churchmen, began to betray their Teutonic independence.
Robert Twenge, the Yorkshire knight, the ringleader
of the insurrection against the Italian intruders into the
English benefices, ventured to Rome, not to throw himself at the Pope's feet and to entreat his pardon, but
with a bold respectful letter from the Earls of Chester,
Winchester, and other nobles, remonstrating against the
invasion of their rights of patronage. Gregory was
compelled to condescend to a more moderate tone; he
renounced all intention of usurpation on the rights of
the barons. Robert Twenge received the acknowledgment of his right to present to the church of Linton.
All the Prelates of the realm, assembled at London,

* Matt. Paris, sub ann. 1239.

disdainfully rejected the claim made for procurations for the Papal Legate Otho, whom two years before they had allowed to sit as Dictator of the Church in the council of London.[f] "The greedy avarice of Rome," they said, "has exhausted the English Church; it will not give it even breathing time; we can submit to no further exactions. What advantage have we from the visitation of this Legate? Let him that sent him here uninvited by the native clergy, maintain him as long as he remains here." The Legate, finding the Prelates obstinate, extorted a large sum for his procurations from the monasteries.

The Emperor highly resented the publication of the sentence of excommunication in the realm of the brother of his Empress Isabella. He sent a haughty message,[g] expostulating with the King for permitting this insult upon his honour; he demanded the dismissal of the Legate, no less the enemy of the kingdom of England than his own;[h] the Legate who was exacting money from the whole realm to glut the avarice of the Pope, and to maintain the Papal arms against the Emperor. Henry III. sent a feeble request to Rome, imploring the Pope to act with greater mildness to Frederick; the Pope treated the message with sovereign contempt. Nor did the Legate behave with less insolent disdain to the King. Henry advised him to

[f] Wilkins, Concilia, 1237. Compare page 216.

[g] Letters to the Barons of England (Rochester, Oct. 29, 1239), Rymer, 1238? To the King, March 16, 1240. Matt. Paris, 1239.

[h] Henry, before the declaration of the Pope against the Emperor, had sent a small force, under Henry de Turberville and the Bishop Elect of Valence, to aid Frederick against the insurgent Lombards. The army was accompanied by a citizen and a clerk of London, John Mansel and W. Hardel, with money.—Paris, sub ann. 1238, Matt. West. The Pope broke out into fury against the King.

quit the kingdom; "You invited me here, find me
a safe-conduct back." In the mean time he proceeded
again to levy his own procurations, to sell (so low was
the Pope reduced), by Gregory's own orders, dispensations to those who had taken on them vows to proceed
to the Holy Land. At length, at a council held at
Reading, he demanded a fifth of all the revenues of the
English clergy, in the name of the Pope to assist him in
his holy war against the Emperor. Edmund Rich the
Primate yielded to the demand, and was followed by
others of the bishops.[1] But Edmund, worn out with
age and disgust, abandoned his see, withdrew into
France, and in the same monastery of Pontigny, imi-
tated the austerities and prayers, as he could not imitate
the terrors, of his great predecessor Becket. The lower
clergy were more impatient of the Papal demands. A
crafty agent of the Pope, Pietro Rosso,[b] (Peter the Red),
travelled about all the monasteries extorting money; he
falsely declared that all the bishops, and many of the
higher abbots, had eagerly paid their contributions.
But he exacted from them, as if from the Pope himself,
a promise to keep his assessment secret for a year. The
abbots appealed to the King, who treated them with
utter disdain. He offered one of his castles to the
Legate and Peter the Red, and to imprison two of the
appellants, the Abbots of St. Edmundsbury and of
Beaulieu. At Northampton the Legate and Peter
again assembled the bishops, and demanded the fifth
from all the possessions of the Church. The bishops
declared that they must consult their archdeacons.
The clergy refused altogether this new levy; they

[1] Edmund had aspired to be a second
Becket; he had raised a quarrel with
the King on the nomination to the
benefices; but feebly supported by
Gregory in his distress, he recoiled
from the contest.   [b] De Rubeis.

would not contribute to a fund raised to shed Christian
blood.   The rectors of Berkshire were more bold; their
answer has a singular tone of fearless English freedom;
" they would not submit to contribute to funds raised
against the Emperor as if he were a heretic; though
excommunicated he had not been condemned by the
judgement of the Church; even if he does occupy the
patrimony of the Church, the Church does not employ
the secular arm against heretics.   The Church of Rome
has its own patrimony, it has no right to tax the
churches of other nations.   The Pope has the general
care over all churches, but no property in their estates.
The Lord said to Peter, ' What you bind on earth shall
be bound in heaven;' not ' What you exact on earth
shall be exacted in heaven.'   The revenues of the
Church were assigned to peculiar uses, for the relief of
the poor, not for maintenance of war, especially among
Christians.   Popes, even when they were exiles and the
Church of England was at its wealthiest, had made no such demands." Yet partly by sowing
discord among his adversaries, partly by flattery, partly
by menace, the Legate continued, to the great indignation of the Emperor, to levy large sums for the Papal
Crusade in the dominions of his brother-in-law.[*]

In France Pope Gregory attempted to play a loftier
game by an appeal to the ambition of the royal house; he would raise up a new French Pepin
or Charlemagne to the rescue of the endan-
gered Papacy.   He sent ambassadors to the court of
St. Louis with this message:—" After mature deliberation with our brethren the Cardinals we have
deposed from the imperial throne the reigning Emperor

---

* M. Paris, sub ann. 1240.

Frederick; we have chosen in his place Robert, brother
of the King of France. Delay not to accept this dignity, for the attainment of which we offer all our
treasures, and all our aid." The Pope could hardly
expect the severe rebuke in which the pious King of
France couched his refusal of this tempting offer.
" Whence this pride and audacity of the Pope, which
thus presumes to disinherit and depose a King who has
no superior, nor even an equal, among Christians; a
King neither convicted by others, nor by his own confession, of the crimes laid to his charge? Even if those
crimes were proved, no power could depose him but a
general council. On his transgressions the judgement
of his enemies is of no weight, and his deadliest enemy
is the Pope. To us he has not only thus far appeared
guiltless, he has been a good neighbour; we see no
cause for suspicion either of his worldly loyalty, or his
Catholic faith. This we know, that he has fought
valiantly for our Lord Jesus Christ both by sea and
land. So much religion we have not found in the
Pope, who endeavoured to confound and wickedly
supplant him in his absence, while he was engaged in
the cause of God." * The nobles of France did more,
they sent ambassadors to Frederick to inform him of
the Pope's proceedings, and to demand account of his
faith. Frederick was moved by this noble conduct.
He solemnly protested his orthodox belief. " May
Jesus Christ grant that I never depart from the faith of
my magnanimous ancestors, to follow the ways of perdition. The Lord judge between me and the man who
has thus defamed me before the world." He lifted his
hands to heaven, and said in a passion of tears: " The

---

* Paris, sub ann. 1239.

God of vengeance recompense him as he deserves. If," he added, " you are prepared to war against me, I will defend myself to the utmost of my power." "God forbid," said the ambassadors, " that we should wage war on any Christian without just cause. To be the brother of the King of France is sufficient honour for the noble Robert."

In Germany the attempt of the Pope to dethrone the Emperor awoke even stronger indignation. Two princes to whom Gregory made secret overtures refused the perilous honour. An appeal to the Prelates of the Empire was met even by the most respectful with earnest exhortations to peace. In one address they declared the universal opinion that the whole quarrel arose out of the unjustifiable support given by the Pope to the Milanese rebels ; and they appealed to the continued residence of the Papal Legate, Gregory of Monte Longo, in Milan as manifesting the Pope's undeniable concern in that obstinate revolt.[a] Popular German poetry denounced the Pope as the favoured of the Lombard heretics, who had made him drunk with their gold.[b] Gregory himself bitterly complains " that the German princes and prelates still adhered to Frederick, the oppressor, the worse than assassin, who imprisons them, places them under the ban of the Empire, even puts them to death. Nevertheless they despise the Papal anathema, and maintain his cause."[c] Gregory was not fortunate or not wise in the choice of his

---

[a] Apud Huba, Monument. t. i. p. 234. "Testimonium generalis opinionis quod in favorem Mediolanensium, et maurum arguendum procurantibus taliter contra eum . . . quod G. de Monte Longo legatus vester, apud Mediolanenses continuam moram trahens, fideles im-

perii modis omnibus, quibus potest, a fide et devotione debitâ nititur revocare."

[b] See the quotation from Bruder Weinher, the Minnsinger, in Giesebr.

[c] Dumont apud Von Raumer.

partisans. One of those partisans, Rainer of St. Quentin,
presumed to summon the German prelates to answer at
Paris for their disloyal conduct to the Pope. The Pope
Albert of
Beham. had invested Albert von Beham Archdeacon
of Passau, a violent and dissolute man, with
full power; he used it to threaten bishops and even
archbishops, he dared to utter sentences of excommunication against them. He alarmed the Duke of Bavaria
into the expression of a rash desire that they had
another Emperor. It was on Otho of Bavaria that
Albert strove to work with all the terrors of delegated
papal power. There was a dispute between the Archbishop of Mentz and Otho concerning the convent of
Laurisheim. Albert as Papal Legate summoned the
Primate to appear at Heidelberg. The archbishop not
appearing was declared contumacious; an interdict was
laid on Mentz. In another quarrel of Otho with the
Bishop of Freisingen the imperialist judges awarded a
heavy fine against Otho. Von Beham, irritated by
songs in the streets, "The Pope is going down, the
Emperor going up," [r] rescinded the decree on the Pope's
authority, and commanded the institution of a new suit.
Von Beham ordered the Archbishop of Saltzburg and
the Bishop of Passau to excommunicate Frederick of
Austria for his adherence to the Emperor; summoned a
council at Landshut; placed Siegfried Bishop of Ratis-
A.D. 1240. bon, the Chancellor of the Empire, under the
ban; threatened to summon the Archbishop
of Saltzburg and the Bishop to arraign them under
processes of treason; "he would pluck their mitres from
their heads." The Bishop of Passau, in his resentment,
threatened to arm his men in a Crusade against Albert

---

[r] "Ruit pars Papalis, prævaluit Imperialis."

von Beham. Albert did not confine himself to Bavaria,
he threatened the Bishops of Augsburg, Wurtzburg,
Eichstadt, with the same haughty insolence. The consequence of all this contempt thus thrown on the greatest
prelates was, that the imperialists everywhere gained
courage. The Emperor, the Landgrave of Thuringia,
the Marquis of Meissen, Frederick of Austria, treated
the excommunication as a vulgar ghost, an old wives'
tale.* But the great prelates did not disguise their
wrath; their dislike and contempt for Von Ikham was
extended to his master. " Let this Roman priest," said
Conrad Bishop of Freisingen, " feed his own Italians;
we who are set by God as dogs to watch our own folds,
will keep off all wolves in sheep's clothing." Eberhard
Archbishop of Saltzburg not only applied the same
ignominious term to the Pope, but struck boldly at the
whole edifice of the Papal power; we seem to hear a
premature Luther. He describes the wars, the slaughters,
the seditions, caused by these Roman Flamens, for their
own ambitious and rapacious ends. " Hildebrand, one
hundred and seventy years ago, under the semblance of
religion, laid the foundations of Antichrist. He who is
the servant of servants would be the Lord of Lords. . . .
This accursed man, whom men are wont to call Anti-

* " Ut tremendum olim excommu-
nicationis numero, nova magis quam
compilatam larvam, aut naviculorum
nambra martuerent, probrorum raid cruda
militarium boniouum pertora capi,
angique religionibus, quas sacrificuli
ut vanissimas superstitiones despue-
rent."—Bruanxu, all., quoted in the
preface to the curious publication of
Höfler, " Albert von Beham," Stuttgard, 1847. Frederick of Austria
held a grave assembly of Teutonic
Knights, Templars, and Hospitallers,
three abbots, five mysts. By them
" Alberti impudentia irrisa; exsibilati
qui hoc misero nundinatori operam
prestarrot cujus merces famosque
prater Bohemum Regem, et Bavuis
Ducem nemo estimaret." — Ibid.
" Neque desunt inter sacrificulas
acurrre qui omnia Alberti fulcins,
separent se vel casu peculiari sibs pro-
curaturos,"—p. xix. Albert was in
poverty and disgrace about the time
of Gregory's death, May 8, 1241.—
Höfler, p. 30.

christ, on whose contumelious forehead is written, 'I am
God, I cannot err,' sits in the temple of God and pretends
to universal dominion."[1] Frederick himself addressed a
new proclamation to the princes of Germany. Its object
was to separate the interests of the Church from those
of the Pope; those of the Bishop of Rome from Gregory.
" Since his ancestors the Cæsars had lavished wealth
and dignity on the Popes, they had become the Emperor's most implacable enemies. Because I will not
recognise his sole unlimited power and honour him
more than God, he, Antichrist himself, brands me, the
truest friend of the Church, as a heretic. Who can
wish more than I that the Christian community should
resume its majesty, simplicity, and peace? but this
cannot be, until the fundamental evil, the ambition, the
pride, and prodigality of the Bishop of Rome, be rooted
up. I am no enemy of the priesthood; I honour the
priest, the humblest priest, as a father, if he will keep
aloof from secular affairs. The Pope cries out that I
would root out Christianity with force and by the
sword. Folly! as if the kingdom of God could be
rooted out by force and by the sword; it is by evil
lusts, by avarice and rapacity, that it is weakened, polluted, corrupted. Against these evils it is my mission
of God to contend with the sword. I will give back to
the sheep their shepherd, to the people their bishop, to
the world its spiritual father. I will tear the mask
from the face of this wolfish tyrant, and force him to
lay aside worldly affairs and earthly pomp, and tread in
the holy footsteps of Christ."[2]

[1] Aventinus, Annal. Brunner doubts the authenticity of this speech of the Archbishop of Saltzburg. It rests on the somewhat doubtful authority of Aventinus. It sounds rather of a later date.   [2] Frederick wrote to Otho of Bavaria (Oct. 4, 1240) to expel Albert von Beham from his dominions.—Aventin. Ann. Prior. v. 3, 5.

On the other hand, the Pope had now a force working
in every realm of Christendom, on every class of man
kind, down to the very lowest, with almost irresistible
power. The hierarchical religion of the age, the Papal
religion, with all its congenial imaginativeness, its
burning and unquestioning faith, its superstitions, was
kept up in all its intensity by the preachers and the
mendicant friars. Never did great man so hastily
commit himself to so unwise a determination as Innocent III., that no new Orders should be admitted into
that Church which has maintained its power by the
constant succession of new Orders. Never was his
greatness shown more than by his quick perception and
total repudiation of that error. Gregory IX. might
indeed have more extensive experience of the use of
these new allies : on them he lavished his utmost
favour; he had canonised both St. Dominic and St.
Francis with extraordinary pomp; he entrusted The Friars.
the most important affairs to their disciples. May 6, 1241.
The Dominicans, and still more the Franciscans, showed
at once the wisdom of the Pope's conduct and their own
gratitude by the most steadfast attachment to the Papal
cause. They were the real dangerous enemies of
Frederick in all lands. They were in kings' courts;
the courtiers looked on them with jealousy, but were
obliged to give them place; they were in the humblest
and most retired villages. No danger could appal, no
labours fatigue their incessant activity. The   Nov. 1246
first act of Frederick was to expel, imprison,
or take measures of precaution against those of the
clergy who were avowed or suspected partisans of
the Pope. The friars had the perilous distinction
of being cast forth in a body from the realm, and
forbidden under the severest penalties to violate its

borders.[u]　In every Guelfic city they openly, in every
Ghibelline city, if they dared not openly, they secretly
preached the crusade against the Emperor.[v]　Milan,
chiefly through their preaching, redeemed herself from
the charge of connivance at the progress of heresy by
a tremendous holocaust of victims, burned without
mercy.　The career of John of Vicenza had terminated
before the last strife;[a] but John of Vicenza was the type
of the friar preachers in their height of influence; that
power cannot be understood without some such example;
and though there might be but one John of Vicenza,
there were hundreds working, if with less authority,
conspiring to the same end, and swaying with their con-
joint force the popular mind.

Assuredly, of those extraordinary men who from time
to time have appeared in Italy, and by their
passionate religious eloquence seized and for a
time bound down the fervent Italian mind, not the least
extraordinary was Brother John (Fra Giovanni), of a
noble house in Vicenza.　He became a friar preacher:
he appeared in Bologna.　Before long, not only did the
populace crowd in countless multitudes to his pulpit;
the authorities, with their gonfalons and crosses, stood
around him in mute and submissive homage.　In a short
time he preached down every feud in the city, in the
district, in the county of Bologna.　The women threw
aside their ribbons, their flowers—their modest heads

John of
Vicenza

---

[u] " Capitula elita sunt, in primis
ut Fratres Prædicatores et Minores,
qui sunt oriundi de terris infidelium
Lombardiæ expellantur de regno."—
Rich. de San Germ.　Gregory asserts
that one Friar Minor was burned.—
Greg. Bull. apud Raynald. p. 220.

[v] It is, however, very remarkable

that even now the second Great Master
of the Franciscans, expelled or having
revolted from his Order, Brother Elias,
a most popular preacher, was on the
side of Frederick.

[a] There is an allusion to John of
Vicenza in a letter of Frederick.—
Höfler, p. 363.

were shrouded in a veil. It was believed that he
wrought daily miracles.[a] Under his care the body of
St. Dominic was translated to its final resting-place with
the utmost pomp. It was said, but said by unfriendly
voices, that he boasted of personal conversation with
Christ Jesus, with the Virgin Mary, and with the angels.
The friar preachers gained above twenty thousand marks
of silver from the prodigal munificence of his admirers.
He ruled Bologna with despotic sway; released criminals; the Podestà stood awed before him; the envious
Franciscans alone (their envy proves his power) denied
his miracles, and made profane and buffoonish verses
against the eloquent Dominican.[b]

But the limits of Bologna and her territory were too
narrow for the holy ambition, for the wonderful powers
of the great preacher. He made a progress through
Lombardy. Lombardy was then distracted by fierce
wars—city against city; in every city faction against
faction. Wherever John appeared was peace. Padua
advanced with her carroccio to Monselice to escort
him into the city. Treviso, Feltre, Belluno, Vicenza,
Verona, Mantua, Brescia, heard his magic words, and
reconciled their feuds. On the shores of the Adige,
about three miles from Verona, assembled the   August 21.
whole of Lombardy, to proclaim and to swear   1233.
to a solemn act of peace. Verona, Mantua, Brescia,

---

[a] But, says an incredulous writer,
"Diceuasi ancora ch' egli curasse ogni
malattia, e che cacciasse i demoni; ma
io non potei vedere alcuno da lui
liberato, benchè pure assai ogni giorno
per vederlo; nè potei parlare con
alcuno chè affermasse con sicurezza di
aver veduto qualche miracolo da lui
operato."—Salimbeni.

[b] " Et Johannes Johanninus
Et saltando choralizat, . .
Modo salta, modo saltas,
Qui cantando per te saltas,
Saltat bos, saltat teke,
Hamultaes cohortes militae,
Saltat chorus Dominianum,
Saltat Dux Venetiarum."

—from Salimbeni, Von Raumer, iii.
p. 656.

Padua, Vicenza, came with their carroccios; from Treviso, Venice, Ferrara, Bologna, thronged numberless votaries of peace. The Bishops of Verona, Brescia, Mantua, Bologna, Modena, Reggio, Treviso, Vicenza, Padua, gave the sanction of their sacred presence. The Podestàs of Bologna, Treviso, Padua, Vicenza, Brescia, Ferrara, appeared, and other lords of note, the patriarch of Aquileia, the Marquis of Este. It was asserted that 400,000 persons stood around. John of Vicenza ascended a stage sixty feet high; it was said that his sermon on the valedictory words of the Lord, "My peace I leave with you," was distinctly heard, wafted or echoed by preternatural powers to every ear.* The terms of a general peace were read, and assented to by one universal and prolonged acclamation. Among these was the marriage of Rinaldo, son of the Marquis of Este, with Adelaide daughter of Alberic, brother of Eccelin da Romano. This was the gage of universal amity; these two great houses would set the example of holy peace. Men rushed into each other's arms; the kiss of peace was interchanged by the deadliest enemies, amid acclamations which seemed as if they would never cease.

But the waters of the Po rise not with more sudden and overwhelming force, ebb not with greater rapidity, than the religious passions of the Italians, especially the passion for peace and concord. John of Vicenza split on the rock fatal always to the powerful spiritual demagogues, even the noblest demagogues, of Italy. He became a politician. He retired to his native Vicenza; entered into the Council, aspired to be Lord and Count;

* Even the Franciscans were carried away by the enthusiasm; they preached upon his miracles; they averred that he had in one day raised ten dead bodies to life.

all bowed before him. He proceeded to examine and
reform the statutes of the city. He passed to Verona,
demanded and obtained sovereign power; introduced
the Count Boniface, received hostages for mutual peace
from the conflicting parties. He took possession of some
of the neighbouring castles; waged fierce war with heretics; burned sixty males and females of some of the
noble families; published laws. Vicenza became jealous
of Verona; Padua leagued with Vicenza to throw off
the yoke. The Preacher, at the head of an armed force,
appeared at the gates, demanded the unconditional surrender of the walls, towers, strongholds of the city. He
was repelled, discomfited, by the troops of Padua and
Vicenza, taken, and cast into prison.

He was released by the intercession of Pope Gregory
IX.[4] The peace of Lombardy was then accordant to
the Papal policy, because it was embarrassing to Frederick II. He returned to Verona; but the spell of his
power was broken. He retired to Bologna, to obscurity.
Bologna even mocked his former miracles. Florence
refused to receive him: "Their city was populous
enough; they had no room for the dead which he would
raise."[*]

Christendom awaited in intense anxiety the issue of
this war—a war which, according to the declaration
of the Emperor, would not respect the sacred person

---

[4] It is said that he was afterwards
commissioned by Innocent IV. to proclaim the Papal absolution in Vicenza,
from excommunication incurred by the
succours furnished by that city to
Frederick II. and Ecelin da Romano.
Tiraboschi has collected all the authorities on John of Vicenza with his usual
industry. — Storia della Lit. Ital.,

vol. xiv. p. 2.

[*] See in Von Raumer how the Gram-
marian Buoncompagni assembled the
people to see him fly, on wings which
he had prepared. After keeping them
some time in suspense, he coolly said,
"This is a miracle after the fashion of
John of Vicenza."—Von Raumer,
from Salimbeni.

of the Pope, and would enforce, if Frederick were
victorious, the absolute, unlimited supremacy of the
temporal power.   This war was now proclaimed and
inevitable.   The Pope must depend on his own armies
and on those of his Italian allies.   The tenths and the
fifths of England and of France might swell the Papal
treasury, and enable him to pay his mercenary troops;
but there was no sovereign, no army of Papal partisans
beyond the Alps which would descend to his rescue.
The Lombards might indeed defend their own cities
against the Emperor,[f] and his son King Enzio,
who was declared imperial vicar in the north
of Italy, was at the head of the Germans and Saracens
of the Imperial army, and had begun to display his
great military skill and activity.   The strength of the
maritime powers, who had entered into the league, was
in their fleets; though at a later period Venetian forces
appeared before Ferrara.   The execution of Tiepolo the
podestà of Milan, taken at the battle of Corte Nuova,
had enflamed the resentment of that republic: they
seemed determined to avenge the insult and wrong to
that powerful and honoured family.   But the Pope,
though not only his own personal dignity, but even the
stability of the Roman See was on the hazard, with the
calm dauntlessness which implied his full reliance on
his cause as the cause of God, confronted the appalling
crisis.   Some bishops sent to Rome by Frederick were
repelled with scorn.   The Pope, as the summer heats
came on, feared not to leave fickle Rome: he retired, as

May 20, 1239.

[f] The legate of the Pope, Gregory
of Monte Longo, at Milan, raised the
banner of the Cross—"complo mandato
ejus signo crucis, et paratis duobus
vexillis cum crucibus et clavibus intus"
—marched towards Lodi, destroying
church towers (turres ecclesiarum) and
ravaging the harvests.—D. Muratori
Chronicon, p. 177.

usual, to his splendid palace at Anagni. During the
rest of that year successes and failures seemed nearly
balanced. Treviso threw off the imperial
yoke; even Ravenna, supported by a Venetian   April, 1239.
fleet, rebelled. The Emperor sat down before Bologna,
obtained some great advantages humiliating to the
Bolognese, but, as usual, failed in his attempt to capture the town. These successes before Bologna
were balanced by failure, if not defeat, before   September.
Milan. Bologna was not so far discomfited but that she
could make an attack on Modena. In November the
Pope returned to Rome : he was received with the
utmost honour, with popular rejoicings. He   Nov. 1239.
renewed in the most impressive form the excommunication of the Emperor and all his sons, dis-
tinguishing with peculiar rigour the King Enzio.

The Emperor passed the winter in restoring peace in
Ghibelline Pisa. The feud in Pisa was closely connected
with the affairs of Sardinia. Pisa claimed the sovereignty of that island, which the all-grasping Papacy
declared a fief of the Roman See. Ubaldo, of the noble
Guelfic house of Visconti, had married Adelasia, the

---

* The castles of Piumazzo and Cre-
vacuore were taken. Piumazzo was
burned; the captain of the garrison
was burned in the castle: 500 taken
prisoners.—July.

b The Sardinian affair was another
instance of the way in which an assertion once made that a certain territory
or right belonged to the See of St.
Peter, grew up into what was held to
be an indefeasible title. The Popes
had made themselves the successors of
the Eastern Emperors. Their own
declaration that Naples was a fief of

the Holy See (having been acknowledged by the Normans to piece out
their own usurpation) became a legal
inalienable dominion. The claim to
Sardinia rested on nothing more than
the assertion that it was a part of the
territory of the Roman See (it was no
acknowledged part of the inheritance
of the Countess Matilda).—Rich. de
San Germ. The strange pretension
that all islands belonged to the See of
Rome, as well as all lands conquered
from heretics, if already heard, was not
yet an axiom of the canon law.

heiress of the native Judge or Potentate of Gallura and
of Tura: he bought the Papal absolution from a sentence of excommunication and the recognition of his
title by abandoning the right of Pisa, and acknowledging the Papal sovereignty. Pisa heard this act of
treason with the utmost indignation. The Gherardesci,
the rival Ghibelline house, rose against the
Visconti. Ubaldo died; and Frederick (this
was among the causes of Gregory's deadly hatred)
married the heiress Adelasia to his natural son, whom
he proclaimed king of Sardinia. The Ghibellines of
Pisa recognised his title.

With the early spring the Emperor, at the head of an
imposing, it might seem irresistible force, advanced into the territories of the Church. Foligno threw open her gates to welcome him. Other
cities from fear or affection, Viterbo from hatred of
Rome, hailed his approach. Ostia, Civita Castellana,
Corneto, Sutri, Montefiascone, Toscanella received the
enemy of the Pope. The army of John of Colonna,
which during the last year had moved into the March
against King Enzio, was probably occupied at some
distance: Rome might seem to lie open; the Pope was
at the mercy of his foes. Could he depend on the fickle
Romans, never without a strong Imperial faction?
Gregory, like his predecessors, made his last bold,
desperate, and successful appeal to the religion of the
Romans. The hoary Pontiff set forth in solemn procession, encircled by all the cardinals, the whole long
way from the Lateran to St. Peter's. The wood of the
true cross, the heads of St. Peter and St. Paul were
borne before him; all alike crowded to receive his benediction. The Guelfs were in a paroxysm of devotion,
which spread even among the overawed and unresisting

Ghibellines.[1] In every church of the city was the solemn mass; in every pulpit of the city the friars of St. Dominic and St. Francis appealed to the people not to desert the Vicar of Christ, Christ himself in his Vicar; they preached the new Crusade, they distributed crosses to which were attached the same privileges of pardon, and so of eternal life, if the wearers should fall in the glorious conflict, awarded to those who fought or fell for the holy sepulchre of Christ.

To these new crusaders Frederick showed no compassion; whoever was taken with the cross was put to death without mercy, even if he escaped more cruel and ignominious indignities before his death.

The Emperor was awed, or was moved by respect for his venerable adversary: he was either not strong enough, or not bold enough to march at once on Rome, and so to fulfil his own menaces. He retired into Apulia; some overtures for reconciliation were made; Frederick endeavoured to detach the Pope from his allies, and to induce him to make a separate peace. But the Pope, perhaps emboldened by the return of some of his legates with vast sums of money from England and other foreign countries, resolutely refused to abandon the Lombard League.[b] Up to this time he had affected to disavow his close alliance, still to hold the lofty tone of a mediator; now he nobly determined to be true to their cause. He bore the remonstrances, on this, perhaps on some other cause of quarrel, of his ablest general, the Cardinal John

March, 1240.

---

[1] According to the B. Mountain Chronicle, he laid down his crown on the reliques and appealed to them— "Vos, Sancti, defendite Romam, si homines Romani nollent defendere."

The greater part of the Romans at once took the Cross, p. 182.

[b] Peter de Vineis, l. 16. Caus. Lect. Œfvls Script. Bohum. l. 608.

Colonna. Colonna had agreed to a suspension of arms,
which did not include the Lombards; this the Pope
refused to ratify. Colonna declared that he would not
break his plighted faith to the Emperor. "If thou
obeyest not," said the angry Pope, "I will no longer
own thee for a cardinal." "Nor I thee," replied Colonna,
"for Pope." Colonna joined the Ghibelline cause, and
carried over the greater part of his troops.[*]

Ferrara in the mean time was for ever lost to the
Imperialist side. Salinguerra, the aged and faithful
partisan of the Emperor, was compelled to
capitulate to a strong force, chiefly of Venetians. They seized his person by an act of flagrant
treachery: for five years Salinguerra languished in a
Venetian prison.

April.

The Emperor advanced again from the South, wasted
the Roman territory, and laid siege to Benevento, which made an obstinate resistance.
The Emperor was at San Germano; but instead of
advancing towards Rome, he formed the siege
of Faenza.

May.

August.

The Pope meditated new means of defence. Imperial armies were not at his command; he determined
to environ himself with all the majesty of a spiritual
sovereign; he would confront the Emperor at
the head of the hierarchy of Christendom;
he issued a summons to all the prelates of Europe for a
General Council to be held in the Lateran palace at
Easter in the ensuing year; they were to consult on
the important affairs of the Church.

A.D. 1241.

The Emperor and the partisans of the Emperor had
appealed to a general Council against the Pope; but a

---

[*] This quarrel was perhaps rather later in point of time.

Council in Rome, presided over by the Pope, was not
the tribunal to which they would submit. Frederick
would not permit the Pope, now almost in his power,
thus to array himself in all the imposing dignity of the
acknowledged Vicar of Christ. He wrote a Sept. 13,
circular letter to the Kings and Princes of 1240.
Europe, declaring that he could not recognise nor suffer
a Council to assemble, summoned by his arch-enemy,
to which those only were cited who were his declared
foes, either in actual revolt, or who, like the English
prelates, had lavished their wealth to enable the Pope
to carry on the war. "The Council was convened not
for peace but for war." Nor had the summons been
confined to hostile ecclesiastics. His temporal enemies,
the Counts of Provence and St. Bonifazio, the Marquis
of Este, the Doge of Venice, Alberic da Romano, Paul
Traversaria, the Milanese, were invited to join this un-
hallowed assembly. So soon as the Pope would abandon
the heretical Milanese, reconciliation might at once
take place; he was prepared to deliver his son Conrad
as hostage for the conclusion of such peace. He called
on the Cardinals to stand forth; they were bound by
their duty to the Pope, but not to be the slaves of his
passion. He appealed to their pride, for the Pope, not
content with their counsel, had summoned prelates from
all, even the remotest parts of the world, to sit in
judgement on affairs of which they knew nothing.[*] To
the Prelates of Europe he issued a more singular warning. All coasts, harbours, and ways were beset by his
fleet, which covered the seas: "From him who spared
not his own son, ye may fear the worst. If ye reach

---

* Quoted from Pet. de Vin. in Bibl. Barberina, No. 2139, by Von Raumer,
p. 96.

Rome, what perils await you! Intolerable heat, foul
water, unwholesome food, a dense atmosphere, flies,
scorpions, serpents, and men filthy, revolting, lost to
shame, frantic. The whole city is mined beneath, the
hollows are full of venomous smokes, which the summer
heat quickens to life. And what would the Pope of
you? Use you as cloaks for his iniquities, the organ-
pipes on which he may play at will. He seeks but his
own advantage, and for that would undermine the
freedom of the higher clergy; of all those perils, perils
to your revenues, your liberties, your bodies, and your
souls, the Emperor, in true kindness, would give you
this earnest warning." Many no doubt were deterred
by these remonstrances and admonitions. Yet zeal or
fear gathered together at Genoa a great concourse of
ecclesiastics. The Legate, Cardinal Otho, brought
many English prelates; the Cardinal of Palestrina
appeared at the head of some of the greatest dignitaries
of France; the Cardinal Gregory, of Monte Longo,
with some Lombard Bishops, hastened to Genoa, to
urge the instant preparation of the fleet, which was to
convey the foreign prelates to Rome.* Frederick was
seized with apprehension at the meeting of the Council.
He tried to persuade the prelates to pass by land
through the territories occupied by his forces; he
offered them safe conduct. The answer was that they
could have no faith in one under excommunication.
They embarked on board the hostile galleys of Genoa.
But Frederick had prepared a powerful fleet in Sicily
and Apulia, under the command of his son Enzio.
Pisa joined him with all her galleys. The Genoese

* The Pope expressed great anger | of overwhelming force. See his con-
against the Cardinal Gregory of Monte | solatory letter to the captive bishops,
Longo, for not having provided a fleet | Raynald, p. 273.

Admiral, who had the ill-omened name Ubbriaco, the
Drunkard, was too proud or too negligent to
avoid the hostile armament. They met off $^{\text{May 3. 1241.}}$
the island of Meloria ; the heavily-laden Genoese vessels were worsted after a sharp contest ; three galleys
were sunk, twenty-two taken, with four thousand
Genoese.[f] Some of the prelates perished in the sunken
galleys ; among the prisoners were three Cardinals, the
Archbishops of Rouen, Bordeaux, Auch, and Besançon ;
the Bishops of Carcassonne, Agde, Nismes, Tortona,
Asti, Pavia, the Abbots of Clairvaux, Citeaux, and
Clugny ; and the delegates from the Lombard cities,
Milan, Brescia, Piacenza, Genoa.[g] The vast wealth
which the Cardinal Otho had heaped up in England
was the prize of the conqueror. The Prelates, already
half dead with sea-sickness and fright, no doubt with
very narrow accommodation, crowded together in the
heat and closeness of the holds of narrow vessels, exposed to the insults of the rude seamen and the lawless Ghibelline soldiery, had to finish their voyage to
Naples, where they were treated with greater or less
hardship, according as they had provoked the animosity
of the Emperor. But all were kept in rigid custody.[h]
Letters from Louis of France, almost rising to menace,
and afterwards an embassy, at the head of which was
the Abbot of Clugny (who himself was released before),
demanded and obtained at length the liberation of the

---

[f] The battle was not likely to be
fought without fury. The Genoese
boasted to the Pope that they had
taken three galleys before the battle
began, imbanded all the men, and sunk
the ships. They then complain of the
barbarity of Frederick's sailors, not
only to the innocent prelates, but to
their conductors.

[g] The Archbishops of St. James (of
Compostella), of Arles, of Tarragona,
of Braga, the Bishops of Phacrutia,
Salamanca, Ovven, Astorga, got back
safely to Genoa.—Epist. Laurent. apud
Raynald. p. 270.

[h] Matth. Paris, sub ann. 1241.

French prelates; but the cardinals still languished in
prison till the death of Gregory.

Faenza and Benevento had withstood the Imperial
arms throughout the winter. Faenza had now
fallen; the inhabitants had been treated with
unwonted clemency by Frederick. Benevento too had
fallen. The Papal malediction might seem to have
hovered in vain over the head of Frederick; Heaven
ratified not the decree of its Vicar on earth. On one
side the victorious troops of Frederick, on the other
those of John of Colonna, were wasting the Papal dominions; the toils were gathering around the lair of the
imprisoned Pope. At that time arrived the terrible
tidings of the progress made by the Mongols in Eastern
Europe: already the appalling rumours of their conquests in Poland, Moravia, Hungary, had reached Italy.
The Papal party were loud in their wonder that the
Emperor did not at once break off his war against
the Pope, and hasten to the relief of Christendom. So
blind was their animosity that he was actually accused
of secret dealings with the Mongols; the wicked Emperor had brought the desolating hordes of Zengis-
Khan upon Christian Europe.* But Frederick would
not abandon what now appeared a certain, an immediate
triumph.

Even this awful news seemed as unheard in the camp
of the Emperor, and in the city where the unsubdued
Pope, disdaining any offer of capitulation, defied the
terrors of capture and of imprisonment; he was near
one hundred years old, but his dauntless spirit dictated
these words: " Permit not yourselves, ye faithful, to be
cast down by the unfavourable appearances of the

---

* Matth. Paris, sub ann.

present moment; be neither depressed by calamity nor
elated by prosperity. The bark of Peter is for a time
tossed by tempests and dashed against breakers; but
soon it emerges unexpectedly from the foaming billows,
and sails in uninjured majesty over the glassy surface."[1]
The Emperor was at Fano, at Narni, at Rieti, at Tivoli:
Palestrina submitted to John of Colonna. Even then
the Pope named Matteo Rosso Senator of Rome in place
of the traitor Colonna. Matteo Rosso made a sally
from Rome, and threw a garrison into Lagosta. The
fires of the marauders might be seen from the walls of
Rome; the castle of Monteforte, built by Gre-   July.
gory from the contributions of the Crusaders
and of his own kindred, as a stronghold in which the
person of the Pope might be secure from danger, fell
into the hands of the conqueror; but still no sign of
surrender; still nothing but harsh defiance. The Pope
was released by death from this degradation.
His death has been attributed to vexation; but   August 21.
extreme age, with the hot and unwholesome air of
Rome in August, might well break the stubborn frame
of Gregory at that advanced time of life. Frederick, in
a circular letter addressed to the Sovereigns of Europe,
informed them of the event. "The Pope Gregory IX.
is taken away from this world, and has escaped the
vengeance of the Emperor, of whom he was the implacable enemy. He is dead, through whom peace was
banished from the earth, and discord prospered. For
his death, though so deeply injured and implacably persecuted, we feel compassion; that compassion had been
more profound if he had lived to establish peace between

---

[1] See letter to the Venetians, Lombards, and Bolognese.—Apud Raynald.
p. 271.

the Empire and the Papacy. God, we trust, will raise up a Pope of more pacific temper; whom we are prepared to defend as a devout son, if he follows not the fatal crime and animosity of his predecessor. In these times we more earnestly desire peace, when the Catholic Church and the Empire are alike threatened by the invasion of the Tartars; against their pride it becomes us, the monarchs of Europe, to take up arms."[a] Frederick acted up to this great part of delivering Christendom from the yoke of these terrible savages. Immediately on the death of Gregory he detached King Enzio with four thousand knights, to aid the army of his son Conrad, King of the Romans. The Mongols were totally defeated near the Delphos, a stream which flows into the Danube; to the house of Hohenstaufen Europe and civilisation and Christendom owed this great deliverance.

Frederick suspended the progress of his victorious arms in the Roman territory that the Cardinals might proceed to the election of a new Pope. There were but six Cardinals in Rome; Frederick consented to their supplication that the two imprisoned Cardinals, James and Otho, giving hostages for their return to captivity, should join the conclave. There were fierce dissensions among these eight churchmen; five were for Godfrey of Milan, favoured by the Emperor, three for Romanus. One died, not without suspicion of poison; the Cardinal Otho returned to his captivity; the Emperor, delighted with his honourable conduct, treated him with respectful lenity.[a] In September, the choice to which the Cardinals were compelled by famine, sickness and violence, fell on Godfrey of Milan, a prelate of

Sept. 22.

a Peter de Vin. l. 11.   a Raynald. p. 277.

gentle character and profound learning; in October
Coelestine IV. was dead. The few remain-
ing cardinals left Rome and fled to Anagni.   Oct. 4, 1241.

For nearly two years the Papal throne was vacant.
The King of England remonstrated with the Emperor,
on whom all seemed disposed to throw the blame; the
ambassadors returned to England, if not convinced of
the injustice, abashed by the lofty tone of Frederick.
The King of France sent a more singular menace. He
signified his determination, by some right which he
asserted to belong to the Church of France, through
St. Denys, himself to proceed to the election of a
Pope. Frederick became convinced of the necessity of
such election; none but a Pope could repeal the excommunication of a Pope. In addresses, which rose above
each other in vehemence, he reproached the cardinals
for their dissensions. "Sons of Belial! animals without
heads! sons of Ephraim who basely turned back in the
day of battle! Not Jesus Christ the author of Peace,
but Satan the Prince of the North, sits in the midst of
their conclave, inflaming their discords, their mutual
jealousies. The smallest creatures might read them
a salutary lesson; birds fly not without a leader; bees
live not without a King. They abandon the bark of
the Church to the waves, without a pilot."[v] In the
mean time, he used more effective arguments;   July, 1242.
he advanced on Rome, seized and ravaged the
estates, even the churches, belonging to the Cardinals.
At length they met at Anagni, and in an evil hour for
Frederick the turbulent conclave closed its labours.
The choice fell on a cardinal once connected with the
interests, and supposed to be attached to the person

---

[v] Pet. de Vin. xiv. 17.

of Frederick, Sinibald Fiesco, of the Genoese house
of Lavagna. He took the name of Innocent
IV., an omen and a menace that he would
tread in the footsteps of Innocent III. Frederick was
congratulated on the accession of his declared partisan;
he answered coldly, and in a prophetic spirit: " In the
Cardinal I have lost my best friend; in the Pope I shall
find my worst enemy.   No Pope can be a Ghibelline."

June, 1243.

CHAPTER V.

Frederick and Innocent IV.

YET Frederick received the tidings of the accession of Innocent IV. with all outward appearance of joy. He was at Amalfi; he ordered Te Deum to be sung in all the churches: he despatched the highest persons of his realm, the Archbishop of Palermo, the Chancellor Peter de Vineâ, Thaddeus of Sucera, and the Admiral Ansaldo, to bear his congratulations to the Pope. "An ancient friend of the noble sons of the Empire, you are raised into a Father, by whom the Empire may hope that her earnest prayers for peace and justice may be fulfilled."

Innocent could not reject these pacific overtures; he sent as his ambassadors to Frederick at Amalfi, the Archbishop of Rouen, William formerly Bishop of Modena, and the Abbot of St. Facundas. They were to demand first the release of all the captive prelates and ecclesiastics; to inquire what satisfaction the Emperor was disposed to offer for the crimes, on account of which he lay under excommunication; if the Church (this could scarcely be thought) had done him any wrong, she was prepared to redress such wrong; they were to propose a General Council of temporal and spiritual persons, Kings, Princes, and Prelates. All the adherents of the Church were to be included in the peace. Frederick demanded the withdrawal of the Papal Legate, Gregory di Monte Longo, from Lom-

lardy; he demanded the release of Salinguerra, the
Lord of Ferrara; he complained that honour was shown
to the Archbishop of Mentz, who was under the ban of
the Empire (he had been appointed Papal Legate in

Aug. 22. Germany); that the Pope took no steps to
suppress heresy among the Lombards; that
the Imperial ambassadors were not admitted to the presence of the Pope. It was answered by Innocent, that
the Pope had full right to send his Legates into every
part of Christendom; Salinguerra was the prisoner of
the Venetians, not of the Pope; the Archbishop of
Mentz was a prelate of the highest character, one whom
the Pope delighted to honour; the war waged by the
Emperor prevented the Church from extirpating the
Lombard heretics; it was not the usage of Rome to
admit persons under excommunication to the holy presence of the Pope.

Frederick might seem now at the summit of his
Frederick's power and glory: his fame was untarnished by
period. any humiliating discomfiture; Italy unable to
cope with his victorious armies: the Milanese had suffered a severe check in the territory of Pavia: King
Enzio had displayed his great military talents with
success: the Papal territories were either in his occupation, or with Rome itself were seemingly capable of
no vigorous resistance: his hereditary dominions were
attached to him by affection, the Empire by respect and
awe. He might think that he had full right to demand,
full power to enforce, in the first place, the repeal of his
excommunication. But the star of the Hohenstaufen
had reached its height; it began to decline, to darken;
its fall was almost as rapid and precipitate as its rise
had been slow and stately.

The first inauspicious sign was the defection of Vi-

terbo. The Cardinal Rainier, at the head of the Guelfic
party, drove Frederick's garrison into the cita- Defection of
del, destroyed the houses of the Ghibellines, Viterbo.
and gathered all the troops which he could to defend
the city. Frederick was so enraged at this revolt, that
he declared, "if he had one foot in Paradise, he would
turn back to avenge himself on the treacherous Viterbans."[*] He immediately, unwarned by perpetual failures,
formed the siege. The defence was stubborn, Sept. 8 to
obstinate, successful; his engines were burned, Nov. 13.
he was compelled to retire, stipulating only for the safe
retreat of his garrison from the citadel. Notwithstanding the efforts of Cardinal Otho of Palestrina, who had
guaranteed the treaty, the garrison was assailed, plundered, massacred. To the remonstrance of Frederick,
the Pope, who was still under a kind of truce with the
Emperor, coldly answered, that he ought not to be surprised if a city returned to its allegiance to its rightful
Lord. The fatal example of the revolt of Viterbo
spread in many quarters: the Marquises of Montferrat
and Malespina, the cities of Vercelli and Alexandria
deserted the Imperial party. Even Adelasia, the wife
of King Enzio, sought to be reconciled with the Holy
See. Innocent himself ventured to leave Anagni, and
to enter Rome; the Imperialists were awed at his presence; his reception, as usual, especially with newly
crowned Popes, was tumultuously joyful. The Nov. 18.
only sullen murmurs, which soon after almost
broke out into open discontent, were among the wealthy,
it was said mostly the Jews, who demanded the payment of 40,000 marks, borrowed in his distress by
Gregory IX. Innocent had authority enough to wrest

* Von Raumer, iv. 128.

Q 2

from the Frangipanis half of the Colosseum, and parts
of the adjacent palace, where they no doubt hoped to
raise a strong fortress in the Imperial interest.

The Emperor again inclined to peace, at least to negotiations for peace. The Count of Toulouse, the
Chancellor Peter de Vineâ, and Thaddeus of
Suessa, appeared in Rome with full powers to conclude,
and even to swear and guarantee the fulfilment of a
treaty. The terms were hard and humiliating. The
Emperor was to restore all the lands possessed by the
Pope and the Pope's adherents at the time of the excommunication; the Emperor was to proclaim to all the
sovereigns of Christendom that he had not scorned the
Papal censure out of contempt for the Pope's predecessor, or the rights of the Church; but, by the advice
of the prelates and nobles of Germany and Italy, treated
it as not uttered, since it had not been formally served
upon him; he owned his error on this point, and acknowledged the plenitude of the Papal authority in spiritual
matters. For this offence he was to make such compen-
sation in men or money as the Pope might require;
offer such alms and observe such fasts as the Pope
should appoint; and respect the excommunication until
absolved by the Pope's command. He was to release
all the captive Prelates, and compensate them for their
losses. These losses and all other damages were to be
left to the estimation of three Cardinals. Full amnesty
was to be granted, the imperial ban revoked against all
who had adhered to the Church since the excommunication. This was to be applied, as far as such offences,
to all who were in a state of rebellion against the Emperor. The differences between the Emperor and his
revolted subjects were to be settled by the Pope and
the College of Cardinals within a limited time to be

Treaty.
March 31.
1244.

fixed by the Pope. But there was a saving clause,
which appeared to extend over the whole treaty, of the
full undiminished rights of the Empire.[b] The Emperor
was to be released from the excommunication by a
public decree of the Church. To these and the other
articles the imperial ambassadors swore in the presence
of the Emperor Baldwin of Constantinople, the Cardinals, the Senators, and people of Rome. The Emperor did not disclaim the terms proposed by his ambassadors; but in the treaty there were some
fatal flaws, which parties each so mistrustful, March 31. 1214.
and justly mistrustful of the other, could not but discern, and which rendered the fulfilment of the treaty
almost impossible. Was the Emperor to abandon all
his advantages, to release all his prisoners (one of the
stipulations), surrender all the fortresses he held in the
Papal dominions, grant amnesty to all rebels, fulfil in
short all these hard conditions at once, and so leave
himself at the mercy of the Pope: then and not till
then, not till the Pope had exacted the scrupulous discharge of every article, was he to receive his tardy
absolution? Nor was the affair of the Lombards clearly
defined. Innocent (perhaps the Emperor knew this)
had from the first declared that he would not abandon
their cause. Was the Emperor to be humiliated before
the Lombards as he had been before the Pope, first to
make every concession, with the remote hope of regain-
ing his imperial rights by the Papal arbitration?[c]

[b] " Jurabit praeviæ stare mandatis
domini Papæ; salra tamen sint et
honores et jura quoad conservationem
integram sine aliqua diminutione Imperii et honorum suorum."—If these
undefined rights were to be respected,
the Pope's decisions concerning the
Lombards were still liable to be called
in question.

[c] " Si latenti morbo, videlicet de
negotio Lombardorum, medicina non
sunt opposita, pax omnino praecedere
non valebit."—Cod. Epist. Vatic. MS.,
quoted by Von Raumer.

According to the Papal account, Frederick began to
shrink back from the treaty to which he had sworn;
the Pope was fully prepared on his part for the last
extremity.[4] He left Rome, where his motions had perhaps been watched; he advanced to Civita Castellana
under the pretext of approaching the Emperor. The
bickerings, however, still continued; the Emperor complained that all the secret terms agreed on with the
Pope were publicly sold for six pennies in the Lateran;
the Pope demanded 400,000 marks as satisfaction for
the imprisonment of the Prelates. The Lombard affairs
were still in dispute. The Pope having seemingly
made some slight concession, proceeded still further to

Flight of the   Sutri. There at midnight he suddenly rose,
Pope.   stole out of the town in disguise, mounted a
powerful horse, like the proud Sinibald the Genoese
noble, he pressed its rocking flanks, so as to escape a
troop of 300 cavalry which the Emperor—to whom

June 28.   perhaps his design had been betrayed—sent to
                 intercept him, outrode all his followers, and
reached Civita Vecchia, where the Genoese fleet of
twenty-three well-armed galleys, which had been long

June 29.   prepared for his flight (so little did Innocent
                 calculate on a lasting treaty), was in the roads.[a]
He was in an instant on board one of the galleys. The

---

4 See Matth. Paris, sub ann. 1244.
"Imperator, ille instigante, qui primos
sperbivit, a forma jurata et humili-
tate satisfactionis compromisse impre-
birndo praiters in feliciter reviluit."
Of course, the biographers of Pope
Innocent are loud on the deceit and
treachery of Frederick (Vit. Innocent. IV.). But if Innocent resolutely
refused (and this seems clear) to revoke
the excommunication until Frederick

had absolutely fulfilled all the stipulations, the charge of duplicity must be
at least equally shared. In truth, if
Frederick was not too religiously
faithful to his oaths, the Pope openly asserted his power of annulling all oaths.
a It was given out that he fled to
avoid being captured by these 300
Tuscan horse, who were sent to seize
him. But the flight must have been
pre-arranged with the Genoese fleet.

next morning, before the anchor was weighed, arrived
five cardinals, who had been outstripped by the more
active Pope.   Seven others made their way to the north
of Italy.   The Pope's galleys set sail, a terrible storm
came on, which threatened to cast them on an
island which belonged to Pisa.   After seven ~~July 1.~~
days they entered the haven of Genoa.   The Genoese
had heard of the arrival of their illustrious fellow-
citizen at Porto Venere.   They received him with a
grand procession of the nobles with the Podestà, the
clergy with the Archbishop at their head.   The bells
clanged, music played, the priests chanted "Blessed is
he that cometh in the name of the Lord."   The Pope's
followers replied, "Our soul is escaped, even as a bird
out of the snare of the fowler: the snare is broken, and
we are delivered." [f]

The Emperor was furious at this intelligence: he too
had his scriptural phrase—"The wicked flees when no
man pursueth."   He complained bitterly of the negligent watch kept up by his armies and his fleets.   He
sent the Count of Toulouse to invite, to press the Pope
to return, and to promise the fulfilment of all the conditions of the truce.   Innocent replied that after such
flagrant violations of faith, he would not expose himself
or the Church to the imminent perils escaped with such
difficulty.   Frederick, in an address to Mantua, denounced the flight of the Pope as a faithless revolt to
the insurgents against the Empire, as though he supposed that Innocent at Genoa, where he remained three
months, would place himself at the head of his Lombard
League.

But he was not safe in Genoa.   The Emperor was in

---

[f] Psalm cxxiv. 7.

Pisa. Through the revolted cities of Asti and Alexandria, by secret ways Innocent crossed the Alps, and on the 2nd of December arrived at Lyons.

July 1.

The Pope at Lyons became an independent potentate. Lyons was not yet within the realm of France, though to a certain degree under her protection. It belonged in name to the Roman Empire; but it was almost a free city, owning no authority but that of the Archbishop. It was proud to become the residence of the Supreme Pontiff.

His reception in France was somewhat more cool than his hopes might have anticipated from the renowned piety of Queen Blanche and her son Saint Louis. The King with his mother visited the monastery of Citeaux; as they approached the church they were met by a long procession of five hundred monks from the convent of that saintly Order, entreating the King with tears and groans to aid the Holy Father of the Faithful against that son of Satan his persecutor, as his ancestor Louis VII. had received Pope Alexander. The first emotion of the King was to kneel in the profoundest reverence. But his more deliberate reply was, that he was prepared to protect the Pope against the Emperor so far as might seem fit to the nobles, his counsellors. The counsellors of Louis refused at once to grant permission that so dangerous and costly a guest should take up his residence in Rheims. The King of Arragon repelled the advances of the Pope. We shall hereafter see the conduct of Henry and the Barons of England. Innocent remained at Lyons; though thus partially baffled, he lost no time in striking at his foe. He summoned all kings, princes, and prelates to a Council on St. John the Baptist's day, upon the weighty

affairs of Christendom; he cited Frederick to appear
in person, or by his representatives, to bear the
charges on which he might be arraigned, and ~~Dec. 27, 1244.~~
to give the satisfaction which might be demanded. In
the mean time meditating a still heavier
penalty, and without awaiting the decree of ~~A.D. 1245.~~
the Council, he renewed the excommunication, and
commanded it to be published again throughout Christendom. In France, Spain, and England many of the
clergy obeyed, but a priest in Paris seems to have
created a strong impression on men's wavering minds.
"The Emperor and the Pope mutually condemn each
other; that one then of the two who is guilty I excommunicate, that one who is guiltless I absolve."[e] But
even in Lyons the haughty demeanour, the immoderate
pretensions, and the insatiable rapacity of Innocent IV.
almost endangered his safety. It is the greatest proof of
the deep-rooted strength of the Papal power, that with
a sullen discontent throughout Christendom, with a
stern impatience of the intolerable burthens imposed on
the Church as well as on the laity, with open menaces
of revolt, it still proceeded and successfully proceeded
to the most enormous act of authority, the deposition of
the Emperor in what claimed to be a full Council of the
Church.

In the short period, since the Pontificate of Innocent
III., a great but silent change had taken place in the
Papacy. Innocent III. was a mighty feudal monarch
at the head of a loyal spiritual aristocracy: the whole
clergy rose, with their head, in power; they took pride
in the exaltation of the Pope; the Pope not merely
respected but elevated the dignity of the bishops and

---

e Matt. Paris. Fleury, lxxxii. c. 17.

abbots; each in his sphere displayed his pomp, exercised his power, enjoyed his wealth, and willingly laid his unforced, unextorted benevolences at the foot of the Papal throne. But already the Pope had begun to be—Innocent IV. aspired fully to become—an absolute monarch with an immense standing army, which enabled him to depress, to humiliate, to tax at his pleasure the higher foundatories of the spiritual realm. That standing army was the two new Orders, not more servilely attached to the Pope than encroaching on the privileges as well as on the duties of the clergy. The elevation of an Italian noble to the Papacy already gave signs of that growing nepotism which at last sunk the Head of Christendom in the Italian sovereign.[b] Throughout the contest Pope Innocent blended with the inflexible haughtiness of the Churchman[1] the inexorable passionate hatred of a Guelfic Burgher towards a rival Ghibelline, the hereditary foe of his house, that of the Sinibaldi of Genoa. There had been rumours at least that Gregory IX. resented the scornful rejection of his niece as a fit bride for a natural son of the Emperor. It was now declared that Frederick had offered to wed his son Conrad to a niece of Sinibald Fiesco, the Pope Innocent IV. That scheme of Papal ambition was afterwards renewed.

Among the English clergy the encroachments of the Pope, especially in two ways, the direct taxation and usurpation of benefices for strangers, had kindled such violent resentment, alike among the Barons and

---

[b] Nic. de Curbio, in Vit. Innocrat. IV.

[1] Innocent held high views of the omnipotence of the Papacy:—" Cum teneat omnium credulitas pia fidelium quod apostolicæ sedis auctoritas in ar- dce018 universis liberam habeat a Dei providentia potestatem; nec arbitrio principum stare cogitur, ut eorum in electionem vel postulationem negotiis requirat assensum."—Ad Regem Henric. MS. B. M. v. 19. Lateran, Feb. 1244.

the Prelates, as almost to threaten that the realm
would altogether throw off the Papal yoke. It was
tauntingly said that England was the Pope's farm. At
this time the collector of the Papal revenues, Master
Martin, was driven ignominiously, and in peril of his
life, from the shores of the kingdom. Martin had
taken up his residence in the house of the Templars in
London. Fulk Fitzwarenne suddenly appeared before
him, and, with a stern look, said, "Arise—get thee
forth! Depart at once from England!" "In whose
name speakest thou?"   "In the name of the Barons of
England assembled at Luton and at Dunstable. If you
are not gone in three days, you and yours will be cut in
pieces." Martin sought the King: "Is this done by
your command, or by the insolence of your subjects?"
"It is not by my command; but my Barons will no
longer endure your depredations and iniquities. They
will rise in insurrection, and I have no power to save
you from being torn in pieces." The trembling priest
implored a safe-conduct. "The devil take thee away
to hell," said the indignant King, ashamed of his own
impotence. One of the King's officers with difficulty
conveyed Martin to the coast; but Martin left others
behind to insist on the Papal demands. Yet so great
was the terror, that many of the Italians, who had been
forced (this was the second grievance) into the richest
benefices of England, were glad to conceal themselves
from the popular fury. The Pope, it is said, gnashed
his teeth at the report from Martin of his insulting
expulsion from England. Innocent, once beyond the
Alps, had expected a welcome reception from all the
great monarchs except his deadly foe. But to the King
of England the Cardinal had made artful suggestions of
the honour and benefit which his presence might confer

on the realm. "What an immortal glory for your
reign, if (unexampled honour!) the Father of Fathers
should personally appear in England! He has often
said that it would give him great pleasure to see the
pleasant city of Westminster, and wealthy London."
The King's Council, if not the King, returned the
ungracious answer, "We have already suffered too much
from the usuries and simonies of Rome; we do not want
the Pope to pillage us."[k] More than this, Innocent
must listen in patience, with suppressed indignation, to
the "grievances" against which the Nobles and whole
realm of England solemnly protested by their proctors:
the subsidies exacted beyond the Peter's-pence, granted
by the generosity of England; the usurpation of benefices by Italians, of whom there was an infinite number;
the insolence and rapacity of the Nuncio Martin.[m]

The King of France, as has been seen, and the King
of Arragon courteously declined this costly and dangerous visit of the fugitive Pope. The Pope, it was
reported, was deeply offended at this stately and cautious reserve; on this occasion he betrayed the violence
of his temper: "We must first crush or pacify the great
dragon, and then we shall easily trample these small
basilisks under foot." Such at least were the rumours
spread abroad, and believed by all who were disposed
to assert the dignity of the temporal power, or who
groaned under the heavy burthens of the
Church. Even Lyons had become, through
the Pope's ill-timed favouritism, hardly a safe refuge.

Church of
Lyons.

---

[k] Matth. Paris, however in some
respects not an absolutely trustworthy
authority for events which happened
out of England, is the best unquestionably for the rumours and impressions

prevalent in Christendom—rumours,
which as rumours, and showing the
state of the public mind, are not to be
disdained by history.

[m] Matth. Paris, 1245.

He had endeavoured to force some of his Italian followers into the Chapter of Lyons; the Canons swore in
the face of the Pope that if they appeared, neither the
Archbishop nor the Canons themselves could prevent
their being cast into the Rhone. Some indeed of the
French prelates and abbots (their enemies accused them
of seeking preferment and promotion by their adulatory
homage) hastened to show their devout attachment to
the Pope, their sympathy for his perils and sufferings,
and their compassion for the destitution of which he
loudly complained. The Prior of Clugny astonished
even the Pope's followers by the amount of his gifts in
money. Besides these he gave eighty palfreys splendidly caparisoned to the Pope, one to each of the twelve
Cardinals. The Pope appointed the Abbot to the office,
no doubt not thought unseemly, of his Master of the
Horse: he received soon after the more appropriate
reward, the Bishopric of Langres. The Cistercian
Abbot would not be outdone by his rival of Clugny.
The Archbishop of Rouen for the same purpose loaded
his see with debts: he became Cardinal Bishop of
Albano. The Abbot of St. Denys, who aspired to and
attained the vacant Archbishopric, extorted many thousand livres from his see, which he presented to the
Pope. But the King of France, the special patron of
the church of St. Denys, forced the Abbot to regorge
his exactions, and to beg them in other quarters. Yet
with all these forced benevolences and lavish offerings
it was bruited abroad that the Church of Rome had a
capital debt, not including interest, of 150,000*l.*

The Council met at Lyons, in the convent of St. Just,
on the Nativity of St. John the Baptist. Around Council of
Lyons,
June 28.
the Pope appeared his twelve Cardinals, two
Patriarchs, the Latin of Constantinople, who claimed

likewise to be Patriarch of Antioch, and declared that
the heretical Greeks had reduced by their conquests his
suffragans from thirty to three, and the Patriarch of
Aquileia, who represented the church of Venice; the
Emperor of Constantinople, the Count of Toulouse,
Roger Bigod and other ambassadors of England who
had their own object at the Council, the redress of their
grievances from Papal exactions, and the canonization of
Edmund Archbishop of Canterbury. Only one hundred
and forty prelates represented the whole of Christendom,
of whom but very few were Germans. The Council and
the person of the Pope were under the protection of
Philip of Savoy at the head of a strong body of men-at-
arms, of Knights of the Temple and of the Hospital.
Philip, brother of the Count of Savoy, was in his character a chief of Condottieri, in his profession an ecclesiastic; he enjoyed vast riches from spiritual benefices,
was high in the confidence of the Pope. Aymori Archbishop of Lyons, a pious and gentle prelate, beheld with
deep sorrow the Pope as it were trampling upon him in
his own diocese, despoiling his see, as he was laying
intolerable burthens on the whole church of Christ. He
resigned his see and retired into a convent. Philip of
Savoy, yet but in deacon's orders, was advanced to the
metropolitan dignity; he was at once Archbishop of
Lyons, Bishop of Valence, Provost of Bruges, Dean
of Vienne. Of these benefices he drained with remorseless rapacity all the rich revenues, and remained at the
head of the Papal forces. And this was the act of a
Pope who convulsed the world with his assertion of
ecclesiastical immunities, of the sacrilegious intrusion
of secular princes into the affairs of the Church. During
four pontificates Philip of Savoy enjoyed the title, and
spent the revenues of the Archbishopric of Lyons. At

length Clement IV. insisted on his ordination and on
his consecration. Philip of Savoy threw off, under this
compulsion, the dress (he had never even pretended to
the decencies) of a bishop, married first the heiress
of Franche Comté, and afterwards a niece of Pope
Innocent IV., and died Duke of Savoy. And the
brother of Philip and of Amadeus Duke of Savoy,
Boniface, was Primate of England.[*]

This then was the Council which was to depose the
Emperor, and award the Empire. Even before the
opening of the Council the intrepid, learned, and eloquent jurisconsult Thaddeus of Suessa, the principal
proctor of the Emperor,[*] advanced and made great
offers in the name of his master: to compel the Eastern
Empire to enter into the unity of the Church: to raise
a vast army and to take the field in person against the
Tartars, the Charismians, and the Saracens, the foes
which threatened the life of Christendom; at his own
cost, and in his own person, to re-establish the kingdom
of Jerusalem; to restore all her territories to the See of
Rome; to give satisfaction for all injuries. "Fine
words and specious promises!" replied the Pope. "The
axe is at the root of the tree, and he would avert it. If
we were weak enough to believe this deceiver, who
would guarantee his truth?" "The Kings of France
and England," answered Thaddeus. "And if he violated
the treaty, as he assuredly would, we should have
instead of one, the three greatest monarchs of Christendom for our enemies." At the next session the Pope in
full attire mounted the pulpit; this was his text: "See,

---

[*] Gallia Christiana, iv. 144. M.
Paris, sub ann. 1251.

[*] Sismondi says that Peter de Vineâ
was one of the Emperor's representatives; that his silence raised suspicion
of his treason. Was he there? The
whole defence seems to have been entrusted to Thaddeus.

ye who pass this way, was ever sorrow like unto my
sorrow." He compared his five afflictions to the five
wounds of the Lord: the desolations of the Mongols;
the revolt of the Greek Church; the progress of heresy,
especially that of the Paterins in Lombardy; the capture and destruction of Jerusalem and the devastation
of the Holy Land by the Charismians; the persecutions
of the Emperor. He wept himself; the tears of others
interrupted his discourse. On this last head he enlarged
with bitter eloquence; he accused the Emperor of
heresy and sacrilege, of having built a great and strong
city and peopled it with Saracens, of joining in their
superstitious rites; of his close alliance with the Sultan
of Egypt; of his voluptuous life, and shameless intercourse with Saracen courtesans; of his unnumbered
perjuries, his violation of treaties: he produced a vast
number of letters, sealed with the imperial seal, as irrefragable proofs of these perjuries.

    Thaddeus of Suessa rose with calm dauntlessness. He
too had letters with the Papal seal, damning
proofs of the Pope's insincerity. The assembly
professed to examine these conflicting documents; they
came to the singular conclusion that all the Pope's
letters, and all his offers of peace were conditional;
those of the Emperor all absolute. But Thaddeus was
not to be overawed; he alleged the clashing and contra-
dictory letters of the Pope which justified his master in
not observing his promises. On no point did the bold
advocate hesitate to defend his sovereign; he ventured
to make reprisals. "My lord and master is arraigned
of heresy; for this no one can answer but himself; he
must be present to declare his creed: who shall presume
to read the secrets of his heart? But there is one strong
argument that he is not guilty of heresy (he fixed his

eyes on the prelates); he endures no usurer in his
dominions." The audience knew his meaning
—that was the heresy with which the whole June 21.
world charged the Court of Rome. The orator justified
the treaties of the Emperor with the Saracens as entered
into for the good of Christendom; he denied all criminal
intercourse with the Saracen women; he had permitted
them in his presence as jongleurs and dancers, but on
account of the offence taken against them he had
banished them for ever from his court. Thaddeus
ended by demanding delay, that the Emperor his
master might appear in person before the Council. The
Pope shrunk from this proposal: "I have hardly escaped
his snares. If he comes hither I must withdraw. I
have no desire for martyrdom or for captivity."
But the ambassadors of France and England July.
insisted on the justice of the demand: Innocent was
forced to consent to an adjournment of fourteen days.
The Pontiff was relieved of his fears. Frederick had
advanced as far as Turin. But the hostile character of
the assembly would not allow of his appearance. "I
see that the Pope has sworn my ruin; he would revenge
himself for my victory over his relatives, the pirates of
Genoa. It becomes not the Emperor to appear before
an assembly constituted of such persons." On the next
meeting this determination encouraged the foes of Frederick. New accusers arose to multiply charges against
the absent sovereign: many voices broke out against the
contumacious rebel against the Church. But Thaddeus,
though almost alone, having stood unabashed before the
Pope, was not to be silenced by this clamour of accusations. The Bishop of Catana * was among the loudest;

---

* Carmola in Guennone.

he charged Frederick with treason against the Church for his imprisonment of the Prelates, and with other heinous crimes. " I can no longer keep silence," broke in Thaddeus, " thou son of a traitor, who was convicted and hanged by the justiciary of my Lord, thou art but following the example of thy father." Thaddeus took up the desperate defence, before such an assembly, of the seizure of the Prelates. The Pope again mingled in the fray; but Thaddeus assumed a lofty tone.

June 20.   " God delivered them into the hands of my master; God took away the strength of the rebels, and showed by this abandonment that their imprisonment was just." " If," replied the Pope, " the Emperor had not mistrusted his own cause, he would not have declined the judgement of such holy and righteous men : he was condemned by his own guilty conscience." " What could my lord hope from a council in which presided his capital enemy, the Pope Gregory IX., or from judges who even in their prison breathed nothing but menace?" " If one has broken out into violence, all should not have been treated with this indignity. Nothing remains but ignominiously to depose a man laden with such manifold offences."

Thaddeus felt that he was losing ground. At the third sitting he had heard that the daughter of the Duke of Austria, whom Frederick proposed to take as his fourth wife (the sister of the King of England had died in childbed), had haughtily refused the hand of an Emperor tainted with excommunication, and in danger of being deposed. The impatient Assembly would hardly hear again this perilous adversary ; he entered therefore a solemn appeal : " I appeal from this Council, from which are absent so many great prelates and secular sovereigns, to a general and impartial

July 17.

Council. I appeal from this Pope, the declared enemy
of my Lord, to a future, more gentle, more Christian
Pope." [1] This appeal the Pope haughtily overruled:
" it was fear of the treachery and the cruelty of the
Emperor which had kept some prelates away: it was
not for him to take advantage of the consequences of his
own guilt." The proceedings were interrupted by a long
and bitter remonstrance of England against the Papal
exactions. The Pope adjourned this question as requiring
grave and mature consideration.

With no further deliberation, without further investigation, with no vote, apparently with no parti-   *Sentence of*
cipation of the Council, the Pope proceeded   *deposition.*
at great length, and rehearsing in the darkest terms all
the crimes at any time charged against Frederick, to
pronounce his solemn, irrefragable decree: " The sentence of God must precede our sentence: we declare
Frederick excommunicated of God, and deposed from
all the dignity of Empire, and from the kingdom of
Naples. We add our own sentence to that of God: we
excommunicate Frederick, and depose him from all the
dignity of the Empire, and from the kingdom of Naples." The Emperor's subjects in both realms were
declared absolved from all their oaths and allegiance.
All who should aid or abet him were by the act itself
involved in the same sentence of excommunication.
The Princes of Germany were ordered to proceed at
once to the election of a new Emperor. The kingdom
of Naples was reserved to be disposed of, as might
seem to them most fit, by the Pope and the Cardinals.

The Council at this sentence, at least the greater

[1] Annal. Caesen. Concil. sub ann.

part, sat panic-stricken; the imperial ambassadors uttered loud groans, beat their heads and their breasts in sorrow. Thaddeus cried aloud, "Oh, day of wrath, of tribulation, and of agony! Now will the heretics rejoice, the Charismians prevail; the foul Mongols pursue their ravages." "I have done my part," said the Pope, "God must do the rest." He began the hymn, "We glorify thee, O God!" His partisans lifted up their voices with him; the hymn ended, there was profound silence. Innocent and the prelates turned down their blazing torches to the ground till they smouldered and went out. "So be the glory and the fortune of the Emperor extinguished upon earth."

Frederick received at Turin the report of his dethronement; he was seated in the midst of a splendid court. "The Pope has deprived me of my crown? Whence this presumption, this audacity? Bring hither my treasure chests." He opened them. "Not one of my crowns but is here." He took out one, placed it on his own head, and with a terrible voice, menacing gesture, and heart bursting with wrath, exclaimed, "I hold my crown of God alone; neither the Pope, the Council, nor the devil shall rend it from me! What! shall the pride of a man of low birth degrade the Emperor, who has no superior nor equal on earth? I am now released from all respect; no longer need I keep any measure with this man."[1]

July 31.

Frederick addressed his justification to all the kings and princes of Christendom, to his own chief officers and justiciaries. He called on all temporal princes to make common cause against this common enemy of the temporal power. "What might not all Kings fear

---

[1] Petur de Vineâ, i. 3.

from the presumption of a Pope like Innocent IV.?"
He inveighed against the injustice of the Pope in all
the proceedings of the Council. The Pope was accuser,
witness, and judge. He denounced crimes as notorious
which the Emperor utterly denied. "How long has
the word of an Emperor been so despicable as not to
be heard against that of a priest?" "Among the
Pope's few witnesses one had his father, son and nephew
convicted of high treason. Of the others, some came
from Spain to bear witness on the affairs of Italy. The
utter falsehood of all the charges was proved by irrefragable documents. But were they all true, how will
they justify the monstrous absurdity, that the Emperor,
in whom dwells the supreme majesty, can be adjudged
guilty of high treason? that he who as the source of
law is above all law, should be subject to law? To
condemn him to temporal penalties who has but one
superior in temporal things, God! We submit ourselves to spiritual penances, not only to the Pope, but
to the humblest priest; but, alas! how unlike the
clergy of our day to those of the primitive church, who
led Apostolic lives, imitating the humility of the Lord!
Then were they visited of angels, then shone around by
miracles, then did they heal the sick and raise the
dead, and subdue princes by their holiness not by arms!
Now they are abandoned to this world, and to drunken-
ness; their religion is choked by their riches. It were
a work of charity to relieve them from this noxious
wealth; it is the interest of all princes to deprive them
of these vain superfluities, to compel them to salutary
poverty." [*]

The former arguments were addressed to the pride of

* Peter de Vin. lib. i. 3.

France; the latter to England, which had so long
groaned under tho rapacity of tho clergy. But it was
a fatal error not to dissever the cause of the Pope from
that of the clergy. To all the Emperor declared his
steadfast determination to resist with unyielding firmness: "Before this generation and the generation to
come I will have the glory of resisting this tyranny;
let others who shrink from my support have the disgrace as well as the galling burthen of slavery." The
humiliation of Pope Innocent might have been endured
even by the most devout sons of the Church; his
haughtiness and obstinacy had almost alienated the
pious Louis; his rapacity forced the timid Henry of
England to resistance. Perhaps the Papacy itself
might have been assailed without a general outburst of
indignation; but a war against the clergy, a war of
sacrilegious spoliation, a war which avowed the necessity, the expediency of reducing them to Apostolic simplicity and Apostolic poverty, was in itself the heresy
of heresies. To exasperate this indignation to the
utmost, every instance of Frederick's severity, doubtless
of his cruelty, to ecclesiastics, was spread abroad with
restless activity. He is said to have burned them by a
slow fire, drowned them in the sea, dragged them at
the tails of horses. No doubt in Apulia and Sicily
Frederick kept no terms with the rebellious priests and
friars who were preaching the Crusade against him;
urging upon his subjects that it was their right, their
duty to withdraw their allegiance. But under all
circumstances the violation of the hallowed person of a
priest was sacrilege: while they denounced him as
a Pharaoh, a Herod, a Nero, it was an outrage against
law, against religion, against God, to do violence to a
hair of their heads. And all these rumours, true or

untrue, in their terrible simplicity, or in the gathered
blackness of rumour, propagated by hostile tongues,
confirmed the notion that Frederick contemplated a
revolution, a new æra, which by degrading the Clergy
would destroy the Church.[1]

The Pope kept not silence; he was not the man who
would not profit to the utmost by this error.   He
replied to the Imperial manifesto: "When the sick
man who has scorned milder remedies is subjected to
the knife and the cautery, he complains of the cruelty
of the physician: when the evil doer, who has despised
all warning, is at length punished, he arraigns his
judge. But the physician only looks to the welfare of
the sick man, the judge regards the crime, not the
person of the criminal. The Emperor doubts and
denies that all things and all men are subject to the
See of Rome. As if we who are to judge angels are
not to give sentence on all earthly things. In the Old
Testament priests dethroned unworthy kings; how
much more is the Vicar of Christ justified in proceeding against him who, expelled from the Church as
a heretic, is already the portion of hell! Ignorant persons aver that Constantine first gave temporal power to
the See of Rome; it was already bestowed by Christ
himself, the true king and priest, as inalienable from
its nature and absolutely unconditional. Christ founded
not only a pontifical but a royal sovereignty, and committed to Peter the rule both of an earthly and a
heavenly kingdom, as is indicated and visibly proved
by the plurality of the keys." 'The power of the

---

[1] "De haeresi per id ipsum se red-
dens suspectum, merito omnem quam
hactenus habebat in omnes populos
igniculum famæ propriæ et sapientiæ

impudenter et imprudenter extinxit
atque delevit."—Matt. Par. p. 459.
Höfler quotes Albert of Beham's MS.

[2] "Non solum pontificalem, sed

sword is in the Church and derived from the Church;'
she gives it to the Emperor at his coronation, that he
may use it lawfully and in her defence; she has the
right to say, 'Put up thy sword into its sheath.' He
strives to awaken the jealousy of other temporal kings,
as if the relation of their kingdoms to the Pope were
the same as those of the electoral kingdom of Germany
and the kingdom of Naples. The latter is a Papal
fief; the former inseparable from the Empire, which
the Pope transferred as a fief from the East to the
West.' To the Pope belongs the coronation of the Emperor, who is thereby bound by the consent of ancient
and modern times to allegiance and subjection."

War was declared, and neither the Emperor nor the
Pope now attempted to disguise their mutual immitigable hatred. Everywhere the Pope called on the
subjects of the Emperor to revolt from their deposed
and excommunicated monarch. He assumed the power
of dispensing with all treaties; he cancelled that of the
city of Treviso with the Emperor as extorted by force;
thus almost compelling a war of extermination;' for if
treaties with a conqueror were thus to be cast
April 14. aside, what opening remained for mercy? In
a long and solemn address, he called on the bishops,
barons, cities, people of the kingdom of Naples and
Sicily to throw off the yoke under which they had so
long groaned of the tyrant Frederick. Two Cardinals,
Rainier Capoccio and Stephen da Romanis, had full

---

regalem constituit principatum, beato Vatican archives, No. 4957, 47, and
Petro ejusque successoribus terreni from the Codex Vindobon. Philol.
simul ac cœlestis imperii commissis p. 178. See also Höfler, Albert von
habenis, quod in pluralitate clavium Beham.
competenter innuitur." This passage * " in feodum transtulit occidentis."
is quoted by Von Raumer from the ⸗ Raynald. sub ann.

powers to raise troops, and to pursue any hostile
measures against the King. The Crusade was publicly
preached throughout Italy against the enemy of the
Church. The Emperor on his side levied a third from
the clergy to relieve them from the tyranny of the
Pope. He issued inflexible orders that every clerk or
religious person who, in obedience to the command of
the Pope or his Legate, should cease to celebrate mass
or any other religious function, should be expelled
at once from his place and from his city, and despoiled
of all his goods, whether his own or those of the Church.
He promised his protection and many advantages to all
who should adhere to his party; he declared that he
would make no peace with the Pope till all those ecclesiastics who might be deposed for his cause should be
put in full possession of their orders, their rank, and
their benefices.[*] The Mendicant Friars, as they would
keep no terms of peace with Frederick, could expect no
terms from him; they were seized and driven beyond
the borders. The summons of the Pope to the barons
of the realm of Sicily to revolt found some few hearers.
A dark conspiracy was formed in which were engaged
Pandolph of Fasanella, Frederick's vicar in Tuscany,
Jacob Morra of the family of the great justiciary, Andrew of Ayala, the Counts San Severino, Theobald
Francisco, and other Apulian barons. It was a conspiracy not only against the realm, but against the life
of Frederick. On its detection Pandolph of Fasanella
and De Morra, the leaders of the plot, fled to, and were
received by, the Pope's Legate. The Cardinal Rainier,
Theobald and San Severino seized the castles of Capoccio and of Scala, and stood on their defence. The

---

* Peter de Vin. l. 4.

loyal subjects of Frederick instantly reduced Scala;
Capoccio with the rebels fell soon after. Fre-

July 10.

derick arraigned the Pope before the world, he
declared him guilty on the full and voluntary avowal of
the rebels,[a] as having given his direct sanction not only
to the revolt, but to the murder of the Emperor.[b]
"This they had acknowledged in confession, this in
public on the scaffold. They had received the cross
from the hands of some Mendicant Friars; they were
acting under the express authority of the See of Rome."
Frederick at first proposed to parade the chief criminals
with the Papal bull upon their foreheads through all the
realms of Christendom as an awful example and a
solemn rebuke of the murtherous Pope; he found it
more prudent to proceed to immediate execution, an
execution with all the horrible cruelty of the times;
their eyes were struck out, their hands hewn off, their
noses slit, they were then broken on the wheel.[c] The
Pope denied in strong terms the charge of meditated
assassination; on the other hand, he declared to Christendom that three distinct attempts had been designed
against his life, in all which Frederick was the acknowledged accomplice. On both sides probably these accusations were groundless. On one part, no doubt, fanatic
Guelfs might think themselves called upon even by the
bull of excommunication, which was an act of outlawry,
to deliver the Church, the Pope, and the world from a
monster of perfidy and iniquity such as Frederick was

---

[a] See in Hofler the letter of the
Pope to Theobald Francisco, and all the
others of the kingdom of Sicily who
returned to their loyalty to the Roman
See: "God has made his face to shine
upon you, by withdrawing your persons
from the dominion of Pharaoh. From

the soldiers of the reprobate tyrant,
you have become champions of our
Lord Jesus Christ."—Appendix, p. 372.

[b] "In prædictæ mortis et exheredita
tionis nostræ summum pontificem assu-
runt authorem."—Peter de Vin. ii. s.

[c] Matth. Paris, sub ann. 1246, 7.

described in the manifestoes of the Pope. Fanatic
Ghibellines might in like manner think that they were
doing good service, and would meet ample even if secret
reward, should they relieve the Emperor from his deadly
foe. They might draw a strong distinction between the
rebellious subject of the Empire, and the sacred head
of Christendom.

The Pope pledged himself solemnly to all who would
revolt from Frederick never to abandon them to his
wrath, never on any terms to make peace with the perfidious tyrant; " no feigned penitence, no simulated
humility shall so deceive us, as that, when he is cast
down from the height of his imperial and royal dignity,
he should be restored to his throne. His sentence is
absolutely irrevocable! his reprobation is the voice of
God by his Church: he is condemned and for ever!
His viper progeny are included under this eternal
immitigable proscription. Whoever then loves justice
should rejoice that vengeance is thus declared against
the common enemy, and wash his hands in the
blood of the transgressor." So wrote the Vicar of
Christ![a]

Frederick took measures to relieve himself from the
odious imputation of heresy. The Archbishop
of Palermo, the Bishop of Pavia, the Abbots of   A.D. 1246.
Monte Casino, Cava, and Casanova, the Friar Preachers
Roland and Nicolas, men of high repute, appeared
before the Pope at Lyons, and declared themselves
ready to attest on oath the orthodox belief of the Emperor. Innocent sternly answered, that they deserved
punishment for holding conference with an excommunicated person, still severer penalty for treating him as

[a] Apud Höfler, p. 383.

Emperor. They rejoined in humility, "Receive us then as only representing a Christian."

The Pope was compelled to appoint a commission of three cardinals. These not only avouched the report of the ambassadors, but averred the Emperor prepared to assert his orthodoxy in the presence of the Pope.

Innocent extricated himself with address: he declared the whole proceeding, as unauthorised by himself, hasty, and presumptuous: " If he shall appear unarmed, and with but few attendants before us, we will hear him, if it be according to law, according to law."[*] Even the religious Louis of France could not move the rigid Pope. In his own crusading enthusiasm, as strong as that of his ancestors in the days of Urban, Louis urged the Pope to make peace with the Emperor, that the united forces of Christendom might make head in Europe and in Palestine against the unbelieving enemies of the Cross. He had a long and secret interview with the Pope in the monastery of Clugny. Innocent declared that he could have no dealings with the perfidious Frederick. Louis retired, disgusted at finding such merciless inflexibility in the Vicar of Christ.[f] But not yet had the spell of the great magician begun to work. The conspiracy in the kingdom of Sicily was crushed; Frederick did not think it wise to invade the territories of Rome, where the Cardinal Rainier kept up an active partisan war. But even Viterbo yielded; the Guelfs were compelled to submit by the people clamouring for bread. Prince Theodore of Antioch entered Florence in triumph. The Milanese had suffered discomfiture; Venice had become more amicable. Inno-

---

* " Ipsum super hoc, u de jure, et sicut de jure fuerit audiamus."—Apud Raynald, 1246.   f Matt. Paris, 1246.

cent had not been wanting in attempts to raise up a
rival sovereign in Germany to supplant the deposed
Emperor. All the greater princes coldly, almost con-
temptuously, refused to become the instruments of the
Papal vengeance: they resented the presumption of the
Pope in dethroning an Emperor of Germany.

The Papal Legate, Philip Bishop of Ferrara, in less
troubled times would hardly have wrought powerfully
on the minds of Churchmen. He was born of poor
parents in Pistoia, and raised himself by extraordinary
vigour and versatility of mind. He was a dark, melancholy, utterly unscrupulous man, of stern and cruel
temper; a great drinker;[x] even during his orisons he
had strong wine standing in cold water by his side.
His gloomy temperament may have needed this excitement. But the strength of the Papal cause was Albert
von Beham.[b] Up to the accession of Innocent IV., if
not to the Council of Lyons, the Archbishops of Saltzburg, the Bishops of Freisingen and Ratisbon and
Passau, had been the most loyal subjects of Frederick.
They had counteracted all the schemes of Albert von
Beham, driven him, amid the universal execration for
his insolence in excommunicating the highest prelates,
and rapacity in his measureless extortions, from Southern
Germany. We have heard him bitterly lamenting his
poverty. Otho of Bavaria, who when once he embraced

[x] " Multas crudelitates exercuit.
Malancholicus, et tristis et furiosus, et
filius Belial. Magnus potator."—Salimbeni, a Papal writer quoted by Von
Raumer, p. 212.

[b] Höfer affirms that because Albert
von Beham, in one of his furious letters
to Otho, calls Frederick the parricide,
the murderer of Otho's father, that it

is a striking proof that Frederick was
guilty of that murder.—p. 118. The
letter is a remarkable one. Höfer's is
one of those melancholy books, showing
how undying is religious hatred. Innocent himself might be satisfied with
the rancour of his apologist, and his
merciless antipathy to Frederick.

the cause of the Hohenstaufen adhered to it with
honourable fidelity, had convicted him of gross bribery,
and hunted him out of his dominions. Albert now
appeared again in all his former activity. He had been
ordained priest by the Cardinal Albano; he was nominated Dean of Passau; but the insatiable Albert knew
his own value, or rather the price at which the Pope
and his cardinals calculated his services: he insisted on
receiving back all his other preferments. The Pope
and the Cardinals held it as a point of honour to
maintain their useful emissary.[1]

Already before the elevation of Innocent, at a meeting at Budweis, a league of Austria, Bohemia,
and Bavaria, had proposed the nomination of
a new Emperor. Eric King of Denmark had refused it
for his son, in words of singular force and dignity. At
Budweis Wenceslaus of Bohemia had fallen off to the
interests of the Emperor: there were fears among the
Papalists, fears speedily realised, of the Imperialism of
Otho of Bavaria. A most audacious vision of Poppo,
the Provost of Munster, had not succeeded in appalling
Otho into fidelity to the Pope. The Queen of Heaven
and the Twelve Apostles sent down from Heaven ivory
statues of themselves, which contained oracles confirm-
ing all the acts of Albert; writings were shown with the
Apostolic seals, containing the celestial decree.[b] Albert
had threatened, that if the electors refused, the Pope

---

[1] He complains that they prevented
him from collecting 300 marks of
silver, which otherwise he might have
obtained. Höfler cannot deny the
venality of Albert von Beham, but
makes a long apology, absolutely start-
ling in a respectable writer of our own
day. The new letters of Albert seem

to me more fatal to his character than
the partial extracts in Aventinus.

[b] "Quorum decreta cum divinæ
mentis decretis examussim conspirantia,
ambobus cœlestis senatus-consulti in
eburneis descripta sigilla, inspiciendi
copiam fecisse." The sense is not quite
clear; I doubt my own rendering.

would name a French or Lombard King or Patrician,
without regard to the Germans.

The meeting at Budweis so far had failed; but a
dangerous approximation had even then been made
between Sifried of Mentz, hitherto loyal to Frederick,
who had condemned and denounced the rapacious
questorship of Albert von Beham, and Conrad of
Cologne, a high Papalist.[*] This approximation grew
up into an Anti-Imperialist League, strengthened as it
was, before long, by the courageous demeanour,
the flight, the high position taken by Innocent   April 28.
at Lyons; still more by the unwise denunciations against
the whole hierarchy by Frederick in his wrath. Now
the three great rebellious temporal princes—Otho of
Bavaria, the King of Bohemia, the Duke of Austria—
are the faithful subjects of Frederick; his loyal prelates,
Saltzburg, Freisingen, Ratisbon, are his mortal enemies.
Not content with embracing the Papal cause, they endeavoured by the most stirring incitements to revenge
for doubtful or mendaciously asserted wrongs, by the
dread of excommunication, by brilliant promises, to stir
up Otho of Bavaria to assume the Imperial crown.
Otho replied, "When I was on the side of the Pope you
called him Antichrist; you declared him the source of
all evil and all guilt: by your counsels I turned to the
Emperor, and now you brand him as the most enormous
transgressor. What is just to-day is unjust to-morrow:
in scorn of all principle and all truth, you blindly follow
your selfish interests. I shall hold to my pledges and
my oaths, and not allow myself to be blown about by
every changing wind." Otho of Bavaria persisted in his
agreement to wed his daughter with Conrad, son of

---

[*] Boehmer, p. 390. See citations.

Frederick. Every argument was used to dissuade him
from this connexion. Three alternatives were laid
before him: I. To renounce the marriage of his
daughter with Conrad, Frederick's son; if so, the Pope
will provide a nobler bridegroom, and reconcile him
fully with Henry, elected King of the Romans. II. To
let the marriage proceed if Conrad will renounce his
father. Albert von Beham was busy in inciting the unnatural revolt of Conrad from his father. III. The
third possibility was the restoration of Frederick to the
Pope's favour: he must await this; but in the mean
time bear in mind that the victory of the Church is
inevitable.* The King of Bohemia, the Duke of Austria,
Brabant, and Saxony, the Margraves of Meissen and
Brandenburg, repelled with the same contemptuous
firmness the tempting offer of the Imperial crown. At
last an Emperor was found in Henry Raspe, Landgrave
of Thuringia. Henry of Thuringia was a man of courage
and ability; but his earlier life did not designate him
as the champion of Holy Church.° He was the brother-
in-law of the sainted Elizabeth of Hungary, now the
object of the most passionate religious enthusiasm, sanc-

---

* " Quia si omne aurum haberet,
quod Rex Solomon habuit, ordinationi
Sanctæ Romanæ Ecclesiæ et divinæ
potentiæ non poteritia repugnare, quia
necesse est ut in omni negotio semper
Ecclesia Dei vincat."—p. 129. The
marriage took place, Sept. 6, 1246.
The rhetorical figures in this address
of Albert of Beham, if it came not
from the Pope himself, were sufficiently
bold: "The Pope would not swerve
from his purpose though the stars
should fall from their spheres, and
rivers be turned into blood. Angels
and archangels would in vain attempt
to abrogate his determination." " Nec
credo angelos aut archangelos sufferre
illi articulo, ut eum possint ad restrum
breve placitum inclinare."

° The electors to the Kingdom of
Germany were almost all ecclesiastics.
The Archbishops of Mentz, Cologne,
Trèves, Bremen; the Bishops of Würtz-
burg, Naumbourg, Ratisbon, Stras-
burg, Henry (Elect) of Spires; Duke
Henry of Brabant, Albert of Saxony;
with some Counts.—May 22.

tioned by the Pope himself. To her, in her desolate
widowhood, Henry had shown little of the affection of a
brother or the reverence of a worshipper; dark rumours
charged him with having poisoned her son, his nephew,
to obtain his inheritance. He had been at one time the
Lieutenant of the Emperor in Germany. Even Henry
at first declined the perilous honour. He yielded at
length as to a sacrifice: "I obey, but I shall not live a
year."

Innocent issued his mandate,[*] his solemn adjuration
to the prelates to elect, with one consent, Henry of
Thuringia to the Imperial crown. He employed more
powerful arguments: all the vast wealth which he still
drew, more especially from England, was devoted to
this great end. The sum is variously stated at 25,000
and 50,000 marks, which was spread through Germany
by means of letters of exchange from Venice. The
greater princes still stood aloof; the prelates espoused,
from religious zeal, the Papal champion; among the
lower princes and nobles the gold of England worked
wonders. On Ascension Day the Archbishops
of Mentz, Cologne, Trèves, and Bremen, the   A.D. 1246.
Bishops of Metz, Spires, and Strasburg, anointed
Henry of Thuringia as King of Germany at
Hochem, near Wurtzburg. His enemies called   August 1.
him in scorn the priest king.[1] The sermons of the
prelates and clergy, who preached the Crusade against
the godless Frederick, and the money of the Pope,
raised a powerful army. King Conrad was worsted in
a great battle near Frankfort; two thousand of his own
Swabian soldiers passed over to the enemy. But the

---

[*] See the very curious letter in Höfler, p. 175, on the determination of the Pope.
[1] Matt. Paris. Chronic. Erphurt. Ann. Argentin. apud Böhmer, Fontes.

cities, now rising to wealth and freedom, stood firm to
Frederick: they defied, in some cases expelled, their
bishops. Henry of Thuringia attempted to besiege first
Reutlingen, then Ulm; was totally defeated
near that city, fled to his Castle of Wartburg,
and died of grief and vexation working on a frame
shattered by a fall from his horse.

Frederick was still in the ascendant, the cause of the
Pope still without prevailing power. The indefatigable
Innocent sought throughout Germany, throughout
Europe: he even summoned from the remote and
barbarous North Hakim King of Norway to assume the
crown of Germany.[*] At last William of Holland, a
youth of twenty years of age, under happier
auspices, listened to the tempting offers of the
Pope; but even Aix-la-Chapelle refused, till after a
siege of some length, to admit the Papal Emperor to
receive the crown within her walls: he was crowned,
however, by the Papal Legate, the Cardinal of St. Sabina.

From this time till Frederick lay dying, four years
after, at Fiorentino, some dire fatality seemed to hang
over the house of Hohenstaufen. Frederick had advanced to Turin; his design no one knew; all con-
jectured according to their wishes or their fears. It
was rumoured in England that he was at the head of a
powerful force, intending to dash down the Alps and
seize the Pope at Lyons. The Papalists gave out that
he had some dark designs, less violent but more
treacherous, to circumvent the Pontiff. Innocent had
demanded succour from Louis, who might, with his
brothers and the nobles of France, no doubt have been
moved by the personal danger of the Pope to take up

[*] Letter to William of Holland.

arms in his cause.[1] Frederick had succeeded, by the
surrender of the strong castle of Rivoli to Thomas Duke
of Savoy, in removing the obstructions raised by that
prince to the passage of the Alps. The Duke of Savoy
played a double game: he attacked the Cardinal
Octavian, who was despatched by the Pope with a strong
chosen body of troops and 15,000 marks to aid the
Milanese. The Cardinal reached Lombardy with hardly
a man; his whole treasure fell into the hands of the
Duke of Savoy. Others declared that Frederick was
weary of the war, and had determined on the humblest
submission. He himself may have had no fixed and
settled object. He declared that he had resolved to
proceed to Lyons to bring his cause to issue in the face
of the Pope, and before the eyes of all mankind.[1] He
was roused from his irresolution by the first of those
disasters which went on darkening to his end. June, 1247.
The Pope was not only Pope; he had powerful
compatriots and kindred among the great Guelfic houses
of Italy. This, not his spiritual powers alone, gave the
first impulse to the downfall of Frederick. In Parma
itself the Rossi, the Correggi, the Lupi, connected with
the Genoese family of the Sinibaldi, maintained a
secret correspondence with their party within the city.
The exiles appeared before Parma with a strong force;
the Imperialist Podestà, Henry Testa of Arezzo, sallied
forth, was repulsed and slain; the Guelfs entered the
city with the flying troops, became masters of the
citadel: Gherardo Correggio was Lord of Parma.

---

[1] Matt. Paris. In the letters to
Louis and to his mother Blanche the
Pope intimates that they were ready to
march an army not only to defend him
in Lyons, but to cross the Alps.

[1] Nicolas de Curbio, in Vit. In-
nor. IV. "Causæ nostræ justitiam
præ-eo-tialiter et potenter in adversarii
nostri facie, coram transalpinis gentibus
pontari."—Petr. de Vin, ii. 49.

This was the turning point in the fortunes of Frederick; and Frederick, by the horrible barbarity
of his revenge against the revolted Parmesans,
might seem smitten with a judicial blindness,
and to have laboured to extinguish the generous sympathies of mankind in his favour. His wrath against
the ungrateful city, which he had endowed with many
privileges, knew no bounds. He had made about one
thousand prisoners: on one day he executed four, on
the next two, before the walls, and declared that such
should be the spectacle offered to the rebels every day
during the siege. He was with difficulty persuaded to desist from this inhuman warfare.
Parma became the centre of the war; on its capture
depended all the terrors of the Imperial arms, on its
relief the cause of the Guelfs. Around Frederick
assembled King Enzio, Eccelin da Romano, Frederick
of Antioch, Count Lancia, the Marquis Pallavicini,
Thaddeus of Suessa, and Peter de Vinea. On the
other hand, the Marquis Boniface threw himself with a
squadron of knights into the city. The troops of
Mantua, the Marquis of Esto, Alberic da Romano, the
martial Cardinal Gregory of Monte Longo at the head
of the Milanese; the Count of Lavagna, the Pope's
nephew, at the head of four hundred and thirty cross-
bow men of Genoa and three hundred of his own,
hovered on all sides to aid the beleaguered city. Parma
endured the storm, the famine. Frederick had almost
encircled Parma by his works, and called the strong
point of his fortifications by the haughty but ill-omened
name of Vittoria. After many months' siege,
one fatal night the troops of Parma issued
from the city, and surprised the strong line of forts, the
Vittoria, which contained all the battering engines,

Turning point to Frederick's fortunes.

August 8.

Feb. 18, 1248.

stores, provisions, arms, tents, treasures, of the Imperial
forces. So little alarm was at first caused, that Thaddeus of Suessa, who commanded in Vittoria, exclaimed,
"What! have the mice left their holes?" In a few
moments the whole fortress was in flames, it was a heap
of ashes, the Imperial garrison slain or prisoners; two
thousand were reckoned as killed, including the Marquis
Lancia; three thousand prisoners.* Among the inestimable booty in money, jewels, vessels of gold and
silver, were the carroccio of Cremona, the Imperial
fillet, the great seal, the sceptre and the crown. The
crown of gold and jewels was found by a mean man,
called in derision "Short-legs." He put the crown on
his head, was raised on the shoulders of his comrades,
and entered Parma, in mockery of the Emperor.
Among the prisoners was the faithful and eloquent
Thaddeus of Suessa. The hatred of his master's enemies was in proportion to his value to his master.
Already both his hands were struck off; and in this
state, faint with loss of blood, he was hewn in pieces.*
And yet could Frederick hardly complain of the cruelty
of his foes—cruelties shown when the blood was still
hot from battle. Only three days before the loss of the
Vittoria, Marcellino, Bishop of Arezzo, a dangerous
and active partisan of the Pope, who had been taken
prisoner, and confined for months in a dungeon, was
brought forth to be hanged. His death was a strange
wild confusion of the pious prelate and the intrepid
Guelf. He was commanded to anathematise the Pope,

---

* Muratori, Annal. sub ann.

* Compare in Höfler's "Albert von
Behem" the curious Latin songs on
the defeat of Frederick before Parma.
All the monkish bards broke out in
gratulant hymns.

" Ambit astrologus et magus et vates,
Berimbub et Astaroth proprios Penates,
Tartarorum convenicon per quos potestates
Sprevorat ecclesiam, et mundi magnates."

he broke out into an anathema against the Emperor. He then began to chant the Te Deum, while the furious Saracen soldiers tied him to the tail of a horse, bound his hands, blindfolded his eyes, dragged him to the gibbet, where he hung an awful example to the rebels of Parma. He was hanged, says the indignant Legate of the Pope, "like a villain, a plebeian, a nightman, a parricide, a murderer, a slave-dealer, a midnight robber." [7]

This was but the first of those reverses, which not only obscured the fame, but wrung with bitterest anguish the heart of Frederick. Still his gallant

May 26, 1249.

son Enzio made head against all his father's foes: in a skirmish before Bologna Enzio was wounded and taken prisoner. Implacable Bologna condemned him to perpetual imprisonment. All the entreaties to which his father humbled himself; all his own splendid promises that for his ransom he would gird the city with a ring of gold, neither melted nor dazzled the stubborn animosity of the Guelfs. A captive at the age

Imprisonment of Enzio.

of twenty-four, this youth, of beauty equal to his bravery—the poet, the musician, as well as the most valiant soldier and consummate captain— pined out twenty-three years of life, if not in a squalid dungeon, in miserable inactivity. Romance, by no means improbable, has darkened his fate. The passion of Lucia Bisdagioli, the most beautiful and high-born maiden of Bologna, for the captive, her attempts to release him, were equally vain: once he had almost escaped, concealed in a cask; a lock of his bright hair

---

[7] Matt. Paris, sub ann. 1249 Letter of Cardinal Rainier. However extravagant this letter, the fact can hardly have been invention. Compare the sermon of the Archbishop of Mentz at Wurtzborg. Ann. Erphardt. Paris, xvi. 58.

betrayed the secret.[*] Nor had Frederick yet exhausted
the cup of affliction; the worst was to come: suspected,
at least, if unproved treachery in another of his most
tried and faithful servants. Thaddeus of Suessa had
been severed from him by death, his son by imprisonment, Peter de Vineâ was to be so, by the most galling
stroke of all, either foul treason in De Vineâ, or in
himself blind, ungrateful injustice. Peter de Vineâ
had been raised by the wise choice of Fre-   Peter de
derick to the highest rank and influence. All   Vineâ.
the acts of Frederick were attributed to his chancellor.[*]
De Vineâ, like his master, was a poet: he was one of
the counsellors in his great scheme of legislation.
Some rumours spread abroad that at the Council of
Lyons, though Frederick had forbidden all his representatives from holding private intercourse with the
Pope, De Vineâ had many secret conferences with
Innocent, and was accused of betraying his master's
interests. Yet there was no seeming diminution in the
trust placed in De Vineâ. Still to the end the Emperor's letters concerning the disaster at Parma are by
the same hand. Over the cause of his disgrace and
death, even in his own day, there was deep doubt and
obscurity. The popular rumour ran that Frederick was
ill; the physician of De Vineâ prescribed for him; the
Emperor, having received some warning, addressed De
Vineâ: "My friend, in thee I have full trust; art thou
sure that this is medicine, not poison?" De Vineâ
replied: "How often has my physician ministered
healthful medicines!—why are you now afraid?"
Frederick took the cup, sternly commanded the phy-

---

[*] Bologna gave him the mockery of
a splendid funeral. "Sepultus est
maximo cum honore."—B. Museum

Chronicon, p. 840.

[*] There is some doubt whether he
was actually chancellor.

sician to drink half of it. The physician threw himself
at the King's feet, and as he fell overthrew the liquor.
But what was left was administered to some criminals,
who died in agony. The Emperor wrung his hands
and wept bitterly : " Whom can I now trust, betrayed
by my own familiar friend? Never can I know security, never can I know joy more." By one account
Peter de Vineâ was led ignominiously on an ass through
Pisa, and thrown into prison, where he dashed his
brains out against the wall. Dante's immortal verse
has saved the fame of De Vineâ : according to the
poet, he was the victim of wicked and calumnious
jealousy.[b]

The next year Frederick himself lay dying at Fiorentino. His spirit was broken by the defeat
of Parma ; a strange wayward irresolution
came over him : now he would march fiercely to Lyons
and dethrone the Pope ; now he was ready to make the
humblest submission ; now he seemed to break out into
paroxysms of cruelty—prisoners were put to the torture, hung. Frederick, if at times rebellious against
the religion, was not above the superstition of his times.
He had faith in astrology : it had also been foretold
that he should die in Firenze (Florence). In Floren-
tino, a town not far from Lucera, he was seized
with a mortal sickness. The hatred which
pursued him to the grave, and far beyond the grave,
described him as dying unreconciled to the Church,
miserable, deserted, conscious of the desertion of all.
The inexorable hatred pursued his family, and charged

b " I son colui, che tenne ambo le chiavi
Del cuor di Federigo, e che le volsi
Serrando e disserrando, sì soavi   *   *

Lo ministro, che mal del ospizio
In Cesare con furon gli occhi putti,

Morte commune, e delle corti vizio
Infiammò contra me l' animi tutti.

E gl' infiammati infiammar sì Au-
gusto,
Che i lieti onor tornaro in tristi lutti,"
et seqq.—Inferno, xiii. 54,

his son Manfred with hastening his death by smothering
him with a pillow.   By more credible accounts he died
in Manfred's arms, having confessed and received absolution from the faithful Archbishop of Palermo.   His
body was carried to Palermo in great state, a magnificent tomb raised over his remains, an epitaph proclaiming his glory and his virtues was inscribed by his
son Manfred.[*]   In his last will he directed that all her
rights and honours should be restored to the Holy
Church of Rome, his mother; under the condition that
the Church should restore all the rights and honours of
the Empire.   In this provision the Church refused to
see any concession, it was the still stubborn and perfidious act of a rebel.   All his other pious legacies for
the rebuilding and endowment of churches passed for
nothing.

The world might suppose that with the death of
Frederick the great cause of hostility had been removed; but he left to his whole race the inheritance of
the implacable hatred of the Papal See; it was extinguished only in the blood of the last of the house of
Hohenstaufen on the scaffold at Naples.

It might indeed seem as if, in this great conflict,
each had done all in his power to justify the extreme
suspicion, the immitigable aversion, of his adversary;
to stir up the elements of strife, so that the whole
world was arrayed, one half against the other, in defence
of vital and absorbing principles of action.   It was
a war of ideas, as well as of men; and those ideas, on
each side, maintained to the utmost imaginable height.
That the justice of Frederick was a stern absolutism

[*] " Si probitas, sensus, virtutum gratia, census,
Nobilitas orti possent obsistere morti
Non foret extinctus Fredericus qui jacet intus."

cannot be denied; that his notion of the Imperial
power was not merely irreconcileable with the fierce
and partisan liberties of the Italian republics, but with
all true freedom; that he aspired to crush mankind
into order and happiness with the iron hand of autocracy. Still no less than autocracy in those times
could coerce the countless religious and temporal feudal
tyrannies which oppressed and retarded civilisation.
The Sicilian legislation of Frederick shows that order
and happiness were the ultimate aim of his rule: the
assertion of the absolute supremacy of law; premature
advance towards representative government; the regard to the welfare of all classes; the wise commercial
regulations; the cultivation of letters, arts, natural
philosophy, science; all these if despotically enforced,
were enforced by a wise and beneficent despotism.
That Frederick was honoured, admired, loved by a
great part of his subjects; that if by one party he was
looked on with the bitterest abhorrence, to others he
was no less the object of wonder and of profound attachment, appears from his whole history. In Sicily and
Naples, though the nobles had been held down with an
inflexible hand, though he was compelled to impose
still heavier taxation, though his German house had
contracted a large debt of unpopularity, though there
might be more than one conspiracy instantly and
sternly suppressed, yet there was in both countries a
fond, almost romantic attachment, to his name and that
of his descendants. The crown of Germany, which he
won by his gallant enterprise, he secured by his affability, courtesy, chivalrous nobleness of character. In
Germany, not all the influence of the Pope could for a
long time raise up a formidable opposition; the feeble
rebellion of his son, unlike most parricidal rebellions of

old, was crushed on his appearance. For a long time
many of the highest churchmen were on his side : and
when all the churchmen arrayed themselves against
him, all, even his most dangerous enemies among the
temporal princes, rallied round his banner; the Empire
was one; it was difficult to find an obscure insignificant
prince, with all the hierarchy on his side, to hazard the
assumption of the Imperial crown.

The religion of Frederick is a more curious problem.
If it exercised no rigorous control over his Religion of
luxurious life, there was in his day no indis- Frederick.
soluble alliance between Christian morals and Christian
religion. This holy influence was no less wanting to
the religion of many other kings, who lived and died in
the arms of the Church. Frederick, if he had not been
Emperor and King of Sicily, and so formidable to the
Papal power, might have dallied away his life in unrebuked voluptuousness. If he had not threatened the
patrimony of St. Peter, he might have infringed on
the pure precepts of St. Peter. Frederick was a persecutor of the worst kind—a persecutor without bigotry :
but the heretics were not only misbelievers, they were
Lombard rebels. How far he may have been goaded
into general scepticism by the doubts forced upon him
by the unchristian conduct of the great churchmen:
how far, in his heart, he had sunk to the miserable
mocking indifference betrayed by some of the sarcasms,
current, as from his lips, and which, even if merely gay
and careless words, jarred so harshly on the sensitive
religion of his age, cannot be known. Frederick certainly made no open profession of unbelief; he repeatedly offered to assert and vindicate the orthodoxy
of his creed before the Pope himself. He was not
superior, it is manifest, to some of the superstitions of

his time; he is accused of studying the influence of the
stars, but it may have been astrology aspiring (under
Arabic teaching) to astronomy, rather than astronomy
grovelling down to astrology.[d]   That which most revolted his own age, his liberality towards the Mohammedans, his intercourse by negotiation, and in the Holy
Land, with the Sultan and his viziers, and with his own
enlightened Saracen subjects, as well as his terrible
body-guard at Nocera, will find a fairer construction in
modern times.   How much Europe had then to learn
from Arabian letters, arts and sciences; how much of
her own wisdom to receive back through those channels,
appeared during the present and the succeeding centuries.   Frederick's, in my judgement, was neither scornful
and godless infidelity, nor certainly a more advanced
and enlightened Christianity, yearning after holiness
and purity not then attainable.   It was the shattered,
dubious, at times trembling faith, at times desperately
reckless incredulity, of a man for ever under the burthen of an undeserved excommunication, of which he
could not but discern the injustice, but could not quite
shake off the terrors : of a man, whom a better age of
Christianity might not have made religious; whom his
own made irreligious.   Perhaps the strongest argument
in favour of Frederick, is the generous love which he
inspired to many of the noblest minds of his time; not
merely such bold and eloquent legists as Thaddeus of
Suessa, whose pride and conscious power might conspire
with his zeal for the Imperial cause, to make him confront so intrepidly, so eloquently, the Council at Lyons;
it was the first bold encounter of the Roman lawyer

---

[d] Read on the religion of Frederick the passage in Ernest Renan's Averroes,
p. 286, et seqq.

with the host of Canon lawyers. Nor was it merely
Peter de Vineâ, whose melancholy fate revenged itself
for its injustice, if he ever discovered its injustice, on
the stricken and desolate heart of the King: but of
men, like Herman of Salza, the Grand Master of the
Teutonic Order. Herman was, by all accounts, one of
the most blameless, the noblest, the most experienced,
most religious of men. If his Teutonic Order owed
the foundation of its greatness, with lavish grants and
immunities, to Frederick, it owed its no less valuable
religious existence, its privileges, its support against the
hostile clergy, to the Popes. Honorius and Gregory
vied with the Emperor in heaping honours on De Salza
and his Order. Yet throughout his first conflict, De
Salza is the firm, unswerving friend of Frederick. He
follows his excommunicated master to the Holy Land,
adheres to his person in good report and evil report;
death alone separates the friends.* The Archbishop of
Palermo (against whom is no breath of calumny) is no
less, to the close of Frederick's life, his tried and inseparable friend; he never seems to have denied him,
though excommunicate, the offices of religion; buried
him, though yet unabsolved, in his cathedral; inscribed on his tomb an epitaph, which, if no favourable
proof of the Archbishop's poetic powers, is the lasting
tribute of his fervent, faithful admiration.

On the other hand, Innocent IV. not only carried the
Papal claims to the utmost, and asserted them   Pope Inno-
with a kind of ostentatious intrepidity: "We   cent IV.
are no mere man, we have the place of God upon
earth!" but there was a personal arrogance in his

---

* In Voigt, Geschichte Preussens, is a very elaborate and interesting account
of Herman of Salza, and the rise of the Teutonic Order.

demeanour, and an implacability which revolted even
the most awe-struck worshippers of the Papal power.
Towards Frederick he showed, blended with the haughtiness of the Pope, the fierceness of a Guelfic partisan;
he hated him with something of the personal hatred of
a chief of the opposite faction in one of the Italian
republics. Never was the rapacity of the Roman See
so insatiate as under Innocent IV.; the taxes levied in
England alone, her most profitable spiritual estate,
amounted to incredible sums. Never was aggression so
open or so daring on the rights and exemptions of the
clergy (during the greater part of the strife the support
of the two new Orders enabled the Pope to trample on
the clergy, and to compel them to submit to extor-
tionate contributions towards his wars): never was the
spiritual character so entirely merged in the temporal
as among his Legates. They were no longer the austere
and pious, if haughty churchmen. Cardinal Rainier
commanded the Papal forces in the state of St. Peter
with something of the ability and all the ferocity and
mercilessness of a later Captain of Condottieri. Albert
von Beham, the Archdeacon of Passau, had not merely
been detected, as we have seen, in fraudulent malversa-
tion and shamefully expelled from Bavaria, but when he
appeared again as Dean of Passau, his own despatches,
which describe his negotiations with the Duke of Bavaria, show a repulsive depth of arrogant iniquity. The
incitement of Conrad to rebellion against his father
seems to him but an ordinary proceeding. The Bishop
of Ferrara, the Legate in Germany, was a drunkard, if
not worse. Gregory of Monte Longo, during the whole
period Papal representative in Lombardy, the conductor
of all the negotiations with the republics, the republics
which swarmed with heretics, was a man of notorious

incontinence; Frederick himself had hardly more concubines than the Cardinal Legate.

Immediately on the death of Frederick, the Pope
began to announce his intention of returning *The Pope*
to Italy. Peter Capoccio was ordered to ascer- *after the death of Frederick.*
tain the state of feeling in the kingdom of Sicily. The
Pope himself raised a song of triumph, addressed to all
the prelates and all the nobles of the realm: "Earth
and heaven were to break out into joy at this great
deliverance."[f] But the greater number of both orders
seem to have been insensible to the blessing; they
were mourning over the grave of him whom the Pope
described as the hammer of persecution. The aged
Archbishop of Palermo and the Archbishop of Salerno
openly espoused the cause of Conrad; the Archbishop
of Bari, Frederick's deadly enemy, seemed to stand
alone in the Papal interest. Strangers, the Subdeacon
Matthew, and a Dominican friar, were sent into Calabria and Sicily to stir up the clergy to a sense of their
wrongs. In Germany Conrad was arraigned as a
rebellious usurper for presuming to offer resistance to
William of Holland. He was again solemnly excommunicated; a crusade was preached against him. The
Pope even endeavoured to estrange the Swabians from
their liege lord: "Herod is dead; Archelaus aspires to
reign in his stead." In an attempt to murder *Dec. 20, 1252.*
Conrad at Ratisbon, the Abbot Ulric is sup-
posed to have been the chief actor; the Bishop of
Ratisbon was awaiting without the walls the glad tidings
of the accomplishment of the assassination.[g] The Archbishop of Mentz, Christian, a prelate of great piety,

[f] Raynald, sub ann. 1251.

[g] " Qui episcopus foras muros civitatis cum multis armatis eventum rei
solicitus expectabat." — Herm. Alt.
apud Boehmer, ii. 507. See Chron.
Salis, Pez, i. 362.

broaches the unpalatable doctrine that, as far as spiritual
enemies, the word of God is the only lawful sword; but
as for drawing the sword of steel, he held it unbefitting
his priestly character. He is deposed for these strange
opinions.[b] A youth, the Subdeacon Gerard, is placed
on the Primate's throne of Germany.

Monarchs, however, seemed to vie in giving honour
to the triumphant Pontiff on his proposed
return to Rome. The Queen-mother Blanche
of France (Louis IX., her son, was now prisoner in the
East) offered to accompany him with a strong body of
French troops. Henry of England expressed his earnest
desire to prostrate himself at the feet of the Holy
Father before he departed for the south. Alphonso of
Castile entreated him to trust to the arms, fleets, and
protection of Spain rather than of France. Before he
bade farewell to the city of Lyons, whose pious hospitality he rewarded with high praise and some valuable
privileges,[i] he had an interview within the city with
his own Emperor William of Holland. After that he
descended the Rhone to Vienne, to Orange, and then
proceeded to Marseilles. He arrived at
Genoa; the city hailed her holy son with
the utmost honours. The knights and nobles of the
territory supported a silken canopy over his head to

---

[b] " At jure episcopatu dejectum ob
principatum conjunctam exploratum
est; cum non modo praesulem sed
etiam principem agere, ac vim insultan-
tium ecclesiis vi repellere oporteret."
Such is the comment of the ecclesiastical annalist Raynaldus, sub ann.

[i] The morals of Lyons were not
improved by the residence of the
Papal court. It was openly declared
by Cardinal Hugo, " Magnam fecimus,
postquam in hanc urbem venimus,
utilitatem et eleemosynam: quando
enim primo huc venimus, tria vel
quatuor prostibula invenimus; sed
nunc recedentes unum solum relinqui-
mus; verum ipsum durat continuatum
ab orientali parte civitatis usque ad
occidentalem."—Matt. Paris, p. 819.

protect him from the sun. On Ascension Day he received the delegates from the cities of Lombardy. Ghibellinism held down its awe-struck   May 17.
and discomfited head. Rome alone was not as yet thought
worthy, or sought not to be admitted to the favour of
his presence, or he dared not trust,[b] notwithstanding
his close alliance with the Frangipani (whom he had
bought), that unruly city. He visited Milan, Innocent
Brescia, Mantua, Ferrara, Modena, everywhere July 31.
there was tumultuous joy among the Guelfs. While
he was at Milan Lodi made her submission: the Count
of Savoy abandoned the party of the Hohenstaufen.
On All-Saints'-Day he was at Faenza; on the 5th of
November he stayed his steps, and fixed his court at
Perugia. For a year and a half he remained in that
city; Rome was not honoured with the presence of her
Pontiff till Rome compelled that presence.

Among the first resolutions of Innocent was the suppression of heresy, more especially in the Ghibelline
cities, such as Cremona. A holocaust of these outcasts
would be a fit offering of gratitude to heaven for the
removal of the perfidious Frederick. It was his design
to strike in this manner at the head of the Ghibelline interests in Lombardy. The sum of Eccelin da
Romano's atrocities, atrocities which, even if blackened
by Guelfic hatred, are the most frightful in these
frightful times, must be still aggravated by the charge
of hereditary heresy. It may well be doubted if such
a monster could have religion enough to be a heretic;
but Eccelin was dead to spiritual censures as to the
reproaches of his own conscience.

But the affairs of the kingdom of Naples occupied the

---

[b] Nic. de Curbio, c. 30.

thoughts of Innocent. Though the firm hand of Manfred
had maintained almost the whole realm in allegiance,
the nominal rule was intrusted by King Conrad to his
younger brother Henry. The denunciations, intrigues,
and censures of the Pope had wrought on certain nobles
and cities. A conspiracy broke out simultaneously in
many places, at the head of which was the Count of
Aquino; in Apulia the cities of Foggia, Andrea, and
Barletta; in the Terra di Lavoro Capua and Naples
were in open rebellion. Capua and Naples defied all
the forces of Manfred. The Pope had already assumed
a sovereign power, as if the forfeited realm had reverted
to the Holy See. He had revoked all Frederick's
decrees which were hostile to the Church: he had invested Henry Frangipani with Manfred's principality of
Tarentum and the land of Otranto; he had bestowed
on the Venetian Marco Ziani, the kinsman of the captain
executed by Frederick, the principality of Lecce.

Conrad had already with some forces crossed the
Alps; he had been received by the few faithful Ghi-
bulline cities in Lombardy, Verona, Padua,
Vicenza. But throughout Central Italy the
Guelfic faction prevailed; the Papal forces were strong.
He demanded of the Venetians, and as they were glad
to get rid of Conrad from the north of Italy, he obtained
ships to convey him to the south; he landed at Siponto,
near Manfredonia. He was received by Manfred and
by the principal nobility as their deliverer.
Aquino, Suessa, San Germano fell before him,
and Capua opened her gates; Naples was
stormed, sacked, and treated with the utmost cruelty.
Innocent beheld the son of Frederick, though under
excommunication, in full and undisturbed possession of
his hereditary kingdom. Innocent looked in vain for

aid in Italy; his own forces, those of the Guelfs, had
not obeyed the summons to relieve Naples. Eccelin da
Romano and the Ghibellines occupied those of Lombardy; the Guelfs of Tuscany and Romagna, now
superior to the Ghibellines, had broken out into factions
among themselves; the fleets of Genoa were engaged
against the infidels. Innocent looked abroad; the
wealth of England had been his stay in former adver-
sities. He had already sent an offer of the kingdom of
Naples to the brother of King Henry, Richard of
Cornwall; but Richard, from timidity or prudence,
shrunk from this remote enterprise. He alleged the
power of Conrad; his own relationship with the house of
Swabia: in his mistrust he went so far as to demand
guarantees and hostages for the fulfilment of
his contract on the part of the Pope. But his
feeble brother, Henry of England, was not
embarrassed by this prudence. He accepted
the offer of the investiture for his second son
Edmund; in his weak vanity he addressed Edmund in
his court, and treated him as already the King of Sicily.
The more prudent Nuncio of the Pope enjoined greater
caution; but all that the King could abstract from his
own exchequer, borrow of his brother Richard, extort
from the Jews, exact by his justices on their circuit, was
faithfully transmitted to Rome, and defrayed the cost of
the Papal armament against Conrad. For this vain title,
which the Pope resumed at his earliest convenience,
Henry III. endangered his own throne: these exactions
precipitated the revolt of his Barons, which ended in the
battle of Lewes.

But while Innocent IV. was thus triumphing over the
fall of his great enemy; while he was levying taxes on
the tributary world; while he was bestowing the empire

T 2

of Germany on William of Holland, assuming the kingdom of Naples as an appanage escheated to the See of
Rome, and selling it to one foreign prince after another,
he was himself submitting to the stern dictation of the
people and the Senator of Rome. The Frangipanis
could no longer repay with their vigorous support the
honours bestowed upon their family by the grant of
the principality of Tarentum. The popular party was
The Senator   in the ascendant. Brancaleone, a Bolognese
Brancaleone.   of great fame as a lawyer, was summoned to
assume the dignity of Senator of Rome. He refused
for a time to place himself at the head of the unruly
people; he consented only on the prudent condition
that thirty hostages of the noblest families in Rome
should be sent to Bologna. Nor would he condescend
to accept the office but for the period of three years.
He exacted a solemn oath of obedience from every
citizen. At first the nobles as well as the people
appear to have acquiesced in the stern, just rule of the
Senator. No rank, no power could protect the high
born; no obscurity, nor the favour of the populace, the
meaner criminal. His first act was to hang from the
windows of their castles some citizens notorious and
convicted as homicides; other rebels he suspended on
gibbets.[*] Among his first acts was to summon the
Bishop of Rome to take up his residence in his diocese;
it was not becoming that the Queen of cities should sit
as a widow without her Pontiff. Innocent hesitated; a
more imperious message summoned him to instant obedience; at the same time the Perugians received a
significant menace; that if they persisted in entertaining
the Pope, the Romans would treat them as they had

---

[*] Raynald. sub ann. 1254.

already treated other cities in the neighbourhood, whom
they had subdued by force of arms. Inno- _{May 22, 1253.}
cent trembled and complied; he entered Rome
with a serene countenance but heavy heart. He was
received with triumph by the Senator and the whole
people. In the spring Innocent again withdrew from
Rome to Assisi; the pretext was the consecration of the
magnificent church of St. Francis.* But the impatient
people murmured at his delay; the Senator Brancaleone
again sent messengers to expostulate in haughty humility
with the Pope; " it became not the pastor to abandon his
flock: he was the Bishop not of Lyons, of Perugia, of
Anagni, but of Rome." The people of Assisi, like those
of Perugia, were warned by the fate of Ostia, Porto
Tusculum, Albano, Sabina, and of Tivoli, against which
last the Romans were in arms. Innocent was compelled
to return; he passed by Narni, and again he was received
with outward demonstrations of joy; but now secret
murmurs and even violent reclamations were heard that
the Pope owed the people of Rome great sums for the
losses sustained by his long absence. Pilgrims and suitors
had been few; they had let no lodgings; their shops had
been without customers; their provisions unsold; their
old usurious profits of lending money had failed. The
Pope could only take refuge in the rigid justice of the Senator; Brancaleone allayed or awed the tumult to peace.

Yet at the same time Innocent was pursuing his
schemes upon the kingdom of Naples without _{Early in 1254. Conrad in Naples.}
fear or scruple. Conrad at first had made
overtures of submission.° He was strong enough to

---

* Matt. Paris, sub ann. 1252.
Carbes, VII. Innocent. IV. Compare
Gibbon, xii. 278, ch. lxix.

° To the Pope's first envoy, ac-

cording to Spinelli, Conrad haughtily
replied, " Ché farei meglio ad impac-
ciarsi con la chierica rasa,"— Darin,
apud Muratori.

indulge the hereditary cruelty which he unhappily displayed in a far higher degree than the ability and
splendour of his forefathers,' and to foster ignoble
jealousy against his bastard brother, Manfred, to whom
he owed the preservation of his realm, but whose fame,
extraordinary powers of body and mind, influence,
popularity overshadowed the authority of the King.
He gradually withdrew his confidence from Manfred,
and despoiled him of his power and honours.' With
admirable prudence Manfred quietly let fall title after
title, post after post, possession after possession; nothing
remained to him but the principality of Tarentum, and
that burthened with a heavy tax raised for the royal
treasury. The King dismissed, under various pretexts,
the kindred of Manfred, Galvaneo and Frederico Lancia,
Bonifacio di Argoino, his maternal uncle. The noble
exiles found refuge with the Empress Constantia, Manfred's sister, at Constantinople: Conrad, by his ambassadors, insisted on their expulsion from that court.

But the Pope, in his despair at this unexpected
strength displayed by the House of Swabia, had recourse to new measures of hostility. Conrad, like his
ally Eccelin, was attainted of heresy; both were summoned to appear before the presence of the Pope to
answer these charges; and to surrender themselves
unarmed, unprotected into the hands of their enemy.
Conrad, whose policy it was rather to conciliate than
irreconcileably to break with the Pope, condescended
to make his appearance by his proctor in the Papal
Court.

But death was on the house of Hohenstaufen. Henry,

' " Vi fece gran giustizia, e grande | di Neocastro, c. 61. Murat., R. I. S.
nobilare."— M. Spinelli, Diario, apud | xiii.
Muratori, R. I. S. xii. Barthelemo   ' Giannone p. 485.

the younger son of Frederick, a youth of twelve years old, came from Sicily to visit his brother Conrad; 'he sickened and died.' No death could take place in this doomed family, the object of such inextinguishable hate, without being darkened from a calamity into a crime. Conrad was accused of poisoning his brother, and by the Pope himself. Even the melancholy of Conrad at the loss of his brother, perhaps a presentiment of his own approaching end, was attributed to remorse. He hardly raised his head again; he wrote letters to the court of England, full of the most passionate grief. In another year Conrad himself was in his grave: he was seized with a violent fever, and died in a few days. Of his death the guilt, for guilt the Guelfs were determined to see, was laid on Manfred.[*] Conradin, almost an infant, not three years old, was the one legitimate heir of Barbarossa and of Frederick II. The consummate sagacity of Manfred led him to declare that he would not accept the Regency of the realm which Conrad (perhaps in some late remorse, or in the desperate conviction enforced on his death-bed, that Manfred alone could protect his son) had thought of bequeathing to him. Manfred awaited his time: he left to Berthold, Marquis of Homburg, the commander of the German auxiliaries of Conrad, the perilous post, knowing perhaps at once the incapacity of Berthold, and the odiousness of the Germans to the subjects of Sicily. Berthold, according to the will of Conrad,

Death of Prince Henry. Dec. 1253.

Of Conrad. May 21, 1254.

Conradin.

---

* Matt. Paris, sub ann. Nic. de Jamsilla. The Pope is said to have proposed to marry his niece to Henry (Paris, p. 832). A treaty was begun. Conrad during the negotiations was poisoned, but recovered. He accused the Pope of this poisoning (Ibid. 851). The Pope himself accused Conrad of poisoning Henry.

* Jamsilla, Malespina.

assumed the Regency, took possession of the royal
treasures, and, in obedience to the dying instructions of
Conrad, sent a humble message entreating peace and
the parental protection of the Pope for the fatherless
orphan. Innocent was said to have broken out into a
paroxysm of joy on hearing the death of Conrad. But
he assumed a lofty tone of compassion; enlarged upon
his own merciful disposition; granted to Conradin the barren title of King of Jerusalem, and
acknowledged his right to the Dukedom of Swabia.
But the absolute dominion of the kingdom of Naples
had devolved to the Roman See: when Conradin
should be of age, the See of Rome might then, if he
should appear not undeserving, condescend to take his
claims into her gracious consideration.

Innocent had again, perhaps on account of the
summer heats, escaped from Rome, and was holding
his court at Anagni. He spared no measures to become
master of the kingdom of Naples. He issued extraordinary powers to William, Cardinal of St. Eustachio,
to raise money and troops for this enterprise. The
Cardinal was authorised to empawn as security to the
Roman merchants, the Church of Rome, all the castles
and possessions of the separate churches of the city,
of the Campagna and the Maritima, and of the kingdom
of Sicily. He was to seize and appropriate to the use
of the war the possessions and revenues of all the
vacant Bishoprics; and of all the Bishoprics, though
not vacant, whose prelates did not espouse the Papal
cause. He had power to levy taxes, and even money
throughout the realm; to confiscate all the estates of
the adherents of Frederick and of his son, who should
not, after due admonition, return to their allegiance to
the Pope. He might annul all grants, seize all fiefs,

and regrant them to the partisans of Rome. By these
exertions, a great army was gathered on the frontier.
From Anagni the Pope issued his bull of excommunication against Manfred, the Marquis of Homburg, and
all the partisans of the house of Conrad.[1] The Regent,
the Marquis of Homburg, found that many of the nobles
were in secret treaty with the Pope; he let the sceptre
of Regency fall from his feeble hands; and amidst the
general contempt abdicated his trust.

All eyes were turned on Manfred; all who were
attached to the house of Swabia, all who abhorred or
despised the Papal government, all who desired the
independence of the realm, counts, barons, many of
the higher clergy, at least in secret, implored   Manfred
Manfred to assume the Regency. Manfred,   Regent.
consummate in the art of self-command, could only be
forced in these calamitous times to imperil his honour
by taking up this dangerous post. Rumours indeed
were abroad of the death of Conradin; and Manfred
was the next successor, according to the will of his
father Frederick.[2] He assumed the Regency; threw a
strong force of Germans into San Germano; fortified
Capua and the adjacent towns to check the   Date comm-
progress of the Papal arms. But everywhere   Feb. 1254.
was rebellion, defection, treachery. The Papal agents
had persuaded or bribed Pietro Ruffo, the Regent,
under Berthold of Homburg, of Calabria and Sicily,
and raised the Papal standard. Berthold's own conduct

---

[1] Apud Raynald. 1254, Sept. 2.

[2] Sic. Jamsilla makes Manfred legitimate; his mother, Bianca Lancia, was the *fifth* wife of Frederick. But Manfred does not seem to have asserted his own legitimacy. Malespini (though Papalist) writes, "Tanquam ex dam-

nato coitu derivatus, defectum nati-
vitas patitur, nobilis tamen naturæ
decus utriusque parentis, qua ortus
ejus esse mereatur generosus, maculam
sere defectûs hujus expiabat."—Apud
Muratori, viii. 787.

indicated treachery; he sent no troops to the aid of
Manfred, but roved about with his Germans, committing
acts of plunder, and so estranging the people from the
Swabian rule. He retained possession of the royal
treasures. Richard of Monte Negro had already, in
hatred of Berthold, made his peace with the Pope; other
nobles were secretly dealing for the renewal of their
fiefs, or for the grant of escheated fiefs, with the Pope,
who claimed the right of universal sovereign. Even in
Capua a conspiracy was discovered against the power
and against the life of Manfred.

Manfred was as great a master in the arts of dissimulation as the Pope himself. He found it
necessary at least to appear to yield. Already
the Papal agents had sounded his fidelity; he now
openly appealed to the magnanimity of the Pope as the
protector of the orphan; he expressed his willingness to
admit the Pope into the realm, reserving his own rights
and those of his royal ward. Innocent was in a
transport of joy. In his most luxuriant language he
dwelt on the moderation, the delight in mercy, the
parental tenderness of the Roman See: he received
Manfred into his highest favour. Not regarding his
grant to the Frangipani, he invested Manfred (Galvano
Fiamma, his uncle, receiving in his name the ring of
investiture) with the Principality of Tarentum, with the
County of Gravino, Tricarico, and the Honour of Monte
St. Angelo: he added the Countship of Andrea, which
he had obtained in exchange for other territories from
the Marquis of Homburg: with this he invested Frederick Lancia, Manfred's other uncle. Manfred met all
these advances with his consummate self-command. He
received the Pope on his entrance into his kingdom at
Ceperano, prostrated himself at his feet, led his horse,

as he passed the bridge over the Garigliano.[a] The
pride of Innocent was at its height in seeing Naples in
his power, the son of Frederick at his feet. He lavished
honours on Manfred; proclaimed him Vicar of the
realm as far as the Faro. Manfred persuaded the Pope
to scatter his forces all through the provinces, and by
their means controlled the Germans, whom he could
not trust, and who began quietly to withdraw to their
own country.[b] The people hailed Manfred as Vicar of
the Pope. They enjoyed again, and under a Swabian
Prince not environed by German soldiery, their full
religious ceremonies.

The Pope entered the kingdom as though to take
possession of the realm; after a short delay at The Pope
Teano from indisposition, he entered Capua Oct. 27, 1254.
in state; he entered Naples in still greater pomp. His
nephew, William Fiesco, Cardinal of St. Eustachio, his
Legate, received the homage of the prelates and the
nobles, with no reservation of the rights of the King or
of the Prince, but absolutely in the name of the Pope,
to whom had devolved the full sovereignty. Manfred
himself was summoned to take the oath of allegiance.
In his deep dissimulation he might have eluded this
trial; he was perhaps awaiting the death of the Pope,
now old and in bad health; but an accidental circum-
stance compelled him prematurely to throw off the
mask. Borello d'Anglone, as the reward of his revolt
to the Pope, had received the grant of the county of
Lesina, an under-fief of Manfred's principality. Manfred
summoned him to do homage; Anglone, confident in
the Pope's favour, returned a haughty denial. Manfred

---

[a] On this homage, says Spinelli, "et onneuno se ne meravigliao assai." —
Apud Muratori.   [b] Giannone, in loc.

appealed to the Pope. The oracle spoke with his usual cautious ambiguity, he had granted to Borello none of the rights of Manfred. Berthold of Homburg was on his way to do homage to the Pope; Manfred withdrew, lest he should encounter him in Capua; his guards fell in with those of Borello; strife arose, Borello, unknown

Death of Borello d'Anglona. Flight of Manfred. to Manfred, was slain. Manfred sent his messengers, declaring himself ready to prove himself before the Pope guiltless of the death of Borello. He was summoned to answer in person. He received secret intelligence from his uncle Galvano Lancia, that the treacherous Berthold of Homburg, instead of espousing his cause, had secretly betrayed it; that his liberty at least was threatened, if not his life. He mounted his horse, with few followers; after many wild adventures, he reached the city of Lucera, occupied chiefly by the Saracenic allies of his father. In despite of the German knights who commanded in the city in the name of Berthold of Homburg, he was received with the loudest acclamations. He was proclaimed Prince and Sovereign. Before the people he swore to maintain and defend the rights and title of the King his nephew, and his own, the liberty and the good estate of the realm, and of the city.

In a short time he was master of Foggia, had gained a brilliant victory over the Papal troops, and those of the Marquis of Homburg.

Innocent had already entered into negotiations with that enemy afterwards so fatal to Manfred. He had once sold the realm of Sicily to Edmund of England,

Dec. 1254. and received at least some part of the price: he had now, regardless of his former obligations, or supposing them forfeited by the inactivity or less lavish subsidies of England, offered the realm to

Charles of Anjou, the brother of the King of France.
All his solemn engagements were, to Innocent IV., but
means to advance his immediate interests. He might
seem as if he would try to the utmost his own power of
absolution, to release himself from the most sacred
obligations.[*]

But death, which had prostrated the enemies of Innocent before his feet, and had reduced the house
of Swabia to a child and a bastard, now laid
his hand on Innocent himself. He died master of
Naples, the city of his great adversary, in the palace of
Peter de Vineâ, the minister of that adversary. He left
a name odious for ambition, rapacity, implacable pride,
to part, at least, of Christendom. In England, where
his hand had been the heaviest, strange tales were
accredited of his dying hours, and of what followed his
death. It was said that he died in an agony of terror
and remorse; his kindred were bitterly wailing around
his bed, rending their garments and tearing their hair:
he woke up from a state seemingly senseless, "Wretches,
why are yo weeping? have I not made you all rich
enough?" He had been, indeed, one of the first Popes,
himself of noble family, who by the marriage of his
nieces, by heaping up civil and ecclesiastical dignities
on his relatives, had made a Papal family. On the very
night of his death a monk, whose name the English
historian conceals from prudence, had a vision. He was
in Heaven, and saw God seated on his throne. On God's
right was the Holy Virgin, on his left a stately and
venerable matron, who held what seemed a temple in

[Death of Innocent, Dec. 7, 1254.]

* Petr. de Vineâ, Epist. ii. 45. I promettait et se retractait avec une
here agree with M. Cherrier : "Trop | rigole facilité, suivant l'état de ses
de faits attestent qu'Innocent IV. | affaires."—t. iii. p. 394.
s'etait montre avec personne ; qu'il

her outstretched hand. On the pediment of this temple
was written in letters of gold, "The Church." Innocent was prostrate before the throne, with clasped and
lifted hands and bowed knees, imploring pardon, not
judgement. But the noble matron said, "O, equitable
judge, render just judgement. I arraign this man on
three charges: Thou hast founded the Church upon
earth and bestowed upon her precious liberties; this
man has made her the vilest of slaves. The Church
was founded for the salvation of sinners; he has degraded
it to a counting-house of money-changers. The Church
has been built on the foundation stones of faith, justice,
and truth; he has shaken alike faith and morals,
destroyed justice, darkened truth." And the Lord
said, "Depart and receive the recompense thou hast
deserved;" and Innocent was dragged away. "Whether
this was an unreal vision, we know not," adds the historian, "but it alarmed many. God grant it may have
amended them."

Nor was this all. The successor of Innocent was himself warned and terrified by a dream of not less awful
import. In a spacious palace sat a judge of venerable
majesty; by his side a stately matron, environed by a
countless company. A bier was carried out by mean-
looking bearers; upon it rested a corpse of sad appearance. The dead arose, cast himself before the throne,
"O God of might and mercy, have pity upon me!"
The judge was silent, the matron spoke: "The time of
repentance is passed, the day of judgement is come.
Woe to thee, for thou shalt have justice, not mercy.
Thou hast wasted the Church of God during thy life;
thou hast become a carnal man; disdained, despised,
annulled the acts of thy holy predecessors; therefore
shall thine own acts be held annulled." The sorere

judge uttered his sentence! The bier was hurried away.
The dead sent to a place which the Christian may
charitably hope was Purgatory. Pope Alexander trem-
blingly inquired who was the dead man. His guide
replied, "Sinibald, thy predecessor, who died of grief,
not for his sins, but for the defeat of his army." The
affrighted Alexander, when he awoke, ordered masses
and alms to mitigate the purgatorial suffering of his
predecessor; he endeavoured to retrieve Innocent's sins
by cancelling some of his acts; to one who offered rich
presents to buy a benefice, the Pope replied, " No, my
friend, he who sold churches is dead."*

Such were the current and popular tales, which
showed that even the Pope could not violate the great
principles of Christian justice and generosity and mercy,
with impunity, or without some strong remonstrance
finding its expression. If Innocent, indeed, had not
trampled on the rights of the clergy, these murmurs
had not been so deep and loud: it was this that imper-
sonated, as it were, the Church, to demand his condemnation. It was not Imperialist or Ghibelline hatred,
but the hatred of churchmen which invented or propagated these legends.

In England, indeed, not only after his death, but
during his life, the courageous English spirit had allied
itself with the profoundest religious feeling to protest
against the rapacity and usurpation of the Italian Pope.
It had found a powerful and intrepid voice in Robert
Grostête Bishop of Lincoln. Robert Grostête, during
his life, had manfully resisted and fearlessly condemned
the acts of the haughty Pontiff: after his death he had
been permitted, it was believed, to appear in a vision.

* All these are from Matt. Paris.

Robert Grostête was of humble birth: at Oxford his
profound learning won the admiration of Roger Bacon.
He translated the book called the Testament of the
Twelve Patriarchs. He went to France to make himself master of that language. He became Archdeacon
of Leicester, Bishop of Lincoln. As Bishop of that
vast diocese he began to act with a holy rigour unprecedented in his times. With him Christian morals
were inseparable from Christian faith. He endeavoured
to bring back the festivals of the Church, which had
grown into days of idleness and debauchery, to their
sacred character; he would put down the Feast of
Fools, held on New Year's Day. But it was against the
clergy, as on them altogether depended the holiness of
the people, that he acted with the most impartial
severity. He was a Churchman of the highest hierarchical notions. Becket himself did not assert the
immunities and privileges of the Church with greater
intrepidity: rebellion against the clergy was as the sin
of witchcraft; but those immunities, those privileges,
implied heavier responsibility; that authority belonged
justly only to a holy, exemplary, unworldly clergy.
Everywhere he was encountered with sullen, stubborn,
or open resistance. He was condemned as restless,
harsh, passionate: he was the Ishmael of the hierarchy,
with his hand against every man, every man's hand
against him. The Dean and Chapter of Lincoln were
his foremost and most obstinate opponents; the clergy
asserted their privileges, the monasteries their Papal
exemptions; the nobles complained of his interference
with their rights of patronage, the King himself that he
sternly prohibited the clergy from all secular offices;
they must not act as the King's justiciaries, or sit to
adjudge capital offences. His allies were the new

Orders, the Preachers and Mendicants. He addressed
letters of confidence to the generals of both Orders.
He resolutely took his stand on his right of refusing
institution to unworthy clergy.[b] He absolutely refused
to admit to benefices pluralists, boys, those employed in
the King's secular service, in the courts of judicature or
the collection of the revenue; in many cases foreigners;
he resisted alike Churchmen, the Chancellor of Exeter;
nobles, he would not admit a son of the Earl of Ferrars,
as under age; the King, whose indignation knew no
bounds; he resisted the Cardinal Legates, the Pope
himself.

As a Churchman, Grostête held the loftiest views of
the power of the Pope: his earlier letters to the Pope
are in the most submissive, almost adulatory tone; to
the Cardinals they are full of the most profound reverence. The Canon Law is as eternal, immutable, universal as the law of God. The Pope has undoubted
power to dispose of all benefices; but for the abuse of
that power hell-fire is the doom.[c] The resistance of
the clergy to their Bishop involved the Bishops and
themselves in vast expense; there was a perpetual
appeal to Rome. Twice Grostête appeared in Lyons:
the second time he was received with respect and
courtesy by the Pope and Cardinals. The Pope even
permitted him to read in his own presence and in the
full consistory, a memorial against the abuses of the
Court of Rome (the Curia), of its avarice and venality,
its usurpations and exemptions, hardly surpassed in its

---

[b] Godwin. de Præsul. Matt. Paris.
[c] "Scio et veraciter scio, domini
Papæ et sanctæ Romanæ Ecclesiæ hanc
esse potestatem, ut de omnibus beneficiis
ecclesiasticis libere possit ordinare, scio |
quousque quod quicquid abutitur hac
potestate, ... ædificat ad ignem
Gehennæ."—Epist. 48, apud Brown.
Fasciculus ii. 339.

vigorous invective in later times. Grostête returned to
England with a decree against the refractory Chapter of
Lincoln, ample powers to reform his diocese, and the
strong support of the seeming favour of the Pope. The
Pope even condescended to limit to some extent the
demands of the Italian clergy on English benefices.
Yet on his return even the firm mind of Grostête was
shaken by the difficulties of his position: he meditated
retirement from the intractable world; but he shook off
the unworthy sloth, and commenced and carried through
a visitation of his diocese unprecedented in its stern
severity. The contumacious clergy were compelled to
submit, and accepted his conditions; the monasteries
opened their reluctant gates, and acknowledged his
authority. In the convents of nuns he is said to have
put their chastity to a strange and indelicate test, which
shows at once the coarseness of the times and the laxity
of morals. Yet he extorted from the monkish historian,
who perhaps had suffered under his rigour, the admission
that his sole object was the salvation of souls.[a]

On Innocent's triumphal return to Italy he had become, as it were, wanton in his invasions on the impoverished English Church. It was rumoured, incredible
as it seems, that he demanded provision for three
hundred of the Roman clergy.[b] Robert Grostête was
summoned to the test of his obedience to the See of
Rome. He had ordered a calculation to be made of the
ecclesiastical revenues possessed by strangers in Eng-

---

[a] Paris, sub ann.
[b] There are many mandates for benefices in favour of Italians.—MS. B. M.
F. g. Stephen the Pope's chaplain to
hold the rich archdeaconry of Canterbury with the archdeaconry of Verona,
et alia beneficia. vii. sub ann. 1232,
p. 110; a Colonna, 213. An Annibaldi
De ——, and John of Civitella, 289;
one or more prebends, with or without
cure of souls.

land. It amounted to 70,000 marks: the King's income
was not one-third of the sum. Grostête received command, through his Nuncio, to confer a canonry of Lincoln on the nephew of Innocent, a boy, Frederick of
Lavagna. Grostête was not daunted by the ascendant
power of the Pope.[f] His answer was a firm, resolute,
argumentative refusal: "I am bound by filial reverence
to obey all commands of the Apostolic See; but those
are not Apostolic commands which are not consonant to
the doctrine of the Apostles, and the Master of the
Apostles, Christ Jesus. The most holy Apostolic See
cannot command that which verges on the odious detestable abomination, pernicious to mankind, opposed
to the sanctity of the Apostolic See, contrary to the
Catholic faith. You cannot in your discretion enact
any penalty against me, for my resistance is neither
strife nor rebellion, but filial affection to my father, and
veneration for my mother the Church."[g]

It was reported in England, that when this letter
reached the Pope, he cried out in a passion of wrath,
"Who is this old dotard who presumes to judge our
acts? By St. Peter and St. Paul, if we were not restrained by our generosity, we would make him a fable,
an astonishment, an example, and a warning to the
world. Is not the King of England our vassal, rather
our slave? Would he not, at a sign from us, throw

---

[f] Paris.

[g] The letter in Brown. Fasciculus, p. 400. There is a point which I find it difficult to explain. In the former epistle to the Legate Otho (quoted above), Epist. 49—seemingly of an earlier period—Grostête writes: "Licet post meam consecrationem in Episcopum serpens Domini Papa promotas

all in eo de optimis pretendis in Lincolniensi Ecclesiâ." This could not be another nephew of Innocent; at the time of his nomination he must have been a boy indeed. Another writer (Ann. Burton) calls him puerulus. Compare Grostête's Letters on the Pope in the Grostête Epistolæ (Rolls publications) page 432.

D 2

this Bishop into prison and reduce him to the lowest disgrace?" With difficulty the Cardinals allayed his wrath: they pleaded the Bishop's irreproachable life, his Catholic doctrine; they more than insinuated the truth of his charges. The condemnation of Grostête might revolt the whole clergy of France and England, "for he is held a great philosopher, deeply learned in Greek and Latin letters, a reader in theology, a devout preacher, an admirer of chastity, a persecutor of Simoniacs." The more moderate or more astute counsels prevailed. Papal letters were framed which in some degree mitigated the abuses of these Papal provisions. The Pope acknowledged, almost in apologetic tone, that he had been driven by the difficulties of the times and the irresistible urgency of partisans to measures which he did not altogether approve. All who possessed such benefices were to be guaranteed in their free enjoyment, all who had expectancies were to be preferred to other persons, but these benefices were not to go down, as it were, by hereditary descent from Italian to Italian: on decease or vacancy the patron, prelate, monastery, or layman, might at once present.[b]

On Grostête's death it was believed that music was heard in the air, bells of distant churches tolled of their

---

[b] This letter is dated Perugia, Ann. Pontific. 10, 1252. It is in the Burton Annals, and in the Additamenta to Paris. In Rymer there is another quite different in its provisions. There the Pope asserts that he has made very few appointments. But Westminster adds to Paris: "Inventum est quod unquam aliquis predecessorum suorum in triplo aliquos sui generis vel patriae tot ditaverat." There is a strange clause in Innocent's letter, expressive of the wild times and the exasperation of the public mind: If a papal expectant should be murdered (si perimi contigerit, as if it were an casual occurrence), no one should be appointed who had not previously cleared himself of all concern in the murder.

own accord, miracles were wrought at his grave and in his church at Lincoln. But it was said likewise that the inexorable Pontiff entertained the design of having his body disinterred and his bones scattered. But Robert Grostéte himself appeared in a vision, dressed in his pontifical robes before the Pope. "Is it thou, Sinibald, thou miserable Pope, who wilt cast my bones out of their cemetery, to thy disgrace and that of the Church of Lincoln? Better were it for thee to respect after their death the zealous servants of God. Thou hast despised the advice which I gave thee in terms of respectful humility. Woe to thee who hast despised, thou shalt be despised in thy turn!" The Pope felt as if each word pierced him like a spear. From that night he was wasted by a slow fever. The hand of God was upon him. All his schemes failed, his armies were defeated, he passed neither day nor night undisturbed. Such was believed by a large part of Christendom to have been the end of Pope Innocent IV.[1]

---

[1] It is a significant fact that Grostéte was never canonised. This honour was granted to the cloistral virtues of his predecessor, Hugh of Lincoln; to his contemporary, Edmund Rich of Canterbury. Edmund had ingloriously retired from his difficult post of primate; his timid piety despaired of reforming his clergy; he was embarrassed between the King and his Barons; between the King compelled to resist the exactions of the Pope, and the Pope whose demands Edmund would have gratified to the full. He took refuge in the retreat of Becket, Pontigny; but with nothing of Becket's character. Yet the mild prelate shared with Becket the honours of a saint. Grostéte was canonised only by the reverence of his country. Even Matthew Paris after his death found out his virtues. Of these not the least was his opposition to the King and to Rome (fuit Domini Papæ et Regis redarguitor manifestus; Romanorum malleus et contemptor) ; the instructor of the clergy, the support of scholars; the preacher of the people; persecutor only of the incontinent. At table he was liberal, plentiful, courteous, cheerful, and affable; in church, devout, tearful, penitent; as a prelate, zealous, venerable, indefatigable.

BOOK XI.

CONTEMPORARY CHRONOLOGY.

POPES.		EMPERORS OF GERMANY.		KINGS OF FRANCE.		KINGS OF ENGLAND.	
A.D.	A.D.	A.D.	A.D.	A.D.	A.D.	A.D.	A.D.
1254 Alexander IV.	1261	Duke William (Conrad)	1256				
1261 Urban IV.	1265	1269 Interregnum	1273	Louis IX.	1270		
1265 Clement IV.	1269			1270 Philip the Hardy	1285		
1269 Vacancy	1271					Henry III.	1272
1271 Gregory X.	1276	1273 Rudolph of Hapsburg	1291			1272 Edward I.	1307
1276 Innocent V, Hadrian V, John XXI.							
						Archbishops of Canterbury.	
1277 Nicolas III.	1281					1264 Boniface of Savoy	1273
1281 Martin IV.	1285						
				1285 Philip the Fair	1314	1273 Robert Kilwardby	1278
1285 Honorius IV.	1288	1291 Adolph of Nassau	1298			1278 Robert Fordham	1294
1288 Nicolas IV.	1292						
1292 Vacancy	1294	1298 Albert of Austria	1308			1294 Robert Winchelsey	1313
1294 Celestine V.							
Boniface VIII.	1303						
1303 Benedict XI.	1304						

KINGS OF SCOTLAND.		KINGS OF SPAIN.		KINGS OF SWEDEN.		EASTERN EMPIRE.	
A.D.	A.D.	A.D.	A.D.	A.D.	A.D.	A.D.	A.D.
		Castile.				*Latin.*	
Alexander III.	1286	1252 Al— XI. the Wise	1284	1250 Waldemar	1276	Baldwin II.	1261
1286 Interregnum	1292	1284 Sancho IV.	1295	1276 Magnus II.	1290	*Greek.*	
1292 John Baliol		1295 Ferdinand IV.	1312	1290 Birger II.		1256 Theodore	1259
1296 Interregnum						1259 John IV.	
		Arragon.				1259 Michael (Palaeologus)	1282
		James I.		KINGS OF DENMARK.			
		Alfonso X.	1276	A.D.	A.D.	1282 Andronicus II. (Palaeologus)	
		1276 Pedro III.	1285	1282 Christopher	1286		
		1285 Alfonso III. the Beneficent	1291	1286 Eric VII.	1319		
		1291 James II., the Just	1312	1319 Olaus IV.	1387		
				1387 Eric VIII.			
		Kings of Portugal.		1396 Hakon II.			
		A.D.	A.D.				
		Alfonso III.	1279				
		1279 Dionysius I.					

BOOK XI.

CHAPTER I.

St. Louis.

THE great fabric of mediæval religion might have suffered a shock from the haughtiness, the rapacity, the
implacability of Innocent IV., which had raised a deep
and sullen alienation even among the clergy, in parts of
Christendom, especially in England and Germany. The
Teutonic pride revolted at the absolute nomination of an
obscure prince to the Empire by the will of the Pope.
The bold speculations, the enlightened studies, promoted
by Frederick II., even the contemptuous indifference
ascribed to him, though outwardly rejected, were working
no doubt in the depths of many minds. Heresy, crushed
in blood in Languedoc, was spreading elsewhere the
more extensively in defiance of the Inquisition, which
was already becoming odious throughout Europe. The
strife of the new Orders with the clergy had weakened
their influence over the popular mind, influence not
altogether replaced by the wonderful numbers, activity,
learning, ubiquity of the Mendicants. In the Franciscan
Order had already begun that schism, which was of far
greater importance than is commonly supposed in religious history.

But there was not wanting the great example of religion to awe and to allure mankind: it was not in the

chair of St. Peter, not at the head of a new Order, but
on the throne of France : the Saint of this period
was a King.   The unbounded admiration of
St. Louis in his own days, the worship of the canonised
Sovereign in later times, was a religious power, of which
it is impossible to trace or define the limits.   Difficult,
indeed, it is to imagine that at the same historic period
lived Frederick II. and Louis IX.   Louis was a monk
upon the throne, but a monk with none of the harshness,
bitterness, or pride of monkery.   His was a frank play-
fulness, or amenity at least of manner, which Henry IV.
never surpassed, and a blamelessness hardly ever before,
till very recent times never after, seen on the throne of
France.   Nor was he only a monk : he had kingly
qualities of the noblest order, gentleness, affability,
humanity towards all his believing subjects, a kind of
dignity of justice, a loftiness of virtue, which prevented
the most religious of men from degenerating into a
slave of the clergy; a simple sincerity even in his
lowest superstitions, an honest frankness, an utter
absence of malignity even in his intolerance, which
holds even these failings and errors high above contempt, or even aversion.   Who can read the Seneschal
Joinville without love and veneration of his master?

Louis was ten years old at the death of his father
Louis VIII.   His mother, Blanche of Castile,
took possession at once of the regency.   Her
firm demeanour awed all ranks; her vigorous administration at once established her power.   Philip the
Rough, the brother of Louis VIII. (the son of Philip
Augustus by Agnes of Meran, but who had been acknowledged as a legitimate prince), submitted sullenly, yet
submitted, to the female rule.   It is strange to contrast
the severe court of the Queen-mother Blanche with that

of Marie de Medicis, or Anne of Austria; the youth of
Louis IX. with that of Louis XIV. or Louis XV.: and
to suppose that the same religion was preached in the
churches, then by a rude Dominican or a homely Franciscan, afterwards in the exquisite and finished language
of Bossuet and Massillon. Blanche of Castile did not
entirely escape the malicious slanders of her enemies.
She was accused of too close an intimacy with the
Legate himself. She fell under stronger suspicion as
the idol of the amorous poetry of the gallant Thiebault,
Count of Champagne, afterwards King of Navarre. But
Thiebault's Platonic raptures were breathed in vain to
the inaccessible matron; it was the policy not the heart
of the Queen Regent which led her not to disdain the
poetic suit of a dangerous subject, constantly falling off
to the enemies of her son, and recalled to his allegiance
by the authority of his mistress. The historian guarantees her chaste and cleanly life.[*] Her treatment of
her son showed no indulgence for such weaknesses.
Once in his early youth he had looked with kindling
eye on some fair damsels. "I had rather he were
dead," said the rigid mother, "than that he should
commit sin." Thus bred a monk, the congenial disposition of Louis embraced with ardour the austere rule.
Had he not been early married, he would have vowed
perpetual chastity. The jealousy of his mother of any
other influence than her own was constantly watching
his most familiar intercourse with his wife, Marguerite
of Provence. He bore it, even the harshness with which
Blanche treated her daughter-in-law at times when
woman's sympathies are usually most tender, with the
meekest filial submission. At all the great religious

---

[*] " Sa vie bonne et nette."—Joinville.

periods, Advent, Lent, the high Festivals, and all holy
days (which now filled no small part of the
year), the youthful King denied himself all con-
nubial indulgences; he would rise from his bed, and
pace the cold chamber till he was frozen into virtue.
His other appetites he controlled with equal inflexibility.
Besides the most rigorous observance of the ordinary
fasts, once only in the year would he allow himself
to taste fruit: he wore the roughest sackcloth next to
his skin. His spiritual teachers persuaded him to less
severe observance, to deny himself only unripe fruit, to
wear haircloth of less coarse texture. On Fridays he
never laughed; if he detected himself in laughter he
repressed and mourned over the light emotion. On
Friday he never changed his raiment. In his girdle he
wore an ivory case of iron-chain scourges (such boxes
were his favourite presents to his courtiers), not for idle
display. Every Friday during the year, and in Lent on
Mondays, Wednesdays, and Fridays, he shut himself up in
his chamber, searching every corner, lest any one should
be present, with his confessor, the Dominican Godfrey of
Beaulieu. The bleeding shoulders of the King attested
his own sincerity, and the singular adulation of the confessor, who knew the King too well not to administer the
discipline with unsparing hand. These more secret acts
of holiness were no doubt too admirable for the clergy to
allow them to remain secret; but the people were no less
edified by his acts of public devotion. It was his constant
practice to visit distant churches with bare feet, or, to
disguise his piety, in sandals without soles. On every
altar he offered profuse alms. One day he walked bare-
foot from Nogent l'Erembert to the church of Our Lady
at Chartres, a distance of four leagues; he was obliged
to lean on his attendants for support. He constantly

Austerities of Louis.

washed the feet of beggars; he invited the poor and the
sick to his table; he attended the hospitals, and performed the most menial and loathsome offices. A leper
on the farther side of a swamp begged of him; the King
crossed over, not only gave him alms, but kissed his
hand. He heard daily two, sometimes three or four,
masses; his whole day might seem one unbroken
service; as he rode, his chaplain chanted or recited the
offices. Even in this respect his teachers attempted to
repress his zeal. A Dominican preacher urged him
from the pulpit not to lower too much the royal dignity,
not to spend the whole day in church, to content himself
with one mass: "whoever counselled him otherwise was
a fool, and guilty of a deadly sin." "If I spent twice as
much time in dice and hawking, should I be so rebuked?"[b] answered the gentle King. He bore even
reproach with meekness. A woman named Sarrette,
pleading in the King's court, said "Fie! you are not
King of France; you are only a king of friars, of priests,
and of clerks. It is a great pity that you are King of
France; you should be turned out of the kingship."[c]
The blessed King would not allow his attendants to
chastise the woman. "You say true! It has pleased
the Lord to make me king; it had been well if it had
pleased him to make some one who had better ruled the
realm." He then ordered his chamberlain to give her
money, as much as forty pence.

Louis had the most religious aversion for all lighter
amusements, the juggler, the minstrel. He was profoundly ignorant of polite letters. His whole time
might seem fully occupied in rehearsing over and over

b Notices et Extraits, ii. 406.
c Life, by the Confessor of Queen Margaret, in Bouquet, p. 366.

the same prayers; yet he is said to have read perpetually
in a Latin Bible with devotional notes, and to have been
deeply versed in the writings of some of the Fathers,
especially St. Augustine. But this learning, whatever
it might be, he acquired with the most reverential
humility; it tempted him to no daring religious specu-
lation, emboldened him to no polemic zeal. " Even
clerks, if not profoundly learned, ought to abstain from
controversy with unbelievers; the layman had but one
argument, his good sword. If he heard a man to be an
unbeliever, he should not dispute with him, he should at
once run that sword into his entrails, and drive it
home." [4] He related with special approbation the anec-
dote of a brave old knight, who broke up a discussion
on the relative excellence of their law between some
Catholic doctors and some Jewish Rabbis by bringing
down his mace upon the head of the principal Jew
teacher. Louis loved all mankind with a boundless
love except Jews, heretics, and infidels, whom he hated
with as boundless hatred.

But above all these weaknesses or exaggerated virtues there were the high Christian graces,
conscientiousness such as few kings are able
or dare to display on the throne, which never swerved
either through ambition or policy from strict rectitude.
No acquisition of territory, no extension of the royal
power, would have tempted Louis IX. to unjust aggression. He was strongly urged to put to death the son of
the chief of the rebels in arms against him, the Count
de la Marche, who had fallen into his hands; he nobly

4 " Mais homme loy (laic) quand il ' l'espee, de quoi il doit donner parmi le
et maudire de la loy crestienne, ne doit ' ventre dedans, tant comme il peut
disputer a culz, ne doit pas defendre la ' entrer."—Joinville, in Bouquet, t. xx.
loy crestienne, ne mais (si non) de p. 198.

replied : " A son could not refuse to obey his father's
orders." The one great war in which he was involved,
before his departure for the Crusade, which ended in
the humiliation of the great vassals of the Crown and
of the leader in that revolt, Henry III. of England, the
chief of these great vassals, was provoked by no oppression or injustice on his part, was conducted with moderation unusual in that age ; and his victory was not
sullied by any act of wanton revenge or abuse of power.
He had no rapacity ; he coveted but one kind of
treasure, reliques ; and no doubt when he bought the
real crown of thorns (the abbey of St. Denys had
already boasted their possession of the authentic crown,
but their crown sank into obscurity, when that of Constantinople arrived in Paris),* when he obtained this
inestimable prize at such enormous cost, there was no
abstemiousness which he would not have practised, in
order so to enrich his beloved France. He plundered
the Jews, but that was on religious grounds; their
tainted wealth might not infect the royal treasury ; he
bestowed the whole on Baldwin of Constantinople.

Yet Louis was no slave of the hierarchy. His religion was of too lofty a cast to submit to the dictates of
a worldly clergy. His own great objects of admiration
were the yet uncorrupt Mendicants, the Preachers and
Minorites ; half his body he would give to St. Dominic,
half to St. Francis. He once gravely meditated the
abandonment of his throne to put on the weeds of one
of these Orders. His laws will afterwards display him,
if not as the founder, the asserter of the liberties of the
Gallican Church, and of the royal power, as limiting
that of the Papacy. Throughout the strife between

---

* Compare Tillemont, Vie de Saint Louis, ii. 337.

Frederick II. and Gregory IX. he maintained an
impartial and dignified neutrality. He had not declined
the summons of the Emperor to hold a meeting of the
temporal Sovereigns of Christendom to resist in common the encroachments of the spiritual power. Nothing
could surpass the calm loftiness with which he demanded the release of the French prelates taken at the
battle of Meloria; he could advance the cogent argument, that he had resisted all the demands and entreaties of the Pope to be permitted to levy subsidies
on the realm of France for the war against the Emperor. He had refused, as we have seen, the offer of
the Imperial crown from Innocent IV. for his brother;
only when Frederick threatened to march on Lyons,
and crush the Pope, did Louis seem disposed to take up
arms for the defence of the Pontiff.[1]

Such a monarch could not but be seized by the yet
unexpired passion for the Crusade. Urban II.,
two centuries before, would not have found a
more ardent follower. It was in St. Louis no love, no
aptitude for war, no boiling and impetuous valour.
His slight frame and delicate health gave no promise of
personal prowess or fame; he was in no way distinguished in, he loved not, knightly exercises. He had
no conscious confidence in his military skill or talent to
intoxicate him with the hopes of a conqueror; he seems
to have utterly wanted, perhaps to have despised, the
most ordinary acquirements of a general. He went
forth simply as the servant of God; he might seem to
disdain even the commonest precautions. God was to
fight his own battles; Louis was assured of victory or
Paradise. All depended on the faith, and the sup-

[1] Tillemont, iii. p. 164.

pression of military licence, at which he laboured with
fond hopes of success, not on the valour, discipline,
generalship of the army. In his determination to embark on the Crusade, Louis resolutely asserted the
absolute power of the monarch: in this alone he resisted the colder caution of his mother Blanche; she
was obliged to yield to the pious stubbornness of her son.
Louis was seized with an alarming illness, he had sunk
into a profound lethargy, he was thought dead; a pious
female had drawn the covering, in sad respect, over
what seemed the lifeless corpse. Another gently withdrew it. The soft but hollow voice of the King was
heard: "God has raised me from the dead: give me
the Cross." His mother wept tears of joy; A.D. 1244.
when she saw the Cross on his breast, she Ætæ. 18.
knew the meaning of that gesture. She shuddered as
if he lay dead before her.[f]

No expedition to the East was so ignominiously disastrous as that of St. Louis: yet none might seem to set
forth under more promising auspices. He was three
years in assembling his forces, preparing arms, money,
horses, soldiers. It was in October (A.D. 1245) that in
the Parliament of Paris he publicly took the Cross.
The princes, the nobles, vied in following his example;
his brother, Robert of Artois, the Duke of Burgundy,
the Duke of Brabant, the Countess of Flanders and her
sons, Peter Mauclerc of Dreux and his son, the Count
of Bretagne, the Counts of Bar, Soissons, St. Pol, de la
Marche, Rhetel, Montfort; the Archbishops of Rheims,
Sens, and Bourges, the Bishops of Beauvais, Laon, and
Orleans, with countless knights and esquires. At
Christmas in the same year Louis practised perhaps

---

[f] Joinville, p. 207.

the only act of treachery of which he was guilty in his
life. It was the custom for the King to distribute, as
his gifts on that day, new robes to the courtiers. He
ordered red crosses to be secretly embroidered between
the shoulders; they were lavished in more than usual
numbers. The courtiers were astonished to find that
the King had thus piously enlisted them; they were
now warriors of the Cross, who could not shrink from
their engagement. It would have been indecent, dis-
graceful, ignoble, to throw aside the crosses; so, with
true French levity, they laughed and wept at once, owning that they were completely entrapped by the King.

From that time the whole thoughts of Louis were
absorbed in the Holy War. He resisted the offers of
Pope Innocent to befriend him in a war against England, even in an invasion of England. He made, as he
hoped, a lasting peace with his neighbour.
He took no part in the confederacy of the
French nobility to resist the exactions of the Pope and
of the hierarchy.[b] He laboured earnestly, though
ineffectually, to reconcile the Emperor and the Pope.

So far, on the other hand, had his strife with the
Emperor absorbed all other religious passions in the
Pope, that not only was there no cordial co-operation
on the part of Innocent in the Crusade of St. Louis, but
exemptions from the Crusades were now notoriously
sold, it was believed to defray the expenses of the war
against the Emperor. The Crusaders in Italy were
urged to join the Pope's forces, with all the privileges
and exemptions of a Crusade to the Holy Land.

Louis himself did not embark at the head of a great

---

b According to Paris, St. Louis favoured the League. Compare Tillemont,
lit. p. 120.

army, like a puissant monarch. The princes, prelates, and nobles were to arrange their own trans- Louis embarks on the Crusade. port. St. Louis passed down the Rhône; he was urged to avenge the death of his father on rebellious Avignon: " I have taken arms to revenge Jesus Christ, not my father." The island of Cyprus was the place of rendezvous. In Cyprus there was a delay of eight months. Want of discipline and a fatal epidemic made great ravages in the army; there seemed a total absence of conduct or command. But for supplies sent by the Emperor Frederick, there had been famine. The grateful Louis made one more effort to mediate between the Pope and the Emperor. The overture was contemptuously rejected.

At length the armament set sail; its object was the conquest of Egypt, as securing that of the Holy June 1. 1249. (Cyprus.) Land. Damietta was abandoned by the Saracens; the Crusaders were masters of that great city.[1] But never were the terror and advantages of a first success so thrown away. Months were wasted; the King was performing the offices of a monk, not of a general. Yet the army of the pious Louis was abandoned to every kind of Oriental luxury.[k] In June they were in Damietta, in November they marched, Nov. 20. (Damietta.) and shut themselves in a camp in a corner between the hills and the canal of Ashmoun. The flying bands of the enemy, with the Greek fire, Feb. 8-11. harassed the camp. Good fortune and the valour of the soldiery extricated them from this diffi-

---

[1] The instant St. Louis landed and saw the Saracens, he drew his sword and was for charging them at once. The wiser "preudhommes" stopped him. This was St. Louis's notion of military affairs.—Joinville, p. 215.

[k] Not a stone's throw from the King the soldiers " tenoient leurs bordiaux." —Joinville, 217.

culty, only to involve them in more fatal disasters. The King's brother, the Count of Artois, fell in a hasty unsupported advance. The unrivalled valour of the French was wasted in unprofitable victories, like those of Mansourah, or in miserable defeats. The camp was in a state of blockade; pestilence,[a] famine, did the

work of the enemy. The King of France was a prisoner to the Sultan of Egypt. Of two thousand three hundred knights and fifteen thousand pilgrims few made their escape. His brothers, Alfonso of Poitou and Charles of Anjou, shared his captivity. His Queen, far advanced in pregnancy, remained with an insufficient force in Damietta. She bore a son prematurely; she called his name "Tristan."

But it was adversity which displayed the great character of St. Louis. He was himself treated at first with courtesy; he was permitted to hear the canonical prayers, after the custom of the Church of Paris, recited by the single priest who had escaped; his breviary, the loss of which he deplored above all losses, was replaced by another. But he had the bitter aggravation of his misery—that, of ten thousand prisoners in Mansourah, all who would not abandon their faith (and some there were guilty of this apostasy) met a cruel death. But to all the courteous approaches of the Sultan, Louis was jealously on his guard, lest he should compromise his dignity as a King or his purity as a Christian: he would not receive the present of a dress from the Unbeliever. To their exorbitant demands and menaces he gave a calm and determined reply. They demanded the surrender of all the fortresses in Syria: these, it was

---

[a] They had no fish all Lent but "bourbrtlcs," which gluttonous fish fed on dead bodies, and produced dreadful maladies.

answered, belonged not to the King of France, but to
Frederick II. as King of Jerusalem. To that of yielding up the castles garrisoned by the Knights of the
Temple and of St. John, the answer was that the
Orders could not surrender them without violating their
vows. The King was threatened with torture—torture
of the most cruel kind—the barnacles, which crushed
the legs. "I am your prisoner," he said, "ye may do
with me as ye will."* It is said that he defied even
the more degrading menace of carrying him about and
exhibiting him as a spectacle in all the cities of Islam.
At length more reasonable terms were proposed; the
evacuation of Damietta, and a large sum of money—for
the King's ransom one million byzantines; for the
captive Barons five hundred thousand French livres.
Concerning his own ransom Louis made some difficulty;
he acceded at once to that of the Barons. "It becomes
not the King of France to barter about the liberty of
her subjects."* The Sultan, Turan-Shah, was moved
by the monarch's generosity; with Oriental magnificence, he struck off one-fifth—two hundred thousand
byzantines—from his ransom.

In the new perils which arose on the murder of the
Sultan Turan-Shah before the deliverance of
the prisoners, the tranquil dignity of the King
of France overawed even the bloody Mamelukes. The
Emirs renewed the treaty; the difficulty was now the
oath. The King demanded, by the advice of Master
Nicolas of Ptolemais, that the Mussulmen should swear,
"that if they broke the treaty they should be dishonoured as the Islamite who should go as a pilgrim

* Joinville, p. 213.
* "Par ma foy largo oal le Franc, quant il en pas bargigné (marchandé) sur
el grant acramo de dealers." So said the Saracens. Joinville, 243.

to Mecca bareheaded, as one who should take back a divorced wife, as one who had eaten swine's flesh." A renegade suggested as an equivalent form to be required of the King, that in like case, should he violate the treaty, "he should be dishonoured as a Christian who had denied God and his Holy Mother, and had severed himself from the communion of God, his Apostles, and Saints; or, in mockery of God, had spat on the Holy Cross and trampled it under foot." Louis indignantly repelled the last clause. The Emirs threatened him with death; he declared that he had rather die than live, after having insulted God and his Holy Mother.[f] His brothers and the other Barons followed the example of his firmness. In vain the Mamelukes seized the Patriarch of Jerusalem, who had come under the Sultan's safe conduct (which they disclaimed) into the camp, a man eighty years old, and tied him to a tent-post with his hands behind his back, till they swelled and almost burst. The Patriarch, in his agony, entreated the King to yield, and offered to take upon himself all the guilt of his oath. The oath was arranged, it is not known how, to mutual satisfaction; but so rigidly scrupulous was Louis that when it appeared that in the payment of part of the ransom the Christians might have gained an advantage, either fairly or unfairly, of ten thousand byzantines in weight, he peremptorily commanded the full payment.

The release of the King on such favourable terms, at a price so much below the value of such a captive, astonished both the Christians and the Mussulmen. Damietta could not have resisted many days. Much was attributed to the awe inspired

Ransom and release.

---

[f] Joinville, p. 246.

by the majestic demeanour and calm self-command of
the King.[4] Joinville, his faithful seneschal and historian, had persuaded himself that the Emirs, after the
murder of Turan-Shah, had determined to offer the
crown of Egypt to the King of France; they were only
deterred by his stern Christianity, which would never
have submitted to the toleration of their creed. The
King himself declared to the Seneschal that he should
not have declined the offer. Happily it was not made,
probably was never contemplated; the death of Louis
would soon have vindicated the affront on Islam. But
all this, no doubt, heightened the religious romance
which spread in Europe around the name of Louis.

Notwithstanding his defeat and humiliation and captivity, the passive courage of Louis was still
unbroken; he persisted, contrary to all counsel, in remaining in Palestine. He would not suppose
that God would utterly abandon his faithful servants;
he would not believe that Christendom would be un-
moved by his appeal; he still would fondly expect that
the irresolute Henry of England would fulfil his vow,
and come to his rescue at the head of his whole realm.[r]
To Henry the summons was earnest and repeated.
Louis made the most advantageous overtures; he even,
to the indignation and disgust of his own subjects,
offered the surrender of Normandy, to which England
still laid claim as her King's hereditary dominions.[s]
He still imagined that the Pope would lay aside all his

*Hopes of
Louis.*

---

[4] The Saracens, according to Joinville, said that if Mohammed had
allowed such sufferings to be inflicted
on them as St. Louis endured, they
should have renounced him.—P. 347.

[r] Henry took the cross (March 6,
1251), says Tillemont, "soit pour

piller plus librement ses sujets, soit
pour quelque meilleur dessein." The
Pope wrote to Henry early in 1251.
Henry swore to go to the Holy Land in
three years.—Paris, p. 834.

[s] Paris, 833, 834.

plans for the humiliation of Frederick, and bo compelled, by his own Apostolic character, and the general voice of Christendom, to sacrifice everything to the recovery of the Holy Land; that there would be but one Crusade under his auspices, and that the legitimate one. Louis was deserted by his brothers, whose light conduct had caused him great vexation; while he was in perpetual self-mortification before God for his sins, which he did not doubt had caused his defeat and bondage, they were playing at dice, whiling away the hours with vain amusements: Almost all the Barons followed the Counts of Poitou and Anjou; Louis was left almost alone with Joinville, his faithful Seneschal. Nor was his weary sojourn in Palestine enlivened by any brilliant successes or gallant feats of arms. For these Louis had neither the activity nor the skill. He was performing the pious office of assisting with his own hands to bury the dead warriors. A hasty pilgrimage in sackcloth to Nazareth was almost the only reward; the only advantage of his residence was the fortification of Cæsarea, Ptolemais, and Joppa. The negotiations with the Sultan of Aleppo on one side, and the Egyptians on the other, by which he hoped to obtain the country west of the Jordan, came to nothing. He is said to have converted many Saracens;[1] he spent enormous sums in the purchase of Mohammedan or heathen slaves, whom he caused to be baptised.[2]

It was only the death of the Queen-mother Blanche, and the imperious necessity for his presence in his kingdom of France, which forced him at last to leave the hallowed soil. He returned—if with-

Marginal notes: Deserted by his brothers. A.D. 1251. Return to Europe. Nov. 1252.

---

[1] Tillemont, from MSS., and Duchesne, p. 405.   [2] Ibid.

out fame for arms, or for the conduct of affairs—with
the profoundest reverence for his sanctity.   Only a few
years before, Frederick II. had come back to Europe,
leaving Jerusalem in the hands of the Christians; the
Christian power in Palestine, but for its own dissensions,
formidable both to the Sultan of Egypt and the Sultan
of Damascus; he had come back still under the sentence
of excommunication, under the reproach with the Papal
party of having basely betrayed the interests of the
Cross and of God.   Louis left Jerusalem unapproachable but with difficulty and danger by the Christian
pilgrim, and the kingdom of Jerusalem visibly trembling to its fall; yet an object of devout respect, having
made some advance at least, to his future canonisation.

The contrast between Frederick and Louis may be
carried on with singular interest, as illustrative
of their times.   It might have been supposed
that Louis would have been the remorseless
persecutor of heretics; Frederick, if not the bold asserter
of equal toleration, which he allowed to Greeks and
Mohammedans, would hardly have been the sovereign
to enact and execute persecuting edicts, unprecedented
in their cruelty, and to encourage the son to denounce
the father.[x]   Happily for Louis, his virtue was not tried
by this sore temptation; it was not under his government that the spiritual ravagers still wasted Languedoc.
After the treaty by which Raymond VII.,
Count of Toulouse, surrendered his principality, he remained with the barren dignity of sovereign,
but without a voice in the fate of a large though concealed part of his subjects.   Bishop Fulk of Toulouse, as
far as actual power, was half sovereign of the land, and

margin notes: Further portrait of Frederick and Louis. / Louis escapes being a persecutor.

---

* See above, p. 150.

the council of that sovereign, which alone displayed
administrative activity, was the Inquisition. Heresy
had been extinguished as far as its public services; but
the Inquisition of Toulouse determined to root it out
from the hearths, from the chambers, from the secret
hearts and souls of men. The statutes of the Council
of Lateran were too merciful. The Inquisition drew up
its code of procedure,[1] a Christian code, of which the
base was a system of delation at which the worst of the
Pagan emperors might have shuddered as iniquitous;
in which the sole act deserving of mercy might seem
to be the Judas-like betrayal of the dearest and most
familiar friend, of the kinsman, the parent, the child.
Though these acts belong neither to Frederick nor to
Louis, they must find their place in our history.

The Court sat in profound secrecy; no advocate might
Form of procedure. appear before the tribunal; no witness was
confronted with the accused: who were the
informers, what the charges, except the vague charge of
heresy, no one knew. The suspected heretic was first
summoned to declare on oath that he would speak the
truth, the whole truth, of all persons whatsoever, living
or dead, with himself, or like himself, under suspicion
of heresy or Vaudism. If he refused, he was cast into
a dungeon—a dungeon the darkest in those dreary
ages—the most dismal, the most foul, the most noisome.
No falsehood was too false, no craft too crafty, no trick
too base, for this calm, systematic moral torture which
was to wring further confession against himself, denun-

---

[1] The two forms of procedure may
be read in Martene and Durand.—
Thesaurus Anecdotorum, t. v. Their
authenticity is beyond dispute. Nothing
that the sternest or most passionate
historian has revealed, nothing that the
most imaginative romance-writer could
have imagined, can surpass the cold
systematic treachery and cruelty of
these, so called, judicial formularies.

ciation against others. If the rack, the pulleys, the
thumbscrew, and the boots, were not yet invented or
applied, it was not in mercy. It was the deliberate
object to break the spirit. The prisoner was told that
there were witnesses, undeniable witnesses, against him ;
if convicted by such witnesses his death was inevitable.
In the meantime his food was to be slowly, gradually
diminished, till body and soul were prostrate. He was
then to be left in darkness, solitude, silence. Then
were to come one or two of the faithful, dexterous men,
who were to speak in gentle words of interest and sympathy—" Fear not to confess that you have had dealings
with those men, the teachers of heresy, because they
seemed to you men of holiness and virtue ; wiser than
you have been deceived." These dexterous men were
to speak of the Bible, of the Gospels, of the Epistles of
St. Paul, to talk the very language, the Scriptural
language of the heretics. " These foxes," it was said,
" can only be unearthed by fox-like cunning." But if
all this art failed, or did not perfectly succeed, then
came terror and the goading to despair. " Die you
must—bethink you of your soul." Upon which if the
desperate man said, " If I must die, I will die in the
true faith of the Gospel "—he had made his confession :
justice claimed its victim.

The Inquisition had three penalties : for those who
recanted, penance in the soverest form which the Court
might enact ; for those not absolutely convicted, perpetual imprisonment ; for the obstinate or the relapsed,
death—death at the stake, death by the secular arm.
The Inquisition, with specious hypocrisy, while it prepared and dressed up the victim for the burning, looked
on with calm and approving satisfaction, as it had left
the sin of lighting the fire to pollute other hands.

Such was the procedure, of which the instructions
may now be read in their very words, which Raymond
of Toulouse must put in execution in his capital city.

A.D. 1231. The death of the Bishop Fulk relieved him
not; an inflexible Dominican sat on the episcopal seat of Toulouse. The Pope, Gregory IX., issued
a bull, in which the Inquisition was placed in the inexorable hands of the Friar Preachers. Two inquisitors
were appointed in every city; but the Bishops needed
no excitement to their eager zeal, no remonstrance
against mistimed mercy to the heretics. At the Council
of Narbonne, presided over by the Archbishops of Narbonne, Aix, and Arles, was now issued a decree, that as
A.D. 1233. there were not prisons vast enough to contain
those who, however they had made submission,
were still unworthy of the absolution of the Church,
and deserved imprisonment for life, further instructions
must be awaited from his Holiness the Pope. But the
contumacious, who refused to submit to imprisonment,
or who broke prison, were to be at once made over to
the secular arm. No plea was to be admitted to release
from imprisonment; not the duty of the husband to the
young wife, of the young wife to her husband; not that
of the parents for the care of their children, nor of
children for the care of their parents; infirmity, age,
dotage, nothing excused, nothing mitigated the sentence. So enormous was the crime of heresy, the infamous, whose witness was refused in all other cases,
were admitted against the heretic: on no account was
the name of a witness to be betrayed.

But the most oppressed may be overwrought to
Rebellion. madness. Witnesses were found murdered;
even the awful persons of inquisitors were not
secure. An insurrection broke out in the suburbs of

Narbonne against the Prior of the Dominicans; the
Archbishop and the Viscount of Narbonne in their
defence suffered a repulse. The insurgents despised the
excommunication of the Archbishop, and fought gallantly against the rest of the city, which espoused the
cause of the Church. Albi was in tumult, even Toulouse
arose. The two great inquisitors, William Arnaud and
Peter Celluni, were compelled to leave the city. They
marched out at the head of the thirty-eight members
of the Inquisition, with the Bishop and the parish priests
in solemn procession; they hurled back an excommunication. Count Raymond compelled the re-admission
of the clergy, but even Rome was appalled: a Franciscan was sent to allay by his gentleness the
popular fury. The proceedings of the Inqui-   A.D. 1237.
sition (this merciful edict was purchased in Rome) were
suspended for a time in Toulouse.[*]

Five years passed. Raymond of Toulouse, under the
shelter, as it were, of the wars between Louis Rising.
IX. and Henry of England, and encouraged by Murder of the
hopes of support from the Spanish kings, aspired at the
head of the league among the great vassals of the south
to throw off the yoke of Northern France. The down-
trodden Albigensians seized their opportunity. They
met at Mirepoix, marched on the castle of Avignonet,
where William Arnaud, the great inquisitor, held his
tribunal. Four Dominicans, two Franciscans, seven
Familiars, the whole terrible court, were hewn to pieces.
That which had thrown a dreadful grandeur over the
murders perpetrated by the inquisitors, gave a majestic
endurance to their own. They died like the meekest

---

[*] Martene, Thesaur. Anecdot., t. 992. Vaissete, Hist. de Languedoc, Appendix xiv.

martyrs: they fell on their knees, crossed their hands
over their breasts, and, chanting the Te
Deum, as wont over their victims, they
awaited the mortal blow.[a] They were not long un-
avenged. Raymond was forced to submit; his act of
subjection to Louis IX. stipulated his abandonment
of the heretics. Two years after, at another
Council at Narbonne, it was enacted that the
penitents, who had escaped from prison, should in mercy
be permitted to wear yellow crosses on their garments,
to appear every Sunday during mass, and undergo
public flagellation: the rest were to suffer life-long in
carceration. At the same time Mont Segur,[b] the last
refuge of the Albigensians, a strong castle on the summit
of a ravine in the Pyrenees, to which most of the Perfect
with their Bishop had fled, was forced to surrender to
the Archbishop of Narbonne, the Bishop of Albi, and
the Seneschal of Carcassonne. All the heretics, with
their Bishop and the noble lady, Esclarmonde, were
burned alive in a vast enclosure of stakes and straw.[c]
Of all these atrocities, however, Louis IX. was guiltless;
he was not yet, or was hardly, of age, and his whole
soul was absorbed in his preparation for his crusade.
Even his brother, Charles of Anjou, who by obtaining
the hand of the heiress of Provence (to which Raymond
of Toulouse aspired) had become lord of that territory,
took no active part in these persecutions.

Yet even in the realm of France a frightful holocaust
was offered near the city of Rheims. In the
presence of the Archbishop and seventeen
Bishops, and one hundred thousand people, on Mont
Aimé near Vertus, one hundred and eighty-three

A.D. 1242

March, 1244.

Persecutions in France.
A.D. 12...

---

[a] Histoire de Languedoc, Preuves, p. 438.   [b] Puy Laurent, c. 46.
[c] Puy Laurent, c. 46.

Manicheans (one Perfect alone) were burned alive with
their pastor, who calmly administered absolution to
them all. Not one but died without fear. But this
execution took place in the territory and under the
sanction of Count Thiebault of Champagne, not of the
King; of Thiebault (the King of Navarre), whose
Troubadour songs were as little respectful to the clergy,
or the Papalists, as those of the other Languedocian bards.[d]
If even under Louis a monk held his court in Paris, and,
unrebuked, inflicted death on many innocent victims,
this seems to have been an exceptional case ; nor is it
quite clear how far it had the concurrence of the King.[e]

Yet for a time suspended, our comparison of Louis
IX. and Frederick II. is not exhausted. As legislators
there is the most striking analogy between these two, in
so many other respects oppugnant sovereigns. The
Sicilian laws of Frederick and the " Establishments " of
St. Louis agree in the assertion (as far as their times
would admit) of the absolute supremacy of the law, the
law emanating from the King, and in the abrogation
(though Louis is more timid or cautious than Frederick)
of the ordeal, the trial by battle, and the still stranger
usage of challenging the judges to battle.

The Justiciaries of Frederick belonged to a more
advanced jurisprudence than the King himself, Frederick
seated on his carpet in the forest of Vincennes and Louis as legislators.
administering justice.[f] But the introduction under his
reign of the civil lawyers, the students and advocates of
the Roman jurisprudence, into the courts of France
(under Philip the Fair will be seen their strife, even
triumph over the canon lawyers), gave a new character

[d] Compare H. Martin, Hist. de Hallam, I. 29, with his authorities.
France.   [e] See the picturesque description in
[f] Raynald, sub ann., I. p. 29. Joinville, p. 199.

to the ordinances of St. Louis, and of far more lasting influence. The ruin of the house of Swabia, and the desuetude into which, in most respects, fell the constitution of Frederick, prevented Naples from becoming a school of Roman law as famous as that of Paris, and the lawyers of the kingdom of Sicily from rising into a body as powerful as those of France in her parliaments.

Both Kings, however, aimed at the establishment of equal justice. They would bring the haughty feudal nobles and even the churchmen (who lived apart under their own law) under the impartial sovereignty of the law of the land. The punishment of Enguerrand de Couci for a barbarous murder attested the firmness of the King. The proudest baron in France, the highest vassal of the crown, hardly escaped with his life. So, too, may be cited the account of the angry baron, indignant at the judicial equity of the King—" Were I king, I would hang all my barons; after the first step, all is easy." " How, John of Thouret, hang all my barons? I will not hang them; I will correct them if they commit misdeeds."

As to the nobles

It was the religion, not the want of religion, in St. Louis which made him determine to bring the criminal clergy under the equal laws of the realm. That which Henry II. of England had attempted to do by his royal authority and by the Constitutions of Clarendon, the more pious or prudent Louis chose to effect with the Papal sanction. Even the Pope, Alexander IV., could not close his eyes to the monstrous fact of the crimes of the clergy, secured from adequate punishment by the immunities of their sacred persons. The Pope made a specious concession; the King's judge did not incur excommunication for arresting, subject to the judgement of the ecclesiastical courts, priests notoriously guilty of capital

As to the clergy.

A.D. 1268.

offences. Alexander threw off too from the Church, and abandoned as scapegoats to the law, all married clergy and all who followed low trades; with them the law might take its course, they had forfeited the privilege of clergy. But neither would Louis be the absolute slave of the intolerance of the hierarchy. The whole prelacy of France (writes Joinville)[1] met to rebuke the tardy zeal of the King in enforcing the excommunications of the Church. "Sire," said Guy of Auxerre, "Christianity is falling to ruin in your hands." "How so?" said the King, making the sign of the cross. "Sire, men regard not excommunication; they care not if they die excommunicate and without absolution. The Bishops admonish you that you give orders to all the royal officers to compel persons excommunicate to obtain absolution by the forfeiture of their lands and goods." And the holy man (the King) said "that he would willingly do so to all who had done wrong to the Church." "It belongs not to you," said the Bishop, "to judge of such cases." And the King answered, "he would not do otherwise; it were to sin against God and against reason to force those to seek absolution to whom the clergy had done wrong."

The famous Pragmatic Sanction contained only the first principles, yet it did contain the first principles, of limitation as to the power of the Court of Rome to levy money on the churches of the realm, and of elections to benefices. It was, in fact, as the foundation of Gallicanism under specious terms of respect, a more mortal blow to the Papal power than all the tyranny, as it was called, exercised by Frederick II. over the ecclesiastics of the kingdom of Naples. Of this, however, more hereafter.

---

[1] P. 200.

CHAPTER II.

Pope Alexander IV.

ON the death of Innocent IV., the Cardinal of Ostia, of
the famous Papal house of Segni, was elected
at Naples: he took the name of Alexander IV.
He was a gentle and religious man, not of
strong or independent character, open to flattery and to
the suggestions of interested and avaricious courtiers.[*]
Innocent IV. had left a difficult and perilous position to
his successor. The Pope could not abandon the Papal
policy: the see of Rome was too deeply pledged, to
retract its arrogant pretensions concerning the kingdom
of Naples, or to come to terms with one whom she
had denounced as an usurper, and whose strength she
did not yet comprehend. But Sinibald could not leave,
with his tiara, his own indomitable courage, his indefatigable activity, his power of drawing resources from
distant lands. Alexander was forced to be an Innocent IV. in his pretensions; he could but be a feeble
Innocent IV. The rapidity with which Manfred after
his first successes overran the whole of the two
Sicilies, implies, if not a profound and ardent
attachment to the house of Swabia, at least an obstinate
aversion to the Papal sovereignty. It seemed a general
national outburst; and Manfred, by circumstances and
by his own sagacious judgement, having separated the

Accession of Alexander IV. Dec. 21. A.D. 1254.

Manfred.

---

* Matt. Paris, sub ann.

cause of the hereditary kings from the odious German tyranny (tho Saracen bands were less unpopular than the Germans), as yet appeared only as the loyal guardian of the infant Conradin. He was already almost master of Apulia; he was with difficulty persuaded to send ambassadors, as sovereign princes were wont to do, to congratulate the Pope. During the next year the legate of the Pope was in person at Palermo; the whole island of Sicily had acknowledged Manfred. His triumph was completed by Naples opening her gates; Otranto and Brundusium followed the example of the capital. Manfred ruled in the name of his nephew from Palermo to Messina, from the Faro to the borders of the Papal States. At the first it was evident that the weak army of the Pope, under the Cardinal Octavian, could not make head against this rising of the whole realm. Berthold of Homburg soon deserted the cause of the Pope.[b] Alexander was trammelled with the engagements of his predecessor, who, having broken off his overtures to Charles of Anjou, had acknowledged Edmund of England king of Sicily. The more remote his hopes of success, the more ostentatiously did Henry III. attempt to dazzle the eyes of his subjects by this crown on the head of his second son. Edmund appeared in public as King of

(margin note: A.D. 1254. March 13.)

(margin note: England.)

---

[b] See the curious letter in Matt. Paris, from which it appears that certain churches and monasteries in England were bound to merchants of Sienna in 2000 marks of new sterling money in favour of Berthold and his brothers. For acts of treason, Berthold and his brothers were declared to have forfeited their claim. But the churches and monasteries were still to discharge the 2000 marks. The Prior and monastery of Durham were amerced at 500 marks; Bath at 400; Tharney at 400; Croyland, 400; Glabora, 300. Durham and Glabora refused payment. This is dated Anagni, June 1258. There is also a letter (MS., B. M.) threatening excommunication against the Prior of Winchester and others, if they do not pay 315 marks to certain merchants of Sienna (sub ann. 1255, in init.).

Sicily, affected to wear an Italian dress, and indulged in
all the pomp and state of royalty. The King himself,
notwithstanding the sullen looks of his Barons, spoke as
if determined on this wild expedition. His ambassadors,
the Bishops of London and Hereford, the Abbot of
Westminster, the Provost of Beverley, accepted the
crown. It was agreed that, as Edmund was not of age,
his father should swear fealty for him.* Yet England
was less liberal than usual of subsidies either to the
Pope or to the King for this senseless enterprise. The
legate, a Gascon, Rustand, had already received a
commission, with the Archbishop of Canterbury and
the Bishop of Hereford, to levy a tenth on England,
Scotland, and Ireland. The King had an offer of an
exemption from his vow of a crusade to the Holy Land,
on condition of his appearing at the head of an army to
subdue Manfred in Apulia. Rustand himself preached
in London and in other places; and made others preach
a crusade against Manfred, the enemy of the Pope and
of their Lord the King of England, a crusade as meritorious as that to the Lord's sepulchre. The honest
English were revolted at hearing that they were to
receive the same indulgences for shedding Christian as
Saracen blood. Rustand received a rich prebend of
York as reward for his services.

Year after year came the same insatiate demands:
ambassador after ambassador summoned the King to
fulfil his engagements; the Pope condescended to

---

* In Rymer, 1254, are the bulls or
terms of grant of the kingdom of
Sicily. See in MS., B. M. (viii. 195),
letter to the King of England to pay
4800 livres Tournois (libræ Turo-
nenses)* for the expenses of W. tar-
rasus (Cardinal of Velletri) " electus
de mandato c. m, Innocent. IV. in
servitium Ecclesiæ pro statu negotio
regni Siciliæ."

* The livre Tournois was about 12 francs.

inform him through what merchants he could transmit
his subsidies to Rome.   The insolence and the falsehood
of Rustand and the other legates, the Archbishop Elect
of Toledo and the Bishop of Bologna, increased the
exasperation.   In the absence of the Primate of England,
Rustand ruled supreme in the Church, and excommunicated refractory prelates, whose goods were instantly
seized and confiscated to the King.   They carefully
disguised the successes of Manfred, and spread rumours
of the victories of the Papal armies.   The King had too
much vanity and too much weakness to resist these
frauds and violences.   The King is said to have bound
himself for two hundred thousand pounds sterling,
besides fifty thousand levied by the Bishop of Hereford.[a]
Even the Cistercian monks could not escape the unusual
and acknowledged alienation of the English clergy from
the see of Rome.   The Pope, or the Nuncio of the
Pope, had recourse to violent measures against Sewal,
the second prelate of the realm, Sewal, Arch- Archbishop
bishop of York.   The words of the English A.D. 1257.
historian show the impression on the public mind:
"About that time our Lord the Pope laid his hand
heavily on the Archbishop of York.   He gave orders
(by a measure so strong and terrible he would daunt his
courage) that Sewal should be ignominiously excommunicated throughout England with the light of torches
and tolling of bells.   But the said Archbishop, taught
by the example of Thomas the Martyr, the example and
lessons of the saintly Edmund, once his master, by the
faithfulness of the blessed Robert, Bishop of Lincoln,
did not despair of consolation from heaven, and patiently
supported the tyranny of the Pope; for he would not

---

[a] Rymer, MS., B. M., sub ann. 1235.

bestow the abundant revenues of the Church on persons
unworthy or unknown, from beyond the Alps, and
scorned to submit himself, like a woman, to the Pope's
will, abandoning his rights. Hence the more he was
anathematised by the orders of the Pope, the more was
he blessed by the people, though in secret for fear of the
Romans." *

But where all this time was the Primate of England,
Boniface, Archbishop of Canterbury. and who was he? On the death of the unworldly and sainted Edmund Rich, the King
and the Pope had forced on the too obsequious, afterwards bitterly repentant, monks of Canterbury, a foreigner, almost an Italian. Boniface, Bishop of Bellay,
was uncle to the Queen, and brother of that Philip of
Savoy, the warlike and mitred bodyguard of Innocent
IV., who became Archbishop of Lyons. Boniface was
elected in 1341, confirmed by Pope Innocent not before
1344. The handsome, proud prelate found that Edmund,
however saintly, had been but an indifferent steward of
the secular part of the diocese. Canterbury was loaded
with an enormous debt, and Boniface came not to England to preside over an impoverished see. He obtained
a grant from the Pope of first-fruits from all the benefices in his province, by which he raised a vast sum.
Six years after, the Primate announced, and set forth
About Michaelmas, a.d. 1294. on a visitation of his province, not as it was
said, and as too plainly appeared, for the glory
of God, but in quest of ungodly gain. Bishops, chapters, monasteries must submit to this unusual discipline,
haughtily and rapaciously enforced by a foreigner.

<hr />

* So writes Paris. " Falso pertinac-
iam illius constantia nomine exornat
(M. Paris) cum justi Pontifex pro
Sicilia, deposita tyranno, in Edmundum
transferenda, a clero Anglicano pecu-
niarum subsidia exigeret." Thus wrote
Raynaldus in the 17th century.—Sub
ann. 1257.

From Feversham and Rochester he extorted large
sums. He appeared in London, treated the Bishop (Fulk
Basset of the old noble Norman house) and his jurisdiction with contempt. The Dean of St. Paul's (Henry de
Cornhill) stood by his Bishop. The Primate appeared
with his cuirass gleaming under his pontifical robes.
The Dean closed the doors of his cathedral against him.
Boniface solemnly excommunicated Henry Dean of
St. Paul's and his Chapter in the name of St. Thomas
the Martyr of Canterbury. The Sub-Prior of St. Bartholomew's (the Prior was dead) fared still worse. He
calmly pleaded the rights of the Bishop; the wrathful
Primate rushed on the old man, struck him down with
his own hand, tore his splendid vestment, and trampled
it under foot. The Bishop of London was involved
in the excommunication. The Dean of St. Paul's
appealed to the Pope; the excommunication was suspended. But Boniface himself proceeded in great pomp
to Rome. The uncle of the Queen of England, the
now wealthy Primate of England, could not but obtain
favour with Innocent. The Dean of St. Paul's was
compelled to submit to the supreme Archiepiscopal
authority. On his triumphant return Boniface continued his visitation. The Chapter of Lincoln, headed
by the Archdeacon (Bishop Grostête was dead), resisted
his demand to dispose of the vacant Prebends of the
Church. The Archdeacon bore his own appeal to
Rome. After three years he obtained (by what means
appears not) what seemed a favourable sentence; but
died, worn out, on his way home. Boniface trampled
on all rights, all privileges. The monks of Canterbury
obtained a Papal diploma of exemption, Boniface threw
it into the fire, and excommunicated the bearers. The
King cared not, for the Pope would not regard the insult.

After the accession of Alexander IV. the Archbishop of Canterbury is in arms, with his brother, the Archbishop of Lyons, besieging Turin, to release the head of his house, the Count of Savoy, whom his subjects had deposed and imprisoned for his intolerable tyranny. The wealth of the Churches of Canterbury and Lyons was showered, but showered in vain, on their bandit army. Turin resisted the secular, more obstinately than London the spiritual arms of the Primate. He returned, not without disgrace, to England. With such a Primate the Pope was not likely to find much vigorous or rightful opposition from the Church of England.[f]

Pope Alexander IV., while he thus tyrannised in England, was not safe in Rome, or even in Anagni. The stern justice of the Senator Brancaleone had provoked resistance, no doubt not discouraged by the partisans of the Pope. The Nobles urged on an insurrection: Brancaleone was seized and thrown into prison. But his wise precaution had secured thirty hostages of the highest Roman patrician houses at Bologna. His wife fled to that city, and roused Bologna with harangues on the injustice and ingratitude shown to her great citizen. The hostages were kept guarded with stricter vigilance. The Nobles appealed to the Pope, who issued an angry mandate to

---

[f] Paris, sub ann. 1241-4, 1250, 1256. See the letter from Pope Alexander, commiserating on the failure before Turin. Godwin de Præsulibus contains a full abstract of the life of Boniface. Compare MS. B. M. vi. p. 347, for the resistance and excommunication (the sentence) of the Dean of St. Paul's: also of Sub-Prior of St. Bartholomew; excommunication of Bishop of London, p. 388. The Archbishop had obtained, under grant of first fruits, "magnam quantitatem pecuniæ," vii. 16. Papal decree against Dean and Chapter of St. Paul's, p. 57. Archbishop Boniface was exempted from visiting his four Welsh dioceses, "propter guerrarum discrimina, penuria victualium," b. vii.

the Bolognese, which they treated with scorn. The
populace of Rome arose and broke the prison of Brancaleone. Brancaleone laid down his senatorship for two
years (during which it was filled by a citizen of Brescia,
who trod in his footsteps) to resume it with still more
inflexible determination. On his reinauguration he
summoned all malefactors before his tribunal,
not the last the authors of his imprisonment. A.D. 1254.
His sentence was inexorable by prayer or bribe. Men
of the highest birth, even relatives of the Pope, were
shown on gibbets. Two of the Annibaldi suffered this
ignoble doom. He destroyed a hundred and forty
castles of those lofty and titled spoilers. The Pope, at
Viterbo, was so unadvised as to issue a sentence of excommunication against the Senator and the people of
Rome. They were not content with treating this sentence with the bitterest derision. The Senator summoned the whole people to assemble, as one man, in
arms; they marched under their banner towards Anagni,
the birthplace of the Pope. The inhabitants of Anagni,
many of them his kindred, implored Alexander with
passionate entreaties to avert their doom. The Pope,
to elude the disgrace of seeing his native city razed to
the earth, was content to send deputies to Brancaleone,
humbly imploring his mercy. The Senator had great
difficulty in restraining the people. An alliance grew
up between Manfred and Brancaleone. The Senator
retained his dignity till his death: his head was then
deposited in a coffer, like a precious relique, and placed,
with all the pomp of a religious ceremony, by the grateful people, on the top of a marble column. Notwithstanding the prohibition of the Pope, the people raised
the uncle of Brancaleone to the Senatorship of Rome.[r]

---

[r] Paris, sub ann. 1258.

Alexander could look for no aid from the Empire.
The Papal Emperor, William of Holland, had fallen in
an expedition against the Frisians. There was no great
German Prince to command the Empire. The
Pope, faithful to the legacy of hatred to the
house of Swabia, contented himself with pro-
hibiting in the strongest terms the election of the
young Conradin. The Germans looked abroad; some
of the divided Electors offered the throne again to
Richard of Cornwall, others to Alfonso King
of Castile. The enormous wealth of Richard
of Cornwall, perhaps his feeble character, attracted the
ambitious Archbishop of Cologne, who hoped in his
name to rule the Empire, and to dispense the
wealth of England. Richard was crowned at
Aix-la-Chapelle. He had before declined the
kingdom of Naples; his avarice had resisted all the
attempts of the King his brother and of the Pope to
employ his riches in the cause of young Edmund; he
retained them to gratify his own vanity.[1]

For seventeen years the Empire was in fact vacant;
better for the Pope such anarchy than a
Swabian on the throne.

France, so long as the treaty existed between the
Pope and England for the investiture of Prince Edmund
with the throne of Sicily, could be roused by no adequate
temptation. The Pope could offer no vigorous resistance,
yet would not make a virtue of necessity and acknowledge the house of Swabia. He had now fully discovered
the weakness, the impotence of the King of England.[2]

---

[1] Paris says that, independent of the
Empire, his revenues would have produced 100 marks a-day for ten years.
[2] "Videns ipsius debilitatem ac im-
potentiam quam publice allegabat."—
MS., B.M. In a letter, b. viii. p. 49,
the Pope recites all the acts of Innocent IV., and the dates.

He had summoned him to execute his contract. Henry
truly, but without shame, pleaded his poverty, and demanded a tenth of the ecclesiastical revenues. The
excommunication hung over the head of the King for
having made a bargain with the Pope which he could
not fulfil.

Manfred had won the crown of Sicily in the name of
his nephew Conradin; he was but Regent of the realm.
Rumours were spread of the death of Conradin; the
enemies of Manfred asserted that they were invented
and disseminated by his astute ambition; his partisans
that he had no concern in their propagation.[a] But
Manfred was necessary to the power, to the independence of the Sicilies. The Prelates, Barons, almost
the whole realm entreated him to assume the Manfred
crown. His coronation took place to the uni- Aug. 11, 1258.
versal joy. Hardly was it over when ambassadors arrived
from the mother of Conradin, and from her son, imploring Manfred not to usurp the rights which he had
defended with so much valour. Manfred received the
ambassadors in a great assemblage of his Barons. "He
had ascended the throne, which he had himself won by
his arms, at the call of his people; their affections could
alone maintain that throne. It was neither for the
interest of the realm nor of Conradin himself that
Naples should be ruled by a woman and an infant: he
had no relative but Conradin, for whom he should
preserve the crown, and faithfully bequeath it on his
death. If Conradin desired to uphold the privileges of
an heir-apparent, he should reside at the court of Manfred,
and win the love of the people whom he was to govern.

---

[a] Jamsilla. Ricordano, c. 147. Le credo le favole. Murat. Ann., sub ann.
1258.

Manfred would treat him as a son, and instruct him in
the virtues of his glorious ancestors." How far Manfred
was sincere, Manfred himself perhaps did not know;
how far, if he had himself issue, his virtue would have
resisted the fondness of a parent for his own offspring,
and that which he might have alleged to himself and to
others as an undeniable truth, the interest of the kingdom. What confusion, what bloodshed might have been
spared to Naples, to Italy, to Christendom, if the crown
of Naples had descended in the line of Manfred; if the
German connexion had been broken for ever, the French
connexion never formed; if Conradin had remained
Duke of Swabia, and Charles of Anjou had not descended the Alps! A wiser Pope, and one less wedded
to the hereditary policy and to the antipathies of his
spiritual forefathers, might have discerned this, and
seen how well it would have coincided with the interests
of the see. Manfred acknowledged and fairly treated
might have softened into a loyal Guelf; he was now
compelled to be the head, a most formidable head, of the
Ghibellines. Alexander lived to see Manfred in close
alliance with Sienna, the stronghold of the exiled Ghibellines of Florence;[a] to see the fatal battle
of Arba, or Monte Aperto, in which the Florentine Guelfs were utterly crushed and forced to
abandon their city. Florence was only saved from
being razed to the earth at the instigation of the rival
cities, Pisa and Sienna, by the patriotic appeal of the
great Ghibelline, Farinata di Uberti, a name which
lives in Dante's poetry.[b] In all the south of Italy
Manfred was supreme: Genoa and Venice were his
allies.

Sept. 4, 1260.

---

[a] See throughout Muratori, who quotes impartially Guelfs and Ghibellines.
[b] Inferno, vi. 79, x. 32.

Nor was it the Guelfic or Papal influence, nor even his own unspeakable cruelties; it was his treachery to his friends alone that in the north of Italy caused the fall of the triumphant champion of the Ghibellines, Eccelin da Romano, and with him of his brother Alberic. The character of Eccelin was the object of the profoundest terror and abhorrence. No human suffering, it might seem, could glut his revenge; the enemy who fell into his hands might rejoice in immediate decapitation or hanging. The starvation of whole cities; the imprisonment of men, women, and children in loathsome dungeons touched not his heart, which seemed to have made cruelty a kind of voluptuous excitement.[*] But what was the social state of this part of Christendom? How had that state been aggravated by the unmitigated dissensions and wars, the feuds of city with city, the intestine feuds within every city! Had the voice of the Father of Christendom, of the Vicegerent of the Prince of Peace ever been earnestly raised in protest or rebuke? Was not the Papal Legate the head of the Guelfic faction, and were the Guelfs on the whole more humane than the Ghibellines? Alexander might have published a crusade against this foe of the human race, and justly might he have offered more splendid promises of pardon and eternal life to him who should rid the world of this monster, than to him who should slay hosts of Moslemin.[P] But a fitter, as an abler leader, might have been found for this enterprise than the Archbishop of Ravenna; and

Eccelin da Romano.

Sept. 27. 1256.

---

[*] It may be doubted whether Eccelin himself was not gradually trained to this habit of barbarity. Frederick II., though severe and merciless to his foes, would hardly have addressed operators

letters, or given his daughter in marriage to a wild beast, such a wild beast as Eccelin appears in his later days.

[P] Compare Alexandri Epist. ad Epis- copos.

when the army of the Archbishop got possession of Padua, the ruthless sacking of the town by his mercenary soldiers made the citizens look back with regret to the iron rule of Eccelin. Nor would Papal anathema or Papal crusade have shaken the power of Eccelin.[a] With the Marquis Pallavicini and Buoso da Doara, the head of the Cremonese Ghibellines, he had become master of Brescia; but Eccelin never conquered save for himself. The flagrant treachery by which he had determined to rid himself of his colleagues was discovered; the indignant Ghibellines made a league against the common enemy of mankind. Eccelin was defeated, sorely wounded, captured. His end was worthy of his life. On the first night of his imprisonment the bells of a neighbouring chapel rang loudly, perhaps rejoicing at his bondage. He woke up in wrath: " Go, hew down that priest that makes such a din with his bells." " You forget," said his guard, " that you are in prison." He inquired where he was taken. " At Bassano." Like most strong minds of the day, Eccelin, who had faith in nothing else, had faith in divination. His astrologer had foretold that he should die in Bassano. The priests and friars thronged around him, urging, threatening, imploring, that he would confess and repent of his sins. " I repent of nothing, but that I have not wreaked full vengeance on my foes; that I have badly conducted my army, and allowed myself to be duped and betrayed."

Alberic de Romano. He would take neither food nor medicine; but death was slow: he tore the dressings from his wounds, and was found a corpse.[b] Alberic,

[a] Rolandini, Monach. Patavin. apud Muratori.

[b] Throughout see Rolandin, xli. c. 13; Chron. Veron., 8. R. T., v. vlil. ; and Muratori, Annali, sub anno 1259, 1260. The B. Museum Chronicle sums up, "nullus in ferocitate et unquam fuit similis."—p. 245.

his brother, once his deadly enemy, was now his ally.
Eccelin wanted but one vice, passion for women, which
might possibly have given some softness to his
heart. No woman was safe from the less san-   A.D. 1260.
guinary Alberic. Alberic was besieged during the next
year in the castle of San Zeno. All hope of succour was
gone; with some remains of generosity he allowed his followers to buy their own free departure by the surrender
of himself and his wife, six sons and two daughters.
He was at first treated with every kind of mockery;
then his six sons slain in his sight, torn in pieces, their
limbs thrust in his face. His wife, his beautiful and
innocent daughters had their lower garments cut off; in
this state of nakedness, in the sight of the whole army,
were bound to a stake and burned alive. Alberic's own
flesh was torn from his body by pincers; he was then
tied to the tail of a horse, and dragged to death.

What wonder that amid such deeds, whatever religion
remained, as it ever must remain in the depths of the
human heart, either took refuge beyond the pale of the
Church, among the Cathari, who never were more
numerous in the cities, especially of northern Italy,
than in these days: or within the Church showed itself
in wild epidemic madness? Against the Cathari the
Friars preached in vain; the Inquisition in vain held its
courts; and executions for heresy added more horrors
to these dire times.

It was at this period too that one of those extravagant outbursts of fanaticism, which constantly   The Fla-
occurred during the middle ages, relieved   gellants.
men's minds in some degree from the ordinary horrors
and miseries. Who is surprised that mankind felt itself
seized by a violent access of repentance, or that repentance disdained the usual form of discipline?

The Flagellants seemed to rise almost simultaneously in different parts of Italy. They began in Perugia. The penitential frenzy seized Rome; it spread through every city, Guelf and Ghibelline, crossed the Alps, and invaded Germany and France. Flagellation had long been a holy and meritorious discipline; it was now part of the monastic system; it had obtained a kind of dignity and importance, as the last sign of subjection to the sacerdotal power, the last mark of penitence for sins against the Church.[*] Sovereign princes, as Raymond of Toulouse; Kings, as Henry of England, had yielded their backs to the scourge. How entirely self-flagellation had become part of sanctity, appears from its being the religious luxury of Louis IX. Peter Damiani had taught it by precept and example.[1] Dominic, called the Cuirassier, had invented or popularised by his fame the usage of singing psalms to the accompaniment of self-scourging. It had come to have its stated value among works of penance.[*]

The present outburst was not the effect of popular preaching, of the eloquence of one or more vehement and ardent men, working on the passions and the fears of a vast auditory. It seemed as if mankind, at least Italian mankind, was struck at once with a sudden paroxysm of remorse for the monstrous guilt of the age, which found vent in this wild but hallowed form of self-torture. All ranks, both sexes, all ages, were possessed with the madness—nobles, wealthy merchants, modest

---

[1] The "Historia Flagellantium" is v. 8. a brief but complete history of religious flagellations, first of legal floggings administered by authority, then of the exopia and practice of self-flagellation.

[1] Epistol. ad Clerum Florentin., p. 85.

[*] "Consequitur ergo ut qui viginti psalteria cum disciplina decantat, centum annorum poenitentiam se persolvisse confidat."—Vit. Damiani Loric.,

and delicate women, even children of five years old.
They stripped themselves naked to the waist, covered
their faces that they might not be known, and went two
and two in solemn slow procession, with a cross and a
banner before them, scourging themselves till the blood
tracked their steps, and shrieking out their doleful
psalms. They travelled from city to city. Whenever
they entered a city, the contagion seized all predisposed
minds. This was done by night as by day. Not only
were the busy mart and the crowded street disturbed by
these processions; in the dead midnight they were seen
with their tapers or torches gleaming before them in
their awful and shadowy grandeur, with the lashing
sound of the scourge and the screaming chant. Thirty-
three days and a half, the number of the years of the
Lord's sad sojourn in this world of man, was the usual
period for the penance of each. In the burning heat of
summer, when the wintry roads were deep in snow, they
still went on. Thousands, thousands, tens of thousands
joined the ranks; till at length the madness wore itself
out. Some princes and magistrates, finding that it was
not sanctioned by the Roman See or by the authority
of any great Saint, began to interpose; that which had
been the object of general respect, became almost as
rapidly the object of general contempt.[a]

[a] " Unda tepescere in brevi orpit reo | multa pecus inter discordantes facis
immoderate concepta."—Herm. Alt. | fluvunt, et multa hora acta sunt."
There are two full descriptions of this | His account is curious.—p. 250. See
singular movement : one by an Italian, | in the Translation of Dr. Hecker's
the Monachus Petavinensis in Muratori, | curious book on the Epidemics of the
viii. 712 ; the other by a German, | Middle Ages much strange matter on
Hermannus Altahensis (Abbot of Nieder | the German Flagellants, and the wild
Altaich), in Böhmer, Fontes, ii. p. | Geisler-Lied, the Hymn of the Flagel-
516. See too B. Museum Chronicle : | lants, with an English version, p. 64.
he adds, " Verumtamen propter hoc |

The Flagellant phrensy was a purely religious movement.[f] It had been preceded by about ten
years by that of the Pastoureaux (the Shepherds) in Flanders and in France. This rising had
something of the fierce resentment of an oppressed and
down-trodden peasantry. But it was a democratic
insurrection, not against the throne, but against the
tyrannous nobles and tyrannous churchmen : it was
among those lowest of the low whom the Friar Preachers
and the followers of St. Francis had not reached, or had
left for higher game. The new Mendicant Orders
were denounced as rudely as the luxurious Cluniacs or
haughty Cistercians. The Shepherds' first declaration
of war was that "the good King Louis was left in
bondage to the Mussulmen, through the criminal and
traitorous remissness of the indolent and avaricious
clergy." They, the peasants of France, had received
the direct mission, a mission from the blessed Virgin
herself, to rescue him from the hands of the Unbelievers.
So sudden, so terrible was the insurrection, that it was
as if the fire had burst out at one instant in remote
parts of the land. It began in Flanders ; at
its head was a mysterious personage, who bore
the name of the Master of Hungary. He was an aged
man with a long beard, pale emaciated face ; he spoke
Latin, French, and German with the same fluent per-
suasiveness ; he preached without authority of Pope or
Prelate ; as he preached, he clasped a roll in his hands,
which contained his instructions from the blessed Virgin.
The Virgin had appeared to him, encircled by hosts of
angels, and had given him his celestial commission to

marginal notes: The Pastoureaux. A.D. 1261. The Master of Hungary.

---

f Affo, Storia di Parma, lit. p. 256, connects the Flagellants with the
believers in the Abbot Joachim. (See forward.)

summon the poor Shepherds to the deliverance of the
good King. Terror spread the strangest rumours of this
awful personage. He was an apostate Cistercian monk ;
in his youth he had denied Jesus Christ ; he had sucked
in the pernicious practices of magic from the empoisoned
wells of Toledo (among the Jews and Arabians of that
city). He it was that in his youth had led the crusade
of children, who had plunged, following his steps, by
thousands into the sea ; he had made a solemn covenant
with the Soldan of Babylon to lead a countless multitude of Christians to certain bondage in the Holy Land,
that they and their King being in his power, he might
subdue Christendom. Since the days of Mohammed, in
the judgement of wise men, no such dangerous scourge
of mankind had arisen in the Church of Christ. His
title, the Master of Hungary, might lead to the suspicion that he was a Bulgarian Manichee, revenging
on the haughty hierarchy the wrongs of his murdered
brethren.[*]

The eloquence and mysterious bearing of the Master
of Hungary stirred the lowest depths of society. The
Shepherds, the peasants left their flocks, their stalls,
their fields, their ploughs ; in vain friends, parents,
wives remonstrated ; they took no thought of sus-
tenance. So, drawing men after him, " as the load-
stone draws the iron," he marched through Flanders
and Picardy. He entered Amiens at the head of thirty
thousand men, was received as the Deliverer with festive
rejoicings. He passed on to the Isle of France, gathering, as some fell off from weakness or weariness, the
whole labouring population in his wake. The villages
and fields were desolate behind them. They passed

---

* Matt. Paris, sub ann.

through the cities (not one dared to close the gates
against them), they moved in battle array, brandishing
clubs, pikes, axes, all the wild weapons they could seize.
The Provosts, the Mayors bowed in defenceless panic
before them. They had at first only the standard of
their Master, a Lamb bearing the banner of the Cross,
the Lamb the sign of humility, the Cross that of victory.

Soon four hundred banners waved above them; on
some were emblazoned the Virgin and the angels appearing to the Master. Before they reached Paris they
were one hundred thousand and more. They had been
joined by all the outlaws, the robbers, the excommunicate, followers more dangerous, as wielding and accustomed to wield arms, the two-edged axe, the sword, the
dagger, and the pike. They had become an army.
They seemed worshippers, it was said, of Mary rather
than of Christ. Blanche, the Queen-Regent, either in
panic or in some wild hope that these fierce hordes
might themselves aid in achieving, or compel others to
achieve the deliverance of her son, professed to believe
their loyal protestations; they were admitted into Paris.

But already they had begun to show their implacable
Hostility to hostility to the Church. They usurped the
the clergy. offices of the clergy, performed marriages, distributed crosses, offered absolution to those who joined
their Crusade. They taunted the Friar Preachers and
Minorites as vagabonds and hypocrites; the White
Monks (the Cistercians) with their covetousness, their
vast possessions in lands and flocks; the Black Monks
(the Benedictines) with gluttony and pride; the Canons,
as worldly, self-indulgent men; Bishops, as hunters and
hawkers, as given to all voluptuousness. No one dared
to repeat the impious reproaches which they heaped on
the Church of Rome.

All this the people heard with the utmost delight.
It was rumoured that the Master miraculously fed the
multitudes; bread, meat, and wine, multiplied under his
hands. They had entered Paris: the Master
was admitted into the presence of the Queen,
and was received with honour and with gifts. The
Master, emboldened, mounted the pulpit in the church
of St. Eustache, with an episcopal mitre on his head,
preached and blessed the holy water. Meantime, his
followers swarmed in the neighbouring streets, merci-
lessly slew the priests who endeavoured to oppose their
fierce fanaticism: the approaches to the University were
closed, lest there should be a general massacre of the
scholars.

The enormous host divided at Paris into three. One
horde went towards Orleans and Bourges, one
towards Bordeaux, one to the sea-coast at
Marseilles. But though Paris, the seat of all wisdom
and of the government, had received them, the southern
cities had more courage; or the strange illusion had
begun to dissipate of itself. The Shepherds entered
Orleans, notwithstanding the resistance of the Bishop
and the clergy; the citizens hailed their approach; the
people crowded in countless numbers and rapt admiration around the Preacher. The Bishop issued his
inhibition to all clerks, ordering them to keep aloof
from the profane assembly: the wiser and older obeyed;
some of the younger scholars were led by curiosity to
hear one who preached unlicensed by Prelate, and who
by his preaching had awed Paris and her famous University. The Master was in the pulpit; he was pouring
forth his monstrous tenets: a scholar rushed forward,
" Wicked heretic! foe to truth; thou liest in thy throat;
thou deceivest the innocent with thy false and trea-

z 2

cherous speech." He had hardly uttered these words, when his skull was cloven by one of the Master's followers. The scholars were pursued; the gates of the University broken in; a frightful butchery followed; their books were thrown into the Loire. By another account, the scholars made a gallant resistance. The Bishop, who had been forced to fly, left the city under an interdict, as having entertained these precursors of Antichrist. The complaints of the Bishop reached the ears of Queen Blanche. Her calm wisdom had returned. " I thought," she said, " that these people might recover the Holy Land in simplicity and sanctity; since they are impostors, be they excommunicated, scattered, destroyed."

They entered Bourges: notwithstanding the denunciations of the Archbishop, the city had opened her gates.

In Bourges.   Here the first act of the Master of Hungary was to penetrate into the Jews' quarter, to plunder their houses, and burn their books. But in Bourges he was so rash, or so intoxicated with success, as not to content himself with the wonders of his eloquence: after the sermon he promised, or was said to have promised, to work the most amazing miracles. The people, eager for the miracles, were perhaps less wrought upon by the sermon: they waited in breathless expectation, but they waited in vain. At that moment of doubt and disappointment, a man (he is called an executioner) rushed forth, and clove the head of the Master with a two-edged axe; his brains were scattered on the pavement; his soul, as all then believed, went direct to hell. The Royal Bailiff of Bourges was at hand with his men-at-arms; he fell on the panic-stricken followers, cast the body into the common sewer to be torn by hounds. The excommunication was read; the whole host were pursued and massacred like mad dogs.

The second squadron met no better fate; Simon de Montfort closed the gates of Bordeaux against them, and threatened to sally out with his knights and behead them all.   Their leader, the favourite companion of the Master of Hungary, was seized, bound hand and foot, and thrown into the Garonne; the scattered followers were seized, hanged; a few found their way home as wretched beggars. Some of these, and part of the third division, reached Marseilles; but the hallucination was over; they were easily dispersed, most perished miserably. So suddenly began, so almost as suddenly ended this religious Jacquerie.[a]

The pontificates of Innocent IV. and of Alexander IV., besides these great insurrections of one order of society—the very lowest against all above them—beheld the growth of a less tumultuous but more lasting and obstinate civil war within the Church itself. The Mendicant Friars, from the humble and zealous assistants, the active itinerant subsidiary force of the hierarchy, rapidly aspired to be their rivals, their superiors—at least equal sharers, not only in their influence and their power, but also in their wealth and pomp; as far, at least, as in their buildings, their churches, their cloisters. They were no longer only among the poorest, the most ignorant of mankind: they were in the lordly halls of the nobles, in the palaces of kings. St. Louis, as we have heard, held them in such devout reverence, that if he could have

(marginal notes:) Bordeaux. Marseilles. Civil war in the Church. Progress of the Mendicant Orders.

---

[a] I have chiefly followed Matt. There is a curious letter about them to Paris and William of Nangis, with Adam de Marisco in the Burton Annals, some few facts from other chronicles. p. 290.

divided his body, he would have given one-half to either
saint, Dominic or Francis.

Not only the Popes, the more religious of the hierarchy and of the old monastic orders, had hailed, welcomed, held in honour these new labourers, who took
the hard and menial work in the lowly and neglected
and despised part of the vineyard. The Popes had the
wisdom to discern at once the power of this vast, silent,
untraceable agency on the spiritual improvement of
Christendom; its power, not only against vice, igno-
rance, irreligion, but against those who dared, in their
independence of thought, to rebel at the doctrines—in
the pride of temporal authority to contest the all-
embracing supremacy of the See of Rome. We have
seen them during the whole war with Frederick II. the
demagogues of refractory subjects, the publishers and
propagators of the fulminations of the Popes in all
lands, the levellers of mankind before the Papal autocracy, the martyrs of the high Papal faith. Those of
less worldly views saw them only as employed in their
holier work. Conrad of Zahringen, the General
of the Cistercian Order, when they established
their first house at Paris, vowed brotherhood with the
Friar Preachers. When Legate at Cologne, a priest
complained that the Preachers interfered in his parish.
"How many parishioners have you?" "Nine thousand." The Legate signed himself with the sign of the
Cross: "Miserable man! presumest thou to complain,
charged with so many souls, that these holy men would
relieve you from part of your burthen?"[b] Yet Conrad
issued his mandates, that though the Friars might preach

General of
Zahringen.

---

[b] Ann. Cistercia. quoted in Hist. Littér. de la France, article "Conrad
of Zahringen."

and administer the sacrament of penance, they should
refuse it to all who withdrew themselves from the care
of their legitimate pastor. Robert Grostète of Lincoln,
as has been said, maintained them against his own
negligent or luxurious clergy.

But their zeal or their ambition was not yet satisfied.
They aspired to the chief seats of learning; *The Universities.*
they would rule the Universities, now rising
to their height of fame and authority. Of all the
universities beyond the Alps, Paris was then the most
renowned. If Bologna might boast her civil *Paris.*
lawyers, Salerno her physicians, Paris might
vie with these great schools in their peculiar studies,
and in herself concentered the fame of all, especially of
the highest—theology. The University of Paris had
its inviolable privileges, its own endowments, government, laws, magistrates, jurisdiction; it was a state
within a state, a city within a city, a church within a
church. It refused to admit within its walls the ser-
geants of the Mayor of Paris, the apparitors of the
Bishop of Paris; it opened its gates sullenly and reluctantly to the King's officers. The Mendicants (the
Dominicans and Franciscans) would teach the teachers
of the world; they would occupy not only the pulpits in
the churches, and spread their doctrines in streets and
market-places, they would lay down the laws of philosophy, theology, perhaps of canonical jurisprudence,
from the chairs of professors; and they would vindicate
their hardy aspirations by equalling, surpassing the
most famous of the University. Already the Dominicans
might put forward their Albert the Great, the nearest
approach to a philosopher; the Franciscans, the Englishman Alexander Hales, the subtlest of the new race of
schoolmen. Aquinas and Bonaventura were to come.

The jealous University, instead of receiving these
great men as allies with open arms, rejected them as
usurpers.[a]

But the University was in implacable war with the
authorities of Paris; there was a perpetual feud, as in
other universities, between the town and the gown.
However wild and unruly the youth, the University
would maintain her prerogative of sole and exclusive
jurisdiction over them. The sober citizens would not
endure the riot, and worse than riot, of these profligate
boys.[b] Their insolent corporate spirit did not respect
the Cardinal Legate.[c] On one occasion (in 1228), in a
fierce fray of many days, two scholars were killed by the
city guard. The University haughtily demanded satisfaction; on the refusal closed her gates, suspended her
lectures, at first maintained sullen silence, and then, at
least a large portion of the scholars shook the dust
from their feet, deserted the dark and ungrateful city,
and migrated to Rheims, Orleans, Angers, even to
Toulouse.[d] The Dominicans seized their opportunity;
they obtained full license for a chair of theology from the
Bishop of Paris and the Chancellor. On the return of

---

[a] Tillemont indeed says, "L'Université les reçut même avec joie dans
ses écoles, parcequ leur vie paroissoit
alors édifiante et utile au public, et
qu'ils sembloient s'appliquer aux
sciences avec autant d'humilité que
d'ardeur et de succès. Mais elle
éprouva bientôt qu'il est dangereux de
donner entrée à des personnes trop
puissantes, et de se lier avec ceux qui
ont des desseins et des intérêts dif-
férens." See the laborious essay on
Guillaume de St. Amour, Vie de
Louis IX., p. 133 et seqq.

[b] The scholars were forbidden to
bear arms in 1218. The Official of
Paris complains "qu'ils enfonçoient et
brisoient les portes des maisons; qu'ils
enlevoient les filles et les femmes."—
Crevier, I. p. 334.

[c] Crevier, p. 335. The dispute was
about the University seal.

[d] Crevier, 341. The reader who
requires more full, learned, and prolix
information, will consult Du Boulay.
Hist. Univers. Paris. Crevier's is a
clear, rapid, and skilful epitome of Du
Boulay.

the University to Paris, they found these powerful rivals in possession of a large share in the theologic instruction. Their re-establishment, resisted by the Crown and by the Bishop of Paris (the Crown indignant that the University had presumed to confer degrees at Orleans and at Angers, the Bishop jealous of their exemption from his jurisdiction), was only effected by the authority of Pope Gregory IX. The Pontiff was anxious that Paris, the foundation of all sound learning, should regain her distinction. His mild and conciliatory counsels prevailed: the University resumed her station, and even obtained the valuable privilege that the Rector and Scholars were not liable to any excommunication not directly sanctioned by the Holy See.

Above twenty years of treacherous peace followed. The Mendicants were gaining in power, fame, influence, unpopularity. They encroached more and more on the offices, on the privileges of the clergy; stood more aloof from episcopal jurisdiction; had become, instead of the clergy and the older monasteries, the universal legatees; obscured the University by the renown of their great teachers. The University raised a loud outcry that there were twelve chairs of theology at Paris: of these, five out of the six colleges of the Regulars—the Cistercians, Premonstratensians, Val de Grace, Trinitarians, Franciscans—held each one, the Dominicans two; the Canons of Paris occupied three; there remained but two for the whole Secular Clergy.[r] They issued their edict suppressing one of the Dominicans: the Dominicans laughed them to scorn. The quarrel was aggravated by the refusal of the Dominican and Franciscan Professors to join the

---

r Crevier, p. 39d.

rest of the University in demanding justice for the death of a scholar slain in a fray.[b] The University passed a sentence of expulsion against the Dominican Professors. The Dominicans appealed to the Pope. They obtained, it was averred by false representations, a favourable award. Europe rang with the clamorous remonstrances of the University of Paris. They issued an address to the whole Episcopate of Christendom. "Would the Bishops, very many of whom had studied at Paris, allow that famous University, the foundation of the faith, to be shaken?"[i] They pressed their appeal before Pope Innocent IV. Innocent, a great student of the canon law, had always looked on the University of Paris with favour. The Mendicants had done their work; Frederick II. was dead; Innocent master of Italy. The Pope, who had alienated the University by his exactions and arrogance, endeavoured to propitiate them by the sacrifice of his faithful allies the Friars. He promulgated his celebrated bull, subjugating the Mendicant Orders to episcopal authority. The next month Pope Innocent was dead. The Dominicans revenged themselves on the ungrateful Pontiff by assuming the merit of his death, granted to their prayers. "From the Litanies of the Dominicans, good Lord deliver us," became a proverbial saying.[k]

Alexander IV. was not the protector only, he was the humble slave of the Mendicants.[m] His first act was to annul the bull of his predecessor

(margin notes: Bull of Pope Innocent. Nov. 1254.)

(margin note: Alexander IV.)

---

[b] The University obtained justice; two were hanged for the offence —Crevier, p. 400.

[i] "Si on attaque le fondement (de l'Eglise) qui est l'Ecole de Paris, tout l'edifice est mis en péril."—See Crevier, p. 407.

"Et ne se fust la bonne garde De l'Université, qui garde La chief de la Chrétienté." Roman de la Rose, l. 12.15.

[k] Antonini. Secunda. in Chronic. Compare Hist. Lit. de la France, xix. p. 197, article William de St. Amour.

[m] The words of Crevier, p. 411.

without reservation." The Mendicants were at once
reinstated in all their power. In vain the eloquent William (called St. Amour, from the
place of his birth in Franche Comté) maintained the
privileges of the University: he returned discomfited,
not defeated, to Paris. He was hailed as the acknowledged champion of the University, and devoted himself
with dauntless courage and perseverance to the cause.[x]
He not only asserted the privileges of the University;
Paris rung with his denunciations of the Mendicants,
of Mendicancy itself. He preached with a popularity
rivalling or surpassing the best preachers of the Orders.
He accused the Friars as going about into houses, leading astray silly women, laden with sins, usurping everywhere the rule over their consciences and men's property, aspiring to tyrannise over public opinion. "And
who were they? No successors of the Apostles; they
presumed to act in the Church with no spiritual lineage,
with no tradition of authority; from them **arose** the
'Perils of the days to come.'"[z]

The Dominicans had boasted, according to the popular
poet,[x] that they ruled supreme in Paris and in Rome:
they had lost Paris, but in Rome they ruled without
rival. The first, the most famous, it is said, of forty
bulls issued by Alexander IV., appeared during the

<hr>

[x] He was elected Dec. 12; revoked the bull Dec. 22.

[x] To William of St. Amour was attributed the bull of Innocent IV.

"S'il n'avait en sa verité
L'accord de l'Université
Et du peuple communément
Qui appelera son prêchement."
Roman de la Rose, l. 12513.

[z] Opera Gulielm. St. Amour, Pref. p. 23.

[x] "Li Jacobin (Dominicains) sont si preu-
dome
Qu'il ont Paris et si ont Rome,
Et si sont roi et Apostole
Et de l'avoir ont il grant somme.
Et qui se morra, se il ne s'assomme
Pour exécuteurs, c'iere lui,
Et sont apostre por parole.
*   *   *   *   *
Lor home n'est pas frivole,
Je, qui redout ces dame folo
Ne vous di plus mès qu'il sont home."
Ruteboeuf, edit. Jubinal, i. 161.

next year.[r] It commenced with specious adulation of
the University, ended with awarding complete victory
to the Dominicans. While it seemed to give full power
to the University, it absolutely annulled their statute of
exclusion against the Dominicans. The Bishops of
Orleans and Auxerre were charged with the execution
of this bull; they were armed with ample powers of
spiritual censure, of excommunicating, or suspending
from their office all masters or scholars guilty of contumacy. The University defied or attempted to elude
these censures. They obstinately refused to admit the
Dominicans to their republic; they determined rather
to dissolve the University; many masters and students
withdrew, some returned and took up again their
attitude of defiance. William de St. Amour was the
special object of the hatred of the Mendicants. He
was arraigned before the Bishop of Paris, at the suit of
Gregory, a chaplain of Paris, as having disseminated a
libel defamatory of the Pope. St. Amour appeared;
but the courage of the accuser had failed, he was not to
be found. St. Amour offered canonical purgation; to
swear on the reliques of the Holy Martyrs that he was
guiltless of the alleged crime. Four thousand scholars
stood forward as his compurgators. The Bishop was
forced to dismiss the charge.[s] In vain the four great
Archbishops of France interfered to allay the strife:
the pulpits rung with mutual criminations.

William of St. Amour and his zealous partisans
arraigned the Mendicants, not merely as usurpers of the
rights, offices, emoluments of the clergy, of heredipety

[r] This bull was called "Quasi lig-
num vitæ." The successive bulls may
be read in the Bullarium.
[s] Crevier, from a letter of the students of the University to the Pope. It
was possibly before the arrival of the
bull.

and rapacity utterly at variance with their ostentatious poverty, but both orders, indiscriminately, Dominicans as well as Franciscans, as believers in, as preachers and propagators of the *Everlasting Gospel*. This book, which became the manual, I had almost said the Bible of the spiritual Franciscans, must await its full examination till those men—the Fraticelli—come before us in their formidable numbers and no less formidable activity. Suffice it here, that the Everlasting Gospel, the   The Eternal Gospel. prophetic book ascribed to the Abbot Joachim, or rather the introduction to the Everlasting Gospel, proclaimed the approach, the commencement of the Last Age of the World, that of the Holy Ghost. The Age of the Father—that of the Law—had long since gone by; that of the Son was ebbing on its last sands; and with the Age of the Son, the Church, the hierarchy, its power, wealth, splendour, were to pass away. The Age of the Holy Ghost was at hand, it was in its dawn. The Holy Ghost would renew the world in the poverty, humility, Christian perfection of St. Francis. The Everlasting Gospel superseded and rendered useless the other four. It suited the enemies of the Mendicants to involve both Orders in this odious charge: the Introduction to the Everlasting Gospel was by some attributed to the Dominicans, its character, its spirit, its tone, were unquestionably Franciscan.[1]

---

[1] Matt. Paris (sub ann. 1256), Richer. Cronic. Senons., and the authors of the Roman de la Rose, attribute the Everlasting Gospel to the Dominicans. Both were the tone in Paris. According, however, to the Roman de la Rose, it had another author:

"Ung livre de par le le grant Diable, Dit l'Evangile pardurable.

Que le Saint Esprit ministre, Bien est digne d'être brulé.
*   *   *   *
Tant seurement ce te l'Evangile, Croit que les quatre Evangiles Jean-Christ livrat a leurs titres."
—L. 12444, &c.

It apparel, according to the poet William de Lorris, in 1250: it was in the hands of every man and woman in the "parvis Notre Dame."

These two rival Orders had followed in their development the opposite character of their founders. To the stern, sober, practical views of Dominic had succeeded stern, sober, practical Generals. The mild, mystic, passionate Francis was followed by men all earnest and vehement, but dragged different ways by conflicting passions: the passion for poverty, as the consummation and perfection of all religion; the passion for other ends to which poverty was but the means, and therefore must be followed out with less rigour. The first General, Elias, even in the lifetime of the Saint, tampered with the vow of holy poverty; he was deposed, as we have heard, became no longer the partisan of the Pope, but of Frederick II., was hardly permitted on his deathbed to resume the dress of the Order.[*] It may be presumed that Crescentius, the sixth General, was, from age or temper, less rigorous as to this vital law. He, too, was deposed from his high place, and John of Parma became General of the Order. John of Parma[*] was, it might be said (if St. Francis himself was not the parent of the Spiritualist Franciscans), that parent; he was the extremest of the extreme. His first act was a visitation of all the monasteries of the Order, the enforcement of that indispensable virtue which would brook no infringement whatever. John of Parma was employed by Innocent IV. in Greece, in an endeavour to reconcile the Oriental schism. In 1251 he was again in Rome. In 1256, exactly the very year in which came forth the daring book of William de St. Amour, there were strange murmurs, sullen suppressed murmurs against John

---

[*] Chroniques des Frères Mineurs, c. xii. p. 27.

[*] The last account which I have read of John of Parma is in the Hist. Littéraire de la France, t. xx. p. 23. But the whole of this development of spiritual Franciscanism will be more fully traced hereafter.

of Parma.   He was deposed, and only by the influence
of the Cardinal Ottobuoni permitted to dwell in retirement at Rieti.   There seems but slight doubt that he
was deposed as the author of the Introduction to the
Everlasting Gospel.[7]   It needed all the commanding
gentleness, the unrivalled learning, the depth of piety,
in St. Bonaventura, the new General, to allay the civil
feud, and delay for some years the fatal schism among
the followers of St. Francis — the revolt of the
Spiritualists from the Order.

The war continued to rage in Paris, notwithstanding
a short truce brought about by the King and the
Bishops.   Bull after bull arrived.[a]   Pope Alexander
appealed at length to the King; he demanded of the
secular power the exile of the obstinate leaders of
the Anti-Mendicant party, William de St. Amour, Eudes
of Douai, Nicolas Dean of Bar-sur-Aube, and Christian
Canon of Beauvais.[a]   Before the King (St. Louis),
whose awful reverence and passionate attachment to
the Mendicant Orders were well known, had determined on his course, William of St. Amour had published his terrible book on the " Perils of the   The Perils of
Last Times."   This book, written in the name,   the Last Times.
perhaps with the aid and concurrence of the theologians
of the University, was more dangerous, because it denounced not openly the practices of the Friars, but it

---

[7] It was the great object of Wadding
and of Staraglia to release the memory
of a General of their order from the
authorship of an heretical book.   It is
attributed to him, or to Gerard da
Borgo san Domnino, under his surplice,
by Nicolas Eymeric.   Direct. Inquis. ii.
v. 24.   Baovius, sub ann. 1259.
Bulæus, p. 299.   See also Tillemont's
impartial summing up. p. 157.

[1] Tillemont, p. 182.

[a] On these men compare Tillemont,
p. 144.   Thomas Cantipratt, among
later writers the great enemy of William
de St. Amour, admits that he endured
the clergy and people of Rome by his
eloquence.

was a relentless, covert, galling exposure of them and
of their proceedings. That they were meant as the
forerunners of Antichrist, the irrefragable signs of the
"perils of the last times," none could doubt. The book
was sent by the indignant King himself to Rome. The
University had endeavoured in vain to anticipate the
more rapid movements of their adversary. They had
despatched a mission (the very four men condemned by
the Pope) to Rome, bearing the Introduction to the
Everlasting Gospel, and demanding the condemnation
of that flagrantly heretical book.[b] They had obtained
letters of recommendation from all the chapters in the
province of Rheims.

Ere they arrived, the all-powerful Dominicans had
struck their blow. The "Perils of the Last Times"
had been submitted to the examination of four Cardinals, one of them a Dominican—Hugo de St. Cher,
who sat as judge in his own cause. It was condemned as unjust, wicked, execrable; it was burned in
the presence of the Pope, before the Cathedral at
Anagni.

William de St. Amour stood alone in Rome against
the Pope Alexander, the Cardinals, and the
Dominicans, headed by Hugo de St. Cher.[c]
He conducted his defence with consummate courage
and no less consummate address. It was impossible to
fix upon him the fatal guilt of heresy.[d] His health
began to fail; he was prohibited for a time from returning to France, perhaps was not sorry to obey the
prohibition. He does not seem even to have been de-

[b] The introduction had been before or was now formally condemned at Rome.
[c] On Hugo de St. Cher, Tillemont, p. 15.
[d] It was condemned "non propter hæresim quam continebat sed quia contra præfatos religiosos militiam et scandala committebat."—G. Nangis.

prived of his benefices.[*] His quiet place of exile was
his native St. Amour, in Franche Comté, not yet in the
dominions of France. He was followed by the respect
and fond attachment of the whole University.

But it is singular that William of St. Amour was not
only the champion of the learned University,   *Popular*
he was the hero of Parisian vulgar poetry.   *party.*
Notwithstanding that the King, and that King St. Louis,
espoused the cause of the Mendicants, the people were
on the other side. The popular Preachers, and the
popular ministers, who had sprung from the people,
spoke the language, expressed at the same time and
excited the sympathies and the religious passions of the
lowest of the low, had ceased to be popular. They had
been even outpreached by William of St. Amour. The
Book of the Perils of the Last Times was disseminated
in the vulgar tongue. The author of the romance of
the Rose,[f] above all, Rutebeuf, in his rude verse addressed to the vulgar of all orders, heaped scorn and
hatred on the Mendicants.[*]

---

[*] Tillemont, p. 312.

[f] "Si j'en devoye perdre la vie,
On entre soye contre droicture,
Comme Saint Pol en chartre obscure,
On entre hastez du Roy enlaus,
A tort, comme fut Maistre Guillaume
De St. Amour, que ypocrisie
Fist taillier par grant ravie."
Roman de la Rose, l. 17183.

Lorris talks of scorning "papelorderie."
Paris writes, "Subannavit populus,
elormosynam consuetas subtrahens, vo-
cans eos hypocritas, antichristi antecessores (antecessores?) pseudo-praedica-
tores."

[*] See especially the two poems, de
Maistre Guillaume de St. Amour,
pp. 71 and 78, "et est en son pais
reclus"—on St. Amour, p. 61.

"On a tel si vaillant homme
Qui por l'apostoille de Romme,
Ne por le roi,
Ne veut destruet son error,
Ainz en a souffert le desror
De perdre honor."—P. 81.

Compare also "La Bataille des Vices
contre les Vertus" (ii. p. 65). "La
Descorde de l'Université et les Jacobins,"
"Les Ordres de Paris," &c. &c., with
constant reference to the notes. The
curious reader will not content himself
with the valuable edition of Rutebeuf
by M. Jubinal; he will consult also
the excellent article by M. Paulin
Paris in the Hist. Lit. de la France, xx
p. 710. Rutebeuf reads to me like
our Skelton; he has the same flowing
rapid doggrel, the same satiric verve,

The war between the University and the Dominicans
Great Schoolmen. continued, if in less active, in sullen obstinacy.
They were still the rival powers, who would
not coalesce, each striving to engross public education.
Yet after all the Mendicants won a noble victory, not
by the authority of the Pope, nor by the influence of
the King, but by outshining the fame of the University
through their own unrivalled teachers. On the death
of Alexander IV., William of St. Amour returned to
Paris; he was received with frantic rapture.[b] His later
book,[c] more cautious, yet not less hostile, was received
with respect and approbation by Pope Clement IV.[d]
Yet who could deny, who presume to question, the
transcendant fame, the complete mastery of the Dominicans in theology, and that philosophy which in
those days aspired not to be more than the humble
handmaid of theology? (Albert the Great might, perhaps, have views of more free and independent science,
and so far, of course, became a suspected magician.)
Who could compete with their Doctors, Hugo de St.
Cher, Albert the Great, Thomas of Aquino? The
Franciscans, too, had boasted their Alexander Hales,

---

with not much of poetry, but both are
always alive. On the whole of this feud,
and its connection with Averroism read
the very remarkable pages of M. Ernest
Renan, Averroes et l'Averroïsme, from
page 259. Paris, 1861.

[b] May 1261. " Debacchantibus
urnomâ in laetitiâ omnibus Magistris
Parisiensibus."—Du Boulay.

[c] Collectiones Catholicæ.

[d] See on this book, and others, Hist.
Lit. de la France, article St. Amour, t.
xix. 197. To his earlier works belongs,
not only the " De Periculis " (In his

works and in Fasciculus of Brown,
who translated it, with some errones),
but also a book, De Antichristo, under
the pseudonyme of Nicolas de Orneme.
The object of this is to show the
coming of Antichrist, of which the
chief signs are the setting up the
Everlasting Gospel against the true
Gospels, and the multitudes of false
preachers, false prophets, wandering
and begging friars.—Ibid. See also
account of the writings of Gerard of
Abbeville, another powerful antagonist
of the Mendicants.

they had now their Bonaventura : Duns Scotus, the
rival of Aquinas, was speedily to come." The University could not refuse to itself the honour of conferring
its degrees on Aquinas," and on Bonaventura. And
still the rivals in scholastic theology, who divided the
world (the barren it might be, and dreary intellectual
world, yet in that age the only field for mental greatness), were the descendants of the representatives of
the two Orders. The Scotists and the Thomists fought
what was thought a glorious fight on the highest meta-
physics of the Faith, till the absorbing question, the
Immaculate Conception of the Virgin, arose to commit
the two Orders in mortal and implacable antagonism.

The hatred of the Mendicants might seem to pass
over to the secular clergy. In every part of *Secular
clergy and
Mendicants.* Europe the hierarchy still opposed with dignity or with passion the encroachments of these fatal
rivals. More than twenty years later met a National
Council at Paris. Four Archbishops and twenty Bishops
took their seats in a hall of the Episcopal Palace. The
Masters, Doctors, Bachelors, and Students of the University, were summoned to hear the decrees of the
Council. The heads of the other religious orders, not
Mendicant, had their writs of convocation. Simon de
Beaulieu, Archbishop of Bourges, took the lead. In a
grave sermon, he declared that charity to their flocks
demanded their interposition ; their flocks, for whom

" Those who esteemed themselves
the genuine Franciscans, always sternly
protested against the pride of learning,
to which their false brethren aspired in
the universities. Hear Jacopone da
Todi :

    "Tal è, qual è, tal è,
    Non c' e religione

Mal vedremo Parigi,
Che n' a destroito Asisi.
Colla sua lettoria
L' ha a messo in mala via."

" Thomas Aquinas condescended to
answer William of St. Amour. See
Adversus Impugnantes Religionem.

2 A 2

they were bound to lay down their lives. He inveighed against the Dominicans and the Franciscans, who were sowing discord in every diocese, in every rank, preaching and hearing confessions without license from the Bishop and the curate. Their insolence must be repressed. He appealed to the University to join in an appeal to the Pope to define more rigidly their asserted privileges. William of Macon, Bishop of Amiens, the most learned jurist in France, followed: he explained the bull of Innocent IV., which prohibited the Friars from preaching, hearing confessions, imposing penance without permission of the Bishop or lawful pastor. The whole clergy of France were ready to shed their blood in defence of their rights and duties.[*]

* This is well related in the Hist. Lit. de la France, t. xxi. article Simon de Desailles.

CHAPTER III.

Urban IV. Clement IV. Charles of Anjou.

ALEXANDER IV. died an exile from Rome at Viterbo. Either from indolence or irresolution, he had allowed the College of Cardinals to dwindle to the number of eight. These eight were of various nations and orders: two Bishops, Otho a Frenchman, Stephen a Hungarian; two Presbyters, John an English Cistercian, Hugo a Dominican from Savoy; four Deacons, Richard a Roman, and Octavian a Tuscan of noble birth, John another Roman, Ottobuoni a Genoese. There was no prevailing interest, no commanding name. More than three months passed in jealous dispute. The strife was fortuitously ended by the appearance of James Pantaleon, the Patriarch of Jerusalem. He was elevated by sudden acclamation to the Papal throne.

The Patriarch was the son of a cobbler at Troyes:[a] and it was a wonderful sight, as it were, a provocation to the first principles of Christianity, to behold in those days of feudal monarchy and feudal aristocracies a man of such base parentage in the highest dignity upon earth. James had risen by regular steps up the ascent of ecclesiastical advancement, a Priest at Laon, a

Death of Alexander IV. June 12, 1261.

[a] " Pauperculi veternamentarii calceamenta resarcientis."—S. Antonin. tit. xiv. p. 59—big words to describe a cobbler. According to the Hist. Littér. (article Urban IV., t. xiv. p. 49), there is a tapestry at Troyes, in the Church of St. Urban, representing Pantaleon (the father) in his shop full of boots and shoes, and his mother spinning and watching little James.

Canon at Lyons, Archdeacon of Liège, a Missionary
Legate in Livonia, Pomerania, and Prussia,[b] a pilgrim
and Patriarch of Jerusalem. Such a man could not so
have risen without great abilities or virtues. But if the
rank in which he was born was honourable, the place
was inauspicious. Had the election not fallen on a
Frenchman, Italy might perhaps have escaped the descent of Charles of Anjou, with its immediate crimes
and cruelties; and the wars almost of centuries, which
had their origin in that fatal event. Any Pope, indeed,
must have had great courage to break through the tra-
ditional policy of his predecessors (where the whole
power rests on tradition, a bold, if not a perilous act).
Urban must have recanted the long-cherished hatred
and jealousy of the house of Hohenstaufen; he must
have clearly foreseen (himself a Frenchman) that the
French dominion in Naples would be as fatal as the
German to the independence of Italy and of the Church;
that Charles of Anjou would soon become as dangerous
a neighbour as Manfred.

Urban IV. took up his residence in Viterbo: already
might appear his determined policy to renew the close
alliance between the Papacy and his native France.
The holy character of Louis, who by the death of Frederick and the abeyance of the Empire, by the wars of
the Barons against Henry of England, had become the
most powerful monarch in Christendom, gave further
preponderance to his French inclinations.[c] He filled
up the College of Cardinals with fourteen new prelates,
at least one half of whom were French.

---

[b] See in Voigt, Geschichte Preussens, ii. p. 591, his wise conduct as a
mediator between the Teutonic Order,
and Swartsbol, Duke of Pomerania.

the ally of the heathen Prussians.
[c] See in Raynaldus the reverse of
Theodoricus Vallicolor, sub ann. 1262,
sub fine.

The Empire still hung in suspense between the conflicting claims of Richard of Cornwall and Alfonso of Castile: Urban, with dexterous skill, perpetuated the anarchy. By timely protestation, and by nicely balancing the hopes of both parties that his adjudication, earnestly and submissively sought by both, would be in favour of each, he suppressed a growing determination to place the crown on the head of young Conradin. Against this scheme Urban raised his voice with all the energy of his predecessors, and dwelt with the same menacing censure on the hereditary and indelible crimes of the house of Swabia: he threatened excommunication on all who should revive the claims of that impious race. After a grave examination of the pretensions of Richard of Cornwall and Alfonso of Castile, he cited both parties to plead their cause before him, and still drew out, with still baffled expectations of a speedy sentence, the controversy which he had no design to close.

The Latin Empire of Constantinople had fallen: Baldwin II. sought refuge, and only found refuge in the West. The Greek Palæologi were on the throne of the East, and seemed not indisposed to negotiate on the religious question with the Pope. The Holy Land, the former diocese of Pope Urban, was in the most deplorable state: the Sultan of Babylon had risen again in irresistible power; he had overrun the whole country; the Christians were hardly safe in Ptolemais. In vain the Pope appealed to his own countrymen in behalf of his old beloved diocese; the clergy of France withheld their contributions, and whether from some jealousy of their lowly countryman, now so much above them; or since the cause had so utterly failed even under their King, it might seem absolutely despe-

rate, the Archbishops of Sens and of Bourges were un-
moved by the Papal rebukes or remonstrances, and
continued, at least not to encourage the zeal of their
clergy.

The affairs of Italy and Naples threatened almost the
personal safety of the Pope. Manfred was at
the height of his power; he no longer deigned
to make advances for reconciliation, which successive
Popes seemed to treat with still stronger aversion.
Everywhere Ghibellinism was in the ascendant. The
Marquis Pallavicini and Buoso da Doara at the head of
the Cremonese, maintained more than an equal balance
in Lombardy. Pisa and Sienna, rampant after the fall
of the Guelfic rule in Florence, received the letters of
the Pope with civil contempt. It might appear that
Manfred was admitted into the rank of the legitimate
Sovereigns of Christendom. In vain the Pope denounced the wickedness, the impiety of a connexion
with an excommunicated family, the King of Arragon
did not scruple to marry his son to the daughter of
Manfred. The marriage of the son of Louis of France
to the daughter of Arragon, increased the jealous alarm
of the Pope. Even Louis did not permit the Papal
remonstrances to interfere with these arrangements.

Miserable, in the meantime, was the state of Italy.
Scarcely a city or territory from the confines
of Apulia to the Alps was undisturbed by one
of those accursed feuds, either of nobles against the
people, or of Guelfs against Ghibellines. Nowhere was
rest. Now one party, now another must dislodge from
their homes, and go into exile. Urban could not remain
in Rome. The stronger cities were waging war on the
weaker. All the labours of the Holy Inquisition and
all the rigour of their penalties, instead of extirpating

the heresy of the Paterins and various Manichean sects,
might seem to promote their increase. In general, it
was enough to be Ghibelline, and to oppose the Church,
down came the excommunication; all sacred offices
ceased. It may be well imagined how deeply all this
grieved religious men, the triumph and joy of the
heretics.[d]

Only to France could the Pope, even if no Frenchman, have looked for succour, if determined to maintain
the unextinguished feud with Manfred. Already the
crown of Naples had been offered to Charles of Anjou.
Urban IV. first laid it at the feet of Louis himself,
either for his brother or one of his sons. But the
delicate conscience of Louis revolted from the usurpation of a crown, to which were already three claimants
of right. If it was hereditary, it belonged to Conradin;
if at the disposal of the Pope, it was already awarded,
and had not been surrendered by Edmund of England;
and Manfred was on the throne, summoned, it might
seem, by the voice of the nation. Manfred's claim, as
maintained by an irreligious alliance with the Saracens,
and as the possession of a Christian throne by one
accused of favouring the Saracens, might easily be
dismissed; but there was strong doubt as to the others.
The Pope, who perhaps from the first had preferred the
more active and enterprising Charles of Anjou, because
he could not become King of France, in vain argued
and took all the guilt on his own head:[e] "the soul of
Louis was as precious to the Pope and the Cardinals as
to himself." Louis did not refuse his assent to the

[d] See this and much more to the
same effect in Muratori, Annal. sub
ann. 1263.

[e] Epist. to Albert of Parma, the

notary who was empowered to treat as
to the conditions of the assumption of
the throne of Naples.—Raynald., sub
ann. 1262.

acceptance of the crown by his brother. It is said, that
he was glad to rid his court, if not his realm, which he
was endeavouring to subdue to monastic gravity, of his
gayer brother, who was constantly summoning tournaments, was addicted to gaming, and every other knightly
diversion.[f]

Charles of Anjou might seem designated for this
service. Valiant, adventurous, with none of that punc-
tilious religiousness which might seem to set itself
above ecclesiastical guidance, yet with all outward
respect for the doctrine and ceremonial of the Church;
with vast resources, holding, in right of his wife, the principality of Provence; he was a leader whom all the
knighthood of France, who were eager to find vent for
their valour, and to escape the peaceful inactivity or
dull control under which they were kept by the scrupulous justice of Louis IX., would follow with headlong
zeal. Charles had hardly yet shown that intense selfish-
ness and cruelty which, in the ally, in the king chosen
by the Pope for his vassal realm, could not but recoil
upon the Pope himself. He had already indeed besieged
and taken Marseilles, barbarously executed all the
citizens who had defended the liberties of their town,
and abrogated all the rights and privileges of that
flourishing municipality. His ambitious wife, Beatrice
of Provence, jealous of being the sister of three queens,
herself no queen, urged her unreluctant husband to this
promising enterprise. But the Pope had still much
to do; there were disputes between the sisters, especially
the Queen of France and the Countess of Provence, on
certain rights as co-heiresses of that land. Though the

[f] "Quia sui regni, quam perturbabat Carolus in tornamentis et aleis."
—Ptolem. Luc. c. xxv.

treaty was negotiated, drawn up, perhaps actually
signed, it was not yet published. It was thought more
safe and decent to obtain a more formal abjuration of
his title from Edmund of England.

Bartholomew Pignatelli, Archbishop of Cosenza, a
Guelfic prelate of noble blood, received a   England.
commission as legate to demand the surrender   A.D. 1763.
of the crown of Sicily. He was afterwards to lay the
result of his mission before Louis of France, in order
to obtain his full consent to the investiture of Charles
of Anjou. Henry III., threatened by the insurrection of
his barons, might well be supposed wholly unable to
assert the pretensions of his son to a foreign crown ; yet
he complained with some bitterness that the treasures
of England, so long poured into the lap of the Pontiff,
had met with such return.[a] Urban endeavoured to allay
his indignation by espousing his cause against the Earl
of Leicester (Simon de Montfort) and the barons of
England: he absolutely annulled all their leagues.[b]
William, Archdeacon of Paris, the Pope's chaplain, had
power to relieve Henry from all his constitutional oaths.[c]
As the war became more imminent, more inevitable,
both before and after the rejection of the award in
favour of the King by the acknowledged arbiter Louis
IX., the Pope adhered with imperious fidelity to the
King. Ugo Falcodi, Cardinal of St. Sabina, was sent
as Legate to command the vassal kingdom to peace:
the rebellious subjects were to be ordered to submit to
their sovereign, and abandon their audacious pretensions

---

[a] See despatch to Archbishop of
Cosenza, MS., B. M., July 25, 1263,
to the King, ibid. v, s.   Instructions at full length, dated Orvieto,
Oct. 4.

[b] "Conjurationes omnes cassamus
et irritamus.   Ad fidem." — MS.,
B. M. 23rd Aug. 1263.

[c] MS., B. M., letter to Archdeacon
of Paris.

to liberty. The Legate was armed with the amplest power to prohibit the observation of all the statutes, though sworn to by the King, the Queen, and the Prince; to suspend and depose all prelates or ecclesiastics; to deprive all counts, barons, or laymen, who held in fee estates of the Church, and to proceed at his discretion to any spiritual or temporal penalties.[h] He had power to provide for all who should accompany him to England by canonries or other benefices.[m] He had power of ecclesiastical censure against archbishops, bishops, monasteries, exempt or not exempt, and all others.[n] He had power to depose all ecclesiastics in rebellion,[o] and of appointing loyal clerks to their benefices.[p] In the case of the rebellion of archbishops or prelates, counts or barons, indulgences were to be granted to all who would serve or raise soldiers for the King, as if they went to the Holy Land:[q] the Friar preachers and Friar minors were to aid the King to the utmost.[r] After the award of the King of France, which the Pope confirmed,[s] Urban becomes even more peremp-

---

[h] "Ad quorum observantiam ipsas decretiones seu tenere, eadem prælatos et clericos per suspensionis ecclesiasticam ab officiis, dignitatibus, honoribus et beneficiis: comites vero, barones et laicos prædictos per privationem feodorum et omnium bonorum, quæ a quibusdam Ecclesiis prædicti regni et aliis detinent et aliis spiritualiter et temporaliter, prout expedire videris."—MS., B. M., Nov. 23, 1263. See also the next letter.

[m] "Non obstante Statuto Ecclesiarum ipsarum de certo clericorum numero, juramento, confirmatione, sive quâcunque firmitate, vallata."—Ibid. v. ii. p. 48.

[n] "Communis universitatis et populos eorum quarumlibet."

[o] Clerks, "indevoti, ingrati, inobedientes."

[p] Even at this time peremptory orders were given for provision for Italian ecclesiastics in the English Church. John de Ebulo claimed the deanery of St. Paul's. The chapter resisted. He resigned the deanery, but accepted a canonry; till a canonry should be vacant, a certain pension.—P. 170.

Orvieto, Nov. 27, 1263.

[q] Ibid., Nov. 27.

[r] Rymer, I. 776, 778, 780, 784.

tory; he commands the infamous provision, one of those
of Oxford, to be erased from the statute book; all those
of Oxford are detestable and impious; he marks with
special malediction that which prohibited the introduction of apostolic bulls or briefs into the realm, and withheld the rich subsidies from Rome.[1] The Archbishop
was to excommunicate all who should not submit to the
award. The King's absolute illimitable power is asserted
in the strongest terms.[2] The expulsion of strangers,
and the assumption of exclusive authority by native
Englishmen, are severely reprobated.[3]

But the Cardinal Legate dared not to land in the
island—even the Archbishop Boniface (of Savoy) would
not venture into his province. Ere long the whole
realm, the King himself, and Prince Edward are in the
power of the Barons. The Legate must content himself
with opening his court at Boulogne. There he issued
his unobeyed citation to the Barons to appear, pronounced against them the sentence of excommunication,
and placed London and the Cinque Ports under an
interdict.[4] Ugo Falcodi, when Pope, cherished a bitter
remembrance of these affronting contempts.

Although the negotiations were all this time proceeding in secret with Charles of Anjou, the Pope cited Man-

---

[1] The Pope's letters, at least, were
after the award. "Nonnulli maledic-
tionis alumni, quaedam statuta ne-
pharia in depressionem libertatis ejusdem
promulgari dicuntur, videlicet quod
quicunque literas apostolicas aut ipsius
archiepiscopi in Angliam deferre prae-
sumpserit, graviter puniatur."—Orvieto, Feb. 20, 1264.

[2] "Plenaria potestate in omnibus et
per omnia."—Ibid.

[3] The King of France "Retractavit
et commisit illud statutum, per quod
regnum Angliae debebat per indigenas
gubernari, et alienigenae tenebantur ab
eodem exire, ad illum minime rever-
suri."—Ibid.

[4] "Propter imminentem turba-
tionem." Feb. 15. His citations were
to be valid, if issued in France. The
Bishop of Lincoln was cited for various
acts of contumacy to the Holy See.—
June 4, 1264.

fred to appear before him to answer on certain charges,

which he published to the world.[a] They comprehended various acts of cruelty, the destruction of the city of Aria by the Saracens, the execution, called murder, of certain nobles, contempt of the ecclesiastical interdict, attachment to Mohammedan rites, the murder of an ambassador of Conradin.[a] Manfred approached the borders; but the Pope insisted that he should be accompanied by only eighty men: Maufred refused to trust himself to a Papal safe-conduct.

But as he was not permitted to approach in peace,

Manfred, well informed of the transactions with Charles of Anjou, threatened to approach in war.[b] From Florence, from Pisa, from Sienna, the German and Saracen, as well as the Apulian and Sicilian forces began to draw towards Orvieto. The Pope hastily summoned a Council: and some troops came to his aid from various quarters. But a sudden event seemed to determine the descent of Charles of Anjou upon Italy, and brought at once the protracted negotiations, concerning the terms of his acceptance of the throne of Naples, to a close. The Roman people, having risen against the nobles, and cast many of them out of the city, determined on appointing a senator of not less than royal rank. One party proposed Manfred, another his

son-in-law, the King of Arragon, a third Charles of Anjou. The Pope was embarrassed: he was compelled to maintain Charles of Anjou against his competitors: and yet a great sovereign as senator of Rome, and for life (as it was proposed), was the death-blow to the Papal rule in Rome. Charles of Anjou felt his strength; he yielded to the Pope's request to limit

---

[a] Oct. 20, 1264.   [a] Raynaldus, sub ann.   [b] Giannone, xix. 1.

the grant of the senatorship to five years; but he seized
the opportunity to lower the terms on which he was to
be invested with the realm of Naples. He demanded a
diminution of the tribute of ten thousand ounces of gold
which Naples was to pay annually to the See of Rome.
Such demand was unjust to him who was about to incur
vast expense in the cause of Rome; unjust to Naples,
which would be burthened with heavy taxation; impolitic, as preventing the new King from treating his
subjects with splendid liberality. He required that the
descent of the crown should be in the female as well as
in the male line: that he should himself judge of the
number of soldiers necessary for the expedition. He
demanded the abrogation of the stipulation, that if any
of his posterity should obtain the Empire, Lombardy or
Tuscany, the crown of Naples should pass from them;
the enlargement of the provision, that only a limited
extent of possession in Lombardy or in Tuscany should
be tenable with the Neapolitan crown.

Charles was so necessary to Urban, the weight of
Urban's influence was so powerful in Rome, that the
treaty was at length signed. Charles sent a representative to Rome to accept the Senatorship.*

Manfred now kept no measures with the hostile Pope.
His Saracen troops on one side, his German on the
other, broke into the Roman territories. But a crusading army of Guelfs of some force had arisen around
the Pope; and some failures and disasters checked
the career of Manfred. Pandolf, Count of Anguillara,
recovered Sutri from the Saracens. Peter de Vico, a
powerful noble, had revolted from the Pope, and having

* Charles agreed to surrender the senatorship when master of Naples.
How far did he intend to observe this condition?—See Sismondi, p. 141.

secret intelligence in Rome, hoped to betray the city
into the power of Manfred: he was repelled by the
Romans. Percival d'Oria, who had captured
many of the Guelfic castles, was accidentally
drowned in the river Negro during a battle near Rieti:
his death was bruited about as a miracle. Yet
was not the Pope safe; Orvieto began to
waver: he set forth to Perugia; he died on the road.

Oct. 2 or 18, 1864.

Death of Urban IV. Oct. 2, 1264.

Christendom at this peculiar crisis awaited with trembling anxiety the determination of the conclave: but this suspense of nearly five months
did not arise altogether out of the dissensions in that
body. Urban IV. had secured the predominance of the
French interest; the election had been long made before
it was published. It had fallen on Ugo Falcodi, that
Papal Legate, who, on the northern shore of France,
was issuing Urban's sentence of excommunication
against the Barons of England, while that Pope was no
longer living. Ugo Falcodi was born at St. Gilles upon
the Rhône: he had been married before he took orders,
and had two daughters. He was profoundly learned in
the law; from the Archdiaconate of Narbonne he had
been brought to Italy, and created Cardinal of S. Sabina.
Of his policy there could be no doubt; Manfred has but
a new and more vigorous enemy; Charles of Anjou a
more devoted friend. The Cardinal of S. Sabina passed
secretly over the Alps, suddenly appeared at Perugia,
accepted the tiara, assumed the name of Clement IV.,
and then took up his residence at Viterbo.

Clement IV. Feb. 5, 1265.

Yet Manfred could hardly have dreaded a foe so
active, so implacable, so unscrupulous, or Charles hoped
for an ally so zealous, so obsequious, above all, so
prodigal. Letters were despatched through Christendom, to England, to France, urging immediate succour

to the Holy See, imperilled by the Saracen Manfred, and trusting for her relief only to the devout Charles. Everywhere the tenths were levied, notwithstanding the murmurs of Bishops and clergy; tenths still under the pretext of aid for Constantinople and Jerusalem. It was rebellion to refuse to pay; the Pope was even lavish of the Papal treasures; he pledged the ecclesiastical estates; usurious interest accumulated on the principal. A loan of 100,000 livres was raised on the security of the possessions of the Church in Rome (in vain many of the Cardinals protested), even on the churches from whence the Cardinals took their titles: St. Peter's, the Lateran, the Hospitals, and the convent of St. George were alone excepted. The Legates, the Prelates, the Mendicants were ordered to preach the Crusade with unwearied activity. They had new powers of absolution; they might admit as soldiers of Christ incendiaries, those excommunicated for refusing to pay tenths, sacrilegious persons, astrologers, those who had struck a clerk, or sold merchandise to Mohammedans, ecclesiastics under interdict, or under suspension, married clerks; those who, in violation of the canons, had practised law or physic. All attempts were made to maintain the Papal interests in Rome, and to excite revolt in the kingdom of Naples.[a]

Charles of Anjou had now declared himself Senator of Rome, and invested with the crown of Naples. He had been long collecting his forces for the conquest. But Italy might seem to refuse access to the stranger. The Ghibellines were in the ascendant in Lombardy. The Marquis Pallavicini and Buoso da Doara, with the Cremonese, watched the passes of the Alps. The fleets

---

[a] Martene. Compare Cherrier, iv. 79.

of Pisa and of Manfred swept the sea with eighty
galleys; the mouth of the Tiber was stopped by a great
dam of timber and stone. But courage and fortune
favoured Charles: he boldly set sail from Marseilles
with hardly more than twenty galleys and one thousand
men-at-arms. A violent storm scattered the fleet of
Pisa and Naples: he entered the Tiber, broke
through all obstacles, and appeared at Rome
at Pentecost, the time appointed for his inauguration as
Senator. He chose for his abode the Pope's Lateran
palace. That was an usurpation which the Pope could
not endure: he sent a strong remonstrance against the
presumption of the Senator of Rome, who had dared
without permission to occupy the abode of the Pope:
he was commanded to quit the palace and seek some
more fitting residence. Yet even at this time Clement
IV. insisted on dictating the terms on which Charles
was to hold the kingdom of Naples, its reversion to the
Papacy in default of heirs of his line, its absolute incom-
patibility with the Empire, the tribute of eight thousand
crowns of gold, the homage and the white horse in
token of fealty. Manfred attempted to provoke Charles
to battle before the arrival of his main army; he
advanced with a large force, many of them Saracens,
to the neighbourhood of Rome. The prudence of the
Pope restrained the impatience of Charles.*

It was not till the end of the summer that the main
army of Charles came down the pass of Mont Cenis into
friendly Piedmont. It was splendidly provided, and
boasted some of the noblest knights of France and
Flanders. The Pope had absolved all those who had
taken the cross for the Holy Land: equal hopes of

---

* Raynaldus, sub ann. 1265.

Heaven were attached to this new Crusade against Manfred, whom it was the policy to represent as more than
half a Saracen. The Legate, Cardinal of S. Cecilia,
had exacted a tenth from the French clergy. Robert
of Bethune took the command ; Guy of Beauvais,
Bishop of Auxerre, was among the most distinguished
warriors; there were Vendômes, Montmorencies, Mire-
poixs, De Montforts, Sullys, De Beaumonts. The Ghibellines made a great show of resistance : the *Advance of
the army.*
Carroccios of Pavia, Cremona, and Piacenza
moved out as to a great battle. But the French army
passed on, threatened Brescia ; Milan and the Marquis
of Montferrat ventured not to take their part openly,
but supplied them with provisions. But through the
treachery of the Ghibellines, bought, according to some
writers of the time, by French gold, or intimidated by
the great French force (which the Chronicles, perhaps
faithfully recording the rumours of the day, represented
as sixty thousand, forty thousand, thirty thousand strong)
the allies of Manfred[1] finally stood aloof in sullen pas-
siveness. The French reached the Po. They advanced
still without serious encounter, and joined their master
in Rome. Charles, though it was the depth
of winter, allowed no long repose. He ad- *In Rome.*
vanced to Ceperano, with the Legate, the Cardinal St.
Angelo, preaching the Crusade on the way. *In Naples.*
Manfred prepared himself for a gallant resistance ; but he had neither calculated on the treachery of
some of his own subjects, nor on the impetuous valour
of the French. The passage of the Garigliano was
betrayed by the Count of Caserta. San Germano, in

---

[1] The annals of Modena give 5000 horse, 15,000 foot, 10,000 bowmen.—
See the Chronicles in Muratori.

which he had secured a strong force and ample stores,
was taken by assault. Manfred's courage was unshaken;
he concentred his army near Benevento, but he sent
messengers to Charles to propose negotiations. "Tell
the Sultan of Nocera that I will have neither peace nor
treaty with him; I will send him to Hell, or he shall
send me to Paradise!" Such was the reply of Charles
of Anjou. The French army defiled into the plain
before Benevento. Manfred is accused of rash-
ness for venturing on a decisive battle. The
French army were in want of money and of provisions;
a protracted war might have worn them out. Manfred's
nephew, Conrad of Antioch, was in the Abruzzi, Count
Frederick in Calabria, and the Count of Ventimiglia in
Sicily; but Manfred perhaps knew that nothing less
than splendid success could hold in awe the wavering
fidelity of his subjects. He drew up his army in three
divisions. On the French side appeared, beside the
three, a fourth. "Who are these?" inquired Manfred.
"The Guelfs of Florence and the exiles from other
cities." "Where are the Ghibellines, for whom I have
done and hazarded so much?" The Germans and the
Saracens fought with desperate valour. Manfred commanded the third army of the Barons of Apulia to move
to the charge. Some, among them the great Chamberlain, hesitated, turned, fled.[a] Manfred plunged
in his desperation into the midst of the fray,
and fell unknown by an unknown hand. The body was
found after three days and recognised by a boor, who
threw it across an ass, and went shouting along, "Who
will buy King Manfred?" He was struck down by one

(margin note: Battle of Benevento. Feb. 6, 1266.)

(margin note: Death of Manfred.)

---

a Dante brands the treason of the Apulians: this was the field
"ove fu bugiardo
Ciascun Pugliese."—*Inferno*, xxviii. 18.

of Manfred's Barons; the body was taken to King
Charles.[k]   Charles summoned the Barons who were
prisoners, and demanded if it was indeed the body of
Manfred.   Galvano Lancia looked on it, hid his face in
his hands, and burst into tears.   The generous French
urged that it should receive honourable burial.   "It
might be," said Charles, "were he not under excommunication."   The body was hastily interred by the
bridge of Benevento: the warriors, French and Apulian,
cast each a stone, and a huge mound appeared,[l] like
those under which repose the heroes of ancient times.
But the Papal jealousy would not allow the Hohenstaufen to repose within the territory of the Church.
The Archbishop of Cosenza, by the command
of the Pope, ordered him to be torn up from
his rude sepulchre.   He was again buried in unconse-
crated ground, on the borders of the kingdom of Naples,
near the river Verde.[k]

    So perished the noble Manfred, a poet like his father,
all accomplished as his father,[m] a man of consummate
courage and great ability.   Naples could hardly have
had a more promising founder for a native dynasty.
But Naples was too near Rome; and the house of
Hohenstaufen had not yet fulfilled its destiny.

    The first act of the triumphant army of the Cross,
under the Pope's ally, was the sacking of the Papal
city of Benevento, a general massacre of both sexes,

Feb. 26

---

[k] Compare the letter of Charles
announcing the victory of the Pope,
before the body was found.
Ricordano Malespini.

[l] " L' ossa del corpo mio sarieno ancora
in co del ponte, presso a Benevento,
sotto la guardia della grave mora;
Or le bagna la pioggia, e muove 'l
vento."

[k] " Lo Re spesso la notte andava per
Barletta, cantando Strambotti e can-
zoni, che ita pigliando il fresco, e con
esso ivano dei Musici Siciliani ch' erano
gran Romanzatori."—Matteo Spinelli.

[footnote right col top] " fuor del regno, quasi lungo 'l Verde
Ove le trasmutò a lume spento."
Dante, Purgat. III, 132.

of all ages, violation of women, even of women dedicated
to God: the churches did not escape the common profanation. Charles was King of Naples: the Capital yielded, Capua surrendered the vast treasures accumulated by Manfred. The King's officers were weighing these treasures. "What need of scales?" said Ugo di Balzo, a Provençal knight: he kicked the whole into three portions: "This is for my Lord the King, this for the Queen, this for your Knights." The whole of Apulia, Calabria, Sicily submitted to the Sovereign invested by the Pope.[a] But they soon began to appreciate the change, to which they had looked as a great deliverance, as the dawn of a golden age of peace and plenty. The French soldiers spread wanton devastation wherever they went, neither respecting property, nor the rights of men nor the honour of women. Naples was at first disposed to admire the magnificence of Charles and his Barons; but those who had reproved the luxuriousness of Frederick's or the ruder splendour of Manfred's court, found that of the Provençal King at least not more favourable to the higher morals.[b] Instead of being relieved from their heavy taxation, they were the prey of still more merciless exaction. King Charles seized the books and registers of the royal revenues in the hands of Gazzolino de Marra. Every royal privilege, subsidy, collection, or

---

[a] Clement writes to Cardinal Ottoboni, Legate in England: "Carissimus in Christo filius R. (C.) Rex Siciliae Illustris tenet totum regnum, illius hominum pestilentis cularer pabulam, uxorem et literas optineas et thesaurum."—MS., B. M., May 1266. The March, Florence, Pistoia, Sienna, Pisa, had returned to their allegiance. Messengers were come from Uberto Pallavicini and the Cremonese. There were hopes of Genoa.

[b] Muratori writes thus:—"Per altro la venuta de' Francesi quella fu, che cominciò ad introdurre il lusso, e qualche cosa di peggio e fors mutar i costumi degl' Italiani."—Sub ann.

tax was enforced with more rigorous severity. New
justiciaries, officers of customs, notaries, and revenue
collectors sprung up in hosts, draining without restraint
the impoverished people. The realm began too late to
deplore its own versatility, to look back on the days of
good King Manfred. Thus are these feelings expressed
by a Guelfic historian: "O King Manfred, little did we
know thee when alive! Now that thou art dead, we
deplore thee in vain! Thou appearedst as a ravening
wolf among the flocks of this kingdom; now fallen by
our fickleness and inconstancy under the present government, after which we groaned, we find that thou wert a
lamb. Now we know by bitter comparison how mild
was thy rule. We thought it hard that part of our substance must be yielded into thy hands, now we find that
all our substance and even our persons are the prey of
the stranger."[s]

Clement IV. could not close his ears to these sad
complaints. He had forced himself to remonstrate on the sack of Benevento; but throughout Italy the Guelfs rose again to power, Florence was
in their hands, Pisa made supplication to the Pope to be
released from excommunication. In Milan there was
a Provençal governor, whose cruelties even surpassed
Italian cruelties. Charles was manifestly aspiring to be
supreme in Italy.[q]

But the Pope did not neglect more remote offences.
The Cardinal of S. Sabina had not forgotten the
contemptuous refusal of the Barons of England
to accept his mediation.[r] Henry III. was too useful, too

---

s Saba Malaspina, iii. 16.
q See all the historians.
r Letter to the Queen, complaining
of the insolence of the Barons, who

had not permitted him to land in
England when Legate.—MS., B. M.,
v. iii. p. 3.

profitable a vassal of the Roman See to be abandoned
to his unruly subjects. Immediately on his accession
the Pope had sent the Cardinal of S. Hadrian (Ottobuoni) as Legate, with the same ample powers with
which himself had been invested.[1] An interdict was
laid upon the island if it refused to admit the Legate.
If the Legate should not be permitted to land, he was
to transmit inhibitions to the clergy, having equal force,
inhibitions to allow no matrimonial rites to the rebels,
or to communicate with them in any way whatever.[2]
He had the same authority to thrust his followers into
dignities or benefices from which the rebellious clergy
or those connected with the rebels were to be ejected.
All sons of rebel Barons or Nobles, all nephews of rebel
Churchmen were to be deprived of their parsonages or
benefices, and declared incapable of holding them.[3]
No promotions were to be made to bishoprics or arch-
bishoprics without express consent of the Holy See.[4] It
was admitted that many bishops were on the side of the
Barons; no favour was to be shown to those of London,
Worcester, Lincoln, or Ely; they were on no account
to be released from excommunication.[5] Tenths were
to be levied for the Holy War.[6] The Legate was to
preach or cause to be preached a Crusade in England
and even in Germany against the insurgent Barons.

[1] The bulls addressed to Ottobuoni
are transcripts of those before addressed
to the Cardinal S. Sabino, in the usual
form, mutatis mutandis.—MS., B. M.
They fill several pages.

[2] Ibid., dated Perugia, June 1, 1265,
p. 119. Since he had excommunicated
"consulles barones et fautores eorum,"
et inhabitatorres Quinque Portuum," if
any of them had obtained letters of
absolution, " in argritudine vel aut

simulata," unless they abandoned the
party of Leicester they were to be as
brethren and publicans.

[3] Ibid., same date.

[4] Ibid., same date.

[5] Ibid., some months later, Oct.
1285.

[6] Ibid., July 1. The Cistercians,
Carthusians, Templars, Hospitallers,
Teutonic Knights, Sisters of S. Clare,
were alone except.

Louis of France was urged to take arms in defence of
the common cause of monarchy against those rebels
who were accused of a design to throw off altogether the
kingly sway. Nothing less than a general league of
Princes could put down those sons of wrath and of
treason, the Barons of England.[a]

The Pope, as Cardinal Legate, had excommunicated
Simon de Montfort, Roger Earl of Norfolk, Hugo the
Chief Justiciary, the City of London, and the Cinque
Ports; he had summoned four of the English Prelates
before him at Boulogne, and ordered them to publish
the excommunication in England. The excommunication had been taken from the unreluctant hands of
the Bishops. The excommunicated had appealed to the
Pope; the appeal was ratified in a convocation of the
clergy. But the excommunication was solemnly confirmed at Perugia. "Nothing could be done unless that
turbulent man of sin (Leicester) and all his race were
plucked up out of the realm."[b] The new Cardinal Legate
was urged to hasten to England to consummate his work.

Ere he had ceased to be Cardinal Legate, the Pope
(Ugo Falcodi) had heard at Boulogne the fatal tidings
of the battle of Lewes, the captivity of the King and of
Prince Edward. Then after his accession had come the
news of the escape of Prince Edward, and the revolt of
the Earl of Gloucester from the Barons. The Pope
wrote in triumph to the Prince,[c] urging him to make
every effort to release his father from slavery; the excommunication was at once removed from the Earl of

[a] Ibid., Perugia, May 6, 1265, p. 75, &c.
[b] Epist. ad Card. S. Hadrian. "Nisi dictus vir pestilens cum totâ suâ progenie de regno Angliæ avellatur."—

July 19, 1265. At this time Manfred was advancing on Rome.
[c] To Prince Edward. The letter enters into some details.

Gloucester.[d] The tidings of the battle of Evesham, of
the death of Simon Earl of Leicester, filled him with
melancholy and joy.[e] Yet extraordinary as it may
seem, Simon de Montfort, excommunicated by the Pope,
to the Pope the Man of Sin, was the Saint and Martyr
of popular love and worship;[f] he was equalled with
Becket.[g] Poetry, Latin, English, French, celebrated,
sanctified, canonised him. His miracles, in their
number, wonderfulness, and in their attestations might
have moved the jealousy of S. Francis or of Becket
himself.[h] Prayers were addressed to him;[i] **prayer was**
offered through his intercession.[k]

The King's victory seemed complete, the Barons
Victory of crushed, the liberties of England buried in the
the King. grave of Simon de Montfort. The Cardinal
Legate crossed to England with the Queen. The Queen
Eleanor was not the least odious of the foreigners who
ruled the feeble mind of the King: to her influence had
The Legate been attributed the unjust, ill-considered award
Oct. 26, 1265. of Louis of France. The Legate assumed a
kind of dictatorial authority.[m] In the church of Westminster, the splendid foundation of Henry III. (under
whose shadow I wrote these lines), he appeared in his

[d] Ibid., p. 191.

[e] " Læta nobis et tristia spartaeris."
—Clement IV., Epist. i. 89.

[f] Rishanger says that all ranks heard
of his death with the most profound
sorrow, "præcipue religiosi, qui parth-
bus illis faverant."—Chronic. p. 48.
Compare also Lords' Report on Dignity
of a Peer. In the Parliament summoned after the battle of Lewes were 23
Barons, 122 Ecclesiastics.—pp. 145-6.

[g] See in Wright's Political Songs
that on the battle of Lewes. After his
death we read in another :—

[11] "Mes par sa mort, le cuens Montfort
Conquist la victoire,
Comme li Martyr de Cantorbyr
Finist sa vie" (p. 125);
and the long Latin poem, p. 71.

[h] See the " Miracula," published by
Mr. Halliwell at the end of Rishanger,
Camden Society, 1840.

[i] " Salve Simon Montefortis,
Totius flos militiæ,
Duras pœnas passus mortis,
Protector gentis Angliæ."

[k] " Ora pro nobis, Beate Simon, ut
digni simus promissionibus Christi."—
Ibid. p. 109.

[m] See the Papal Bulls, gratulatory

full scarlet pontifical robes, recited the act of excommunication passed on Simon de Montfort and all his adherents, abrogated all the oaths sworn by the King, declared null and void all the constitutions and provisions of the realm.[a] At Northampton he held a council, and by name confirmed the excommunication of the Prelates who had made common cause with the Barons, Winchester, Worcester, London, Chichester.[b] The Pope, while he made large grants of the tenths, and triumphed in the King's triumph, in more Christian spirit enjoined him to use his victory with mercy and moderation.[c] If any mercy was shown to the persons (and this is doubtful, for all the bravest and most formidable had perished in the field), there was none to their estates. The obsequious Parliament passed a sweeping sentence of confiscation on the lands of all who had joined or favoured De Montfort. The Legate was not less severe against the obnoxious clergy.[d] There was a wide and general ejection of all who had been or were suspected of having been on the proscribed side. The Pope is again busy in reaping for his own colleagues and followers some grains of the golden harvest. Demands are made, at first modest for prebends, for pensions in favour of Roman ecclesiastics.[e] He is compelled by the poverty of the Car-

---

to the King and Prince, and admonitory to the Barons to return to the King's allegiance.—Rymer, i. 817, 819.

[a] Wilkes, 72. [b] Rishanger, p. 47.

[c] Rymer, loc. cit.

[d] "Qui non solum et post terras et possessiones occisorum in bello et captivorum merceserie etiam tam tam spiritualia quam temporalia religiosorum videtur, nulli parcentes ordini, dignitati, vel ecclesiastica libertati . . .

infinitam pecuniam ab eis immeriti corditer extorserunt, ablatas et quacunque domos religiosas tantæ supplicationi mancipando quod vix aut nunquam poterunt resplicare."—Rishanger, p. 48.

[e] MS., B. M., p. 202. Assignment of 260 marks on England to the Bishop of Ostia and Velletri, "propter egestatem." One or two benefices to be obtained in England to make up

dinals to become more pressing, more exorbitant in his
exactions.

During the next year there is a formidable reaction;
a wide and profound dissatisfaction had spread
through the realm. The discontented are de-
fending themselves with desperate resolution in the isle
of Ely.   Rome is alarmed by the gloomy news from
England: the Pope is trembling for the lives of the
King, the Queen, and the Prince; he is trembling for
the irrecoverable loss of that noble fief of the See of
Rome.[*] The affrighted Cardinal is disposed to abandon
his hopeless mission. The Pope reproves him for his
cowardice, but leaves it to his discretion whether he will
remain or not in the contumacious and ungrateful
island.[*]

The King's cause again prospers: at Christmas the
King and the Legate are seen dining together in public
at Westminster. The indignant people remark that
the seat of honour, the first service of all the dishes are
reserved to the Legate; the King sits lower, and par-
takes of the best fare, but after the Legate.[*] At St.
Edmondsbury the ecclesiastics resisted the demand not
only of the tenths, but of thirty thousand marks more,

---

this sum. "In eundem modum pro
domino retornass (Velletri) ccccxvi.
marks." He intends to write, on account of the general poverty of the
Cardinals, not only "pro duobus, pro
pluribus, licet non in tanta summa
sed minore."—Peragia, Oct. 26, 1265,
p. 117. "Importabilis fratrum per-
suasio, quam sensi literalitatis ipsius
qui ad Romanam Ecclesiam de mundi
diversis partibus fuerre conservit, pene,
vel quam pralitas arefacto, crescit, nec
crescet cessavit."—P. 223.

[*] "Nihil aliud sunt penitus, nisi
totum everti negotium, Regem, Re-
ginam et illorum tradi morti, et
Ecclesiæ Romanæ feudum tam nobile
sine spe qualibet recuperationis amitti."
—MS., B. M., p. 233.

[*] Ibid., May 16, 1266.

[*] "Legato in sedili regis collocato,
singulisque ferculis coram eo primitus
appositis, et postremo coram rege,
unde murmurabant multi in aulâ
regiâ."—Wikanger, p. 59.

•

claimed by the Pope as arrears of the **King's debt** for
the subjugation of Naples.

About a year and a half after, at the close **of the**
Pontificate of Clement IV., the Cardinal Legate Council in
holds a Council of the Church of England and St. Paul's.
Ireland in the cathedral of St. Paul. The famous constitutions of Ottobuoni, the completion and Constitutions
confirmation of those of Cardinal Otho, are of Ottobuoni.
passed, which were held for some time as the canon law
of England. Of these constitutions some must be
noticed, as giving a view of the religion of the times.
I. The absolute exemption of the property of the Church
from all taxation by the state, the obedience of the laity
to the clergy, were asserted in the fullest and most
naked simplicity. II. One was directed against the
clergy bearing arms. Some of the clergy are described
(awful wickedness!) as little better than robber chief-
tains. It was forgotten that but a few years before the
Archbishop of Canterbury had been in arms with the
Archbishop of Lyons before Turin; that French Bishops
were in the army of Charles of Anjou, the army blessed,
sanctified by the Pope! III. Pluralities were generally
condemned: pluralities without Papal dispensations

Bishanger, p. 61.

April 21, 1268. Wilkins' Concilia. It has been suggested to me
that the author of these constitutions
may have been no less than Benedetto
Gaetani, afterwards Boniface VIII. He
was the companion and counsellor of
Ottobuoni in England.

"Nec alieui liceat censum ponere
super ecclesiam Dei. Admonemus
Regem et principes et omnes qui in
potestate sunt, ut cum magna humili-
tate archiepiscopis canonibusque aliis
episcopis obediant."

"In his ergo tam horrendis sce-
leribus clericis debacchantes?"—they
had been described as joining bands
of robbers—"prosequimur excommu-
nicatione, deprivatione."—Art. viii.

John Mansel is described (Bishanger, p. 12) as "multarum in
Anglia rector ecclesiarum et possessor
reddituum quorum vix erat numerus,
ita quod ditior clericus eo non in orbe
videretur." Mr. Halliwell quotes the
Chron. Mailros, as giving him 700
livings, bringing in 18,000 marks. I
cannot find the passage.

altogether proscribed.[c] IV. There was a strong canon
against the married clergy: not merely were many
clergy married,[d] but the usage existed to a great extent
of the transmission of benefices from father to son, and
these benefices were not seldom defended by violence
and force of arms.[e]

We return to Italy, with a glance at Spain, and the
James of carlier years of Clement's Pontificate. The
Arragon. triumphs of James, the King of Arragon, over
the Saracens of Spain, and the capture of Murcia, called
forth the triumphant gratulations of the Pope. But
James of Arragon was not to be indulged in weaknesses
unbecoming a Christian warrior. The Pope summoned
him to break the chains in which he was fettered by a

---

[c] Henry de Wingham is a good
example of what might be and was
done by Papal dispensations (MS.,
B. M., ix. p. 314). Wingham has
licence to hold the deanery of St.
Martin's-le-Grand, the chancellorship
of Exeter, a prebend of Salisbury, ac
universos alios permutatio, etiam alia
beneficia (dated Anagni, July 23, 1259).
A month after De Wingham (of whom
Paris speaks as a disinterested man,
sub eras, 1257) is bishop elect of
London: he petitions to hold all these
benefices with London for five years.
He was also Lord Chancellor. The
nephew of this poor man, holding only
two livings, has Papal licence to hold two
more.—P. 411. Anagni, Aug. 28, 1259.

[d] "Nisi clerici et maxime qui in
sacris ordinibus constituti, qui in
dominibus suis detinent publicé concu-
binas."—Art. viii.

[e] The MSS., B. M., are full of notices
of married clergy in England. Letter
to the Archbishop of York (xi. 124).

Some succeeded to their fathers' benefices, "quidam in ecclesiis, in quibus
patres ministraviat eorum, se immo-
diatá patribus ejus substituti, tanquam
jure hereditá possidere sanctuarium
Dei." The same in diocese of Lincoln,
p. 133; Worcester, p. 136; Carlisle,
p. 177. Complaints to Bishop of
Salisbury of priests who have "fa-
caria." To Bishop of Coventry, of
their holding these benefices "violenter
et armatá manu," Dec. 21, 1235. So
also to Bishop of Norwich, June 12,
1240; Winchester, p. 5 and 35, 1243.
The Synod of Exeter (Wilkins, Concilia, c. xviii. p. 142) complains of
clerks on their deathbeds providing for
their concubines and children out of
the ecclesiastical revenues, "praeoccup-
tione tam damnatá in extremis labor-
antes, et de infernis minimé cogitantes
.... in sub ultima voluntatibus ....
bona ecclesiae concubinis reliuqeere non
formidant." These wills were declared
illegal.

beautiful mistress, and to return to his lawful wife: he
urged him to imitate the holy example of Louis of
France. King James pleaded that his wife was a
leper, and demanded the dissolution of the marriage.
"Thinkest thou," rejoined the Pope, "that if all the
Queens of the earth were lepers, we would allow Kings
to join in adulterous commerce with other women?
Better that all the royal houses should wither root and
branch." He put the obedience of the King of Arragon
to another test: he ordered him inexorably to expel all
Mussulmen from his dominions, to depose all the Jews
from the high places which they held in this as in
many of the Spanish kingdoms.[f]

In less than two years after the conquest of Naples,
the insupportable tyranny of the French under
Charles of Anjou, and the resentment of the
Ghibellines throughout Italy, had wrought up a spirit
of wide-spread revolt. The young Conradin could alone
deliver Sicily from the foreign yoke, check the re-
vengeful superiority of the Guelfs, and restore the now
lamented house of Hohenstaufen. Many secret mes-
sages were sent from Tuscany and Lombardy. Galvano
and Frederick di Lancia, and the two chiefs of the
house of Capece, whose lives had been excepted from
the general proscription of Manfred's partisans, found
their way to Germany. They called on Conradin to
assert his hereditary rights; to appear as a deliverer
from foreign oppression. The youth, not yet sixteen,
listened with too eager avidity. At the head
of four thousand German troops he crossed
the Alps, and held his court at Verona.

Pope Clement heard the intelligence with dismay.

f Clement Epist. Raynaldus, sub ann.

He instantly cited the presumptuous boy, who had dared
to claim a kingdom granted away by the See
of Rome, to answer before his liege lord at
Viterbo. There, in the Cathedral of Viterbo, in May,
and on the festival of St. Peter and St. Paul, he proclaimed his excommunication. He wrote to Florence
to warn the Republic of "the young serpent which had
sprung up from the blood of the old." He wrote to
Ottocar, King of Bohemia, to make a diversion by
attacking the Swabian possessions of Conradin. He
declared Conradin deposed from the kingdom of Jerusalem. At the same time he wrote to Charles of Anjou,
in terms which showed his own consciousness that the
danger was in the tyranny and in the hatred of Charles
rather than in the strength or popularity of Conradin.
He entreated him "to moderate the horrible exactions
enforced under the royal seal;[a] to listen to the petitions of his people ; to put some check on the wasteful
extravagance of his court; to keep a balance of his
receipts and expenditure; to place on the seat of justice
men of incorruptible integrity, with ample salaries, so
as to be superior to bribery ; not to permit unnecessary
appeals to the King; to avoid all vexatious inquisi-
tions; not to usurp the guardianship of orphans; to
punish all attempts to corrupt magistrates ; not to
follow the baleful example of his predecessor in encroaching on the rights of the Church."[b] Yet this
King, who needed these sage admonitions as to the
administration of his kingdom, was raised at this very
juncture by the Pope to the extraordinary office now
vacant—an office the commanding title of which was

---

[a] "Sigillo tuo legem impera, ut
tollatur infamia de horrendis exactioni-
bus eo nomine factis," et sqq. Clem.
Ep.

[b] See the letter of Pope Clement in
Martene, and in Raynaldus, sub ann.

ill-suited to the man and to the times—that of Peace-maker,[1] or Conservator of the Peace throughout Tuscany and all the provinces subject to the Roman empire; in other words, to keep down the Ghibellines, and by force of arms to compel them to lay down their arms.[k] King Alfonso of Castile heard with jealousy of this new title, which sounded as though Charles of Anjou was usurping the prerogative of the Empire, if not intending to supplant both himself and his competitor, Richard of Cornwall. The Pope was compelled at once to soothe and to alarm the Spaniard; to allay his fears as to any designs of Charles upon the Empire, not without some significant hint that the coronation by the Archbishop of Cologne was indispensable for a just title to the Empire; and the Archbishop of Cologne had crowned Richard. Alfonso was awed into silence, if not satisfied.[m]

But, not at the instigation, nor with any encouragement from the King of Castile, two of his brothers had become the most dangerous adversaries of the Pope. Henry and Frederick of Castile had been driven from their native land,[n] had taken to a wild adventurous life,

---

[1] "Paciarius non partiarium."

[k] There is a curious letter from the Pope to the Cardinal S. Hadrian. MS., B. M. When he had created Charles paciarius, "opponentibus Senensibus, Pisanis et pluribus Ghibellinis." The Romans, under the Senator, Henry of Castile, were in league with the Ghibellines. Henry had taken some cities, and seized in Rome the brothers Napoleon and Matthew Orsini, Angelo Malebranca, John Savelli, Peter Stefaneschi, Richard Annibaleschi, some of whom he had sent by night prisoners

to Monticelli. "We would, as far as possible, war with the Romans: Conradin is in Verona with all Lombardy, except Pavia, and the march of Treviso. Sicily is in full revolt under Frederick of Castile." "God's will be done," concludes the devout Pope.—Vitterbo, Nov. 23, 1267.

[m] Clement, Epist.

[n] They seem to have been at the head of a constitutional opposition against their brother Alfonso, who aspired to rule without the Cortes.

and found hospitality at the court of the King of Tunis.
It was said that they had adopted at least Mohammedan
manners, attended Mohammedan rites, and more
than half embraced the Mohammedan creed.[*] They
returned to Europe. Frederick landed in Sicily, where
some short time after he raised the standard of Conradin.
Henry went on to Italy; he was received by
his cousin, Charles of Anjou, who bestowed on him
sixty thousand crowns. Henry had hopes, fostered by
the Papal Court, if not by the Pope, of obtaining the
investiture of Sardinia, which the Pope would fain wrest
from the rule of Ghibelline Pisa. But Charles of Anjou

Henry of Castile. grew jealous of Henry of Castile; he too had
pretensions on Sardinia; it was withdrawn
from the grasp of Henry; and the Castilian was brooding
in dissatisfaction and disappointment, when the
opportunity of revenge arose. The people of Rome
were looking abroad for a Senator. Charles had surrendered
or forfeited his office when he became King of
Naples. A short lived rule of two concurrent Senators
had increased the immitigable feud. Angelo Capucio
was a noble Roman, still attached to the fallen fortunes
of Manfred. By his influence, notwithstanding the
repugnance of the rest of the nobles, and strong opposition
from some of the Cardinals, Henry of Castile was
chosen Senator of Rome. He commenced his rule
with some of those acts of stern equity which over
overawed and captivated the Roman people. Clement
too late began to suspend his design of investing
Charles of Anjou with the throne of Sardinia, to which

---

[*] Mariana describes Henry as "in rebus bellicis potens et strenuus, et animum callidus, and scelerattissimus et in fidei catholicæ cultu non diligens."   For private reasons for the hatred of Henry and Charles, see Hispan. Illustrat. ii. p. 647; Amari, Vespro Siciliano, ch. p. 30.

Henry might again aspire. But the hatred of Charles
was deep in Henry's heart; he openly displayed the
banner of Conradin. Galvano Lancia, the *Rome for Conradin.*
kinsman and most active partisan of Manfred,
hastened to Rome; and the Pope heard with indignation that the Swabian standard was waving from the
hallowed Lateran, where Lancia had taken up his
quarters, and was parading his forces before it.[f] The
censures of the Pontiff addressed to the authorities of
Rome made no impression. The Senator summoned
the people to the Capitol; his armed bands were in
readiness; he seized two of the Orsini, and sent them
prisoners to the strong castle of Monticelli, near Tivoli;
two of the Savelli were cast into the dungeons under
the Capitol, many others into different prisons; Henry
of Castile took possession of St. Peter's and of the
Papal palaces.[4]

The few German troops with which Conradin had
crossed the Alps fell off for want of pay:[r] but the
Ghibelline interest, the nobler feelings, awa- *Movements of Conradin. A.D. 1268.*
kened in favour of the gallant boy thus
cruelly deprived of his inheritance, and the growing
hatred of the French, soon gathered an army around
him. He set out from faithful Verona; he was received in Pavia, in Pisa, in Sienna, as the champion of
Ghibellinism; as the lawful King of Sicily.[s] In Apulia,

---

[f] " Ac loca, specialiter Lateranal ad
quæ ingrediunda viri etiam justi vix
digni sunt habiti, pomplis lascivientibus
circuire, ac ibidem hospitium accipere
non expavit."—Lib. Pontif. quoted in
Raynald. 1267.

[4] See note above from MS., B. M.

[r] It is curious to observe (in Boh-
mer's Register), of the few arts of

Conradin in Italy, how large a part
are on the pawning (Verpfändung) of
estates or rights for sums of money.—
p. 287.

[s] In Pavia, March 22; in Pisa,
April 4; in Sienna, July 7; in Rome,
July 7 or August 11. In Rome he is
said to have had 3000 German knights,
Henry of Castile 800 Spaniards.

2 o 2

the Saracens of Lucera were in arms; in Sicily, Frederick of Castile, with the Saracens and some of Manfred's partisans, who had taken refuge in Africa and now returned. The island was in full revolt; the Lieutenant of Charles was defeated; except Messina, Palermo, and Syracuse, Sicily was in the power of Conradin. Already, in his agony of apprehension, the Pope, finding that Charles was still in Tuscany, pressing his advantages in favour of the Guelfs of Florence, hastily summoned him to return to Naples. "Why do we write to thee as King, while thou seemest utterly to disregard thy kingdom? It is without a head, exposed to the Saracens and to the traitorous Christians; already exhausted by your robberies, it is now plundered by others. The locust eats what the cankerworm has left. Spoilers will not be wanting, so long as its defender is away. If you love the kingdom, think not that the Church will incur the toil and cost of conquering it anew; you may return to your Countship, and, content with the vain name of king, await the issue of the contest. Perhaps, in reliance on your merits, you expect a miracle to be wrought in your favour; that God will act in your behalf, while you thus follow your own counsels, and despise those of others. I had resolved not to write to thee on this affair: my venerable brother, Rudolph, Bishop of Alba, has prevailed on me to send you these few last words."[1]

Charles obeyed, and returned in all haste to Naples; he formed the siege of Lucera, the stronghold of his most dangerous foes, the Saracens. Conradin advanced towards Rome; he marched under the walls of Viterbo, intending perhaps to insult or intimi-

[1] Clement, Epist. apud Raynald. A.D. 1269, p. 233.

date the Pope, who had a strong garrison in the city.
The affrighted Cardinals thronged around the Pope,
who was at prayer. "Fear not," he said; "they will
be scattered like smoke." He even ascended the walls,
beneath which Conradin and his young and faithful
friend Frederick of Austria were prancing on their
stately coursers. "Behold the victims for the sacrifice." [a]

The dark vaticinations of the Pope, though sadly
verified by the event (perhaps but the echo of the
event), if bruited abroad in Rome, had no more effect
than the ecclesiastical thunders which at every onward
step Clement had hurled with reiterated solemnity at
the head of Conradin. Notwithstanding these excommunications, the Romans welcomed with the loudest
acclamations Conradin, called by the Pope "the accursed branch of an accursed stem, the manifest enemy
of the Church:" "Rome had calmly seen that son of
malediction, Galvano Lancia, who had so long walked
the broad road to perdition, from whose approach they
should have shrunk with scorn, displaying the banner
of Conradin from the Lateran." It was an event as
yet unheard, which disturbed the soul of the Pontiff,
that although occasional discords, and even the scandal
of wars, had taken place between the Pope and his
City, now their fidelity should revolt to the persecutor
of the Church; that Rome should incur the guilt of
matricide. [b] Yet not the less did the Senator and
Rome welcome the young Swabian. Henry the Senator
marched at the head of the Roman forces in Conradin's
army, having first plundered the churches and monasteries. The Pope heard with deeper resentment that

---

[a] Raynald. c. xiii. Fraher.   [b] Apud Raynald. A.D. 1269.

the Lateran, the churches of St. Paul, St. Basil on the
Aventine, Santa Sabina, and other convents, had been
obliged to surrender their treasures, which were expended upon the army of the excommunicate.[7]

But the destiny which hovered over the house of
Hohenstaufen had not yet exhausted its vials
of wrath. At the battle of Tagliacozzo, the
French for once condescended to depend not on their
impetuous valour alone, but on prudence, military skill,
and a reserve held by the aged Alard de St. Valery, a
French knight, just returned from that school of war,
Palestine. St. Valery's eight hundred men retrieved
the lost battle. Conradin, Frederick of Austria, Henry
of Castile, were in the hands of the remorseless conqueror. Conradin had almost bribed John Frangipani,
Lord of Astura, to lend him a bark to escape. The
Frangipani sold him for large estates in the princedom
of Benevento.[8]

Battle of Tagliacozzo.

Christendom heard with horror that the royal brother
of St. Louis, that the champion of the Church,
after a mock trial, by the sentence of one
judge, Robert da Lavena—after an unanswerable pleading by Guido de Suzaria, a famous jurist—had condemned the last heir of the Swabian house—a rival
king, who had fought gallantly for his hereditary
throne—to be executed as a felon and a rebel on a
public scaffold. So little did Conradin dread his fate,
that when his doom was announced, he was playing at

Execution of Conradin.

[7] Apud Raynald. A.D. 1269.
[8] "En 1256, quatre ans après les
Vêpres Siciliennes, un amiral de
Jacques d'Arragon emporta Astura,
qu'il réduisit en cendres. Les biens
des Frangipani furent ravagés; Jacob,
le fils de Jean, périt dans le combat.
Sa postérité s'éteignit, et, de cette
branche, dont le blason était taché du
sang royal, il ne reste qu'un souvenir
de déshonneur." Astura was near the
spot where Cicero was killed.—Char-
rier, iv. p. 212.

chess with Frederick of Austria. "Slave," said Conradin to Robert of Bari, who read the fatal sentence,
"do you dare to condemn as a criminal the son and
heir of kings? Knows not your master that he is my
equal, not my judge?" He added, "I am a mortal,
and must die; yet ask the kings of the earth if a
prince be criminal for seeking to win back the heritage
of his ancestors. But if there be no pardon for me,
spare, at least, my faithful companions; or if they must
die, strike me first, that I may not behold their
death."[a] They died devoutly, nobly. Every circum-
stance aggravated the abhorrence: it was said—perhaps
it was the invention of that abhorrence—that Robert
of Flanders, the brother of Charles, struck dead the
judge who had presumed to read the iniquitous sentence.[b] When Conradin knelt, with uplifted hands,
awaiting the blow of the executioner, he uttered these
last words—"O my mother! how deep will be thy
sorrow at the news of this day!"[c] Even the followers of Charles could hardly restrain their pity and
indignation. With Conradin died his young and valiant
friend, Frederick of Austria, the two Lancias, two of
the noble house of Donaticcio of Pisa. The inexorable
Charles would not permit them to be buried in consecrated ground.

The Pope himself was accused as having counselled
this atrocious act. One of those sentences, which from
its pregnant brevity cleaves to the remembrance, lived

[a] Bartholomæo di Neocastro apud
Muratori, p. 1027.

[b] There is evidence, it appears, that
this judge, or prothonotary, was alive
some years after.

[c] "Ad cœlum jungebat palmas,

mortemque inevitabilem patienter ex-
pectans, suum Domino spiritum com-
mendabat: nec divertebat caput, sed
exhibebat se quasi victimam et cœneris
trucos ictus in patientiâ expectabat."
—Malaspina apud Muratori, viii. 851.

long in the memory of the Ghibellines: "The life of
Conradin is the death of Charles, the death of Conradin
the life of Charles." But to have given such advice,
Clement must have belied his own nature, his own previous conduct, as well as his religion. Throughout he
had been convinced of the impolicy, and was doubtless
moved with inward remorse at the cruelties of Charles
of Anjou. Clement had tried to mitigate the tyranny
of the King. Even the colder assent, at least the
evasive refusal to interfere on the side of mercy—
"It becomes not the Pope to counsel the death of
any one," is hardly in the character of Clement IV.[4]
There is another, somewhat legendary, story. Ambrose of Sienna, afterwards a Saint, presented himself
on the first news of the capture of Conradin before
the Pope; he dwelt on the parable of the prodigal
son, received with mercy into his father's house.
"Ambrose," said the Pope, "I would have mercy,
not sacrifice." He turned to the Cardinals, "It is
not the monk that speaks, it is the Spirit of the Most
High." [5]

But if he was responsible only for not putting forth
the full Papal authority to command an act of wisdom
as of compassion, Clement himself was soon called to
answer before a higher tribunal. On the 29th October
the head of Conradin fell on the scaffold; on the 29th
November died Pope Clement IV. It is his praise that
he did not exalt his kindred—that he left in obscurity
the husbands of his daughters.[6] But the wonder be-

---

[4] Compare the fair and honest Tillemont, Vie de Saint Louis, vi. 129.
Poor Conradin had said in one of his
proclamations of Clement's hostility.
" Clemens cujus nomen ab effectu non

modicè distat."—B. Museum Chronicon, p. 273.
[5] Vit. S. Ambrosii Senen. apud
Bollandistas, c. iii.
[6] " Nec invenitur exaltâsse parentes,

trayed by this praise shows at once how Christendom
had already been offended; it was prophetic of the
stronger offence which nepotism would hereafter entail
upon the Papal See.

totus Deo dicatus." — Ptolem. Luc.
annelli. Tillemont has collected the
passages (and they are many) to the
praise of Clement IV. Tillemont is
not perhaps less inclined to admire him
because he was a Frenchman.—Vie de
St. Louis, iv. p. 350 et seq.

CHAPTER IV.

Gregory X. and his Successors.

AFTER the death of Clement IV. there was a vacancy of more than two years in the Pontificate. The cause of this dissension among the fifteen Cardinals[a] nowhere transpires: it may have been personal jealousy, where there was no prelate of acknowledged superiority to demand the general suffrage. The French Cardinals **may** have been ambitious, under the dominant influence **of the** victorious Charles of Anjou, to continue the **line** of French Pontiffs: the Italians, both from their Italian patriotism and their jealousy of the power of Charles, may have stubbornly resisted such promotion. During this vacancy, Charles of Anjou was revenging himself with his characteristic barbarity on his rebellious kingdom, compressing with an iron hand the hatred of his subjects, which was slowly and sullenly brooding **into** desperation. He was thus unknowingly preparing his own fall by the terrible reaction of the Sicilian Vespers. He was becoming in influence, manifestly aspiring to be, through the triumphant Guelfic factions, the real master of the whole of Italy.

At this period was promulgated an Edict, **before** briefly alluded to,[b] apparently unobserved; but **which,**

---

[a] Ciacconius gives 17.—See 6 French, 4 Romans.—p. 178.

[b] See back, page 313. Ordonnances des Rois, i. 97, March, 1268. Sis-mondi, viii. p. 106. I cannot see the force of the objection to the authenticity of the Ordinance, to which Mr. Hallam seems to give some weight.

nevertheless, in the hands of the great lawyers, who
were now establishing in the minds of men, especially
in France, a rival authority to that of the clergy, became a great Charter of Independence to the Gallican
Church.   The Pragmatic Sanction, limiting   Pragmatic
the interference of the court of Rome in the   Sanction.
elections of the clergy, and directly denying its right of
ecclesiastical taxation, being issued by the most religious of Kings, by a King a canonised Saint, seemed so
incongruous and embarrassing, that desperate attempts
have been made to question its authenticity: Louis IX.
might seem, in his servile time, himself servilely religious, to be suddenly taking the lofty tone of Charlemagne.   But it was this high religiousness of Louis
which suggested, and which enabled him to promulgate
this charter of liberty: as he intended none, so he
might disguise even to himself the latent, rather than
avowed hostility to the power of Rome.   Among the
dearest objects to the heart of Louis was the reformation of the clergy; that reformation not aiming at the
depression, but tending to the immeasurable exaltation
of their power, by grounding it on their piety and
holiness.   It is to this end that he asserts the absolute
power of jurisdiction in the clergy, the rights of patrons,
the right of free elections in the cathedrals and other

---

that St. Louis had not any previous
differences with the See of Rome.   The
right of patronage seems to have been
a standing cause of quarrel throughout
Christendom, as we have seen in
England.   See, too, in Tillemont,
iv. p. 408–412—the king (Louis)
asserting his rights of patronage to the
prebends of Rheims and the archdeaconry of Sens against the Pope.
Tillemont does not doubt its authenticity, and refers to these disputes as a
possible cause.   See also the strange
account of John of Canterbury, who
paid 10,000 livres Tournois for confirmation in the Archbishopric of
Rheims.   John had expended it for the
honour of his Holiness and the Roman
court.   The Pope blushed at this great
expense for his honour. — p. 410.
Clement, Epist. p. 308.

churches. The Edict was issued in the name of "Louis by the grace of God, King of the French. To ensure the tranquil and wholesome state of the Church in our realm; to increase the worship of God, in order to promote the salvation of the souls of the faithful in Christ; to obtain for ourselves the grace and succour of Almighty God, to whose dominion and protection our realm has been ever subject, as we trust it will ever be, we enact and ordain by this edict, maturely considered and of perpetual observance :—

" I. That the prelates, patrons, and ordinary collators to benefices in the churches of our realm, have full enjoyment of their rights, and that the jurisdiction of each be wholly preserved.

" II. That the cathedral and other churches of our realm have full freedom of election in every point and particular.

" III. We will and ordain that the pestilential crime of simony, which undermines the Church, be for ever banished from our realm.

" IV. We will and ordain in like manner that promotions, collations, provisions and dispositions of the prelacies, the dignities, the benefices, of what sort soever, and of the ecclesiastical offices of our realm, be according to the disposition, ordinance, and determination of the common law, the sacred Councils of the Church of God, and the ancient institutions of the Holy Fathers.

" V. We will that no one may raise or collect in any manner exactions or assessments of money, which have been imposed by the court of Rome, by which our realm has been miserably impoverished, or which hereafter shall be imposed, unless the cause be reasonable, pious, most urgent, of inevitable necessity, and recognised by our express and spontaneous consent, and by that of the Church of our realm.

" VI. By these presents we renew, approve, and confirm the liberties, franchises, immunities, prerogatives, rights, privileges, granted by the Kings our predecessors of pious memory, and by ourselves to all churches, monasteries, holy places, religious men and ecclesiastics in our realm."

This Edict appeared either during the last year of Clement IV., when the Pope absolutely depended on the protection of Charles of Anjou against the reviving Ghibellinism under Conradin, and he might be reduced to take refuge under the tutelage of Louis; or during the vacancy in the Pontificate. In either case it would have been dangerous, injurious, it would have been resented by the common voice of Christendom, if the acts of Louis had been arraigned, or even protested against, as impious aggressions on the rights of Rome. The Edict itself was profoundly religious, even submissive in its tone; at all events, the assertion of the supremacy, of the ultimate right of judgement in the temporal power, was very different coming from Louis of France than from Frederick II., or any of his race. Louis was almost Pope in the public mind; his piety, his munificence, his devotion to the Crusade, in which he was again about to embark, his profound deference in general to the clergy and to the Pope himself, which had almost already arrayed him in worshipped sanctity, either allayed the jealousy of the Roman See, or made it imprudent to betray such jealousy. Hence it was that neither at the time of its publication, nor subsequently, did it provoke any counter protestation; it had already taken its place among the Ordinances of the realm, before its latent powers were discovered,

denounced, condemned. Then, seized on by the Parliaments, defended, interpreted, extended by the legists,
strengthened by the memorable decree of the *Appeal
against abuses*, it became the barrier against which the
encroachments of the ecclesiastical power were destined
to break; nor was it swept away till a stronger barrier
had arisen in the unlimited power of the French crown.

During this vacancy in the Pontificate, St. Louis
 closed his holy life in the most ignoble, and
not the least disastrous of the crusades, into
Africa. It was the last, except the one desperate (in
some degree brilliant) struggle, which was even now
about to take place under our Prince Edward, for the
narrow remnant of the Holy Land. Again the beauty
of the passive virtues of Louis, his death, with all the
submissive quietness of a martyr, blinded mankind to
his utter incompetency to conduct a great army, and
to the waste of noble blood; the Saint in life assumed
in the estimation of mankind the crown of martyrdom.*
Nothing was wanting but his canonisation; and canonisation could add no reverence to the name of St. Louis.

Year after year had passed, and still the stubborn
fifteen Cardinals persisted in their feud; still
Christendom was without a Pontiff; and
might discover (at least the dangerous question might
arise) the fatal secret that a supreme Pontiff was not
necessary to Christendom. They withstood the bitter
mockery of one of their brethren, the Bishop of Porto,
that it were well to remove the roof of their chamber,
that the Holy Ghost might descend upon them. The
Franciscans seem to have been astonished that the

---

* Joinville. Tillemont has collected all the striking circumstances of the
death of St. Louis.—Vol. v. p. 169.

virtues and learning of the pride of their order, S. Bonaventura, did not command the general homage. They
fabled, at least the annalist of the Church declares it a
fable, that Bonaventura would not condescend to the
proffered dignity.[d] At length the Cardinals determined
to delegate to six of their members the full power of the
conclave.

The wisdom or felicity of their choice might, if ever,
justify the belief in a superior overruling Gregory X.
counsel. It fell upon one, towards whom it is
difficult to conceive how their thoughts were directed, a
man neither Cardinal nor Prelate, of no higher rank
than Archdeacon of Liège, and dispossessed of his Archdeaconry by the unjust jealousy of his bishop; upon one
now absent in the Holy Land on a pilgrimage. Gregory X., such was the name he assumed, was of a noble
house, the Visconti of Piacenza, but having early left
his country, was not committed to either of the great
Italian factions: he was unembarrassed with family
ties; he was an Italian, but not a Roman, not therefore
an object of jealousy and hatred to rival houses among
that fierce baronage. He had been a canon of Lyons,
but was by no means implicated with French interests.
One great religious passion possessed his soul. The Holy
Land, with its afflictions and disasters, its ineffaceable
sanctity, had sunk into the depth of his affections; the
interests of that land were his highest duties. It was
to this end that Gregory X. devoted himself with all the
energy of a commanding mind, or rather to a prepara-
tory object, perhaps greater, at all events indispensable
to that end. It was in order to organise a Crusade,
more powerful than any former Crusade, that he aspired

* Raynald. sub ann.

to pacify, that he succeeded for a time in pacifying, Western Christendom. This greatest of pontifical acts, but this alone, Gregory X. was permitted to achieve.

The reception of this comparatively obscure eccle- siastic, thus suddenly raised to the chair of St. Peter, might encourage his most holy hopes. He landed at Brundusium, was escorted by King Charles to Capua, and from thence, passing by Rome, to Viterbo, where the Cardinals met him with reverential unanimity.

He was crowned at Rome with an elaborate ceremonial, published by himself as the future code, according to which the Roman Pontiffs were to be elected, inaugurated, invested: the most minute particulars of dress were arranged, and the whole course of processional service.* Gregory X. took up his residence at Orvieto.

Gregory had hardly ascended the Pontifical throne, when he determined to hold a great Œcumenic Council. That it might be a Council worthy of the title, he summoned it for two years later. The pacification of Christendom was the immediate, the reconquest of the Holy Land the remote, object of this great diet of Christendom. The place of the Council was debated with grave prudence. Within the Alps it was more convenient, perhaps it was more dignified, for the Pope to receive the vassal hierarchy; but beyond the Alps alone was there hope of re-awakening the slumbering enthusiasm for the sepulchre of the Saviour.

(margin notes: Inauguration. Jan. 31, 1272. / March 27, 1272. / Determination to hold a Council.)

---

* The Jews were to offer, as a regular part of the ceremony, their congratulations, and to present the book of the Old Testament. The Pope was seated on the Sedes Stercoraria, emblematic of the verse in the Psalm "de stercore erigit pauperem." This is noticed on account of misapprehensions sometimes prevalent on this singular usage. See on the Sedes Stercoraria, Mabillon, Iter Italicum, p. 59.

Lyons was the chosen city. **Gregory** in the mean time laboured assiduously at the **great work which was** to be consummated in the **Council—the pacification** of Christendom.   Three measures **were** necessary: I. The extinction of the wars and **feuds in** Italy. II. The restoration of the Empire, in the person of a great German Prince.   III. The acknowledgment of the Greek Emperor of Constantinople, and the admission of that Emperor into the league of Christian princes; with the reunion of the Greek and Latin Churches.

Gregory began his work of pacification in Lombardy: he did not at once withdraw himself from the head of the Guelfic confederacy; he still asserted the power of Charles of Anjou as Vicar of the Empire; he even confirmed the excommunication against the Ghibelline cities, Pisa, Pavia, Verona, and the Duke of Tyrol: **nor** did **he take** up the cause of Otho Visconti, the **exiled Ghibelline** Archbishop of Milan, against **the** Della Torres, who held that city.[f]   But he began gradually to feel his strength.   He negotiated peace between Genoa and Venice, rivals for the mastery of the sea;   A.D. 1272. between Venice and Bologna, rivals for the command of the navigation of the Po.   Pisa was re-conciled to the Church; the archiepiscopal dignity restored to the city.   In Florence, on his way to the Council, Gregory attempted to awe into peace the Guelfs and Ghibellines.   The Guelfs heard this strange doctrine applied to their enemies, "They are Ghibellines, it is true, but they are citizens, men, Christians."[g]   He made the two factions, both at Florence and Sienna, swear to a treaty of peace, and to the re-admission of

[f] Annal. Mediolan. Muratori, Ann., sub ann. 1272.
[g] S. Antonin. iii. tit. 20, c. 2.

the exiles on both sides, in his own presence and in that
of Charles of Anjou, and Baldwin of Constantinople.
But the hatred of Guelf and Ghibelline was too deeply
rooted; Charles of Anjou openly approving the treaty,
secretly contrived a rupture; the Ghibellines were
menaced with assassination: the Pope paused on his
journey to cast back an excommunication on forsworn
and disobedient Florence. Nor would Genoa enter into
terms of reconciliation with Charles of Anjou. Yet on
the whole there was at least a surface of quiet; though
under the smouldering ashes lay everywhere the fire,
nursing their strength, and ready to burst out again in
new fury.

Richard, Earl of Cornwall, died, having squandered
his enormous wealth for the barren honour of
bearing the imperial title of King of the
Romans for fourteen years, and of displaying in London
the splendour and majesty of his imperial pomp.[b] Notwithstanding the claim of Alfonso of Castile, who had
exercised no other right than sending a few troops into
Lombardy, the Pope commanded a new election.
Perhaps he already anticipated the choice of Rodolph
of Hapsburg, the founder of the great house
of Austria. The Pope confirmed the choice;
he tried all means of soothing the pride; he used the
gentlest, most courteous persuasions, but he paid no
regard to the remonstrances of the King of Castile.
Rodolph of Hapsburg, whose great activity and abilities
had been already displayed in the internal affairs of
Germany, who had commanded the suffrages of all the

April 2, 1272.

Sept. 29, 1273.

* The Germans soon saw, according
to Paris, the contempt in which
England held Richard of Cornwall;
and withdrew, ashamed of their Emperor. He proved as much theirs in
England as in Germany.—Matt. Paris,
pp. 953-4.

electors, except the hostile Ottocar, King of Bohemia,[1] was the sovereign whose accession any Pope, especially Gregory X., might hail with satisfaction. He seemed designated as the chief who might unite Christendom in the Holy War.[2] He had none of the fatal hereditary claims to possessions in Italy, or to the throne of Naples. In the north of Italy he might curb the insatiate ambition, the restless encroachments of Charles of Anjou: the Pope exacted his promise from Rudolph that he would not assail Charles in his kingdom of Sicily or in Tuscany. Gregory X. aspired to include within the pale of the great Christian confederacy, to embark in the common crusade, even a more useful ally, the Greek Emperor of Constantinople. A Greek was again Emperor of the East; Michael Palæologus ruled in Constantinople; Baldwin II., the last of the Latin emperors, was an exile in Europe. Instead of espousing his cause, or encouraging the ambition of Charles of Anjou, who had married his daughter to the heir of Baldwin, and aspired to the dominion of the East in the name of his son-in-law, Gregory embraced the wiser and bolder policy of acknowledging the title of the Greek. Palæologus consented to pay the great price of this acknowledgment,

A.D. 1273.

---

[1] The electors were Werner of Eppstein, Archbishop of Mentz; Henry of Frislingen, Archbishop of Treves; Engelbert of Falkenstein, Archbishop of Cologne; Louis, Palatine of the Rhine and Duke of Bavaria; John, Duke of Saxony; John, Margrave of Brandenburg. According to some authorities, Ottocar, King of Bohemia, declined the crown. The reader will find a fair popular account of the elevation of Rodolph of Hapsburg in

Coxe's House of Austria.

[2] Rodolph was besieging the Bishop of Basle when he received the intelligence of his election. The city at once surrendered to the King of the Romans. The Bishop was furious. "Sit firm," he cried, "O Lord God, or Rodolph will occupy thy throne." "Sede firmiter, Domine Deus, vel locum Rodolfus occupabit tuum."—Albert. Argentin. p. 100.

no less than submission to the Papal supremacy, and
the union of the Greek with the Latin Church."
Palæologus had no great reason for profound attachment
to the Greek clergy. The Patriarch Arsenius, with
boldness unusual in the Eastern hierarchy, had solemnly
excommunicated the Emperor for his crime in cruelly
blinding the young John Lascaris, in whose name he
held the empire. Arsenius had been banished on a
charge of treason; a new patriarch sat on the throne,
but a powerful faction of the clergy were still Arsenites.
On his death, they compelled the burial of the banished
prelate in the sanctuary of Santa Sophia; absolution
in his name alone reconciled the Emperor to God.
Palæologus, though the ruling Patriarch was more
submissive, might not be disinclined to admit larger
authority in a more remote power, held by a Pope in
Italy rather than a Patriarch in Constantinople. By
every art, by bribery, intimidation, by skilfully softening
off the points of difference, and urging the undoubted
blessings of union, he wrung a slow consent from the
leading clergy of the East: they were gradually taught
to consider that the procession of the Holy Ghost, from
the Father and the Son, was not a doctrine of such
repulsive heterodoxy, and to admit a kind of vague
supremacy in the Pope, which the Emperor assured
them would not endanger their independence, as dear
to him as to themselves." Ambassadors arrived at

" Pachymer, ii. 15; iii. 1, 2;
v. 10; p. 369, &c. Nicephorus Gre-
goras, lib. i; iv. 1, Gibbon, edit. Milman, xi. 313, et seq.

" Pachymer complains, not without
bitterness, that the Latins called the
Greeks, in their contempt, " white Ha-
garenes." τοωσλεταντε γὰρ τὸ σνδε-

Βαλοσ,καὶ τὸ Ανυκοβς 'Αγαρηνοὺς εἶναι
Γραικοὺς παρ' ἑαυτοῖς μείζον ἔχετε.—
Lib. v. p. 367, edit. Bonn. The Greek
clergy were secretly determined to
maintain their independence, to acknowledge no primacy, and not to subject
themselves to the judgment of traitors
and low men. I presume they thought

Rome with splendid offerings for the altar of St. Peter,
and with the treaty of union and of submission to the
Roman see, signed by the Emperor, his son, thirty-five
archbishops and metropolitans, with their suffragan
synods. The Council of Lyons witnessed with joy this
reunion—a reunion unhappily but of few years—of the
Church of Basil, the Gregories, and Chrysostom, with
that of Leo and Gregory the Great.

Nothing could contrast more strongly than the first
and second Councils of Lyons. The first was   *Council of*
summoned by Innocent IV., attended by   *Lyons.*
hardly one hundred and fifty prelates, to represent the
whole clergy of Christendom; its aim to perpetuate a
desperate war, and to commit the Empire and the
Papacy in implacable hostility; its authority disclaimed
by the larger part of Christendom, cordially and fully
accepted by scarcely one of the great kingdoms. At
the second Council of Lyons, Gregory X. took his seat
at the head of five hundred bishops, seventy abbots, and
at least a thousand dignified ecclesiastics. Every
kingdom of the West acknowledged its œcumenic power.
The King of Arragon was present; the Latin patriarchs
of Constantinople and of Antioch, fourteen cardinals,
ambassadors from Germany, France, England, Sicily,
the Master of the Templars, with many knights of St.
John. Of the two great theologic luminaries   *May 7, 1274.*
of the age, the Dominican Thomas Aquinas
and the Franciscan Bonaventura, Thomas died on his
way to the Council:[a] Bonaventura was present, preached

---

all Italians like the Genoese of Pera, merchants. ἀλλὰ μένειν καὶ ἀθεῖς ἐν τῇ πυρᾷ τὴν ἐκκλησίαν ἡγούμενοι, αἰδοῖ καὶ ἀρχῆθεν εἶχε, καὶ μὴ παρὰ πενήλμεν αἰσθητικεῖν ἀφίενται

καὶ βαρυδέων.—p. 368. Strange collision of Greek and Roman pride! The sovereign did not like the ἀρχηεραι who were very busy.

[a] Dante has given perpetuity to the

during its sittings, but died before its dissolution.
The Council of Lyons aspired to establish peace
throughout Christendom; the recognition of an Emperor,
elected with the full approval, under the closest bonds of
union with the Pope; the re-admission of the Eastern
Empire, and of the Greek Church, within the pale of
Western Christendom. Such was the function of this
great assembly, perhaps the first and last Council which
was undisturbed by dispute, and uttered no sentence of
interdict or excommunication. The declared objects for
which the Council was summoned were succour to the
Holy Land, the reconciliation of the Greek Church, the
reformation of manners. The session opened with great
solemnity. The Pope himself officiated in the religious
ceremonial, assisted by his cardinals. For the first
object, the succour to the Holy Land, a tenth of all
ecclesiastical revenues was voted for six years. The
Council, as it awaited the arrival of the Greek ambassadors, occupied itself on regulations concerning the
discipline and morals of the clergy. On the 24th June
arrived the ambassadors. After the edict of the Emperor
of Byzantium, sealed with a golden seal, had been ex-
hibited and read, the act for the union of the two
Churches was solemnly passed; the Pope himself intoned
the *Te Deum* with tears of joy; the Latin clergy
chanted the creed in Latin; the Greek, those of the
embassy, assisted by the Calabrese bishops, chanted it
in Greek. As they came to the words, "who proceedeth

charge against Charles of Anjou of
having poisoned St. Thomas; added
also by Villani, lib. 218 :—

"Carlo venne in Italia, e per ammenda
Vittima fe di Curradino, e poi
Ripinse al ciel Tommaso per ammenda."
                          Purgat. xx. 67.

Compare commentary of Benvenuto da
Imola (apud Muratori). The Guelf
Villani assigns as a motive the fear
that St. Thomas (a Neapolitan), the
oracle of Christendom, would expose
the cruelty and wickedness of Charles.
It is probably an invention of the profound Neapolitan hatred.

from the Father and the Son," they repeated it, with
more emphatic solemnity, three times. The representative of the Eastern Emperor acknowledged in ample
terms (such were his secret instructions) the supremacy
of St. Peter's successor.

Gregory X. did not permit this Council to be dissolved until he had secured the Papacy from *Law of Papal
Election.* the scandals which had preceded his own election; but to the stern law with which he endeavoured
to bind the cardinals, he found strong opposition. It
was only by his personal authority with each single
prelate, that he extorted their irrevocable signature and
seal to the statute which was to regulate the proceedings of the conclave on the death of a Pope. The
statute retained to the cardinals the proud prerogative
of sole election; but it ordained that only ten days after
the death of the Pope they were to be shut up, without
waiting for absent members of the college, in a single
chamber in the deceased Pope's palace, where they were
to live in common; all access was to be strictly prohibited, as well as writing or message: each was to have
but one domestic; their meals were to be received
through a window too narrow to admit a man. Any
communication with them was inhibited under the
menace of interdict. If they agreed not in three days,
their repast was to be limited, for five days, to a single
dish; after that to only bread and wine; so they were
to be starved into unanimity. If the Pope died out of
Rome, in that city where he died was to be this imprisonment of the conclave, under the municipal magistrates, who were sworn to allow the liberty permitted
by statute, but no more. All offenders against this
decree, of whatever rank, were at once excommunicate,
infamous, and could rise to no dignity or public office;

any fief or estate they might hold of the Church of
Rome, or any other Church, was forfeit. All former
pacts, conventions, or agreements, were declared null
and void; if under oath, the oath was abrogated, annulled. In every city in Christendom public prayers
were to be offered up to God to infuse concord, speedy
and wise decision, into the hearts of that venerable conclave.[p] So closed the second Council of Lyons. One
act of severity alone, the degradation of Gregory's old
enemy, the Bishop of Liège, appears in the annals of
this Council. The Christian world was, on the other
hand, highly edified by the appearance and solemn
baptism of certain Tartars.

Gregory X., after an interview with the King of
Castile at Beaucaire, whom he strove to reconcile to the loss of the Empire, and an interview
with the Emperor Rodolph at Lausanne, repassed the
Alps. He was received with deserved honours; only
into excommunicated Florence — excommunicated, no
one could deny, with perfect Christian justice—the
peaceful prelate refused to enter. The world was
anxiously awaiting the issue of these sage and holy
counsels. The pontificate of peace, peace only to be
broken by the discomfiture of the infidels in the East,
was expanding, it was to be hoped, into many happy
and glorious years. Suddenly Gregory sickened on his
road to Arezzo; he died, and with him broke
up the whole confederation of Christendom.
The world again, from the conclave to the remotest
limits not of Europe alone, but of Christianity, became
one vast feud. With Gregory X. expired the Crusades;
Christianity lost this principle of union, the Pope this

p Mansi et Labbe, sub ann.

principle of command, this title to the exaction of tribute from the vassal world. From this time he began to sink into an Italian prince, or into the servant of one of the great monarchies of Europe. The last convulsive effort of the Popedom for the dominion of the world, under Boniface VIII., ended in the disastrous death of that Pope; the captivity of the Papacy at Avignon.

After the death of Gregory X., in hardly more than three years three successive Popes rose and passed like shadows over the throne of St. Peter, and a fourth commenced his short reign. The popular superstition and the popular hatred, which, unallayed by the short-lived dignity, holiness, and wisdom of Gregory X., lay so deep in the public mind, beheld in these deaths which followed each other in such darkening rapidity, either the judicial hand of God or the crime of man. The Popes were no sooner proclaimed than dead, either, it was believed, smitten for men's sins or their own, or cut off by poison.[a] The first of these, Peter of Tarantaise (Innocent V.), was elected in January, took up his residence in Rome, and died in June. Ottobuoni Fieschi, the nephew of Innocent IV., answered his kindred, who crowded around him with congratulations on his election, "Would that ye came to a cardinal in good health, not to a dying Pope." He just lived to take the name of Hadrian V., to release his native Genoa from interdict, and to suspend with his dying breath the constitution of Gregory X. concerning the Conclave. He was not crowned, consecrated, or even ordained priest. Hadrian V. died at Viterbo.

Rapid succession of Popes.

Innocent V. 1276.

Hadrian V. Elected July 8, died Aug. 18.

---

[a] "Papa quatuor mortui, duo divino judicio, et duo veneno exhausti."—Chronic. Foro Livien. Muratori, S. I. xiil.

The immediate choice of the cardinals now fell on
Pedro Juliani, a Portuguese, the Cardinal
Bishop of Tusculum. Though the cardinals had
already obtained from the dying Hadrian the suspension
of the severely restrictive edict of Gregory X. concerning the Conclave, the edict was popular abroad. There
were many, and among them prelates who declared
that, excepting under that statute, and in conformity
with its regulations, the cardinals had no right to the
sole election of the Pope.[1] There was a great uproar in
Viterbo, instigated by these prelates. The Archbishop
of Corinth, with some other ecclesiastics who were sent
forth to read the suspension of the edict by Hadrian V.,
confirmed by John XXI., the new Pope, was maltreated;
yet, even if the ceremonial was not rigidly observed,
there had been the utmost speed in the election of
John XXI. The Pope was a man of letters, and even
of science; he had published some mathematical trea-
tises which excited the astonishment and therefore the
suspicion of his age. He was a churchman of easy
access, conversed freely with humbler men, if men of
letters, and was therefore accused of lowering the dignity
of the Pontificate. He was perhaps hasty and un-
guarded in his language, but he had a more inexpiable
fault. He had no love for monks or friars: it was supposed that he meditated some severe coercive edicts on
these brotherhoods. Hence his death (he was crushed
by the falling of the roof in a noble chamber which he
had built in the palace of Viterbo) was foreshown by

John XXI.

---

[1] "In tantam prorupere temeritatis
insaniam, ut in dubium auctoritatem
et jurisdictionem collegii ejusdem Ecclesiæ revocarent, et de illis in deroga-
tionem ipsarum disputantes utilibet,
enervare immo et evacuare pro viribus
niterentur insulsis argumentis."—Re-
script. Joann. XXI., apud Raynald.
1276.

gloomy prodigies, and held either to be a divine judgement, or a direct act of the Evil One.   John XXI. was contemplating with too great pride the work of his own hands, and burst out into laughter; at that instant the avenging roof came down on his head.   Two visions revealed to different holy men the Evil One bowing down the supports, and so overwhelming the reprobate Pontiff.   He was said by others to have been, at the moment of his death, in the act of writing a book full of the most deadly heresies, or practising the arts of magic.[*]   *May 16 (?) 20? 1277.*

For six weeks, the Cardinals, released from the coercive statute, met in conclave without coming to any conclusion.   At length the election fell on John Gaetano, of the noble Roman house, the Orsini, a man of remarkable beauty of person and demeanour.   His name, "the Accomplished," implied that in him met all the graces of the handsomest clerks in the world; but he was a man likewise of irreproachable morals, of vast ambition, and of great ability.   *Nov. 25, 1277. Nicolas III. "Compositus."*   This age of short-lived Popes was the age of magnificent designs as short-lived as their authors.   The nobler, more comprehensive, more disinterested scheme of Gregory X. had sunk into nothing at his death; that of Nicolas III. had deeper root, but came not to maturity during his reign, or in his line.   An Italian, a Roman, was again upon the throne of St. Peter.   The Orsini at first took up his residence at Rome.   He built a splendid palace, the Vatican, near St. Peter's, with gardens around, and fortified with a strong wall.[*]   He repaired, enlarged, and strengthened the Lateran Palace.

---

* Ptolem. Loc. xxvi. Nangis, however, says that he died " perceptis omnibus sacramentis ecclesiasticis."—

* Sub ann. 1277. Sifftel. in Chronic.

* Bunsen and Platner, Roms Beschreibung, ii. p. 211.

Unlike his rash predecessor, he was a friend to the great
monastic orders: he knew how completely the preachers
and other mendicants still, notwithstanding the hatred of
the clergy, now they had taken possession of the high
places of theology, ruled the public mind. To Thomas
Aquinas and S. Bonaventura the world looked up as to
its guiding lights; nor had they lost their power over
the popular passions.

Nicolas III. did not in any degree relax the Papal
superintendence over Christendom to its extreme limits:
he is interfering in the affairs of Poland and Hungary,
mediating in the wars between France and Spain,
watching over the crumbling wreck of the Christian
possessions in the Holy Land. In the East he not
merely held the justly alarmed Emperor, Michael
Palæologus, to his plighted fidelity and allegiance, but
insisted on the more ample recognition of the Papal
supremacy.* He demanded that a solemn oath of
subordination should be taken by the Patriarch and
the clergy. To the prudent request of the Emperor,
that the obnoxious words which asserted the procession
of the Holy Ghost from the Son, should not be forced
at once into the creed, he returned a haughty reply
that no indulgence could be granted, though some
toleration might be conceded for a time on the other
points in which the Greek differed from the Roman
ritual. He even required that the Greek Church
should humbly seek absolution for the sin of their long
schism. A strong faction broke out in the Empire,
in Constantinople, in the Court, in the family of the

---

* Raynald. sub ann. 1279, 60.
Pachymer (vi. 10. p. 461) calls the
Pope πρᾶκτωρ. The Jesuit Possin,
Chronol. in Pachymerum, conjectures
Oeconomus, the Orator — perhaps a
blunder of the Greeks. The whole
long intrigue may be traced through
two or three books of Pachymer.

Emperor. They branded the Pope, the Patriarch, the
Emperor, as heretics. Palæologus became that most
odious of persecutors, a persecutor without the excuse
of religious bigotry; confiscation, scourging, mutilation,
punished the refractory assertors of the independence
of the Greek Church. The Pope's Legates were
gratified by the sight of four princes of the blood
confined in a loathsome prison. But discontent led
to insurrection. The Prince of Trebisond, who had
always retained the title of Emperor, espoused the
cause of Greek orthodoxy. His generals betrayed
the unhappy Palæologus: his family, especially his
nieces, intrigued against him. He hesitated; for his
hesitation he was excommunicated at Rome by
Martin IV., the slave of his enemy Charles of Anjou.
On his death the Greeks with one consent Return of
threw off the yoke; the churches were puri- the Greek
fied from the infection of the Latin rites; the dependence
creed resumed its old form; Andronicus, the son of
Palæologus, refused burial to his schismatic father.[*]

But Italy was the scene of the great achievements,
it was to be that of the still greater designs, of Nicolas III. The Emperor Rodolph was not yet so
firmly seated on his throne (he was involved in a
perilous war with Ottocar of Bohemia) as to disdain
the aid of the Roman Pontiff. He could not but look
to the resumption at least of some imperial rights in
Lombardy; if the Pope should maintain the cause
of Charles of Anjou, Italy was entirely lost. From
the magnificence, the policy, or the fears of Rodolph,
the Pope extorted the absolute cession to the Roman
See, not only of Romagna, but of the exarchate of

[*] Raynald. 1279. 8.

Ravenna. The Chancellor of the Emperor had exacted
an oath of allegiance from the cities of Bologna, Imola,
Faenza, Forli, Cesena, Ravenna, Rimini, Urbino, and
some other towns. Rodolph disclaimed the
acts of his Chancellor, recognised the donation
of the Emperor Louis, and made a new donation, in
his own name, of the whole territory from Radicofani
to Coperano, the march of Ancona, the duchy of
Spoleto, the county of Bertinoro, the lands of the
Countess Matilda, the exarchate of Ravenna, the
Pentapolis, Ferrara, Commachio, Montefeltro, and Massa
Trabaria, absolutely; and with all his full rights to the
See of St. Peter. The Pope obtained a confirmatory
acknowledgment of his sovereignty, as well as over
Sardinia, Corsica, and Sicily, from the great electors
of the Empire.[f] This document is signed by the
Archbishop of Saltzburg, and other prelates, by the
Chancellor of the Empire, by Albert the eldest, and
Hartman the second son of the Emperor,
by many of the nobles with their own hand, by
some with that of their notaries.[g] This cession Nicolas
determined should not be, as it had heretofore been,
an idle form in the officers of the Empire; and the
Legates of the Pope presented themselves at the gates
of the greater cities, demanding the acknowledgment
of the Papal sovereignty. The independent principalities, the republics which had grown up in these
territories, made no resistance; they were released
from their oath to the Emperor, and took the oath
to the Pope; even Bologna submitted on certain terms.
The Pope was actual ruling sovereign of the whole of

(margin: May 30, 1278.)
(margin: Feb. 18, 1279.)

---

[f] Raynald. p. 473.

[g] Rohrmer observes of this document that the two sons of the Emperor
could write: the Bargrave of Nurem-
burg and the Archbishop of Saltzburg 1
could not.—Regesta, p. 94.

the dominions to which the Papal See had advanced
its pretensions.[a] The extent of this sovereignty was
still vague and undefined : the princes maintained their
principalities, the republics their municipal institutions
and self-government. They admitted no rulers appointed by the Pope; his power of levying taxes was
certainly not unrestricted, nor the popular rule absolutely abrogated. Thus strong in the manifest favour
of the Emperor Rodolph, Nicolas III. made a great
merit to Charles of Anjou that he had stipulated that
the Emperor should abstain from all warlike operations
against Charles. The ambitious Frenchman overawed,
quietly allowed himself to be despoiled first
of his vicariate of Tuscany, and then of his
senatorship of Rome. Charles humbly entreated that
he might not suffer the indignity of surrendering that
office, which, on the expulsion of Henry
of Castile, had been regranted to him for ten
years by Pope Clement IV., before the expiration of
that term, now almost elapsed. Nicolas condescended
to grant his humble petition; but on the abdication
of Charles he passed a rigorous edict that the senatorship from that time should never be held by emperor,
king, prince, marquis, duke, count, or baron, or any
man of great rank or power, or even by their brother,
son, or grandson ; no one could hold it for above a year ;
no one without special licence of the Apostolic See.[b]
This hostility to Charles may have been the deliberate
policy of the Pope: it was said that the Pope had
demanded the niece of Charles in marriage for his
nephew; Charles contemptuously answered, the Pope

---

[a] " Ma quello, che i chierici prendono, tardi sanno rendere."—Villani, vii. 53.
[b] Nicolai III., Regesta. Raynald. sub ann.

was no hereditary prince, and that notwithstanding
the red shoes he wore, he must not presume to mix
his blood with that of kings.[a] There can be no doubt
that Charles had used his influence in the conclave to
oppose the elevation of the Roman Orsini.

Charles retired to his dominions to brood over revenge, to meditate a league against the Eastern Empire
which was to compensate for his losses in the West.
The Popes had taken the reconciled Greeks, the
submissive Palæologus (the fear of Charles had been
a chief motive for the religious tractableness of the
Greeks[b]), under their protection. Gregory X. had
refused to sanction or to consecrate the banner which
Charles was prepared to unfold in the name of the
Latin Philip; Charles had been seen to gnaw his
ivory sceptre in wrath, in the antechamber of the Pope,
at this desertion of what he asserted to be the cause
of legitimate right and orthodox belief.[c] Charles was
now negotiating with the Latins of the Eastern Empire
and the republic of Venice to take arms and replace
the son of Baldwin on the throne of Constantinople.
Even in Sicily Charles of Anjou was not absolutely
secure: the Pope was understood to entertain secret
relations with the enemies of the French rule.

But Nicolas III. had ulterior schemes, which seem
Nepotism of to foreshow and anticipate the magnificent
Nicolas III. designs of later nepotism. Already, under
pretence of heresy, he had confiscated the castles of
some of the nobles of Romagna, that particularly
of Suriano, and invested his nephews with them. The
castle of St. Angelo, separated from the Church, was

[a] Ricordano Malaspina, 204. Villani, vii. 53.

[b] This appears throughout the Byzantine accounts.

[c] Pachymer, v. 26, p. 410.

granted to his nephew Orso. His kinsmen were by various means elected the Podestàs of many cities. Three of his brethren, four more of his kindred, had been advanced to the Cardinalate. Bertoldo Orsini, his brother, was created Count of Romagna. His favourite nephew, by his sister's side, Latino Malebranca (a Brancaleone), the Cardinal Bishop of Ostia, a powerful preacher, had great success in allaying the feuds in many of the cities,[f] even in Bologna, wearied by the long strife of the Lambertazzi and the Gieromei; wherever the Cardinal established peace, the Count of Romagna assumed authority. Himself he had declared perpetual Senator of Rome. His nephew Orso was his vicar in this great office. But these were but the first steps to the throne which Nicolas III. aspired to raise for the house of Orsini. It was believed that he had laid before the Emperor Rudolph a plan by which the Empire was to become hereditary in his house, the kingdom of Vienna was to be in Charles Martel, grandson of Charles of Anjou, the son-in-law of the Emperor. Italy was to be divided into the two kingdoms of Insubria and Tuscany, besides that of Sicily; and on these thrones were to be placed two of the house of Orsini.[g]

A sudden fit of apoplexy at his castle of Soriano cut short all these splendid designs.[h] From this   Aug. 22, 1280. Death of Nicolas III. favourite residence he had dated his Bulls, a practice which had given great offence.   The Pope

[f] Villani, b. c. 53. Villani calls Bertoldo Orsini nepote of Nicolas III.

[g] Muratori, Annal. sub ann. 1280, with authorities.

[h] Nicolas is in Dante's hell for his unmeasured nepotism —

"Sappi ch'io fui vestito del gran manto;
E veramente fui figliuol dell'Orsa,
Cupido sì per avanzar l'Orsatti,
Che su l'avere, e quì me misi in borsa."
Inferno, xix. 69.

"Poichè il sin; e ché in; ...... podeste,
E guarda ben la mal tolta moneta,
Ch'esser ti fece contra Carlo ardito."—xx.97.

was, as it were, merging himself in the stately Italian sovereign.

Charles of Anjou heard with the utmost joy the un-expected tidings of the death of his enemy Nicolas III. He instantly took measures to secure himself against the calamity of a second hostile Pope, to wrest the Pontificate from the aspiring family of the Orsini, and form an independent Italian interest.[1] The family of the Annibaldeschi rivalled that of the Orsini in wealth and power. There was a rising in Rome; the divided people had recourse to the vain step for the preservation of peace, the creation of two Senators, one out of each of the rival houses. This, as might have been expected, increased the confusion; Rome became a scene of strife, murder, anarchy. But Viterbo, where the conclave of Cardinals was assembled, was even of more importance, an Annibaldeschi was Lord of that city.[2] The people of Viterbo were won, by force or bribery, to the party of Charles. The constitution of Gregory X. was utterly forgotten; the conclave prolonged its sittings. The Pope had crowded the college with Orsinis and their dependants. The Viterbans surrounded the chamber; they accused the Orsini Cardinals as disturbing or arresting the freedom of election, dragged forth two of them, and cast them into prison. With them they seized and incarcerated Malebranca the Cardinal Bishop of Ostia: the rest were kept on the statutable bread and wine; the French Cardinals, it was said, were furtively provided with better viands. Yet the strife endured for nearly six months before the stubborn conclave would yield to the election of the Cardinal of Santa

The conclave at Viterbo.

Feb. 22, 1281.
Latino Malebranca.

---

[1] Villani, vii. c. 57.   [2] Muratori, sub ann. 1281.

Cecilia, a Frenchman, the slave and passive instrument
of Charles of Anjou.

Martin IV. was born at Mont Pencé in Brie; he had
been Canon of Tours. He put on at first the
show of maintaining the lofty character of   Martin IV.
the Churchman.   He excommunicated the Viterbans
for their sacrilegious maltreatment of the Cardinals;
Rinaldo Annibaldeschi, the Lord of Viterbo, was compelled to ask pardon on his knees of the Cardinal
Rosso, and forgiven only at the intervention of the
Pope.[a] Martin IV. retired to Orvieto.

But the Frenchman soon began to predominate over
the Pontiff; he sunk into the vassal of Charles of
Anjou. The great policy of his predecessor, to assuage
the feuds of Guelf and Ghibelline, was an Italian
policy; it was altogether abandoned. The Ghibellines
in every city were menaced or smitten with excommunication; the Lambertazzi were driven from Bologna.
Forli was placed under interdict for harbouring the
exiles; the goods of the citizens were confiscated for
the benefit of the Pope. Bertoldo Orsini was deposed
from the Countship of Romagna: the office was bestowed on John of Appia, with instructions everywhere
to coerce or to chastise the refractory Ghibellines.[b]
The Pope himself was elected Senator of Rome, in
defiance of the decree of Nicolas III.; Charles of
Anjou was his vicegerent. Nor did excommunication
confine itself to Italy; Charles was now in a state to
carry on his league for the subjugation of the Eastern
Empire, in conjunction with the exiled Latin Sovereign
and the Venetian republic. Palæologus, who had sur-

---

[a] Ptolem. Luc. xxiv. 2.

[b] " Che votò l' erario delle munichz
per fulminar tutti i Ghibellini, e
chiunque era semico o poco amico del
medraimo Rè Carlo," So scrive the
calm Muratori, p. 185.

rendered the liberties of the Greek Church to the
supremacy of Rome, who, at the command of the Pope,
had persecuted, had provoked his subjects, his kindred
to rebellion, had raised up a rival Greek Patriarch to
contest Constantinople, who had been denounced as
worse than a heretic, as an apostate, was now, because
something was yet thought wanting to his base com-
pliance, or rather because he maintained his throne in
defiance of Charles of Anjou, solemnly excommunicated
by Martin IV.* The last hope of union between the
Churches was thus cut away by the Pope's suicidal
hand; Palæologus died repudiated as a renegade by
his own Church, under the interdict of the Church of
Rome. His son Andronicus, as has been said, dissolved
the inauspicious alliance; and the Churches were again
for above two centuries in implacable oppugnancy.

Charles of Anjou, with the Pope as his obsequious
minister, might seem reinstated in more than his
former plenitude of power; he resided with the Pope
at Orvieto, as it were to dictate his counsels. Though
Martin did not yet venture to dispossess the Emperor
Rodolph of the Vicariate of Tuscany, Charles might
have been justified in the noblest hopes of his ambition
in Italy, but he was looking with more wide-grasping
predilection to the East. Under the pretext of a Crusade to the Holy Land, he was aspiring to add Constantinople to his realm.

* This passionate and partial excommunication shocked his own age. From
the date of this act, writes Ptolemy of Lucca, all went wrong with Charles
and the Church. See back, 413.

CHAPTER V.

Sicilian Vespers.

BUT a mine had long been working under his throne, which in the next year burst with all the suddenness and terror of one of his kingdom's volcanoes. While he contemplated the sovereignty of the East, Sicily was lost to his house. Around one man has gathered all the glory of this signal revolution; John of Procida has been handed down as almost the sole author of the expulsion of the French, and the translation of the crown of Sicily to the house of Arragon: Peter of Arragon, the Emperor Palæologus, Nicolas III., the revolted Barons of Sicily were but instruments wielded by his strong will, brought into close alliance through negotiations conducted by him alone; excited, sustained, guided by his ubiquitous presence. Even the Vespers of Palermo were attributed to his secret instigation. John of Procida perhaps achieved not all which is ascribed to him alone; in the vast system of secret agency he was not the sole mover; much which was traced to his suggestion arose out of natural passions, resentment, revenge, ambition, interest, patriotism, love of power and glory in those who conspired to this memorable work. A fatal revelation, but too trustworthy, shows John of Procida in his early career (he had been already physician to Frederick II. and to Conrad, and confidential counsellor of Manfred) as basely abandoning the cause

of the fallen Manfred, crouching at the feet of the Pope
at Viterbo, protesting that he had only bowed beneath
the storm of Manfred's tyranny; he was commended to
the mercy of Charles of Anjou by the Pope, as his
beloved son, as the future faithful servant of King
Charles. How far he was admitted to favour appears
not, but three years after he is involved in a charge of
high treason, and flies from Naples. But however base
instead of noble, revenge disappointed treachery and
ambition are hardly less strong and obstinate motives
to action than generous indignation at tyranny, and
holy love of country.[a]

In all the conspiracy, a conspiracy of thoughts,
feelings, passions, if not of compacts and treaties, the
most fatal to Charles was the insupportable,
unexampled, acknowledged tyranny of the
French dominion.[b] Sicily had groaned and bled under
the cruel despotism of the Emperor Henry; the German rudeness aggravated the harshness of his rule.
Frederick II., as also his son, had been severe, though
just; if his fiscal regulations were oppressive, they
were repaid by the brilliancy of his court, by his wise
laws, by noble foundations, by the national pride in
beholding Naples and Sicily the most civilised kingdom
in the world. Charles and his French and Provençal
nobles, with the haughtiness and cruelty of foreign
rulers, indulged without restraint those outrages which
gall to madness. Charles from the first treated the
realm as a conquered land; after the insurrection in

(marginal note: Tyranny of the French.)

---

[a] See the document among the
Pièces justificatives in Cherrier, iv. 524.
from a copy in the Royal Library at
Paris. Compare Amari's preface and
document first edit, iv., Florence, 1851;

St. Priest, Histoire de la Conquête de
Naples, Paris, 1847.

[b] "Sub tyrannica turbine tem-
pestatis."

favour of Conradin, as a revolted kingdom. The insurgents, or reputed insurgents, were hunted down, torn from their families: happy if only put to a violent death![b] To the exactions of Charles there were no limits. The great fiefs seized, confiscated on the slightest suspicion of disaffection, were granted to French nobles; the foreign soldiers lived at free quarters; they were executioners commissioned to punish a rebellious race. To all complaints of cruelty, outrage, extortion, Charles replied with a haughty scoff, as though it were fit treatment for the impious rebels against himself and the Pope. The laws, severe enough before, were aggravated by still more sanguinary enactments, and by their execution with refined mercilessness. But there were worse cruelties than these; those women only were safe who, being heiresses, were compelled to marry French nobles; of these there was a regular register; of all others the honour was at the mercy of those who in this respect knew no mercy: there was no redress, no pity; it might seem as if Sicilian women were thought honoured by being defiled by French and Provençal brutality.[c] Over this tyranny, which himself had inflicted on this beautiful land, Clement IV. had groaned in bitter remorse. Charles in his impartial rapacity spared not the property of the Church; if in his cruelty he respected the sacred persons of ecclesiastics, he taxed even the Templars and Knights of St. John. The Pope had sent remonstrances, embassies, to warn, to threaten, but in

[b] Amari, c. iii., for a full account of these horrors, with his authorities.

[c] See these enactments, quoted in Amari. On the forced marriages, p. 61. His fourth chapter we read with a revulsive shudder, and would fain disbelieve; but the industry of Amari has been too searching, his facts and documents are too strong even for charitable palliation.

vain.* He had entreated the intervention of the holy
Louis. Gregory X. menaced that for the tyrannies of the
same kind which Charles exercised in Tuscany the wrath
of God would fall on such a tyrant. "I know not,"
answered Charles, "what that word tyrant means; this
I know, that so far I have been protected by God; I
doubt not that he will still protect me." The Archbishop of Capua denounced him at the Council of
Lyons; he laughed to scorn the complaints of the Prelates, the Legates of the Council, the letters of the
Pope to Philip of France. In Sicily all the abuses of
the government were felt in their extreme weight.
Naples was the residence of the court, and derived
some glory or advantage from its splendour; Palermo
sank to a provincial town, Sicily to a province. The
Parliament had fallen into desuetude; it was an iron
reign of force without justice, without law, without
humanity, without mercy, without regard to morality,
without consideration of any one of the rights, or of the
interests or the welfare of mankind.

The race of Sicily's old kings was not utterly extinct.
In Constance, the daughter of Manfred, the
wife of Peter of Arragon, lingered the last
drops of Swabian blood: it was said that on the scaffold
Conradin had cast down his glove, to be borne to the
King of Arragon, as the heir of his rights, the avenger
of his death. To the court of the King of Arragon had
fled those Sicilians of the Swabian party who had the
good fortune to become exiles—among these three of
great name, Roger Loria, Conrad Lancia, John of
Procida. John of Procida was an exile soon after the

* See two letters especially, in Raynaldus, 1267; also in Martene and
Durand, Thes. Nov. Anecd. ii. 530, 537, &c.

failure and death of Conradin. His hatred to the French
is said to have been deepened by the worst outrage,
perpetrated on his wife and his daughter. Existing
grants to his wife Landolfina intimate that she was
under the protection of some powerful influence, not
improbably of a French paramour.[f] John of Procida
was born at Salerno; though a noble, he was profoundly skilled, as in other learning, in the science of
his native city, that of medicine. He rose in the favour
of Peter of Arragon, became his bosom counsellor, was
endowed with lands, the lands of Luxen, Benezzano,
and Palma, in the kingdom of Valencia; he was a
Valencian noble.[g]

Peter of Arragon, with his court and his confidential
council, thus occupied by Sicilian exiles, who   Peter of
were constantly urging upon him the odious   Arragon.
tyranny of Charles the usurper, and the discontent, disaffection, despair of the Sicilians; with his Queen not
likely to forget her own hereditary claims, or the wrongs
of her noble father Manfred and his ancient house; lord
but of his own narrow kingdom hardly won from the
Moors, and held, as it were, in a joint sovereignty with
his Nobles, was not likely to avert his eyes from the
prospect of a greater monarchy, which expanded before
him. He had made treaties of peace with the rival
Kings his neighbours, a treaty for five years with the
King of Granada, a league with Castile; and over King
Sancho of Castile he held the menace of letting loose
the two young princes, nearer to the throne than
Sancho, and resident at the court of Arragon.[b] He kept
up friendly relations with Philip of France, the husband

[f] Amari, note, p. 82.   [g] See Amari's note, p. 81.
[b] Montaner, c. 40, 45; in Buchon, Collection des Mémoires, D'Esclot, c. 76.

of his sister; he even made advances to Charles of
Anjou; there was a proposal of marriage between his
son and the daughter of Charles. Peter was embarked
in suspicious negotiations with the Saracens in Tunis.[1]
At the same time he was making great preparations for
war; in his arsenals in Valencia, Tortosa, and Barcelona
was gathering a powerful fleet; his subjects granted
subsidies; provisions, stores, arms, accontrements of
war were accumulated as for some momentous design.
How far John of Procida instigated these designs, or
only encouraged the profound ambition of the King for
dominion, of the Queen for revenge for her injured
house, none can know: nor how far Procida acted from
his own intense patriotism or revenge, or but as an
instrument in the hand of others.

There can be no doubt that there was a secret understanding, that there was direct communication between
the enemies of Charles, the Emperor of the East, Pope

John of
Procida.

Nicolas III., the King of Arragon, perhaps the
Sicilian nobles, Alaimo de Lentini and his
colleagues: Procida may have been, no doubt was, one
of the chief of those agents;[2] if not actually commissioned, tacitly recognised. He was once, if not twice,
at the court of Constantinople. There he needed not to
rouse the fears and jealousy of Palæologus; the designs
of Charles against the Eastern Empire were, if not
avowed, but half disguised. Charles was the open ally
of Philip, the Latin claimant of the Empire. Palæolo-

---

[1] Amari, p. 80, with his notes.

[2] Amari is inclined to treat as romance this primary organisation of the
whole confederacy by John of Procida;
his ubiquitous agency; his disguises;
especially his frequent intercourse with
the Sicilian nobles. But there seems a

great difficulty as to the growth of this
romance, and this elevation of Procida
into the sole hero of the war and the
great deliverer, after his apostasy from
the cause of Arragon, and after he had
incurred the hatred of the Arragonese
party.

gus might well enter into correspondence, or admit to a
secret interview, the bosom counsellor of King Peter of
Arragon. To Procida Palæologus may have entrusted
his secret offers of large sums of money for the Pope,
the hundred thousand byzantines, not to detach him
from the interests of Charles of Anjou, against whom he
had already taken hostile measures, but to enable him
to defy the power of the Angevine.* Procida, according
to the common account—an account contradicted only
by the silence of other writers—left Constantinople, pretending to be driven away by the Emperor; he disguised
himself as a Mendicant Friar, reached Malta, landed
in Sicily, had frequent interviews with the disaffected
nobles, Walter of Caltagirone, Palmerio Abbate, Alaimo
da Lentini. From them he obtained an invitation to
Peter of Arragon to advance his claims to the inheritance of his wife. In the friar's garb he made his way to
Nicolas III. in Soriano, revealed himself to the Holy
Father, explained the extent, the success of his negotiations; laid the treasures of Palæologus at his feet.
Nicolas consented to recognise the claims of Peter of
Arragon, and by letters of the most profound secrecy
promised him the investiture of the realm. Procida
appeared at Barcelona with these animating tidings to
rekindle the somewhat slumbering ambition of the
King. The warlike preparations were urged with
greater activity. Procida set forth on a second mission:
he landed at Pisa; at Viterbo he saw the Pope; at
Trapani conferred with the Sicilian nobles; passed to
Negropont undiscovered, reached Constantinople. He
was welcomed by the Emperor; negotiations were com-

---

* " E guarda ben in mal tolta moneta,
Ch' oggue ti fann contra Carlo ardito."
Dante, *Inf.* xix. 99.

Amari's new interpretation of this verse is to me quite unsatisfactory.

menced for an alliance by marriage between the courts
of Arragon and Constantinople. Accardo, a Lombard
knight, was secretly despatched by the Emperor to the
court of Peter with thirty thousand ounces of gold.
Procida embarked on board a ship of Pisa, Accardo was
concealed in the ship. At Malta they met the Sicilian
conspirators, with the news of the death of Nicolas III.
The Sicilians would have abandoned the hopeless enterprise; Procida reinvigorated them by the introduction
of Accardo, and the sight of the Byzantine gold. All
Procida's eloquence, all his ability, it is said, but very
improbably, was needed to dissuade the King of Arragon
from the abandonment of the hopeless enterprise. Again
the plan was fully organised; the manner, the time of
the insurrection arranged.*

It is certain that the warlike preparations of the King
of Arragon had not escaped the jealous observation of
Charles of Anjou; he could not but know the claims,
the wrongs, of the Queen of Peter of Arragon and the
stern, reserved, ambitious character of Peter; perhaps
he had obtained some clue to the great league which
was secretly forming against him. The vague rumours
industriously propagated of designs against the Saracens
of Africa by Peter of Arragon, however at other times
they might have justified vast and secret armaments,
could not blind the Angevine's keen apprehensions.
Charles had himself demanded explanations. Among
the first acts of Martin IV. was to require, through
Philip of France, and from Peter himself directly, the
scope and object of these menacing preparations: if
they were against the infidels, he offered his sanction,

---

* The sons of Manfred were living, but in prison, from whence they never
came forth.

his prayers, his contributions. Peter baffled his inquiries
with his dexterous but inflexible reply. He implored
the prayers of the Pope on his design; "but if he
thought his right hand knew his secret, he would cut it
off, lest it should betray it to his left."

Charles, on his part, had been making great preparations; he had a large fleet in the ports of Sicily and
Naples; a powerful land force was assembled for embarkation. He had increased the burthens of the kingdom to provide this army, compelled the Sicilian nobles
to furnish vessels; and he was as little disposed to dis-
close his own secret objects as the King of Arragon.
The ostensible object was the deliverance of the Holy
Land; the immediate one the subjugation of the Greek
Empire. These forces were still in the garrisons and
towns of Sicily. Forty-two castles had been built, either
in the strongest positions, or to command the great
cities, and were held by French feudatories. They were
provided with arms, and could summon at an instant's
notice all their French sub-feudatories, or the Sicilians
on whom they could depend for aid. Heribert of
Orleans, the King's Lieutenant, was in Messina; in
Palermo, John di San Remi, the Justiciary of the Val di
Mazzara.

At this juncture the crisis was precipitated by one of
those events which no sagacity could have
foreseen,* which all the ubiquitous activity
ascribed to John of Procida could not have devised—
an outburst of popular fury excited by one of those acts
of insulting tyranny which goad an oppressed people to

---

* Amari, c. v. p. 89. "Le trame
col Ghibellini e con alcuni Baroni di
Napoli o di Sicilia, non al presente
ormai rivocare in dubbio. Falso è che
la pratica, si strettamente condotta,
fosse a punto rimessa a produrre lo
scoppio del Vespro." I fully subscribe
to this latter class.

madness. The insurrection of Palermo received the darkly famous name of the "Sicilian Vespers."

The Sicilians still crowded to their religious festivals with all the gaiety and light-heartedness of a southern people. Even their churches, where they assembled for the worship of that God whose representative on earth had handed them over to their ruthless tyrant, where alone they found consolation under the grinding tyranny, were not secure against the all-present agents of that tyranny. The officers of the revenue watched the doors of the churches: as all who had not paid their taxes went in or came forth, even from within the sanctuary itself they dragged off their miserable victims, whom they branded with the name of heretics—"Pay, ye Paterins, pay!"

It was at a festival on Easter Tuesday that a multitude of the inhabitants of Palermo and the neighbourhood had thronged to a church, about half a mile out of the town, dedicated to the Holy Ghost. The religious service was over, the merriment begun; tables were spread, the amusements of all sorts, games, dances under the trees, were going gaily on; when the harmony was suddenly interrupted, and the joyousness chilled by the appearance of a body of French soldiery, under the pretext of keeping the peace. The French mingled familiarly with the people, paid court, not in the most respectful manner, to the women; the young men made sullen remonstrances, and told them to go their way. The Frenchmen began to draw together. "These rebellious Paterins must have arms, or they would not venture on such insolence." They began to search some of them for arms. The two parties were already glaring at each other in angry hostility. At that moment the beautiful daughter of Roger Mas-

March 31.

trangelo, a maiden of exquisite loveliness and modesty, with her bridegroom, approached the church. A Frenchman named Drouet, either in wantonness or insult, came up to her, and under the pretence of searching for arms, thrust his hand into her bosom. The girl fainted in her bridegroom's arms. He uttered in his agony the fatal cry, "Death to the French!" A youth rushed forward, stabbed Drouet to the heart with his own sword, was himself struck down. The cry, the shriek, ran through the crowd, "Death to the French!" Many Sicilians fell, but of two hundred on the spot, not one Frenchman escaped. The cry spread to the city: Mastrangelo took the lead; every house was stormed, every hole and corner searched; their dress, their speech, their persons, their manners denounced the French. The palace was forced; the Justiciary, being luckily wounded in the face, and rolled in the dust, and so undetected, mounted a horse, and fled with two followers. Two thousand French were slain. They denied them decent burial, heaped them together in a great pit. The horrors of the scene were indescribable: the insurgents broke into the convents, the churches. The friars, especial objects of hatred, were massacred; they slew the French monks, the French priests. Neither old age, nor sex, nor infancy, was spared; it is a charge more than once repeated in the Papal acts, that they ripped up Sicilian women who were pregnant by Frenchmen, in order to exterminate the hated brood. A government was hastily formed; Roger Mastrangelo, Arrigo Barresi, Niccoloso d'Ortoleva (knights), with Niccolo de Ebdemonia were summoned by acclamation to be Captains of the people. They then proclaimed the "Good estate and liberty," unfolded the banner of the city, an eagle on a field of gold; the keys of the Church were still quartered upon it.

The Justiciary was pursued to Vicari, thirty miles
distant; the people rose at the cry of "Death
to the French!"[p] The garrison at first refused to capitulate, and to be sent safe to Provence; it
was now too late, the Justiciary was shot down by a
random arrow, every Frenchman massacred. Sicily
was everywhere in arms; Corleone first followed the
example of Palermo. Everywhere the French were
hunted down and murdered. One man alone was
spared. William Porcelet, Governor of Calatafimi, who
had ruled with justice and humanity, was, by common
consent, sent safe on board ship by the Palermitans,
and returned to Provence. In Messina was the strength
of the French force, under the Viceroy, Heribert of
Orleans. Messina rose. Heribert was compelled to
submit to terms; he swore to transport himself and all
his soldiers to Aigues Mortes, in Provence. He broke
his oath, and landed in Calabria; the Messinese revenged his perjury on every Frenchman who was left
behind. In one month, that of April, Sicily was free;
the French had disappeared.

Such was the revolution which bears in history the
appalling name of the Sicilian Vespers, sudden, popular,
reckless, sanguinary, so as to appear the unpremeditated
explosion of a people goaded to phrensy by intolerable
oppression; yet general, simultaneous, orderly, so as to
imply, if not some previous organisation, some slow and
secret preparation of the public mind. John of Procida, the barons in league with John of Procida, appear
not during the first outburst; the fleets of Peter of
Arragon are yet within their harbours. The towns take

---

[p] Moriam le Francese! In this account I am quite with Amari against
Mon. de St. Privat, who cannot forget to be a Frenchman.—See Amari's authorities, p. 103, and Appendix.

the lead: they assert their own independence, and form
a league for mutual defence. Acts are dated as under
the rule of the Church and the Republic. The Church
is everywhere respected; it might seem as if the Sicilians
supposed Nicolas III. still on the Pontifical throne, or
that they would not believe that the Pope was so servile
an adherent of the Angevine. They were soon dis-
abused. When Charles first heard of the
revolt, of the total loss of Sicily, and the massacre of at least two thousand Frenchmen, he lifted
his eyes to Heaven in devout prayer: "O Lord God, if
it hath pleased thee to visit me with adverse fortune,
grant at least that it may come with gentle steps."[1]
As though he had satisfied his religion by this one stern
act of humility, no sooner had he reached Naples than
he burst into the most furious paroxysms of wrath.
Now he sat silent, glaring fiercely around him, gnawing
the top of his sceptre; then broke forth into the most
horrible vows of vengeance: "if he could live a thousand years, he would go on razing the cities, burning
the lands, torturing the rebellious slaves. He would
leave Sicily a blasted, barren, uninhabited rock, as a
warning to the present age, an example to the future."
Pope Martin, less violent in his demeanour, was hardly
less so in his public acts. The Palermitans sent an
embassy declaring their humble submission to the Papal
See. The messengers were monks. They addressed
the Pope—"O Lamb of God, that takest away the sins
of the world, have mercy upon us!" Martin compared
them to the Jews, who smote the Saviour, and cried
"Hail, King of the Jews."[2] His Bull of excommunication describes in the blackest terms the horrors

Conduct of Charles of Anjou

---

[1] Villani, vii. 71.   [2] Ibid, 62.

of the massacre." A crusade was proclaimed against
the Sicilians: all ecclesiastics, archbishops, bishops,
abbots, who favoured the insurgents, were at once deprived and deposed; all laymen stripped of their fiefs
or estates. The people of Palermo sternly replied, that
"they had unfolded the banner of St. Peter, in hopes,
under that protection, to obtain their liberties; they
must now unfold the banner of another Peter, the King
of Arragon." [1]

Charles made the most vigorous preparations for war.
The age and state of the public mind are singularly illustrated by the following story: a
Mendicant Friar, Bartolomeo Piazza, appeared in his
camp, a man of blameless morals and some learning; he
disdained the disguise of a spy. He was led before the
King. "How darest thou," Charles abruptly accosted
him, "come from that land of traitors?" "Neither am
I a traitor, nor come I from a land of traitors. I come,
urged by religion and conscience, to warn my holy
brethren that they follow not your unjust arms. You
have abandoned the people committed by God to your
charge to be torn by wolves and hounds; you have
hardened your heart against complaints and supplica-
tions; they have avenged their wrongs, they will
defend, they will die for, their holiest rights. Think of
Pharaoh!" Either awe, or the notion that Bartolomeo
would bear back a true account of his overwhelming
forces, induced the King to endure this affront; the
Friar returned to Messina. [2]

Before Messina appeared Charles with all his army,
burning for revenge. At first he obtained some suc-

<hr>

[1] Saba Malaspina. The Bull in
Raynald, sub ann. 1282.

[2] Compare Amari, Documento 1. a long oration, assuredly made after the time.

[3] Bartolom. de Neocastro, cap. 33, 34.

ceases; but the popular leader, Manfrone, was deposed, the Noble Alaimo da Lentini placed at the head of the garrison. The resistance became obstinate. The women were most active, as perhaps most exposed to the vengeance of the French. Their delicate hands bore stones, ammunition; they tended the sick and wounded.[*] The Legate of the Pope, the Cardinal Gerard, accompanied the King; he was armed with the amplest powers. He demanded, or was invited to enter the city. He was received with general jubilation, and escorted to the Cathedral; Alaimo da Lentini laid at his feet the keys of the city and his own staff of command. They entreated him to accept the dominion of the city in the name of the Church, to appoint a governor: "to the Church they would willingly pay their tribute, but away with the French! in the name of God let them be driven from the lands of the Church!" Gerard replied, if not in the fierce and criminatory tone ascribed to him by one historian as to insolent rebels, yet with a haughty condescension.[*] "Heinous as were their sins, they were not beyond the mercy of their mother the Church; he would reconcile the Messinese to their King; subjects must not speak of terms to their sovereign. Let them trust the magnanimity, the clemency of Charles; the savage murderers alone would meet with condign punishment. Let Messina lay herself in the lap of the Church; in her name to be restored to King Charles." "To Charles! Never!" shouted Alaimo; he seized his staff from the hand of the astonished Prelate. "To the French, never! so

margin note: Charles before Messina.

* "Deh cum' egli è gran pietate,
    Delle donne de Messina,
    Vegurudole sempligliate,
    Portando pretia e carina.
    Iddio gli dia briga a travagtia,
    A chi Messina vuol guastar."

—Popular song, quoted by Villani, cii. 77.

f Neocastro, Villani, Malaspina, &c.

2 F 2

long as we have blood to shed and swords to wield."
The whole people took up the cry; Gerard made one
more effort: thirty citizens were appointed to treat with
the Legate; but all was in vain. They knew too well
the mercy of Charles. "O, candid counsel of the Church
to lay our necks down before the headsman! We are
sold to the French; we must ransom ourselves by arms.
We offer to the Pope the sovereignty of the land:
Martin declines it. Instead of being the mild and
gentle Vicar of Christ, he is but the tool of the French.
Go and tell the Angevine tyrant that lions and foxes
shall never more enter into Messina."

In the mean time, the fleets of Peter of Arragon were
Peter of Arragon. upon the seas; still disguising his aim, as if he
June 3. designed to make war only on the Saracens of
June 29. Africa, he landed his forces on the coast of
Tunis. He appeared as the ally of the Prince
of Constantina. He disembarked in the Port of Collo:
he had some vigorous engagements with the Saracens.[1]
He despatched ambassadors to Rome to implore the
blessing of the Pope on his Crusade against the infidels,
the protection of the Church for his dominions in Spain,
the presence of a Legate, the right to levy the tenths
for a war against the infidels. This specious embassage
was received with specious civility by the Pope at Monte
Fiascone.

The Parliament had met at Palermo; it had been
King of Sicily. determined to offer the throne of Sicily to
Peter. He received the ambassadors of the
Sicilians with grave solemnity; as offering to him unex-
pected, unsolicited honours. The Holy War was at an
end; Peter and his fleet in the port of Trapani. At

Palermo he was saluted by acclamation King of Sicily.
The relief of Messina was the first aim of the
new King.   He ordered a general levy of all   Aug. 30.
who could bear arms: men crowded to his banner.   To
Charles he sent an embassy of the noble Catalonians,
Pietro Queralto, Ruy Ximenes de Luna, William Ay-
meric, Justiciary of Barcelona.   He demanded safe-
conduct by two Carmelite Friars.   In two days Charles
declared that he would give them audience ;
two days—during which he hoped to find him-   Sept. 11.
self master of Messina.   But his terrific assault by sea
and land was repelled ; instead of receiving the ambassadors of the King of Arragon as a haughty conqueror,
he received them weary with toil, boiling with rage and
baffled pride.   He was seated on his bed, which was
covered with rich silk drapery.   He threw disdainfully
aside on his pillow the letter of the King of Arragon:
he awaited the address of the ambassador Queralto.
Queralto's words were doubtless those of the letter, they
ran thus: "The illustrious Peter, King, by the grace of
God, of Arragon and Sicily, commands you, Charles,
Count of Provence and King of Jerusalem, to depart
from his kingdom; to give him free passage into his
city of Messina, which you are besieging by sea and
land; he is astonished at your presumption in impeding
the passage of the King through his own dominions." *
The ambassadors no doubt asserted the here-   Ambassadors
ditary claim of the King of Arragon.   Charles,   to Charles.
with the gesture constantly ascribed to him, bit his
sceptre in his wrath ; his reply had his usual pride, but,
by one account, something of dejection.   He told the
ambassadors to survey his vast forces; he expressed

* See, in Amari, the variations in the copies of this letter, p. 166, note.

utter astonishment that the King of Arragon should presume to interfere between him and his rebellious subjects; he held Naples and Sicily as a grant from the Pope; but he intimated that he might withdraw his weary troops to refresh them in Calabria: it would only, however, be to return and wreak his vengeance on Sicily; the Catalonian dominions of the King of Arragon would not be safe from his resentment.

From this period the mind of Charles, never strong, but so insolent and tyrannical in prosperity, sunk into a strange prostration, in which fits of an absurd chivalry alternated with utter abjectness. He would neither press vigorously, nor abandon the siege of Messina. Now he wreaked his vengeance on all the lands in his possession, burned churches and monasteries; now offered advantageous terms to the Sicilians; now endeavoured openly to bribe Alaimo da Lentini, who cast back his offers with public scorn. At length, threatened by the fleets of Arragon, he withdrew to his continental dominions.

The climax of this strange state of mind was his challenge to the King of Arragon, to determine their quarrel by single combat. In vain the Pope denounced the impiety, and remonstrated against the wild impolicy of this feudal usage, now falling into desuetude. The King of Arragon leaped at the proposition, which he could so easily elude; and which left him full time to consolidate undisturbed his new kingdom, to invade Calabria, to cover the sea with his fleets. This defiance to mortal combat, this wager of battle, was an appeal, according to the wild justice of the age, to the God of Battles, who, it was an established popular belief, would declare himself on the righteous side. Charles of Anjou had the opportunity of publicly arraigning before Chris-

tendom his hated rival of disloyal treachery, of secret
leaguing with his revolted subjects, of falsehood in his
protestations of friendship. The King of Arragon stood
forth on the broad ground of asserting his hereditary
right, of appearing as the deliverer of a people most
barbarously oppressed, as summoned to the crown by
the barons and people of Sicily. He was almost
admitted as possessing an equal claim with him who
had received the Papal investiture. The grave and
serious manner in which the time, the place, the manner
of holding those lists were discussed might seem to
portend a tragic close; this great ordeal would be commended to still greater honour and acceptance by the
strife of two monarchs for one of the noblest kingdoms
of the earth, the kingdom of Naples. Italy itself offered
no fair or secure field. The King of England, Edward I.,
was the one powerful and impartial monarch, who might
preside as umpire; his Gascon territories, a neutral
ground, on which might be waged this momentous combat. All proceeded with the most serious and solemn
dignity, as if there could be no doubt that the challenge
so given, so accepted, would come to direct and inevitable issue. Bordeaux was chosen as the scene of the
kingly tournament. The lists were prepared at great
cost and with great splendour. Each King proceeded
to enrol the hundred knights who were to have the
honour of joining in this glorious conflict with their
monarch. The noblest and bravest chivalry of France
offered themselves to Charles of Anjou; his nephew,
Philip the Hardy, offered to enter the lists with him.
On the side of Peter of Arragon were the most valiant
Spanish knights, men accustomed to joust with the Moor,
to meet the champions of the Crescent from Cordova or
Granada. A Moorish Prince presented himself; if God

gave the victory to Peter, not only would the Moor
share the triumph, but submit to baptism in the name
of the Christian's God. The Pope was over-
borne; the Church had pronounced its condemnation on judicial combats. Martin had
condemned this on general grounds[b] and on the special
objection, that it was setting on the issue of arms that
which had already been solemnly adjudged by the
supreme Pontiff; it was to call in question the Pope's
right of granting the kingdom of Naples. He commanded Charles to desist from the humiliating comparison of himself and his heaven-sanctioned claims, with
those of a presumptuous adventurer, of one already
under the censure, under the excommunication of the
Roman See; he offered to absolve the King from all his
oaths: yet even on this point the Pope was compelled to
yield his reluctant consent to the imperious will of his
master.

The wrath of the Pope on the first intelligence of the
insurrection, still more at the invasion of the realm by
Peter of Arragon, had been hardly less violent than that
of Charles of Anjou. At Orvieto he proclaimed more
than the excommunication, the degradation of
Peter. He denounced again the crime of the
Palermitans in the massacre of the French;
the impious rebellion of the realm of Sicily; he boasted
the mild attempts of the Church, especially through
Cardinal Gerard in Messina, to reconcile them to their
lawful Sovereign. "Since Peter, King of Arragon,
under the false colour of an expedition to Africa, has
invaded the island of Sicily—the peculiar territory of

---

[b] Martin writes to King Edward of England that he had power " impedimenti
tam detentanda tam activa."—MS., B. N., vol. xiv. Orvieto, April 15, 1284.

the Roman Church—with horse and foot; has set up
the claim of his wife, the daughter of the accursed Manfred, to the throne; has usurped the name of King of
Sicily; [c] has openly countenanced the Messinese as he
before secretly instigated the Palermitans to rebel
against their Sovereign: he has incurred the severest
penalties, of usurpation, sedition, and violence. His
crime is aggravated by the relation of the crown of
Arragon to the See of Rome. That crown was granted
by the Pope; his grandfather, Peter of Arragon, received
it from the Pope, and swore fealty in his own name and
in that of his successors to the successor of St. Peter."
The King was now not only in rebellion; he had practised an impious fraud on his holy Father; he had
implored the aid of the Pope, his blessing on his army,
as though designed against the African barbarians.
For these reasons not only was Peter adjudged a lawless
usurper of the realm of Sicily, but deposed from his
kingdom of Arragon; his subjects were discharged from
all their oaths of fealty. His kingdom was to be seized
and occupied by any Catholic Sovereign, who should be
duly commissioned to that end by the Pope. The Cardinal of St. Cecilia was sent into France to offer the
forfeited throne of Arragon to any one of the King's
sons who would undertake the conquest: the only provision was the exclusion of the heir to the French
throne: the two kingdoms could not be united under
the same Sovereign. The subjugated realm was to be
held of Pope Martin and his successors in the Apostolic

---

[c] The Pope seems here to charge
Peter of Arragon with being the prime
mover of the rebellion. " Sicque non
solum Panormitanos ecclesiam, quos alias
pluries ad hæc solicitasse per nuncios
dicebatur, in inchoata contra p. a fatum
regem seditionis et rebellionis contu-
macià obfirmavit," &c. &c.—Raynald.
1283, xls.

See. The forfeiture comprehended the whole dominions of Peter, the kingdom of Arragon, the kingdom of Valencia, Catalonia, and Barcelona.

The wager of battle between the Kings, which

Wager of battle. maintained its solemn dignity up almost to the appointed time, ended in a pitiful comedy, in which Charles of Anjou had the ignominy of practising base and disloyal designs against his adversary; Peter, that of eluding the contest by craft, justifiable only as his mistrust of his adversary was well or ill grounded, but much too cunning for a frank and generous knight. He had embarked with his knights for the South of France; he was cast back by tempests on the shores of Spain. He set off with some of his armed com-

Peter at Bordeaux. panions, crossed the Pyrenees undiscovered, appeared before the gates of Bordeaux, and summoned the English Seneschal. To him he proclaimed himself to be the King of Arragon, demanded to see the lists, rode down them in slow state, obtained

May 31. an attestation that he had made his appearance within the covenanted time, and affixed his solemn protest against the palpable premeditated treachery of his rival, which made it unsafe for him to remain longer at Bordeaux. Charles, on his part, was furious that Peter had thus broken through the spider's web of his policy. He was in Bordeaux, when Peter appeared under the walls, and had challenged him in vain. Charles presented himself in full armour on the appointed day, summoned Peter to appear, proclaimed him a recreant and a dastardly craven, unworthy of the name of knight.

Pope Martin's enmity was as indefatigable as the ambition of Peter of Arragon. He strained his utmost power to break off a marriage proposed between Alfonso,

the elder son of Peter, with Eleonora, the daughter of
Edward of England. He expostulated with Edward on
the degradation of allying his illustrious house with
that of an excommunicated prince; he inhibited the
marriage as within the fourth degree of consanguinity.
By enormous charges on the Papal treasury he bought
off the Venetians from a treaty, which would have
placed their fleet on the enemy's side.[d] He borrowed
still larger sums on the security of the Papal revenues,
above 28,393 ounces of gold: the tenths decreed by the
Council of Lyons were awarded to this new Crusade.
The annual payment of 8000 ounces of gold for the
kingdom of Naples was postponed, on account of the
inability of the Prince of Salerno to discharge the debt.
Thrice in the following year, on Holy Thurs-
day, on Ascension Day, on the Dedication of   A.D. 1283
St. Peter's church, the excommunication was promulgated at Orvieto, in Rome, in every city in Italy which
would admit this display of Papal authority. The
Cardinal Gerard, of S. Sabina, was commissioned to
preach everywhere the Crusade: he might offer unlimited indulgences to all who would take up arms
against Peter and the Sicilian rebels. The kingdom of
Arragon, with the county of Barcelona and the kingdom
of Valencia were solemnly adjudged to Charles of Valois,
the son of the King of France. Great forces were prepared in France to invade these Spanish realms of
Peter. But in the mean time, Martin himself might
tremble in his dominions. Guido of Montefeltro was
in arms, hardly kept in check by John of Epps, the
Papal General. At Rome were threatening commo-

<hr>

[d] Five thousand ounces of gold, which were likewise to hire and man
twenty galleys for the fleet of Charles.

tions: the Pope endeavoured to maintain his influence
by the purchase of corn in great quantities in Apulia
during a famine, its free or cheap distribution, and by
other concessions. But the King of Arragon was not
without his secret allies within the city.

Worse than this, Charles of Anjou returned to Italy;
he was met by the disastrous tidings of the utter destruction of his fleet by Roger Loria, and the capture of
his son Charles, Prince of Salerno. This precious
hostage was in the power of his enemies; on him they
might wreak their vengeance for the death of the young
Conradin. Charles put on a haughty equanimity: "I
had rather have heard of his death than of his captivity." He overwrought this proud endurance. He
assembled the nobles; he enjoined them to rejoice with
him that he had lost a priest, who had only impeded the
vigour and success of his arms.[*] He entered Naples,
and declared it mercy that he impaled only one out of
a hundred and fifty, who were suspected or accused of
tampering with the victorious Arragonese.

But his arms were to be arrested by a mightier power.
One fatal year was to witness the death of all the great
personages engaged in this conflict; it was to be bequeathed to a new generation of combatants. In the
midst of his preparations for a more determined invasion
of Sicily, Charles, exhausted by disappointment and sorrow, died at Foggia: the Papal writers aver
he made a most Christian end. Philip of
France, after a doubtful campaign in Catalonia, for the
conquest of the Spanish dominions of Peter of
Arragon, in behalf of his brother, Charles of Valois, died at Perpignan: Peter of Arragon about a month

Feb. 7, 1345.

Oct. 5.

Nov. 11.

---

[*] Ptolem. Luc. xiv. 8. Compare throughout Raynaldus, and Muratori,
Annal. sub annis, with their authorities.

later at Villa Franca di Penades. Alfonso, the elder son, quietly succeeded to his father's Arragonese crown; the infant James, according to his father's will, to that of Sicily. On the 29th of March before had died at Orvieto Pope Martin IV., who had emptied the whole armoury of excommunication against the enemies of Charles of Anjou.[f] Such was the issue of all the interdicts, the anathemas, the crusades, and all the blood shed to determine the possession of the throne of Sicily.

There was now no commanding interest to contest the Pontificate. The Emperor Rodolph did not busy himself much in Italian politics. A Roman Prelate, John Boccamuzza, Archbishop of Monreale, Cardinal Bishop of Tusculum, resided as Legate in Germany; he presided over a Council at Wurtzburg, in the presence of the Emperor Rodolph. A chronicler of the times compares him with the Dragon in the Revelations, dragging his venomous tail (a host of corrupt Bishops) through Germany, which he contaminated with his simoniac perversity, amassing riches from all quarters, selling privileges, which he instantly revoked to sell them again, bartering with utter shamelessness the patrimony of the Crucified: he was insulted by the lofty German Prelates; he retired muttering vengeance.[g] In Italy the Angevine cause was paralysed by the death of Charles, and the imprisonment of his son. The house of Arragon had no footing in the conclave. Under such circumstances the great families of Rome had usually some Prelate of sufficient weight and character, if parties among themselves were not too equally balanced, to advance to the highest eminence in the Church.

---

[f] Muratori, sub ann. 1285.

[g] Gothofridus Vam. apud Boehmer, Fontes, ii. 111. Labbe, Concil. sub ann. 1286.

An Orsini had but now occupied the Papal throne,

Honorius IV.
April 2, 1285. then a Savelli, and then a Pope of humble birth, enslaved by a nepotism of favour, not of blood, to the family of Colonna, followed in rapid succession. The Savelli, Honorius IV., was a man of great ability, a martyr to the gout. Almost his only important acts were the publication of two Edicts, matured under his predecessor Martin, which if issued and carried out under the Angevine reign in Naples and Sicily, might perhaps have averted the revolt. One was designed to propitiate the clergy of the realm: it asserted in the highest terms their independence, immunities, freedom of election, and other privileges. The second re-enacted the laws, and professed to renew the policy of William

James
crowned
Feb. 2, 1286. the Good, the most popular monarch who had ever reigned in Sicily.[1] But they came too late. Sicily first under James, the second son of Peter of Arragon, afterwards, on the accession of James to the throne of Arragon, under Frederick, defied the Papal authority, and remained an independent kingdom. The captive Charles, now King of Naples, had framed a treaty for his own deliverance; he bought it at the price of his kingdom of Sicily and the city of Reggio. Although the Pope annulled the treaty which granted away the dominion of the Apostolic See, it was held to be of force by the contracting parties. This was the last act of Honorius IV.[1]

The Conclave met; for months, the hot summer months, they rate in strife: six of them died. The Cardinal Bishop of Præneste, by keeping a constant fire in his chamber, corrected the bad air, and maintained his vigour; the rest fled in fear. In February they met

---

[1] Raynald. sub ann. Sept. 17.   [1] He died April 3, 1287.

again: their choice fell on the Cardinal of Præneste, the General of the Franciscan Order, the first of that Order who had ascended the Papal throne. The Bishop of Præneste, born, it is said, of lowly race, at Ascoli, owed his elevation to the Cardinalate to the Orsini, Nicolas III. In gratitude to his patron he took the name of Nicolas IV. His first promotion of Cardinals, though it seemed impartially distributed among the great local and religious interests, betrayed his inclinations. There was one Dominican, Matthew Acquasparta, the General of the Order; an Orsini, Napoleon; one of the house of Colonna, Peter; there was one already of that house in the Conclave, Jacobo Colonna. On the Colonnas were heaped all the wealth and honours; under their safeguard the Pope, who at first took up his residence at Rieti, ventured to occupy the Papal palace at Rome.

The liberation of Charles the Lame, the King of Naples, from his long captivity, was the great affair of Christendom. The mediation of Edward of England, allied with the houses of Arragon and of Anjou, and now the most powerful monarch in Europe, was employed to arrange the terms of some treaty which should restore him to freedom. The King of Arragon would not surrender his captive, still in prison in Catalonia, but at the price of the recognition of the Arragonese title to the kingdom of Sicily; Charles, weary of bondage, had already at Oleron acceded to this basis of the treaty.

By the treaty of Oleron,[k] Charles was to pay fifty thousand marks of silver. He pledged himself to arrange a peace in a manner satisfactory to the Kings of Arragon and of Sicily: in the mean time

---

[k] The treaty and documents in Rymer, 1286-7.

there was to be a truce between the two realms, including
Sicily. Charles was to obtain the ratification of the
Pope, and the cession of Charles of Valois, who still
claimed, as awarded by the Pope, the crown of Arragon;
or at the close of that period he was to return into captivity. He was to surrender his three sons, and sixty
Provençal Nobles and Barons, as hostages: the Sene-
schals of the fortresses in Provence were to take an
oath that if the King did not terminate the peace or
return into bondage, they were to surrender those
fortresses to the King of Arragon. This treaty had
been annulled first during the vacancy by the College
of Cardinals, again at Rieti by Nicolas IV. The King
of England was urged to find some other means of releasing the royal captive. King Alfonso was forbidden
to aid the cause of his brother James of Sicily; in that
cause Alfonso himself had grown cool. A new treaty
was framed at Campo Franco; it was written by a Papal
notary. Charles was to pay at once twenty thousand
marks (England lent ten thousand); he was to
give security for the rest. He was to pledge
his word to the other conditions of the compact.* In
this treaty there was a vague silence concerning the
kingdom of Sicily: within one year Charles
was bound to procure peace between France
and Arragon: for this he left his three sons
as hostages; and solemnly swore that if this peace was
not ratified, he would return to his prison. He obtained
his freedom.

Oct. 20, 1288.

Liberation of Charles the Lame. Nov. 1288.

Nicolas IV. on his accession had not dared to take up
his residence at Rome; Charles appeared before him at

* Rymer, p. 368 et seq. The whole progress of the negotiation is
well and accurately traced by Amari, in a note to c. 13, p. 321.

llicti. He was crowned, if not in direct violation of the
words, of the whole spirit of the treaty, King of Naples
and Sicily; for the whole of the dominions claimed by
the house of Anjou he did homage and swore fealty to
the Pope.* The Pope boldly and without scruple annulled the treaty written by his own notary, signed,
executed without any protest on his part, by which
Charles the Lame had obtained his freedom. This
decree of Nicolas was the most monstrous exercise of
the absolving power which had ever been advanced in
the face of Christendom: it struck at the root of all
chivalrous honour, at the faith of all treaties. It declared, in fact, that no treaty was to be maintained with
any one engaged in what the Holy See might pronounce
an unjust war, that is a war contrary to her interests—a
war such as that now waged between James of Arragon,
as King of Sicily, and the crusading army of the son of
Charles the Lame. The war of the house of Arragon
against the house of Anjou being originally unjust, no
compact was binding. The kingdom of Naples, including
Sicily, having been granted by the Holy See as a fief,
the title of Charles was indefeasible; himself had no
power of surrendering it to another. It declared that
all obligations entered into by a prince in captivity were
null and void, even though oaths had been interchanged
and hostages given for their performance. Charles had
no right to pledge the Roman See and the King of
France, and the King of Arragon (Charles of Valois had
assumed that title) to such terms. If Charles had sworn
that should those Kings not accede to the treaty, he
would return into captivity, the Pope replied that the
imprisonment having been from the first unjust, Charles

* May 29 (Muratori), June 19 (Amari), 1289.

was not bound to return to it: his services being imperiously demanded as a vassal and special athlete for the defence of the Church, he was bound to fulfil that higher duty.[c] On these grounds Pope Nicolas IV. declared the King and his heirs altogether released from all obligations and all oaths. He went further; he prohibited Charles the Lame from observing the conditions of the treaty, and surrendering his eldest son, according to the covenant, as one of the hostages. Nor was the Pope content with thus entirely abrogating the treaty; he anathematised King Alfonso for exacting, contrary to the commands of the Church, such hard terms; he ordered him, under pain of the highest ecclesiastical censure, to release Charles from all the conditions of the treaty; he even threatened the King of England with interdict, if, as guarantee of the treaty, he should enforce its forfeitures. But Charles the Lame himself would not be content with the Papal absolution: he satisfied his chivalrous honour with a more miserable subterfuge. He suddenly appeared near the castle of Panicus, on the borders of Arragon, proclaimed that he was come in conformity to his oath to surrender himself into captivity. But as no one was there on the part of the King of Arragon to receive him, he averred that he had kept his faith, and even demanded the restoration of the hostages and of the money left in pawn.

Spring, 1288.

The war continued: James, not content with the occupation of Sicily, invaded Apulia; before Gaeta he suffered an ignominious failure. Charles, weakly, to the disgust of the Count of Artois and his other French followers who returned to France,

[c] "Nominatæ Ecclesiæ incommoda multa provenirent, dum ipse ejusdem ecclesiæ vassallus præcipuus, et specialis athleta ab illius per hoc defensione subtrahitur."—Bulla Nicolai IV. Compare Raynaldus, sub ann.

agreed to a truce of two years. The death of his brother
Alfonso made James King of Arragon: he 1289-1291.
left his younger brother Frederick his Viceroy June 14,1291.
in Sicily. Frederick became afterwards the founder of
the line of Arragonese Kings of the island.

Nicolas IV. closed his short Pontificate in disaster, shame, and unpopularity. He had in some respects held a lofty tone; he had declared the kingdom Close of Crusades.
of Hungary a fief of the Holy See; and re-
buked the Emperor Rodolph for causing his son, Albert,
without the Pope's permission, to be chosen King of the
Romans.[p] But the total loss of the last Christian possessions in the East, the surrender of Berytus, Tripoli,
even at last Acre,[q] to the irresistible Saltan: the fatal
and ignominious close of the Crusades, so great a source
of Papal power and Papal influence, the disgrace which
was supposed to have fallen on all Christendom, but
with special weight upon its Head, bowed Nicolas down
in shame and sorrow. The war between Edward of
England and Philip of France, in which his mediation,
his menace, were loftily rejected or courteously declined,
destroyed all hopes of a new Crusade; that cry would
no longer pacify ambitious and hostile Kings.

Nicolas had become enslaved to the Colonnas. No
doubt under their powerful protection he had Nicolas IV. and the Colonnas.
continued to reside in Rome.[r] They were
associated in his munificence to the Churches. On the
vault of S. Maria Maggiore, repaired at their common

---

[p] Raynald. sub ann.

[q] Read the siege of Acre (Ptolemais) in Michaud, iv. 458 et seq.
Wilken, vii. p. 735 et seq. Acre fell,
May 18, 1291. Michaud quotes the
emphatic sentence of a Mussulman

writer on this, a serious, final close of
the Crusades;—"Les choses, s'il plait
à Dieu, resteront ainsi jusqu'au dernier
jugement."—P. 497.

[r] Franciscus Pipin., S. R. I., t. ix.

cost, appeared painted together the Pope and the Cardinal James Colonna.   John Colonna was appointed
Marquis of Ancona, Stephen Colonna Count of Romagna : this high office had been wrested from the
Monaldeschi. Cesena, Rimini after some resistance,
Imola, Forli were in his power. In attempting to seize
Ravenna he was himself surprised and taken prisoner
by the sons of Guido di Polenta. But they were afterwards overawed by the vigorous measures of the Pontiff,
urged by the Colonna. Ildobrandino da Romagna,
Bishop of Arezzo, was invested with the title of Count
of Romagna ; the subject cities leagued under his influence ;[*] the sons of Polenta were compelled to pay
three thousand florins of gold for their daring attack on
the Pope's Court.[*] The Romans seemed to enter into
the favouritism of the Pope. James Colonna was created
Senator ; he was dragged, as in the guise of an Emperor, through the city, and saluted with the name of
Cæsar ; he gratified the Romans by marching at their
head to the attack of Viterbo and other cities over which
Rome, whenever occasion offered, aspired to extend her
sovereignty.[*]

There were acts in these terrible wars that raged in
almost every part of Italy which might have grieved the
heart of a wise and humane Pontiff more than the loss
of the Holy Land. The mercy of Christendom might
seem at a lower ebb than its valour. The Bishop of
Arezzo, an Ubaldini, was killed in a battle against the

[*] Muratori, sub anno 1290, 1291.
[*] Rubeus, Chronic. Ravennat., Chronic. Parm., Chronic. Forliviens. S. R. I.
xxii.
[*] The play upon the name of Colonna,
which Petrarch afterwards enshrined
in his noble verse, had long occurred to

the Saturnalian wit of Rome. In the
frontispiece of a book, entitled " The
Beginning of Evils," the Pope Nicolas IV. was represented as a column
crowned by his own mitral head, and
supported by two other columns.—
Muratori.

Florentines; the Florentines slung an ass, with a mitre
fastened on his head, into his beleaguered
city.[b] The Marquis of Montferrat, the most   A.D. 1290.
powerful prince in northern Italy, was taken prisoner
by the Alexandrians, shut up in an iron cage, in which
he languished for nearly two years and died.[f] Dante
has impressed indelibly on the heart of man the imprisonment and death of the Pisan Ugolino (a man, it is
true, of profound ambition and treachery) with that of
his guiltless sons.

Nicolas is said to have died in sorrow and humiliation; he died accused by the Guelfs of unpapal
Ghibellinism,[b] perhaps because he was more   April 4, 1292.
sparing of his anathemas against the Ghibellines, and
had consented, hardly indeed, but had consented to the
peace between France and Arragon, Naples and Sicily:
still more on account of his favour to the Colonnas,
Ghibelline by descent and by tradition, and hereafter to
become more obstinately, furiously, and fatally Ghibelline in their implacable feud with Boniface VIII.[a]

---

[b] 1289. Villani, vii. c. 130. Muratori, sub ann.
[f] Annal. Mediolanens. S. H. T. t. xvi.
[b] Rudolph of Hapsburg, the Emperor, died July 15, 1291.
[a] "Ma molto favoreggiò i Ghibellini." So writes the Guelf Villani,
vii. c. 150.

CHAPTER VI.

Cœlestine V.

NICOLAS IV. died on the 4th of April, 1292. Only
twelve Cardinals formed the Conclave. The
constitution of Gregory X. had been long
suspended, and had fallen altogether into disuse. Six
of these Cardinals were Romans, of these two Orsinis
and two Colonnas; four Italians; two French.[a] Each
of the twelve might aspire to the supreme dignity.
The Romans prevailed in numbers, but were among
themselves more implacably hostile: on the one side
stood the Orsinis, on the other the Colonnas.[b] Three

[a] The list is Ciaconius:—

Romans.

1. Latino Malebranca, a Franciscan, Cardinal of Ostia, the nephew of, and created by, Nicolas III.

2. John Boccamazza, Cardinal of Tusculum (once Legate in Germany), created by Martin IV.

3. Jacobo Colonna, Cardinal of S. Maria in Viâ Latâ, created by Nicolas III.

4. Peter Colonna, Cardinal of S. Eustachio, created by Nicolas IV.

5. Napoleon Orsini, Cardinal of S. Hadrian, created by Nicolas IV.

6. Matteo Rosso (Rubeus), Cardinal of S. Maria in Portico, created by Urban IV.

Italians.

7. Gerard Bianchi of Parma, Car-

dinal Sabinus, created by Honorius IV.

8. Matthew Acquasparta, Cardinal of Porto, created by Nicolas IV.

9. Peter Peregrosso, a Milanese, Cardinal of S. Mark, created by Nicolas IV.

10. Benedetto Gaetani of Anagni, Cardinal of S. Silvester (afterwards Boniface VIII.), created by Martin IV. He was dangerously ill, retired to his native Anagni, and recovered.

Frenchmen.

11. Hugh de Billiom, Cardinal of S. Sabina, created by Nicolas III.

12. Jean Cholet, Cardinal of S. Cecilia, died of fever in Rome, Aug. 2, 1292.

[b] The proceedings of each member of the Conclave, during this interval,

times they met, in the palace of Nicolas IV., near S.
Maria Maggiore, in that of Honorius IV. on the Aventine, and in S. Maria sopra Minerva.* The heats of
June, and a dangerous fever (of which, one, the Frenchman, Jean Cholet, died), drove them out of Rome; and
Rome became such a scene of disorder, feud, and murder
(the election of the Senator being left to the popular
suffrage), that they dared not reassemble within the
walls. Two rival Senators, an Orsini and a Colonna,
were at the head of the two factions.[d] Above a year
had elapsed, when the Conclave agreed to *Oct. 18, 1292.*
meet again at Perugia. The contest lasted *R. Luke's day.*
eight months more. At one time the two Colonnas and
John of Tusculum had nearly persuaded Hugh of
Auvergne and Peter the Milanese to join them in
electing a Roman, one of the Colonnas. The plan was
discovered and thwarted by the Orsini, Matteo Rosso.
The Guelfic Orsini were devoted to the interests of
Charles, the King of Naples; they laboured to advance
a prelate in the Angevine interest. The Colonnas,
Ghibelline because the Orsini were Guelf, were more
for themselves than for Ghibellinism. Charles *in Perugia.*
of Naples came to Perugia, by his personal
presence to overawe the refractory members of the
Conclave. The intrepid Benedict Gaetani, the future

---

are described in the preface to the poem
of the Cardinal St. George.—Muratori, v. p. 616. The Cardinal describes
himself as being " veluti præsens,
videns, ministrans, palpans, et audiens,
notusque Pontifici, quia Pontificibus
carus."—P. 614.

c The Cardinal of St. George highly
disapproved of the building of new
palaces, by Honorius IV. on the Aventine, by Nicolas IV. near S. Maria

Maggiore. It implied the desertion of
the Lateran and the Vatican :—

"ore utile mundo
Exemplum, tanta quânque mus (ut) ducet in
aliam
Ædem, et capitis Petri delubra relinquent.
At Lateranense palas, tramita donis,
[respiciet, gaudens proprios habitare pa-
nales."—P. 631.

d One of the Senators was Peter the
son of Stephen, father of the author;
the other, Otho de San Eustazio.—See
Cardinal St. George.

Boniface VIII., haughtily rebuked him for presuming to interfere with the office of the Holy Spirit. No one of the Cardinals would yield the post to his adversary, and expose himself to the vengeance of a successful rival; yet all seemed resolute to confine the nomination to their own body.

Suddenly a solitary monk was summoned from his cell, in the remote Abruzzi, to ascend the Pontifical throne. The Cardinal of Ostia, Latino Malo- Malebranca. brunca, had admired the severe and ascetic virtues of Peter Morrone, a man of humble birth, but already, from his extraordinary austerities, held by the people as a man of the highest sanctity. He had retired from desert to desert, and still multitudes had tracked him out in vast swarms, some to wonder at, some to join his devout seclusion. He seemed to rival if not to outdo the famous anchorites of old. His dress was haircloth, with an iron cuirass; his food bread and water, with a few herbs on Sunday.

Peter Morrone has left an account of his own youth. Peter Morrone. The brothers of his Order, who took his name, the Cœlestinians, vouched for its authenticity. His mother was devoutly ambitious that one of her eleven children should be dedicated to God. Many of them died, but Peter fulfilled her most ardent desires. His infancy was marked with miracles. In his youth he had learned to read the Psalter; he then knew not the person of the Blessed Virgin, or of St. John. One day they descended bodily from a picture of the Crucifixion, stood before him, and sweetly chanted portions of the Psalter. At the age of twenty he went into the desert: visions of Angels were ever round him, sometimes showering roses over him. God showed him a great stone, under which he dug a hole, in which he

could neither stand upright, nor stretch his limbs, and
there he dwelt in all the luxury of self-torture among
lizards, serpents, and toads. A bell in the heavens
constantly sounded to summon him to prayers. He was
offered a cock; he accepted the ill-omened gift; for his
want of faith the bell was thenceforth silent. He was
more sorely tried; beautiful women came and lay down
by his side.* He was encircled by a crowd of followers,
whom he had already formed into a kind of Order or
Brotherhood; they were rude, illiterate peasants from
the neighbouring mountains.†

Either designedly or accidentally the Cardinal Malebranca spoke of the wonderful virtues of the hermit,
Peter Morrone; the weary Conclave listened with
interest. A few days after the Cardinal declared that a
vision had been vouchsafed to a Holy Man, that if before
All-Saints' Day they had not elected a Pope, the wrath
of God would fall on them with some signal chastisement. "This, I presume," spake Benedetto Gaetani,
"is one of the visions of your Peter Morrone." In truth
it was; Malebranca had received a letter purporting to
be in his hand. The Conclave was in that perplexed
and exhausted state, when men seize desperately on
any strange counsel to extricate themselves
from their difficulty. To some it might seem
a voice from heaven. Others might shelter their own
disappointment under the consolation that their rivals
were equally disappointed: all might think it wise to

Election of
Coelestine V.

---

* One vision is too coarse almost to
allude to; but how are we to judge of
the times or the men without their
coarseness? The question was whether
he should offer mass "pro pollutione
nocturnam." The vision which sets
his mind at rest is that of "smelli

stercoravit" on the steps of a palace,
that of the Holy Trinity. One of
these awful persons is represented as
pointing the moral of this foul imagination.

† "Non erds mihi ed rustica turba
Montibus aldgents."—Card. St. George.

elect a Pope without personal enmity to any one. It
might be a winning hazard for each party, each interest,
each Cardinal; the Hermit was open to be ruled, as
ruled he would be, by any one. Malebranca saw the
impression he had made; he pressed it in an eloquent
speech. Peter Morrone was declared supreme Pontiff
by unanimous acclamation.[*]

The fatal sentence was hardly uttered when the brief
unanimity ceased. Some of the cardinals began to
repent or to be ashamed of their precipitate decree. No
one of them (this they were hereafter to rue) would
undertake the office of bearing the tidings of his elevation to the Pope. The deputation consisted of the
Archbishop of Lyons, two Bishops, and two notaries of
the Court.

The place of Morrone's retreat was a cave in a wild
mountain above the pleasant valley of Sul-
mona. The ambassadors of the Conclave
having achieved their journey from Perugia, with
difficulty found guides to conduct them to the solitude.
As they toiled up the rugged ascent, they were over-
taken by the Cardinal Peter Colonna, who had followed
them without commission from the rest, no doubt to
watch their proceedings, and to take advantage of any
opportunity to advance his own interests. The cave, in
which the saint could neither sit upright nor stretch
himself out, had a grated window with iron bars, through
which he uttered his oracular responses to the wondering
people. None even of the brethren of the order might
penetrate into the dark sanctuary of his austerities.
The ambassadors of the Conclave found an old man with

a long shaggy beard, sunken eyes overhung with
heavy brows, and lids swollen with perpetual *Ambassadors*
weeping, pale hollow cheeks, and limbs meagre *before him.*
with fasting: they fell on their knees before him, and
he before them.   The future Cardinal-Poet was among
the number: his barren Muse can hardly be suspected
of invention.[b]

So Peter Morrone the Hermit saw before him, in
submissive attitudes, the three prelates, attended by
the official notaries, who announced his election to the
Papacy. He thought it was a dream: and for once
assuredly there was a profound and religious reluctance to accept the highest dignity in the world. He
protested with tears his utter inability to cope with the
affairs, to administer the sacred trust, to become the
successor of the Apostle.[i]   The news spread abroad;
the neighbouring people came hurrying by thousands,
delighted that they were to have a saint, and their own
saint, for a Pope.   The Hermit in vain tried to escape;
he was brought back with respectful force, guarded with
reverential vigilance.   Nor was it the common people
only who were thus moved.   King Charles himself may
not have been superior to the access of religious wonder,
for to him especially (if indeed there was no design in
the whole affair) this sudden unanimity among the
ambitious Cardinals might pass for a miracle, more
miraculous than many which were acknowledged by
the common belief.   The King of Naples, accompanied
by his son, now in right of his wife entitled King of

[b] Cardinal St. George, apud Muratori.

[i] The Cardinal St. George, however,
asserts that Celestine hardly affected
reluctance; and the Cardinal says that

he was among a great multitude of all
ranks, who clambered up the mountain,
"cerns conspirantes montem
Glitorabas vates, nemubris vultusque reve-
dens."
to catch a glimpse of the Pope.

Hungary, hastened to do honour to his holy subject, to
persuade the Hermit, who perhaps would be dazzled by
royal flatteries into a useful ally, to accept the proffered
dignity. The Hermit-Pope was conducted from his
lowly cave to the monastery of Santo Spirito, at the
foot of the mountain. He still refused to be invested
in the pontifical robes. At length arrived the Cardinal
Malebranca: his age, dignity, character, and his language, urging the awful responsibility which Peter
Morrone would incur by resisting the manifest will of
God, and by keeping the Popedom longer vacant (for
all which he would be called to give account on the day
of judgement), prevailed over the awe-struck saint. Not
the least earnest in pressing him to assume at once the
throne were his rude but not so unambitious hermit
brethren: they too looked for advancement; they
followed him in crowds wherever he went, to Aquila
and to Naples. Over his shaggy sackcloth at
length the Hermit put on the gorgeous attire
of the Pontiff; yet he would not go to Perugia to
receive the homage of the Conclave. Age and the
heat of the season (he had been accustomed to breathe
the mountain air) would not permit him to undertake
the long unwonted journey. He entered the city of
Aquila riding on an ass, with a King on each side of
him to hold his bridle. Some of the indignant clergy
murmured at this humiliation of the Papal majesty
(the successor of St. Peter was wont to ride on a stately
palfrey), but they suppressed their discontent.

If there had been more splendid, never was there so
popular an election. Two hundred thousand spectators
(of whom the historian, Ptolemy of Lucca, was one[1])

Peter Mor-
rone Pope.

[1] "Quibus ipse interfui."—Ptolem. Luc.

crowded the streets. In the evening the Pope was compelled again and again to come to the window to bestow his benediction; and if hierarchical pride had been offended at the lowliness of his pomp, it but excited greater admiration in the commonalty: they thought of Him who entered Jerusalem "riding on an ass's colt." Miracles confirmed their wonder: a boy, lame from the womb, was placed on the ass on which the Pope had ridden; he was restored to the full use of his limbs.

But already the Cardinals might gravely reflect on their strange election. The Pope still obstinately refused to go to Perugia, or even to Rome, though they suggested that he might be conveyed in a litter. The Cardinals declared that they were not to be summoned to the kingdom of Naples. Two only, Hugh of Auvergne and Napoleon Orsini, condescended to go to Aquila. Malebranca probably had begun to droop under the illness which ere long carried him off. But the way in which the Pope began to use his vast powers still more appalled and offended them. He bestowed the offices in his court and about his person on rude and unknown Abruzzese; and to the great disgust of the clergy, appointed a layman his secretary. High at once in his favour rose the French Prelate, Hugh Ascalon de Dilliom, Archbishop of Benevento under Nicolas IV., Cardinal of S. Sabina. He had been the first to follow Malebranca in the acclamation of the Pope Morrone. On the death of Malebranca he was raised to the Bishopric of Ostia and Velletri, and became Dean of the College of Cardinals. Large pensions, charged on great abbeys in France, gilded his elevation. The Frenchman seemed destined to rule with undivided sway over the feeble Cœlestine:

the Italians looked with undisguised jealousy and aversion on the foreign prelate.[a]

The Cardinal, Napoleon Orsini, assisted at the inauguration, gave to the Pope the scarlet mantle, the mitre set with gold and jewels; he announced to the people that Peter had taken the name of Cœlestine V. The foot of the lowly hermit was kissed by kings, cardinals, bishops, nobles. He was set on high to be adored by the people.[b] The numbers of the clergy caused singular astonishment; but the Cardinals, though reluctant, would not allow the coronation to proceed without them; they came singly and in unwilling haste.[c] Last of all came Benedetto Gaetani: he had deeply offended Charles of Naples by his haughty rebuke at Perugia. Yet still, though all assisted at the ceremony, the place of honour was given to the French Cardinal: he anointed the new Pope, but the Pontiff was crowned by Matteo Rosso, after Malebranca's death, probably the elder of the Cardinals present.[d]

Coronation.

A few months showed that meekness, humility, holiness, unworldliness might make a saint; they were not the virtues suited to a Pope. To Naples he had been led, as it were, in submissive triumph by King Charles; he took up his residence in the royal palace, an unsuspecting prisoner, mocked

Cœlestine V. in Naples.

---

[a] Compare on Hugh Ascalon de Billom Hist. Littér. de la France, xx. 73.

[b] " Quod stupori erat videre, quia tergis renitebant ad suam obtinendam benedictionem, quam pro prebendæ acquisitione."—Ptolem. Luc.

[c] " Domini Jacobus de Colonna, et Dominus Matheus, et Dominus Hugo de Ascalon "—(he must have been there before)—" Aquilam veniant, factique sunt domini Curiæ, quod alii Cardinales videntes Aquilam properant."—Ptolem. Luc. Annal. p. 1298.

[d] Hæc postquam videre Rubei, seu morte Latini
Prævii solymos, coierunt ad tanta pericula curiæ.—Cardin. S. George, p. 649.

[e] He was created by Urban IV.

with the most ostentatious veneration. So totally did
the harmless Cœlestine surrender himself to his royal
protector, that he stubbornly refused to leave Naples.
His utter incapacity for business soon appeared; he
lavished offices, dignities, bishoprics, with profuse hand;
he granted and revoked grants, bestowed benefices,
vacant or about to be vacant.[a] He was duped by the
officers of his court, and gave the same benefice over
and over again; but still the greater share fell to his
brethren from the Abruzzi. His officers issued orders
of all kinds in his name. He shrank from
publicity, and even from the ceremonial duties　*His conduct.*
of his office; he could speak only a few words of bad
Latin. One day, when he ought to have sat on the
pontifical tribunal, he was sought in vain; he had
taken refuge in the church, and was with difficulty
persuaded to resume his state. His weakness made
him as prodigal of his power as of his gifts.[b]　*Sept. 1294.*
At the dictation of King Charles he created
at once thirteen new Cardinals, thus outnumbering the
present conclave.[c] Of these, seven were French; the

[a] " Dabat enim dignitates, prela-
tiones, officia et beneficia, in quibus
non expectabatur curize consuetudinem,
sed potius quorondam suggestionem, et
seam rudem simplicitatem."—Jacob.
a Vorag. apud Muratori S. R. T. ix.
p. 54. " Multa fecit de plenitudine
potestatis sed plura de plenitudine
simplicitatis," *ibid.* The favouritism of
the French Cardinal of S. Sabina, by
this author's account, was generally
odious.

[b] "O quam multiplices indeas potentia formas
Edidit, indulgens, donans, fariansque re-
creat,
Atque vacaturus concedens atque va-
cantes."—Card. St. George.

—See also Ptolem. Loc. lxxiv. c. 29.

[b] There was a small monkish tyranny
about the good Cœlestine. He compelled the monks of the ancient and
famous abbey of Monte Casino to wear
the dress of his own order. The
Cardinal-Poet is pathetic on this :—

"Syd-rei colla. Montisque Casini
Congulit, heu! monachos habitus sanc-
tare fratrem.
Depretum sub tegu Petri : (Morrone) nov-
ellos ab inde,
Unto parvre brygat, monachos : tunc excolat.
O quam
Decliperis !"

[c] See the list in Ciacconius. One, a
Beneventan, Cardinal of S. Vitale, died
the next year.

rest Italians; of the latter, three Neapolitans, not one
Roman. In order to place the Conclave more completely in the power of Charles, who intended to keep
him till his death in his own dominions, he re-enacted
the Conclave law of Gregory X.

The weary man became anxious to lay down his
Wishes to   heavy burthen. Some of the Cardinals urged
abdicate.   upon him that he retained the Papacy at the
peril of his soul. Gaetani's powerful mind (once at
Benedetto   Naples, he resumed the ascendancy of his
Gaetani.   commanding abilities) had doubtless great influence in his determination. He was soon supposed
to rule the Court and the Pope himself, to be Cœlestine's
bosom counsellor.¹ It was reported, and the trick was
attributed to Gaetani his ambitious successor, that
through a hole skilfully contrived in the wall of his
chamber, a terrible voice was repeatedly heard at the
dead of night, announcing itself as that of a messenger
of God. It commanded the trembling Pontiff to
renounce the blandishments of the world, and devote
himself to God's service. Rumour spread abroad that
Cœlestine was about to abdicate. The King secretly,
the monks of his brotherhood openly, worked upon the
lower order of Naples, and instigated them to a holy
insurrection. Naples was in an uproar at this rumoured
degradation of the Pope. A long and solemn procession
of all the clergy, of whom Ptolemy of Lucca was one,
passed through the city to the palace. A Bishop, a
kind of prolocutor, addressed him with a voice like a
trumpet, urging him to abandon his fatal design. The
speech was heard by Ptolemy of Lucca. Another

¹ " Gaetani—eo quod Regem Carolum Perusii multum exasperavit, qui
statim sub ministeriis et artibus factus est Dominus Curiæ et serviens Regis."
—Ptolem. Luc. p. 1299.

Bishop from the walls announced that the Pope had
no such intention. The Bishop below immediately
broke out into a triumphant *Te Deum*, which was taken
up by a thousand voices. The procession passed away."

But Advent was drawing on. Cœlestino would not
pass that holy season in pomp and secular
business. He had contrived a cell within the
royal palace, from whence he could not see the sky.
He had determined to seclude himself in all his wonted
solitude and undisturbed austerities, like a bird, says
the Cardinal-Poet, which hides its head from the fowler,
and thinks that it is unseen." He had actually signed
a commission to three Cardinals to administer during his
seclusion the affairs of the Popedom : it wanted but the
seal to be a Papal Bull. But this perhaps more dangerous
step of putting the Papacy in commission was averted.

Long and inconclusive debates took place on the
legality of a Papal abdication. Could any human
power release him who was the representative
of Christ on earth from his obligations? Could the
successor of St. Peter, of his own free will, sink back
into the ordinary race of men? Holy Orders were
indelible : how much more indelible must be the consecration to this office, the fount and source of all
Apostolic ordination? Cœlestino himself, from irresolution doubtless rather than artful dissimulation, had
lulled his supporters, even the King himself, into
security." On a sudden, on the day of S. Lucia, the
Conclave was summoned to receive the abdication

* Ptolem. Luc. apud Muratori.
" P. 638.
r " Dissimulans, ceu vera loquens, alie-
que venire Gallicitus, quo ad illa damna secreta,
l'altrenym

Crediderat, immo nolle quidem dimit-
tere personam.
Canxque foret generalis fides, ceniteres es
potierat,
Sed etiam, cmlet exoplens oblivia terU,
Immemorum varietasque l'ytrum, &c."
Card. SL. George.

of the Pope. The trembling Cœlestine alleged as the
cause of his abdication, his age, his rude manners and
ruder speech, his incapacity, his inexperience. He
confessed humbly his manifold errors, and entreated
the Conclave to bestow upon the world of Christendom
a pastor not liable to such infirmities. The Conclave
is said to have been moved to tears, yet no one (all
no doubt prepared) refused to accept the abdication.
But the Pope was urged first, while his authority was
yet full and above appeal, to issue a Constitution declaring that the Pope might at any time lay down his
dignity, and that the Cardinals were at liberty to
receive that voluntary demission of the Popedom. No
sooner was this done than Cœlestine retired;
Abdication. he stripped off at once the cumbrous magnificence of his Papal robes and his two-horned mitre;
he put on the coarse and rugged habit of his brotherhood. As soon as he could, the discrowned Pope withdrew to his old mountain hermitage.

The abdication of Cœlestine V. was an event unprecedented in the annals of the Church, and jarred
harshly against some of the first principles of the Papal
authority. It was a confession of common humanity,
of weakness below the ordinary standard of men, in
him whom the Conclave, with more than usual cer-
titude, as guided by the special interposition of the
Holy Ghost, had raised to the spiritual throne of the
world. The Conclave had been, as it seemed, either
under an illusion as to this declared manifestation of
the Holy Spirit, or had been permitted to deceive itself.
Nor was there less incongruity in a Pope, whose office
invested him in something at least approaching to
infallibility, acknowledging before the world his utter
incapacity, his undeniable fallibility. That idea,

formed out of many conflicting conceptions, yet forcibly harmonised by long traditionary reverence, of unerring wisdom, oracular truth, authority which it was sinful to question or limit, was strangely disturbed and confused, not as before by too overweening ambition, or even awful yet still unacknowledged crime, but by avowed weakness, bordering on imbecility. His profound piety hardly reconciled the confusion. A saint, after all, made but a bad Pope.

It was viewed, in his own time, in a different light by different minds. The monkish writers held it up as the most noble example of monastic, of Christian perfection. Admirable as was his election, his abdication was even more to be admired. It was an example of humility stupendous to all, imitable by few.[a] The divine approval was said to be shown by a miracle which followed directly on his resignation;[a] but the scorn of man has been expressed by the undying verse of Dante, who condemned him who was guilty of the baseness of the "great refusal" to that circle of hell where are those disdained alike by mercy and justice, on whom the poet will not condescend to look.[b] This sentence, so accordant with the stirring and passionate soul of the great Florentine, has been feebly counteracted, if counteracted, by the praise of Petrarch in his declamation on the beauty of a solitary life, for which the lyrist professed a somewhat hollow and poetic admiration.[c] Assuredly there was no magnanimity contemptuous of the Papal

How thought of in his own time.

Dante.

Petrarch.

---

[a] "Præbuit humilitatis exemplum, stupendum cunctis, imitabile paucis." —Jordan. MS., quoted by Raynaldus.

[a] Bernard, in Chron. Roman. Pontif.

[b] "Che fece per viltà il gran rifiuto." *Inferno*, iii. 60.

I cannot for an instant doubt the allusion to Celestine; perhaps it was embittered by Dante's hatred of Boniface VIII.

[c] "Petrarch de Vità solitarià," a rhetorical exercise.

greatness in the abdication of Cœlestine: it was the weariness, the conscious inefficiency, the regret of a man suddenly wrenched away from all his habits, pursuits, and avocations, and unnaturally compelled or tempted to assume an uncongenial dignity. It was the cry of passionate feebleness to be released from an insupportable burthen. Compassion is the highest emotion of sympathy which it would have desired or could deserve.

But coeval with Dante there was another, a ruder poet, who must be heard, that we may fully comprehend the times. Jacopone da Todi, the Franciscan, had been among those who hailed with mingled exultation and fear the advancement of the holy Cœlestine.[a] "What wilt thou do, Peter Morrone, now that thou art on thy trial?" "If the world be deceived in thee, malediction! Thy fame has soared on high; it has spread through the world. If thou failest, there will be confusion to the good. As the arrow on its mark, the world is fixed on thee. If thou holdest not the balance right, there is no appeal but to God." "The Court of Rome is a furnace which tries the fine gold." "If thou takest delight in thine office (there is no malady so infectious), accursed is that life

---

[a] "Che farai, Pier da Morrone?
Se' venuto al paragone.

Sa 'l mondo è di te ingannato,
Sequirà maledizione..
    La tua fama alta è salita,
E 'e multo peste el è gito
se el tenir a la fonta,
A l'tua a sarai conturbate.
    Como arme a mugliere,
Fretto 'l mondo a te si affitta,
Se non tien bilance ritta,
a Dio ne 'tu appellazione.

Questa sorte e una focina,
Ca 'l buon uro si el afina
    *   *   *   *
Se l'offici- ti diletta,
Di alte malanno più infetta;

Peno è vita maledetta,
Perder lihe per tal baccenne.

Che 't hal punto giego la suglia,
Ha 'mmer' ina dannatione.

L' ordine Cardinalate,
Pusto ha in bono stato !
Chi suo parentado
D' arriccar in' intentiome.
    *   *   *   *
Guardati de baratiere,
Ch' el suo biasmo fan stiere ;
Se non ti sai ben schermaire,
Ca teval mala amaure."—Satir. xv.

There are other passages which betray the pride in the elevation of Pier Morrone.

which for such a morsel loses God." "Thou hast put
the yoke on thy neck, must we not fear thy damna-
tion?" "The order of Cardinals has sunk to the
lowest level: their sole aim is to enrich their kindred."
"Guard thyself from the traffickers who make black
white. If thou dost not guard thyself well, and will
be the burthen of thy song." Yet in these mistrustful
warnings of the poet there is the manifest pride and
hope of a devoted partisan that a new era has begun,
that Peter Morrone is destined to regenerate the
Papacy. The abdication, no doubt, was the last event
to which these hermit followers of Peter Morrone looked
forward. Bitter must have been their disappointment
when he himself thus frustrated their pious expectations, their passionate vaticinations; yet they adhered
to him in his self-chosen lowliness; they were still his
stedfast admirers; they denied his right to abdicate,
no doubt they disseminated the rumours of the arts
employed to frighten him from the throne. Their
hatred of Boniface, who supplanted him, was as deep
and obstinate as their love of Cœlestine. This poet
will appear as at least cognisant of the formidable
conspiracy which threatened the power of Boniface VIII.
Nor was the poet alone: his was but the voice which
expressed, in its coarse but vigorous strains, the sense
of a vast and to a certain extent organised party, in
every rank, in every order, but especially among the
low, and the lowest of the low.

END OF VOL. VI.

LONDON: PRINTED BY WILLIAM CLOWES AND SONS, STAMFORD STREET,
AND CHARING CROSS.

VOL. VI.   2 I

www.ingramcontent.com/pod-product-compliance
Lightning Source LLC
Chambersburg PA
CBHW031815270326
41932CB00008B/433